Praise for *Breaking the Color Barrier*

"My first personal experience with racial integration began when an African American student, Wesley Brown, entered the U.S. Naval Academy in 1945. We both ran cross-country during the year that we spent together in Annapolis. A few members of my senior class attempted to find ways to have him discharged, but Brown's good performance prevailed and he became the Academy's first black graduate. *Breaking the Color Barrier* describes Brown's experiences, the travails of his predecessors, and, through the African American community's efforts to integrate the Academy, black people's dream of achieving equality."
　　　　—Jimmy Carter

"This highly readable narrative combines an impressive amount of archival research with firsthand accounts from participants to tell the story in human terms."
　　　　—Paul Stillwell, editor of *The Golden Thirteen: Recollections of the First Black Naval Officers*

Breaking the Color Barrier

The U.S. Naval Academy's
First Black Midshipmen and
the Struggle for Racial Equality

Robert J. Schneller, Jr.

NEW YORK UNIVERSITY PRESS
New York and London

NEW YORK UNIVERSITY PRESS
New York and London
www.nyupress.org

Library of Congress Cataloging-in-Publication Data
Schneller, Robert John, 1957–
The U.S. Naval Academy's first Black midshipmen and the struggle
for racial equality / Robert J. Schneller, Jr.
p. cm.
Includes bibliographical references and index.
ISBN 0–8147–4013–8 (cloth : alk. paper)
1. African American midshipmen—Maryland—Annapolis.
2. United States Naval Academy—Admission.   3. United States
Naval Academy. Brigade of Midshipmen—Membership.
4. Discrimination in higher education—United States.
5. United States—Race relations.   I. Title.
V415.L1S36   2005
359'.0092'396073—dc22   2004023711

New York University Press books are printed on acid-free paper, and
their binding materials are chosen for strength and durability.

Manufactured in the United States of America

10 9 8 7 6 5 4 3 2 1

To Wesley Brown

Contents

All illustrations appear as an insert following p. 172.

Preface

When Wesley A. Brown took the midshipman's oath on 30 June 1945, he became the sixth African American to enter the U.S. Naval Academy since its establishment one hundred years earlier. Although quite moved by the occasion, he must also have experienced trepidation, for he knew what had happened to blacks who had entered service academies in years past.

Until World War II, black people were persona non grata at the Naval Academy, unless they were employed as janitors, as launderers, or in some other menial capacity. No African Americans served on the Academy's faculty or uniformed staff, except for the black Navy stewards who waited on the midshipmen in the mess hall.[1]

African Americans had been struggling since Reconstruction to integrate the Naval Academy as a step toward the ultimate goal of securing full civil rights. By the end of World War II, their efforts resulted in the appointment of more than two dozen young black men to the Academy. Only five of these young men were admitted, however, and none of them succeeded in graduating. Each of these black midshipmen was hazed unmercifully because of his race and left Annapolis under dubious circumstances. To varying degrees, the Academy's leadership condoned this discrimination.

White midshipmen present during Wesley Brown's "plebe" year—as freshman year was called then and now—heard "horror stories" about the hazing his black predecessors had suffered. The most common story had it that upperclassmen tied one black plebe to a buoy out in the Chesapeake Bay. Some say that the victim died; others say that he was rescued, but the incident prompted him to resign. Nothing found in the documentary record substantiates any version of this story, but its prevalence reflected racial attitudes at the Academy through World War II.

During the war, the Navy's racial policy evolved from exclusion of blacks outside the messman branch, where they functioned as officers' servants, to full integration by early 1946, at least in writing. In the wake of this "revolution," and with the support of Representative Adam Clayton Powell, Jr. (D-NY), Secretary of the Navy James V. Forrestal, and future President Jimmy Carter (while still a midshipman), among others, Wesley Brown survived an attempt by a group of upperclassmen to run him out of the Naval Academy and in 1949 became its first African American graduate.

Breaking the Color Barrier examines the black community's efforts to integrate the Naval Academy as well as the experiences of the first six black midshipmen. It analyzes how the Academy's culture and racial policies responded to demands for the integration of African Americans and affected the lives of black midshipmen. It argues that a black midshipman's success in any given period depended upon national politics, the Navy's racial policy, other midshipmen's racial attitudes, and the black midshipman's own abilities and survival skills.

Most institutional history is written from the top down, while most social history is written from the bottom up. Based on the documentary record as well as on the memories of scores of midshipmen and naval officers, *Breaking the Color Barrier* includes both perspectives. This approach permits a much fuller exploration of the dynamics of racial integration of an American institution than is possible with either a top-down or a bottom-up approach alone. Examining both the institutional and individual levels produces a much more realistic picture of what it took to break the color barrier at the Naval Academy.

In a broader sense, the story of the first black midshipmen sheds light on the American racial dilemma itself. The convergence of forces that leveled the playing field for Wesley Brown at the Naval Academy—a push from the black community, national political imperatives, a shift in racial attitudes among the American people, direct intervention by leaders, and the strengths and abilities of individuals in the trenches—presages the convergence of forces that brought about America's "Second Reconstruction." The story of the first black midshipmen is a microcosm for understanding racism in America and provides a unique window into the underpinnings of the civil rights movement.

Acknowledgments

I am privileged to work for the United States Naval Historical Center, the U.S. Navy's official history office. Many people at the Center helped this book come to be. I thank Dr. William Dudley, Director of Naval History, for his leadership and encouragement from the book's inception. I also thank William Vance, Jay Thomas, Todd Creekman, James Carlton, Andy Hall, and Duane Heughan, who served as successive deputy directors during the research and writing phases. I am particularly grateful to Gary Weir and Ed Marolda, my current and former bosses in the Contemporary History Branch, for their guidance and support.

Every one of my friends and colleagues at the Naval Historical Center helped in one way or another. Several of them deserve special mention. For invaluable research support, I am indebted to Gina Akers, Bernard Cavalcante, John Hodges, Ariana Jacob, Ken Johnson, Kathy Lloyd, Mike Walker, and Wade Wyckoff of the Operational Archives, as well as Barbara Auman, David Brown, Davis Elliott, Glenn Helm, Jean Hort, Shirley Martyn, Heidi Myers, Young Park, and Tonya Simpson of the Navy Department Library. I thank Jeff Barlow, Bob Cressman, Mike McDaniel, Randy Papadopoulos, Rick Russell, and John Sherwood of the Contemporary History Branch for research leads and constructive criticism. I am grateful to Senior Editor Sandy Doyle for editorial advice. I thank Sabreena Edwards, Jack Green, Jill Harrison, Ruby Hughlett, Ella Nargele, Randy Potter, Donna Smilardo, and Maxine Ware for providing various kinds of administrative support.

I thank Gina Akers, Alan Gropman, Diane Batts Morrow, Alex Roland, and John Sherwood for reviewing the entire manuscript and offering valuable suggestions for its improvement. Although these people helped make this book better, responsibility for its flaws remains with me.

I thank the staffs of the Charles Sumner School Museum and Archives, the Chicago Historical Society, the D.C. Public Library, Dunbar Senior

High School, the Library of Congress, Howard University's Moorland-Spingarn Research Center, the Naval Historical Foundation, Princeton University's Seeley G. Mudd Library, the National Archives, the U.S. Naval Academy's Nimitz Library, the Franklin Delano Roosevelt Library, the U.S. Naval Institute, and the University of North Carolina library for their help with documentation and images. I am particularly indebted to Gary LaValley and Beverly Lyall of Nimitz Library's Special Collections and Archives Division for preserving and making available the Naval Academy's records. Special thanks also go to Paul Stillwell and the U.S. Naval Institute Oral History Program for preserving and making available naval officers recollections.

I thank Deborah Gershenowitz at New York University Press for shepherding this book into print.

I am particularly grateful to the alumni of the U.S. Naval Academy who shared their recollections with me, both on paper and on tape. Their names appear in the bibliography.

Most of all I wish to express my gratitude to Wesley Brown for sharing his recollections and answering countless questions. His magnanimity, inspiration, and encouragement made *Breaking the Color Barrier* possible. Without his help, I would never have been able to write the book.

PART I

The Glorious Failure

Reconstruction and the
Naval Academy, 1872–1876

1

"Not . . . Their Equals *Socially*"

African Americans have long had a tradition of looking upon military service as an opportunity to strike a blow against racism and prove their value and loyalty to their country. After the Civil War, ex-slaves, northerners, and white southerners struggled to shape the meaning of freedom, the consequences of emancipation, and the social, political, and economic systems that replaced those that died with slavery. Freedpeople strove to secure all the rights, privileges, and opportunities available to white American citizens, including the opportunity to become officers in the United States Navy.

Legislation passed during Reconstruction held the promise of making such dreams seem possible. In the last days of the war the government established the Freedmen's Bureau, which provided food and clothing to ex-slaves and opened hospitals and schools for blacks across the South. The ratification of the Thirteenth Amendment in December 1865 abolished slavery throughout the United States. The next year Congress adopted the Fourteenth Amendment, which established equality before the law as a fundamental right of American citizens and shifted responsibility for protecting citizens' rights from the states to the federal government. In 1867, Congress adopted the Reconstruction Act, temporarily barring many ex-Confederates from voting or holding office, helping to create new southern state governments, and demanding suffrage for blacks. In 1869, Congress adopted the Fifteenth Amendment, which prohibited the federal and state governments from depriving any citizen of the right to vote because of race.

In the South, a politically mobilized black community joined with white allies to bring the Republican Party to power. More than fifteen hundred African Americans held office in the Reconstruction South. Although Democrats cried that "Negro rule" had come to the South, blacks nowhere controlled state governments, nor did they hold office in numbers equal to their proportion of the total population. Nevertheless, their political empowerment represented a stunning departure in American government.

African Americans attacked racial segregation throughout the country. Before the war, discriminatory laws excluded blacks from both public and private facilities almost everywhere in the United States. In the South, Reconstruction governments outlawed racial discrimination by railroads, hotels, and other institutions. In the North, black citizens forced state governments to amend or abolish many regulations concerning segregation. At the federal level, the Civil Rights Act of 1875 prohibited racial discrimination in places of public accommodation.

Freedom to former slaves also meant independence from white control. Freedpeople refused to labor in gangs under an overseer in cotton fields anymore. Instead of working someone else's land, they sought to purchase their own. Black parents resisted efforts to force their children into involuntary labor through court-ordered apprenticeships and insisted on deciding for themselves when their children should go to work. Black Christians left white churches and established their own places of worship. Most of all, freedpeople thirsted for the education that had been denied to them under slavery. The new southern state governments established the region's first state-supported public schools, and although the schools were generally segregated by race, they enabled more than 50 percent of black children to attend school in a region that had outlawed learning for blacks in the antebellum era.

Most white southerners refused to believe that African Americans deserved the same political rights and economic opportunities as they had. Some of those who simply could not accept the idea of former slaves voting, holding office, and enjoying equality before the law worked to reestablish a system of white supremacy as close to slavery as possible. Opponents of Reconstruction reacted violently when freedpeople tried to exercise their new civil rights. Many assaulted and some even murdered black men and women for refusing to give way to whites on sidewalks, using "insolent" language, sending their children to school, leaving plantations, challenging contract settlements, or attempting to buy land.

After 1867, the violence became more pervasive, organized, and politically motivated. In many areas of the South, opponents of Reconstruction unleashed a campaign of terror and violence aimed at overthrowing the new governments and restoring white supremacy. Secret societies emerged to keep blacks from voting and to assassinate local Republican

Party leaders and officials. The most notorious such organization, the Ku Klux Klan, was founded as a social club in Tennessee in 1866 and quickly degenerated into an organization whose members were willing to use any terrorist tactic necessary to maintain white supremacy. Led by planters, merchants, certain Democratic politicians, and some ex-Confederate officers, Klan terrorists committed some of the most brutal crimes against African Americans and sympathetic whites in American history. Klansmen whipped, tortured, and murdered individuals and sometimes assaulted whole black communities, particularly singling out black churches and schools.

In 1872, numerous prominent Republicans, alienated by corruption within President Ulysses S. Grant's administration (1869–1877), denounced Reconstruction and bolted from the party. Their actions diverted northern attention from Reconstruction and contributed to a resurgence of racism above the Mason-Dixon Line. An economic depression that began in 1873 also competed with Reconstruction for northerners' attention. Meanwhile, terrorism against African Americans and white Republicans continued in the South. When Mississippi governor Adelbert Ames frantically appealed to the federal government for help, President Grant replied that the northern public was "tired out" by southern problems and would condemn any interference from Washington. On election day in Mississippi in 1875 and in South Carolina in 1876, Democrats destroyed ballot boxes, drove former slaves away from the polls, and intimidated freedpeople. Because of the renewed violence, the economic blow dealt by the depression, and factionalism among southern Republicans, the Reconstruction governments fell like dominoes.

To succeed Grant in 1876, the Republicans nominated Ohio governor Rutherford B. Hayes. Samuel J. Tilden, New York's governor, was his Democratic opponent. At this juncture only South Carolina, Florida, and Louisiana remained under Republican control. The election was so close that whoever carried these states—and both candidates claimed to have done so—would become president. To head off a political and constitutional crisis, perhaps even another civil war, Republicans and Democrats struck the infamous "Bargain of 1877." In return for the Democrats' ceding the presidency to Hayes, the Republicans agreed to recognize Democratic control of the remaining southern states. The Redeemers, as the southern Democrats who overturned Republican governments called themselves, now ruled the entire South, thus bringing down the curtain on Reconstruction.[1]

Historians have termed Reconstruction a "glorious failure." "Glorious," in the words of Peggy Lamson, "because it was a beginning, a noble experiment which encouraged Negroes to look forward to the day when race would no longer be a factor in judging men and their capabilities; a failure because in the end it only served to sharpen, perhaps irrevocably, the subtle antagonisms which divided whites and blacks."[2]

Nevertheless, freedpeople striving for equality during Reconstruction succeeded in breaking the color barrier on several fronts. For the first time in American history, all southern black males had the right to cast ballots, sit on juries, and hold political office. The short-lived biracial Reconstruction governments rebuilt and expanded public facilities, established school systems, and purged legal codes of racism. For a fleeting moment, some African Americans enjoyed all the rights and privileges of United States citizens.

African Americans also sought equal opportunities in the Navy during Reconstruction. While the Union navy had permitted a degree of integration of black and white sailors on board its ships during the Civil War, it had excluded blacks from its officer corps. After the war, African Americans sought to redress the imbalance.

The Navy's enlisted service had long been integrated. Wooden ships had reigned supreme in the antebellum era. To man them, the Navy had sought sober, able-bodied mariners who were quick to obey and willing to endure discomfort and danger, and who had mastered the generalized skills involved in working sails and smoothbore guns. Race remained a secondary consideration, particularly in wartime. Accordingly, black sailors fought in every American conflict before the Civil War. At sea, blacks and whites shared the same mess and hung their hammocks side by side on warships. Although black sailors did not have the same opportunities as whites, nor did they ever totally escape prejudice, they were not burdened by segregation on board ship.

From the beginning of the Civil War, southern blacks flocked to the vessels patrolling Confederate waters. Perpetually short-handed Union naval commanders could not resist putting them to work. In September 1861, Secretary of the Navy Gideon Welles declared that escaped slaves could be enlisted, but at a lower rate of pay. The Union navy subsequently enlisted a greater proportion of blacks into its ranks than did the Union army. Even though most black sailors occupied the lowest enlisted ratings of boy and landsman during the war, a few did become petty officers. And while most black petty officers served as cooks and stewards, a small number became captains of the hold, captains of the foretop, carpenter's mates, coxswains, and even gunner's mates and quartermasters. On warships, black sailors accounted for between 10 and 24 percent of the crew, depending on time and place. The proportion rose even higher on service craft and sailing vessels. On 1 April 1865, the crew of the mortar schooner *Adolph Hugel* numbered forty-eight men, forty-six of whom were African American. Given the increasing opportunities accorded black sailors during the war, it seemed logical that the next step would be to commission African Americans.[3]

To enter the Navy's officer corps, African Americans first had to break the color barrier at the United States Naval Academy. In the "Old Navy," officer candidates had learned their trade on board warships. Berthed in the steerage between the officers and enlisted men, they were called "midshipmen." The establishment of the Naval Academy in 1845 at old Fort Severn on the west bank of the Severn River in Annapolis was a milestone in the professionalization of the Navy's officer corps and one of several events that marked the passing of the Old Navy. Regulations put into effect in 1851 shaped midshipmen's experiences for generations. They established the uninterrupted four-year curriculum with summer "practice" cruises and coined the terms "fourth classman," "third classman," "second classman," and "first classman" in place of "freshman," "sophomore," "junior," and "senior." One provision made the Naval Academy the Navy's sole source of line officers. With a few wartime exceptions, the Academy's monopoly remained unbroken until the establishment of the Naval Reserve Officer Training Corps in 1925. During the 1870s, midshipmen were called "cadet midshipmen," "cadets," and "naval cadets."[4]

To stand a realistic chance of admission into the Naval Academy, a prospective officer candidate had to have political influence. By the end of the Civil War, the duty and privilege of appointing midshipmen to the Academy had fallen to the president, congressmen, and territorial representatives. The president could appoint one naval cadet from the District of Columbia, ten enlisted men who had spent at least one year at sea, and ten men "at large." Each senator and representative essentially "owned" one opening, and as soon as his previous appointee graduated or "bilged out" (failed), he could nominate another cadet midshipman. Normally, a young man interested in becoming a naval officer applied to his congressman for an appointment. A few politicians selected their appointees on the basis of competitive examinations, but usually the appointment depended on a candidate's political connections, not his potential as a naval officer. Some politicians did not even try to hide the fact that patronage was the primary consideration. One congressman told an unsuccessful applicant during the Civil War that he had "promised his most intimate friends to use his influence to get appointments for their sons."[5]

African Americans lacked a friend who could appoint them to the Naval Academy until 1870, when Robert Brown Elliott won a seat in the U.S. House of Representatives. A pioneer in his own right, Elliott was the first black person elected to Congress. Born around 1842 in Liverpool, England, Elliott received a classical education, worked for a time as a printer, and served in the Royal Navy. He emigrated to Boston shortly after the Civil War and then moved to South Carolina. Elliott entered politics in his adopted state and helped establish the Republican Party there. In 1868, he became a leading figure in the state constitutional convention, where he advocated compulsory public education and defeated the imposition of a poll tax and literacy test for voters, both of which threatened to disfranchise blacks. That same year, he won a seat in South Carolina's House of Representatives. In 1869 he became assistant adjutant general of South Carolina, with authority to organize a state militia to protect citizens from Ku Klux Klan violence.

At age twenty-nine, Elliott was sworn in as a representative of South Carolina's third district on 4 March 1871 along with the rest of the Forty-second Congress. A young Afro-Anglo-Yankee whose speeches contained classical allusions delivered without a discernable Boston, English, or African American accent, Elliott must have mystified his racist opponents. The highlight of his congressional career came during his second term, when he spoke in favor of the Civil Rights Act of 1875. Replying to Georgia representative and former Confederate Vice President Alexander Stephens, he declared that the true meaning of the Civil War lay in the struggle to secure liberty and equal rights for any American citizen who had experienced discrimination.[6]

As one way of translating his civil rights rhetoric into action, Elliott strove to break the color barrier at the Naval Academy. In June 1872, he nominated James Henry Conyers as a cadet midshipman. Born on 24 October 1855, Conyers had received his early education at Avery Normal Institute, an all-black secondary school and teachers' college with a classical curriculum founded by northern missionaries in Charleston in 1865. Thereafter he had worked as a messenger in the office of the secretary of state of South Carolina.

Why Elliott chose Conyers remains unclear. Whether the appointment resulted from political patronage or the two simply crossed paths in some South Carolina state office is unknown. In a letter acknowledging receipt of his entrance examination permit, Conyers described Elliott as "my friend and patron." Obviously Elliott believed that Conyers was qualified for the pioneering role. A letter that Conyers wrote to his mother hints that the congressman had approached him with the idea of breaking the color barrier at the Naval Academy, rather than the other way around. Elliott indicated on the recommendation form that his nominee was a resident of Columbia, the capital of South Carolina. Where Conyers was born or whether he was raised a slave or a free black remains unknown. Nothing else is known about Conyers's life before he arrived in Annapolis.[7]

Conyers's success at the Naval Academy would depend not only on his own ability, but on the good graces of the officers who ran the Academy as well as the support or at least passive acceptance of his fellow cadet midshipmen. One of the Academy's most important functions in those days was to socialize prospective officers into the Navy's culture. Cadet midshipmen brought to Annapolis the mores and behavioral patterns that they had learned at home. Some of these mores and patterns meshed with those of the Navy; others clashed. The Academy's officers deemed it necessary to employ strict measures to mold incoming cadet midshipmen into the Navy's cultural image, "because without right living," as one contemporary observer put it, "civilization cannot exist."[8]

The Academy's organization was structured around teaching cadet midshipmen to "live right." Regulations placed the Academy "under the direct care and supervision of the Secretary of the Navy." George M. Robeson held this post throughout Grant's eight years in office. A Princeton dropout, lawyer, and New Jersey attorney general before assuming the post, Robeson was a terrible secretary. Fond of good living and loyal to his friends, Robeson embodied the worst behavior of Grant's scandalous administration, using his office for personal financial gain while allowing the Navy to languish. He possessed none of the qualities of a reformer and proved incapable of checking abuses within his department.[9]

The superintendent, the Academy's highest ranking officer, reported directly to the secretary of the Navy. The superintendent set the course for the Academy and the general state of affairs there reflected his personality and leadership. He handled the overall administration, commanded the officers assigned there, and supervised all the civilian employees. Since the student body in those days rarely numbered more than 250 cadet midshipmen, he was more involved in the naval cadets' day-to-day affairs than his twentieth-century successors were, particularly in matters of discipline. The commandant of cadets,[10] the second ranking officer, served as the superintendent's executive officer and as department head and principal instructor in seamanship, gunnery, naval and infantry tactics, drill, and "the art of defense." Other officers attached to the Academy served as academic department heads, instructors, medical officers, paymasters, and administrative officers. Civilians played academic and administrative roles too.[11]

When Conyers entered the Naval Academy, John Lorimer Worden was superintendent. Worden was a bona fide naval hero. Born in New York, Worden had entered the Navy in 1834 at age sixteen. At the outbreak of the Civil War, he was a 43-year-old lieutenant. In January 1862, through an old family friend, Worden received command of the *Monitor,* an experimental turreted ironclad warship then being built at Greenpoint, Long Island. On the evening of 8 March 1862, Worden's newly completed warship arrived in Hampton Roads. Earlier that day, the Confederate ironclad *Virginia* had dealt the Navy the worst blow it had yet received, sinking two wooden warships, the *Congress* and *Cumberland,* and damaging a third, the *Minnesota.* On 9 March 1862, when the Confederate ironclad reappeared to finish off the blockading fleet, the *Monitor* stood out to meet her. Thus began history's first battle between ironclad warships. For more than four hours the two ships blasted away at each other, but neither sustained serious damage. Toward the end of the duel a Confederate shell exploded directly outside the vision slit in the *Monitor*'s pilothouse, driving powder fragments into Worden's face. Temporarily blinded, with blood streaming from his wounds, Worden staggered backward, urging his subordinates to save the *Minnesota.* The battle proved a strategic victory for the Union, since the blockade held. Congress and President Lincoln thanked Worden for his efforts to save the country. The northern public showered him with praise, congratulations, and sympathy. The state of New York gave him a sword and a testimonial. After briefly commanding the monitor *Montauk,* Worden spent the rest of the war in various shore billets.

Despite the fame it brought him, the duel between the *Monitor* and the *Virginia* shattered Worden's life. "My head was all knocked to pieces at Hampton Roads," he recalled in 1895. "For three months, I lay unconscious and when I woke to life again, I was a mental wreck. Since then I have never known the time when I wasn't suffering both physical and mental pain." Powder granules from the exploding shell had destroyed his left eye and remained permanently embedded in his cheeks, giving him a gray-hued complexion that matched his general mood. For the first few years after the Civil War the Navy assigned him easy duty and allowed him to rest, but he never regained his health. Worden became superintendent of the Naval Academy on 1 December 1869. Conservatism characterized his tour there, for he preferred to follow the course set by his predecessor than to chart a new one.[12]

The typical midshipman of the Reconstruction era came from the nation's financial, commercial, industrial, and professional elite. His parents were well-to-do, white, Episcopalian Anglo-Americans with political connections or influence. Although 51 percent of mature American males worked as unskilled factory operatives or agricultural laborers in 1870, fewer than 1 percent of their sons became cadet midshipmen. Similarly, fewer than 1 percent of naval officers between 1845 and 1915 rose from the enlisted ranks. No African American had become a naval cadet before Conyers, and Conyers remained the only black midshipman throughout his first year.[13]

Even for the children of the elite, the Naval Academy was tough. Candidates for admission had to be between fourteen and eighteen years old and of sound mind and body and "good moral character." To enter the Academy, appointees had to pass an entrance exam in reading, writing, spelling, arithmetic, geography, and grammar. Once admitted, cadet midshipmen faced many more academic hurdles. The course of instruction included seamanship, gunnery, naval and infantry tactics, mathematics, steam engineering, astronomy, navigation, surveying, physics, English, geography, history, and a host of other subjects. The academic year began on 1 October and consisted of two terms. The first term ended with the "semiannual examination," held between 15 January and 15 February; the second ended in June with the "annual examination." These were final exams in the courses taught that term. Those who failed were held over to retake the exams, "turned back" to the incoming class, or dismissed, depending on the recommendation of the Academic Board and the ruling of the secretary of the Navy. The Academic Board included the superintendent, the commandant, and several other executive officers and department heads. During the first half of the 1870s, more cadet midshipmen failed than succeeded. The classes of 1873 through

1876 averaged thirty graduating and forty-one nongraduating cadet midshipmen and eight graduating and four nongraduating cadet engineers.[14]

Incoming cadet midshipmen learned the art of "right living" through both formal and informal means. Written regulations governed almost every aspect of a naval cadet's life. They dictated how he spent his day, what he wore, how he kept his room, how he ate, and when and where he could study, play a musical instrument, or take a bath. For offenses that were considered serious, such as intoxication and dueling, a cadet could be court-martialed or dismissed from the service. For lesser infractions a midshipman received a certain number of demerits, depending on the severity of the offense. Demerits served as a record of conduct. Cadet midshipmen worked off demerits by performing "guard duty"—"hours of weary pacing of the brick walks around the grounds"—during their free time. Other punishments included confinement to quarters, public reprimand, and deprivation of liberty or recreation, depending on the offense. Academy officers investigated all reports of infractions. The accused had the right to present an explanation to the superintendent.[15]

To help them enforce the rules and regulations, the Academy's officers assigned formal leadership roles to the cadet midshipmen and made them responsible for policing themselves. For the purposes of indoctrination, drill, and general order, the midshipmen were organized into a structure patterned after a first-class sloop of war. The basic unit was the "gun crew," numbering eighteen naval cadets. Five gun crews formed a division (or a company for infantry drill). The entire student body formed a battalion of four divisions. First-class "cadet officers" led the various units during gunnery exercises and infantry drills. Cadet midshipmen appointed as "superintendents of rooms," "superintendents of buildings," and the "officer of the day" maintained order and reported infractions in individual rooms and on the Academy grounds. Section leaders marched their sections to class and reported infractions to the cadet midshipman officer of the day. These responsibilities helped train the cadets to become officers.[16]

Unwritten rules supplemented regulations in teaching midshipmen to live right. Upperclassmen enforced these rules through hazing. Introduced to the Academy by naval cadets who had attended private school before coming to Annapolis, the practice expanded after the Civil War. Hazing functioned to indoctrinate new cadets into the Academy's culture and inculcate deference to higher ranks, respect for discipline, and conformity to service traditions. It also served to induce those with low "aptitude for the service"—those who did not fit in—to resign. Hazing had both mental and physical aspects, some harmless, others brutal. Officers assigned to the Academy were well aware of its existence. Some condoned it; others deplored it.

Worden detested hazing. He likened it to the strong picking on the weak. In the tradition that he inherited, third classmen did most of the hazing, subjecting fourth classmen or "plebes" (a term adapted from a Latin word denoting society's lowest class) to a broad range of indignities. A plebe might be made to climb on top of a wardrobe and sing; to wear his coat and pants inside out; to drink an entire pitcher of water; or to dance to the point of exhaustion. If the plebe remained defiant, he might be "passed around"—shoved roughly from one third classman to the next, sometimes into a wall. In the fall of 1871, upperclassmen handled some of the incoming plebes so roughly that their parents flooded the Navy Department with complaints. Worden issued a series of orders expressly forbidding hazing and promising to punish anyone reported for doing so, but these failed to inhibit the practice. After a major outbreak of hazing occurred in the spring of 1874, Worden dismissed the ringleaders and canceled summer leave for the entire third class. The following June, Congress passed what became known as the "Hazing Law," which declared hazing a court-martial offense and empowered the superintendent to dismiss any cadet midshipman found guilty of the practice. Even these measures failed to deter upperclassmen. Hazing remained embedded in the Naval Academy's culture through most of the next century.[17]

While hazing caused Worden the most heartache during his superintendency, race ran a close second. The Academy had always permitted African Americans inside its walls, but only as servants, stewards, or slaves. Annapolis's black population depended largely upon the Academy for its livelihood, while the Academy depended largely upon Annapolis's black population for menial labor.[18] Until the ratification of the Thirteenth Amendment, slavery, with all its attendant barbarism, remained legal in Annapolis inside the Academy as well as outside. In 1857, Lieutenant William H. Parker, an instructor in navigation and astronomy, reported Navy surgeon Dr. Solomon Sharp to the Secretary of the Navy for "unofficerlike and ungentlemanly conduct" because Sharp beat his "negro girl (a slave)" with a cane "without sufficient provocation."[19] On another occasion, Midshipman Henry D. Foote, a nongraduate of the class of 1861, beat a black female servant so severely that his classmates tarred and feathered him.[20]

Four of the five antebellum superintendents of the Naval Academy were born in southern states and harbored southern sentiments. Maryland-born Commander Franklin Buchanan, the Academy's first superintendent, owned slaves, assessed political candidates on the basis of their commitment to slavery, and served in the Confederate navy, including commanding the CSS *Virginia* in Hampton Roads, where he was wounded on 8 March 1862 and just missed making the next day's duel between the ironclads also a duel between once and future superintendents.[21] Commander Louis Goldsborough, another Maryland native and superintendent from 1853 to 1857, ran a cotton plantation in Florida with his slave-owning father-in-law during the 1830s, defended fugitive slave laws, and, even though he ultimately remained loyal to the Union, in January 1861 urged his well-connected wife Elizabeth to obtain for him "the highest berth you can in the Southern Navy."[22]

Racial attitudes of many of the naval officers and midshipmen at the Academy reflected the kinds of attitudes that had given rise to slavery and the Ku Klux Klan. In 1847, Midshipman Charles P. McGary called free black James Holliday a "damned black son of a bitch" and threatened to assault him physically over a minor mail-delivery problem. In recounting the incident Commander George P. Upshur, the superintendent, described Holliday as "remarkable" for his "uniformly respectful, humble, and submissive deportment to his superiors."[23] Upshur's "Uncle Tom" characterization of Holliday was just as racist as McGary's verbal assault. Racist, too, was one officer's characterization of the midshipmen's pet monkey as an African cousin of the Academy's black servants.[24] During the crisis of secession, more than one hundred midshipmen resigned from the Academy and "went south."[25] Most who did so served in the Confederate navy. During Reconstruction, many southern midshipmen's families had formerly owned slaves, were actively engaged in trying to relegate black people to a condition resembling slavery, and passed their racism on to their sons.

Northerners brought racist attitudes into the Academy as well. Rear Admiral David D. Porter, Worden's predecessor as superintendent, was born in Pennsylvania to a powerful naval family and himself became a prominent member of what one historian has called "the naval aristocracy."[26] Porter led two of the Union navy's largest commands during many of the war's most significant naval operations and emerged as the most important naval officer after David G. Farragut. Like many of his northern peers, Porter harbored racial prejudice and often used the word "nigger" when referring to black people. In the fall of 1862, Porter began substituting blacks for white firemen and coal heavers, the dirtiest jobs on a steamer, noting that the blacks' lower pay reduced expenses. In July 1863, the admiral began recruiting large numbers of blacks for service in the Mississippi Squadron because "white men cannot stand the Southern sun." Porter warned that blacks were not "naturally clean in their persons" and insisted that they be "exercised separately at great guns and small arms" and "kept distinct from the rest of the crew." In November 1864, he issued an order prohibiting his skippers from posting black sailors as lookouts, "as they are not fit to [be] intrusted [sic] with such important duty."[27] Such attitudes ensured that racism remained embedded in the Academy's culture long after the Civil War.

As the first African American midshipman, James Henry Conyers introduced the struggle for black equality to the Naval Academy, and in the process collided head-on with the Academy's institutional racism. If an African American cadet midshipman were to graduate, the ramifications would affect the entire Navy. "All race and political questions aside," wrote a Class of 1867 alumnus, "the issue was presented of whether or not a negro could take his place in the hierarchy of a warship and secure not only the necessary recognition from his immediate associates, but be able to maintain the discipline and enforce the respect incident thereto from the crew."[28]

Conyers arrived in Annapolis on 21 September 1872 and reported to the superintendent. Worden told him that if he treated the other cadet midshipmen "with politeness," the "same would be shown to him." Conyers was surprised and gratified at the kindness with which Worden, the other Academy officers, and the midshipmen treated him while he took the entrance examinations. Newspapers picked up the story and reported favorably about Conyers's first few days at the Academy. "He is of good form," read one account, "has a complexion about browned coffee color, with the usual curly hair of his race, and stands about five feet three inches." He was sixteen years old.[29]

Conyers passed the entrance exams and was sworn in on 24 September 1872. "The place was in an uproar at once," noted one of the instructors, Lieutenant Commander Robley D. "Fighting Bob" Evans.

The excitement among all classes was intense. As I walked along the row of officers' quarters, all the colored servants were at the front gate discussing the news. When I reached my own quarters my dining room boy, a small, copper-coloured imp, with his eyes sticking out of his head, said to me, "My Lord, Mr. Evans, a nigger done enter the Naval Academy!" That was what we were all feeling, though we expressed ourselves somewhat differently.

A southerner who had remained loyal to the Union, Evans had been severely wounded at Fort Fisher and emerged from the Civil War a hero, but had retained his antebellum views on race.[30]

Conyers was assigned to Room 64 on the fourth deck of the New Quarters. A four-story red brick building constructed in 1869 with an illuminated clock tower and an iron veranda extending across all 293 feet of its face, the New Quarters housed midshipmen in Victorian comfort. The basement boasted a steam room, laundry, and bathrooms with running water. The ground floor contained offices, reception and recitation rooms, and a mess hall. The cadet midshipmen lived, two to a room, in the upper stories. Another socially undesirable naval cadet, variously described as a "bootblack" or a "street tough" from New York City, was assigned as Conyers's roommate. Each resented having to room with the other. They did not get along.[31]

Robley Evans noted that "the question of colour was one we were not prepared to tackle." Secretary of the Navy George Robeson had made it clear to the officers at the Academy "that no imposition or indignity upon this Cadet, on account of his race, would be permitted from any one." From Evans's perspective, this order translated into a twofold mission. The first was

to see that no bodily harm came to the lad. . . . Our second thought was for the reputation of the naval school, that nothing unworthy its grand record should take place. The great danger was from the system of hazing, which had grown to very deplorable proportions, and which we were bending our energies to destroy.[32]

Evans was right about the danger to Conyers from hazing. Some of it seemed to be the usual type by which upperclassmen indoctrinated new plebes into the fold. On one cold, raw night, Conyers went missing. After an unsuccessful search, Evans was preparing to report the matter to the commandant when he heard a curious noise outside. Upon investigation, he found Conyers "in the top of a tree, very scantily clad, and barking with all his might because some senior classmen had told him to do it."

Adhering to the tradition of "never bilge a shipmate," Conyers refused to name the upperclassmen.[33]

But from the start, most of the indignities that Conyers suffered were racially motivated and perpetrated by fellow plebes. During their first few days as naval cadets, white fourth classmen frequently muttered "black son-of-a-bitch," "moke,"[34] or "damned nigger" to each other when Conyers passed by. Conyers often overheard them. Once when he entered the water closet, one of his classmates said to another, "lookout, there is a moke." On another occasion Conyers happened upon a group of plebes talking about him. "Are you speaking to me, gentlemen?" he said. One of the plebes called him a "damned black son-of-a-bitch" and threatened to whack him in the head with a chair. Other midshipmen expressed their racism by holding their noses or hissing when they encountered him. Several made a pointed effort not to stand beside him in formation. Most avoided him.[35]

Violence soon erupted. Friday evening, 11 October 1872, found Conyers and other fourth classmen at the gymnasium, taking a dancing lesson. Afterward, they formed up and began the ten-minute march back to quarters, with Conyers near the rear. Behind him marched George W. Collamore, Albert B. Crittenden, and George E. Goodfellow. Collamore had been born in Boston and raised in Kansas, where Confederates had killed his father in the "Quantril Raid" during the Civil War. President Grant appointed him to the Academy in 1870, but Collamore had failed the entrance exam. With the help of radical Republican Benjamin F. Butler, Collamore received another appointment from Grant in 1871. The Academic Board found Collamore deficient in his first annual exam and turned him back to the Class of 1876. Crittenden, born in Kentucky and raised in Mississippi, had likewise entered the Naval Academy with the Class of 1875 but had been turned back to the Class of 1876 because of academic problems. His grandfather, John J. Crittenden, who was a U.S. congressman from Kentucky and had served as U.S. Attorney General before the Civil War, had authored the "Crittenden Compromise," one of several last-ditch efforts to resolve the secession crisis of 1860–1861 by political negotiation. Goodfellow had entered the Class of 1876 with an appointment from Nevada representative C. W. Kendall. Like Collamore, Goodfellow's family had connections to Grant.[36]

Soon after moving out, several plebes behind Conyers began to push and insult him. Then a scuffle broke out, with Collamore and Goodfellow kicking and punching Conyers. A black steward named Brooks happened by. Thinking that Brooks was coming to Conyers's aid, Collamore, Crittenden, and Goodfellow grabbed boards from a temporary railing near the bandstand and threatened to beat Conyers and Brooks. Conyers said that he would report them if they did. They threatened to kill him if he reported them. At this point Cadet Midshipman First Class William Winder, the cadet officer in charge, heard the disturbance and ran back from the front rank. "What's all this?" he shouted. "Get to your places." Conyers said that he had been jostled out of ranks but would not say by whom; then he and the others fell in and resumed marching. Soon, Collamore and a few other plebes began throwing stones at Conyers. Winder reappeared to investigate this new disturbance, but all he saw were several cadet midshipmen behind Conyers snickering. Upon returning to quarters, Conyers went up the stairs backwards, fearing that someone would attack him from behind if he ascended face forward. Winder and Conyers reported the incident to the officer on watch.[37]

That night, in despair, Conyers wrote his mother Catherine a letter that must have horrified her. "The boys here are cursing me from morning to night," he began, then described the march back from the gymnasium in vivid detail. He added,

> If I had thought that there would have been so much trouble, I never would have accepted the appointment. I suppose you will say it is a great honor for me to be a pioneer of my race, but it don't pay for a man to be kicked around even if he is a leader. You hear it is a great glory to die for ones race or country; but when it comes down to stubborn facts it loses all its beauty. . . . You need not get frightened mother dear, for although I am beaten now and then, it will pass away in a year or two.

Catherine Conyers gave the letter to Frederick A. Sawyer, a white, Massachusetts-born, Harvard-educated U.S. senator from South Carolina.[38]

After seamanship drill five days later, Conyers and other plebes formed up to march back to quarters. Conyers fell in toward the rear beside Robert D. Digges, a Maryland native who, like Collamore and Crittenden, had entered with the Class of 1875 but had been turned back to the Class of 1876. Not wanting to march beside Conyers, Digges told him to go to the front rank. Conyers refused. They returned to quarters without incident and broke ranks. Digges turned toward Conyers. "The next time I tell you to get into the front rank," he hissed, "you go." Conyers said that his place was in the rear. Digges called him a "black son-of-a-bitch."

Conyers returned the insult. Digges kicked him and punched him in the mouth. Conyers drew back his fist, but then walked away and reported the incident.[39]

Meanwhile, stories about Conyers's treatment had broken in Baltimore and Philadelphia newspapers. Then as now, the press brought national attention to stories and, as often as not, spun them for political purposes. Exactly how the press got Conyers's story remains unclear, but it is likely that Senator Sawyer had something to do with it. For the most part the newspapers condemned Conyers's attackers. One account reported that on 11 October, twenty white cadet midshipmen set upon Conyers and "kicked [him] about the grounds until a cadet officer with a drawn sword had to interpose to put a stop to the assault." The paper denounced the perpetrators as "cowardly," "unmanly," and "un-American." An article entitled "Negrophobia at Annapolis" demanded that Conyers "be protected in his rights," even if it became necessary to expel every white cadet midshipman to do so. Another article declared that Conyers had as much right to be at the Academy as any other citizen. "There is no question here about the policy of admitting colored youth to the national academies," it asserted. "The people have decided." The article reported that President Grant had taken a personal interest in the case but did not mention his connections to the perpetrators.[40]

The *Army and Navy Journal* reported that if the cadet midshipmen were "abusing this negro cadet on account of the accident of his color, they are making a foolish mistake." Since African Americans had won the right to vote, the Academy could expect a succession of black cadet midshipmen. "The colored population has surely its right to seek representation in the Army and Navy."[41]

Navy Department officials were well aware of the political implications of Conyers's case. On 18 October, Acting Secretary of the Navy A. Ludlow Case wrote Worden that the "alleged ill treatment of Conyers . . . has gone through the press of the country like wildfire; and it is thought, by some, for political purposes, to influence the votes of the colored people, at the coming election." Case told Worden to keep the department "fully and daily advised" of any further mistreatment of Conyers.[42]

Worden had already ordered a board to investigate the attacks as well as the general treatment of Conyers. The three-man board included Lieutenant Commander Winfield Scott Schley, head of the Department of Modern Languages, who later achieved prominence during the Spanish-American War as commander of the "Flying Squadron," which patrolled the east coast of the United States. The board convened on the 17th. Schley and the other board members heard testimony from Conyers and twenty-five other plebes, fifteen upperclassmen, and three officers. Eventually they asked every cadet at the Academy whether he ever saw Conyers "molested, maltreated, or annoyed by gestures or otherwise, or ever heard him in any way abused by insulting epithets applied to him, so that [he] might hear, or so that they were intended for him to hear."

The majority admitted that they had heard Conyers regularly spoken of as "a black son-of-a-bitch, a nigger, or a moke," but not in his presence. The board believed most of the upperclassmen's testimony but found "a want of frankness" and "contradictions and evident desire to conceal what they knew" among many of the plebes. Collamore, Crittenden, and Goodfellow denied any wrongdoing. William Winder never mentioned drawing his sword during the altercation on 11 October, nor did anyone else.

Conyers claimed that he could not identify his attackers on the march back from the gymnasium because it had been too dark to make out their faces and because he had no desire to accuse the wrong person. When asked if others had "annoyed" him, he said that upperclassmen and cadet officers generally treated him with civility. The bulk of his problems came from fellow plebes. He named no one in particular except Digges. The board concluded,

> Cadet Midshipman Conyers has not been subjected to assaults and abuse from any inherent offensiveness, nor from any want of amiability, or ill temper on his part, but simply and solely on account of the color of his skin. His persecutors are left then without excuse or palliation except the inadmissible one of prejudice—therefore we think the severest punishments should be given, for by adopting stringent measures, Cadet Midshipman Conyers will be sooner secured in his rights, and be the sooner freed from molestation.

The board recommended dismissing Collamore, Crittenden, Goodfellow, and Digges from the Academy. As for other cadet midshipmen found guilty of insulting or mistreating Conyers, the board recommended dismissing two, confining four to the Academy grounds for seven months, and giving two ten demerits and a public reprimand. The board believed that only extreme measures would give Conyers a fair chance of succeeding or failing on his own merit.[43]

Shortly thereafter Worden forwarded the proceedings and recommendations of the board to the Navy Department. He told Robeson that he knew of no "organized combination to persecute" Conyers. "That [Conyers] is disagreeable to many, on account of his race and color, there seems to be no doubt," he lamented, "and while we may confess, that this arises from a most unwarrantable prejudice, it cannot be denied that, it is the growth of more than a century, and is not limited to any section of our country, nor to any class of people, but is wide spread and embraces all conditions of men."

Nevertheless, Worden believed that the board had recommended overly harsh punishments simply because Conyers was black. Considered without reference to race, he argued, the offenses did not merit such severe chastisement. "If *all* Cadet Midshipmen at the Academy are *equally* protected by the law, without regard to 'race, color, or previous condition,'" he reasoned, "an offense should be considered by itself, without regard to its affecting a white, or colored Cadet Midshipman." Ignoring the racial component, he characterized Conyers's ill treatment as hazing. He upheld the recommendations to dismiss Collamore, Goodfellow, and Digges but suggested that Crittenden be confined to the Academy grounds for four months. Similarly, he advised reducing the restriction for the others. He proposed that all the offenders be "reprimanded in General Orders by the Secretary of the Navy."[44]

Robeson followed Worden's advice. In his order of reprimand he pointed out that recently passed laws had abolished "all political distinctions of race" in the United States. Because of repeated warnings not to mistreat Conyers, those who had done so had acted in "a spirit rebellious of authority." Their action represented an "unmanly" and "impotent protest against the spirit of national law." While the Navy could not "control the personal feelings, nor regulate the personal associations of any of its officers," it could not condone defiance of authority. Robeson dismissed Collamore, Goodfellow, and Digges and punished the others as Worden had recommended.[45]

Goodfellow and Collamore immediately mounted a campaign to reenter the Academy. Both wrote Robeson expressing regret and begging for reinstatement. A Democratic representative from New Hampshire, a Republican representative from Vermont, and a Republican senator from New Hampshire all endorsed Collamore's request. Goodfellow's mother, Mrs. M. P. Goodfellow, personally appealed to Julia Grant for help in persuading the president to reinstate her son. While the assault on Conyers was unjust, she reasoned, it was not an "unpardonable sin."

> We can not blame boys for not looking upon colored cadets as their equals *socially* any more than we would wish our *daughters* to mingle with them and consider them suitable as husbands or our *sons* to select one of that class for wives. Would you like your son "Fred" [then a West Point cadet] to go around commanded by a negro even though he's superior in every way?

Mrs. Goodfellow closed her letter by reminding the First Lady of their mutual friends. Despite this influence, Collamore and Goodfellow were not reinstated. Robeson later dismissed Crittenden for academic deficiency.[46]

As the months passed, Conyers struggled to succeed. He struggled alone, for his classmates continued to shun him, speaking to him only when official business demanded it. "The agreement of the class," a fellow plebe later noted, "is to avoid him in every way." In reporting this fact, the *Army and Navy Journal* echoed Robeson's justification of Conyers's silencing: "Young gentlemen cannot, of course, be controlled in the selection of friends among the students." Even those cadet midshipmen who might have spoken to Conyers under other circumstances probably chose not to do so for fear of ostracism.[47]

Conyers found solace at the home of the Bishop family, where he spent his leisure hours. The Bishops were a wealthy African American family with branches in Baltimore and Annapolis. James Bishop, the best-known member of the Annapolis branch, manufactured sugar and cigars. He lived in an imposing house directly across the street from St. Anne's Episcopal Church.[48]

At the end of May, Conyers and his classmates took the dreaded annual examination. For the black naval cadet, it lived up to its reputation. The Academic Board found Conyers "badly deficient" in algebra, geometry, and French, with "no aptitude" for the service and "no promise" of improvement. Worden and the other board members recommended that the secretary dismiss Conyers. Instead, Robeson ordered that Conyers "be retained at the Academy for study; be examined in October and, if passed, go on with his class—if not, be dropped." Why Robeson overruled the board remains unclear, but the answer probably lies in the reality of congressional politics. Senator Sawyer had written to him about the

11 October incident and it is possible that other Republicans had spoken to him about the matter. Robeson undoubtedly hoped to avoid any more bad press like that which had appeared in the wake of the assault on Conyers the previous fall. One newspaper reported that Robeson's "leniency has been granted" because Conyers's failure "was not so signal as the majority." Whatever the reason, Conyers remained at the Academy.[49]

Unflattering pictures of Conyers emerged in the wake of the annual exam and Robeson's action. The *Baltimore American and Commercial Advertiser* attributed Conyers's failure to "a lack of brains." Robley Evans later recalled that "in our efforts to protect the colored boy we ran into the error of favouring him too much, and he soon came to give himself undue importance. He fancied that he was an issue which the authorities of the school dared not meet." Evans personally found Conyers to be "unbearable."[50]

Many of Conyers's classmates shared this opinion. The Academic Board had found Harry N. Butterfield, John F. Cheek, Francis H. Duer, Boyd Ewing, Louis C. Fletcher, William Lockett, John T. O'Keefe, Andrew Summers Rowan, and William T. Young academically deficient in the annual exam and had recommended their dismissal. These plebes represented a cross-section of American society in terms of geographic origin and social class. Butterfield hailed from Kansas, Cheek from Indiana, Duer from New Jersey, Ewing from Nashville, Fletcher from Philadelphia, Lockett from Georgia, O'Keefe from New York City, Rowan from West Virginia, and Young from Mississippi. O'Keefe had grown up in poverty, became a "newsboy," and won his appointment in a competitive exam. His low social standing was so unusual for a cadet midshipman that it had elicited comments from the press when he matriculated. Young originally hailed from Indiana, but his family had acquired the Magnolia Bluff Plantation near Natchez, Mississippi, in 1868. Young's father had been a surgeon in the Sixty-sixth Illinois Regiment during the Civil War until illness compelled him to leave the service after the battle of Shiloh. Following the war he became a planter. Duer had been appointed "at large" by President Grant; the rest had been appointed by their congressmen. They all had one thing in common: racism.[51]

Perhaps feeling that Robeson was going to dismiss them anyway, these nine plebes lost whatever inhibitions they might have had about harassing Conyers. At about 4:00 in the afternoon of Wednesday, 4 June, Conyers went to the boat house to go swimming. When he arrived, Butterfield, Cheek, Duer, Ewing, Fletcher, Lockett, O'Keefe, Rowan, and Young were in the water or getting dressed in the boat house. O'Keefe told Conyers that he had no right to swim there. Conyers said that he had just as much right to be there as any of them. When Conyers tried to step outside to the float on the water, Cheek and Duer placed oars across the doorway to bar his way. Conyers called Cheek a damned fool. "We don't want cursing about here," Lockett said. Waving a cane, Ewing threatened to hit Conyers if he tried to take down the oars. Conyers ducked under the oars, went out onto the float, and dove into the water. As Conyers was diving, O'Keefe threw a stone that hit him in the back. When Conyers surfaced, he shouted that whoever had thrown the stone was a coward. At that point the nine whites broke for the outer door. Young paused to kick one of Conyers's shoes into the water. Once everyone got outside, O'Keefe barred the door. Duer headed to town while the rest strode over to the wharf, which lay eight feet from the float.

Conyers climbed out of the water and put on his clothes. O'Keefe jumped back into the water from the wharf. Conyers asked for the missing shoe. The others laughed. Conyers tried to leave the boat house but found the outside door locked. Swimming nearby, O'Keefe made fun of his black classmate, calling him "nigger" and other names. Conyers grabbed an oar, returned to the float, and tried to pole it over to the wharf. O'Keefe climbed onto the float, grabbed an oar, and poled in the opposite direction, preventing Conyers from reaching the wharf.

Meanwhile, some of those on the wharf shouted insults at Conyers. Others evinced amusement at his predicament. A few remained impassive. None tried to help Conyers.

Nearby, a group of African American masons and a white foreman, P. H. Gibbs, were working on a seawall and saw the ugly scene unfold. Their stomachs must have burned with anger and disgust. One of the black masons, Joseph Sommers, happened to be rowing a boat toward the wharf. Conyers asked the mason to pick him up. Sommers turned toward the float. "You have no right to come here," shouted O'Keefe. Calling Sommers a "black bastard" and threatening to capsize the boat if the mason came any closer, O'Keefe jumped back into the water. Some of the cadet midshipmen on the wharf also began shouting threats and curses at the mason. Sommers hauled off. Just then the captain of the watch happened by, saw what was happening, and ran to fetch the officer in charge.

Meanwhile, the foreman had had enough. He told Sommers to head back and pick up Conyers. The boat drew alongside the float. As Conyers turned his back and stepped into the boat, Butterfield, Rowan, and Fletcher threw stones and chunks of dirt at him. One stone struck him in the head, drawing blood; another hit him in the wrist. Still another struck Sommers in the hand. Conyers shouted that whoever had thrown the stones was a "damned dog." The mason rowed Conyers away and landed him on the new seawall without further incident. Conyers returned to the boat house to look for his shoe, but couldn't find it. At this point the officer in charge appeared and ordered Conyers to report the incident. Conyers was not seriously injured. The whole affair had lasted some thirty to forty-five minutes.

The next day Admiral Worden ordered an investigation. A three-man board convened at 9:00 A.M. on 6 June and heard testimony from all parties involved. The officers concluded that "the undoubted animus which actuated the assault" was "Mr. Conyers' color." They identified O'Keefe and Ewing as the "ringleaders." They recommended that Butterfield, Cheek, Duer, Ewing, Fletcher, O'Keefe, and Rowan be dismissed from the Academy without being allowed to resign, a face-saving gesture normally accorded those found academically deficient.[52]

Worden forwarded their report along with his own recommendations to Robeson on 10 June. He declared that Butterfield, Cheek, Duer, Ewing, Fletcher, Lockett, O'Keefe, Rowan, and Young were guilty of throwing stones at Conyers or "deliberately aiding and abetting in annoying and attempting to prevent him from enjoying a privilege he was entitled to, equally with themselves." He supported the board's recommendations. The secretary dismissed all nine.[53]

The assault and its denouement made headlines. Most newspapers condemned the perpetrators. The parents of the boat house nine castigated the naval authorities for dealing with them so summarily.[54]

Five of the boat house nine quickly sought reinstatement. Butterfield's father visited Robeson in Washington and made a personal appeal on behalf of his son, which he followed up with a letter. Senator William M. Stewart, a Republican from Nevada, asked Robeson "as a personal favor" to reinstate Boyd Ewing. Worden recommended against reappointing Butterfield and Ewing. To restore them to the service, he argued, would hurt the Academy and embarrass the Navy Department. They did not return.

It was a different story for Fletcher, Rowan, and Duer. Representative Samuel Jackson Randall, a Democrat from Pennsylvania, renominated

Louis Fletcher in June 1873. Fletcher entered with the Class of 1877, did poorly in his studies, and resigned in May 1876. Representative Frank Hereford, a West Virginia Democrat, reappointed Rowan in September 1874. Rowan too had academic problems and resigned in February 1876. He later joined the Army and became a symbol for accomplishing a difficult mission without complaint by delivering a message during the Spanish-American War from President William McKinley to a Cuban insurgent named Garcia after a three-week trek through hostile territory. The feat, immortalized in Elbert Hubbard's pamphlet "A Message to Garcia," became required reading for twentieth-century midshipmen.[55]

President Grant became personally involved in Duer's case. His action reflected his general approach as president to the issue of race. Although he had supported the Fifteenth Amendment and civil rights legislation and had fought the Klan, he typically backed down when he anticipated that the cost of racial progress would be too high.

Grant had followed a parallel course when a racial problem had arisen at West Point. The Military Academy had admitted its first black cadet, James Webster Smith, in 1870. A northern philanthropist characterized Smith as "a remarkable scholar" of "excellent character." White cadets had abused Smith from the moment he arrived and threw a pail of excrement over him one night as he slept. They regularly forced him to take his meals cold and to drill alone and constantly reminded him that he was "nothing but a damned nigger." Several cadets had conspired to drive him from the Military Academy and extricated a pledge from the entire first class to silence him. President Grant's son, Frederick, seems to have participated in the effort to oust Smith. The lad undoubtedly inherited his prejudice from his mother Julia, who considered blacks inferior and whose family had owned slaves before the war. Fred supposedly told his father that "no damned nigger will ever graduate from West Point." President Grant could have taken decisive action to stop the harassment of Smith, but he did nothing, doubtless because any ax that fell on Smith's persecutors might also have struck his own son. Instead, Grant blamed Smith's problems on Smith himself, for Fred had declared that the black cadet was "very objectionable." Ultimately Smith was forced to leave West Point for dubious academic reasons.[56]

Similarly, Grant took no action on behalf of Conyers. While he had placed family concerns above black rights at West Point, he now placed political concerns above black rights at Annapolis. Duer wrote directly to President Grant asking for reinstatement. Robeson, Secretary of State

Hamilton Fish, and Secretary of the Interior Columbus Delano supported Duer's appeal. Grant reappointed Duer in June 1874. Duer washed out academically and resigned a year later.[57]

For Conyers, the lonely struggle continued. Soon after the boat house incident, he asked permission to return home for the summer for additional academic instruction. Robeson granted his request and Conyers returned to South Carolina. Conyers must have been relieved to be free of the Academy's stifling racist environment for a few months.[58]

2

"Speechless Walls as Companions"

While the first black midshipman was studying for the October reexamination, another African American was preparing for the Naval Academy's entrance examination. Alonzo Clifton McClennan was born on 1 May 1855 in Columbia, South Carolina, orphaned in childhood, and raised by his uncle, Edward B. Thompson, a prosperous free black barber. McClennan began his education at age ten at Benedict Institute, a Baptist school founded in Columbia by a Rhode Island philanthropist to educate newly freed slaves. Through the influence of another uncle, Samuel B. Thompson, a South Carolina state representative, McClennan later landed a job as a page in the South Carolina state legislature.[1]

There McClennan met Richard Harvey Cain, an African American minister and politician. Born on 12 April 1825 in Greenbriar County, Virginia, Cain moved with his family to Ohio, received a basic education, and worked on steamboats in the Ohio River. In 1841 he decided to become a minister and for the next two dozen years he preached in the Midwest and New York City. In 1865 his church sent him to Charleston, where he entered Republican Party politics. He became editor of the *South Carolina Leader*, with Robert B. Elliott as his assistant. Between 1868 and 1872 he served as a state senator, and it was during this period that he and McClennan became friends, probably as a result of crossing paths in the state house.

In 1872 the people of Charleston elected "Daddy" Cain as their representative to the Forty-third Congress. In Washington Cain championed land reform, suffrage, labor, and civil-rights issues and advocated honesty in government. Like Elliott, Cain wanted to send African Americans to the service academies, and in the summer of 1873 he announced that he intended to nominate candidates to Annapolis and West Point. Since the Thompsons could not afford to send McClennan to college, they urged him to seek an appointment. McClennan had long dreamed of becoming a physician and figured that a service academy education would be a good step toward that goal. He went to see Cain. The congressman said that he would like to send McClennan to West Point or Annapolis but felt obliged to hold a competitive exam for the appointments. Cain prided himself on never asking for political patronage and believed that merit should outweigh influence in determining whom to send to the service academies. McClennan studied hard, and on the appointed day, he and three others took the exam at the state house. One of McClennan's competitors stood first and chose West Point. McClennan, who placed second, accepted the Naval Academy appointment.[2]

McClennan spent the rest of the summer studying for the entrance examination. In late September he boarded a train for Annapolis. He must have felt apprehensive, for he had heard about Conyers's woes, probably from reading newspapers and hearing stories circulating in Columbia's black community. On the 22nd he and the other appointees reported for the entrance examination. To McClennan's surprise, none of the other prospective plebes exhibited hostility toward him. In fact, they chatted freely with him during the two days of the exam. McClennan began to believe that he would have an easier time at the Academy than had Conyers.

McClennan passed the entrance exam. He and the other new plebes spent the 24th being measured for uniforms, receiving bedding and shoes, and otherwise getting squared away, during which process a classmate from Maine befriended McClennan and offered to room with him. Instead, the commandant assigned McClennan to Room 64 in the New Quarters with Conyers, no doubt to avoid having blacks and whites living together.

Things changed drastically the next day, when an article identifying McClennan as "a bright mulatto" appeared in the *Baltimore American and Commercial Advertiser.* Although indeed an African American, McClennan had blond hair, blue eyes, and a fair complexion. Everyone knew that a black from South Carolina had been appointed to the Academy, but almost nobody could tell that McClennan was black by looking at him. One or two of the white midshipmen with darker complexions had been mistaken for the new black naval cadet. But with the publication of the article, everyone quickly learned who McClennan was. The fact that he towered above most of the others at a height of five feet eleven inches made him easy to pick out in a crowd. The boy from Maine who had offered to be his roommate refused to speak to him or even look at him, doubtless because he hadn't known before that McClennan was black. "I was now alone," McClennan recalled. "The acquaintances I had made at the examination had deserted me . . . with no one to give me pleasant smiles or recognition or the friendly grasp of the hand. Everybody looked to be strangers . . . and in one day the whole world, it seemed, had changed. I felt very sad and regretted that I had left my home."[3]

Conyers's return to Room 64 brought an unimaginable sense of relief to McClennan. "Conyers," McClennan said, "I am glad you have come and hope that you will be with me during the year, as I find it very lonesome in this large building." To McClennan's alarm, Conyers replied that although he had been studying all summer, he doubted he could pass the exam. Nevertheless, Conyers helped McClennan with his studies and showed him the ropes.

But Conyers could not always be there for him. Since one was a third classman and the other a plebe, they attended different classes, drills, and formations. Fellow plebes tried to avoid lining up next to McClennan in ranks. The section leaders proved unable to prevent McClennan's classmates from "insulting or annoying" him "in many ways." Even with Conyers present, upperclassmen made a habit of bursting into Room 64 and making McClennan snap to attention and remove his hat.[4]

Conyers, on the other hand, found that his classmates' behavior toward him had changed. They had stopped calling him names and otherwise mistreating him. He noticed that he "had it quite easy" compared to before. Then as now, midshipmen were most vulnerable to separation from the Academy during plebe year. It could be that Conyers's classmates figured that if they hadn't been able to provoke him into committing an offense that would have gotten him kicked out during plebe year, they wouldn't be able to do so thereafter, either, so they stopped trying. Or it could be that they had developed a grudging respect for him.[5]

Whatever the reason, academic problems still plagued Conyers. Sadly, as he had predicted, the extra summer instruction did not help. On 1 October 1873, he retook the exams in algebra, geometry, and French. The Academic Board found him deficient in all three, and again recommended dropping him. Robeson concurred. The secretary allowed Conyers to submit a resignation in lieu of suffering the ignominy of dismissal. Conyers did so on 10 November. Robeson approved it the next day. Conyers was out.[6]

Conyers's departure "demoralized" McClennan and made him "homesick." He was now "alone in Room 64" with "nothing but the bed and books and the speechless walls as companions." The only person who spoke to him was the African American servant who periodically blacked his boots and emptied the slops in his room. His only solace came from visiting the Bishops and receiving "cheering letters" from friends in Columbia. But he had nothing else to "assist in propping up the human building that soon gave signs of collapse."[7]

Academic trouble made the silence even more deafening. Although McClennan had studied hard to win his appointment and pass the entrance exam, he still felt "handicapped with the lack of sufficient preparation." Having not begun his education till age ten, he stood well behind his classmates in the quantity of schooling he had had before entering the Academy. He also lacked the same quality of education. In Columbia's public schools and in the Benedict Institute he had been "king bee," but at the Academy he "did not even stand well at the foot" of his class. He had studied arithmetic before coming to Annapolis, for example, but had never even seen a geometry or algebra problem.

McClennan's relative lack of preparation depressed him and, combined with his classmates' treatment of him, made him belligerent. "When one of the cadets interfered with me I resented it at once," he recalled. He resolved that if he were to leave Annapolis without "the honors of a diploma from the great American Naval School," he would return home "with the honor of having protected myself by muscular force."[8]

Because of McClennan's race and attitude, upperclassmen frequently reported him for infractions. McClennan began to accumulate demerits at an alarming rate. The extra duty imposed as punishment robbed him of time he might otherwise have spent studying, thus rendering his academic picture even bleaker. On several occasions he denied committing the offense cited in a report. Although the commandant of cadets, Commander Kidder R. Breese, ruled in McClennan's favor in these instances, he began to harbor doubts about the black plebe's defiant nature.[9]

In January 1874, McClennan took his first semiannual exam. The Academic Board found him deficient in algebra, history, grammar, and

French and noted that he had "very little" aptitude for study and no aptitude for the service. Since McClennan had accumulated 174 demerits during the first semester, the board also cited him as being "very inattentive to Regulations" and recommended dropping him.[10]

A discipline matter that Admiral Worden was already reviewing strengthened the case for dismissal. On 31 December 1873, McClennan's section leader had reported him for breaking ranks before the order was given to do so. Fuming, McClennan had fired off a letter of denial to the commandant. This time Breese did not give him the benefit of the doubt because several of McClennan's classmates had confirmed the section leader's story. Breese told Worden that McClennan was "guilty of uttering a falsehood."[11]

Worden ordered Commander Samuel Dana Greene, who had served with him on board the *Monitor* at the battle of Hampton Roads, Lieutenant Commander Schley, and another officer to investigate Breese's charge. The board convened on 6 January 1874 and heard testimony from McClennan, five other plebes, and a third classman. McClennan maintained that he had not broken ranks before the order was given. The others maintained that he did. The board confirmed Breese's finding that McClennan was guilty of lying.[12]

Whereas Worden had exhibited some sympathy for Conyers, he had none for McClennan. No doubt McClennan's more aggressive attitude put him off. "Cadet-Midshipman McClennan has nothing to recommend him to the clemency of the Department," Breese wrote Robeson at Worden's direction, "and his dismissal from the service is respectfully urged."[13]

McClennan considered the matter a "put up job." He wrote to Congressman Cain, explaining what had happened and asking him to intercede on his behalf with the secretary of the Navy. Cain, in turn, fired a letter to Robeson. "I do not controvert the statement of so many witnesses," he wrote, "but I respectfully submit whether such a misunderstanding between students, *colored* with their Prejudices against him, should drive McClennan from the academy [and] deprive him of his just rights." Driven by political imperative, personal feeling, or both, Robeson overruled the Academic Board and allowed McClennan to stay.[14]

Trouble continued to stalk McClennan. One evening about a month later, he sat down to supper in the mess hall beside Spencer Langdon Blodgett, a classmate from Pennsylvania. Blodgett insisted that McClennan move to the next chair so that an empty seat stood between them.

McClennan refused. Blodgett pushed on his arm and called the waiter over to tell him to move. McClennan threatened to strike Blodgett if he continued to annoy him. Blodgett kept pushing. "I tapped him lightly," McClennan recalled. "He was assisted to his seat with the help of some fellow cadets."

Worden ordered McClennan court-martialed. Witnesses testified that Blodgett had done nothing—that the black plebe had struck him without provocation. It astonished McClennan that no one told the truth. He decided not to speak in his own defense "as everything seemed to be onesided as far as the testimony was concerned." The court found him guilty and confined him on board the *Santee* for six months.

The old sailing frigate *Santee* served the Academy as a gunnery practice ship and a punishment barracks. Cadets confined there attended recitations and meals as usual, but slept on board in hammocks. McClennan liked living on the *Santee* better than living in the New Quarters, for the sailors posted there talked to him and the midshipmen could not bother him.[15]

Two of McClennan's instructors, Professors Freeman Snow and Frank H. Foster, paid him several visits on board the *Santee*. They said that although they would like to see him succeed, "it is useless for any Colored boy to attempt to go through because of the strong prejudice against [him]." They made McClennan an attractive offer. If he would resign from the Academy, they would see that he received an education.[16]

McClennan accepted. "I was not stuck on the navy and was not particular about being an officer if the way was made clear for me to get an education," he recalled. He wrote to his uncle about the decision. Although Edward Thompson had had his heart set upon his nephew's becoming a naval officer, he told him to do what he thought best. "What Ever you do I hope you will Let me know at once as I am very anxious about your future welfare," he wrote. "If you Resign I hope you will com home, for I think that we wold all be so glad to see you."[17]

On 11 March 1874, McClennan submitted his resignation. Robeson accepted it. "I left the Academy with no one within its walls to regret my departure," he recalled, "but, oh, my God, what a weight had been taken off my head and shoulders."[18]

Professors Snow and Foster kept their promise. They sent McClennan to Wesleyan Academy in Wilbraham, Massachusetts, for the rest of 1874. The next year McClennan entered the University of South Carolina, where he remained until Wade Hampton and his Democratic "red shirts" excluded African Americans from the university after taking office in 1877. McClennan moved to Washington and enrolled at Howard University, where he pursued his lifelong ambition to become a physician. After graduating with honors and degrees in medicine and pharmacy from the Howard University School of Medicine in 1880, he established a practice in Augusta, Georgia. In 1884, he moved to Charleston, where he soon rose to prominence among the city's black elite. That same year, he established Charleston's first black drug store and, in 1897, founded the Hospital and Training School for Nurses in that city. McClennan managed the hospital and school until his death in 1912. Charlestonians commemorated his contributions by naming the McClennan-Banks Memorial Hospital (1959) and McClennan-Banks Ambulatory Center (1992) for him.[19]

The next African American midshipman came hard on McClennan's heels. In June 1874, white congressman Henry W. Barry appointed Henry Edwin Baker, Jr., to the Academy. A self-educated man born in upstate New York in 1840, Barry moved to Kentucky at age eighteen and became principal of Locust Grove Academy. When the Civil War began he entered the Union army as a private, rose rapidly in the ranks, served as an officer in a succession of black units, and became a brevet brigadier general of volunteers on 13 March 1865. As a colonel he had organized Kentucky's first regiment of African American troops. After the war he studied law at the Columbia Law College (now George Washington University), moved to Mississippi as an agent of the Freedmen's Bureau, entered politics (naturally as a Republican), and from 1870 until his death on 7 June 1875 served in the House as a representative from Mississippi. In Washington Barry blended practical politics with genuine concern for black rights. "The colored vote of the South," he told fellow congressmen in 1871, "was necessary to balance the rebel vote and to prevent that section of our common country from falling into hands hostile to our Union."[20]

The *Army and Navy Journal* described Barry's nominee as "so civil and intelligent that his graduation is by no means impossible. He is from Mississippi, about seventeen years old, coffee colored, and the most superior specimen of his race that has ever presented for examination." Born on 18 September 1857, Henry Baker was living in Columbus, Mississippi, when Barry appointed him. It is not clear whether Baker approached Barry for the nomination or vice versa. In any case, Baker passed the entrance exam and was sworn in as a cadet midshipman on 25 September 1874.[21]

Baker received the same sort of welcome as had Conyers and McClennan. "No one ever addressed me by name," Baker recalled years later. "I was called the Moke usually, the Nigger for variety. I was shunned as if I were a veritable leper and received curses and blows." The other naval cadets mutilated his books and cut up his clothes, sometimes beyond repair. At one point things got so bad that the officers at the Academy had to detail a marine to escort him to and from meals. Only once during his time at the Academy did another midshipman talk to Baker outside of official business. On that occasion, a Pennsylvania boy appeared in his room at midnight with a piece of birthday cake. The act of kindness surprised Baker and aroused his suspicions until the lad said that his mother had asked him to share a slice with "the colored cadet who was without friends."[22]

As with Conyers and McClennan, the Academy's leadership convened a series of boards to investigate incidents involving Baker. The first occurred on 26 October 1874, when James Henry Glennon, a plebe from North Carolina, reported Baker for calling him a "son of a bitch." Rear Admiral Christopher Raymond Perry Rodgers, who had replaced Worden as superintendent on 22 September 1874, ordered a board to investigate the charge "and also whether Cadet-Midshipman Baker is at times exposed to insults, and whether he provokes them, as alleged by Cadet-Midshipman Glennon."

A nephew of Commodores John Rodgers, Oliver Hazard Perry, and Matthew C. Perry, C. R. P. Rodgers awed the cadet midshipmen with his aristocratic bearing. During his superintendency Rodgers thoroughly revamped the Academy's curriculum to provide a modern, professional education, leading one historian to dub him "Mentor of the New Navy." Rodgers took a strong personal interest in routine matters, fostered "official reserve and distance" between the first class and the lower three in an effort to develop leadership traits, and emphasized self-control as the first duty of cadet officers.

Commander William T. Sampson, later renowned for his great victory at the battle of Santiago during the Spanish-American War, presided over the board, which convened on 28 October. For two days the board heard testimony from Baker, Glennon, five other plebes, and two second classmen. Glennon claimed that he never heard Baker call him the name. "I have always avoided Mr. Baker," he said, "and know of no reason why he should call me such a name." The other plebes said that they had heard Baker mutter the epithet, but that Glennon had not heard it. They also testified that naval cadets routinely referred to Baker as the "moke" or the "nigger," sometimes within his hearing. They said that they had never heard Baker swear before. "My observation is that he is quiet but he knows the feeling of the class against him and he tries to find amusement out of it," reported Illinois-born plebe George H. Stafford. "The general bearing of the class towards him is never to associate with him. Everybody seems to have an aversion to him because of his race or color." A second classman reported that "the bearing of Mr. Baker towards the Midshipmen is that of supreme contempt I should say. The bearing of the Midn. towards him so far as I can see is not to take much notice of him."

Baker denied swearing at Glennon. "In coming from the Hall that night as on most others," he said, "the Midn. behind me were singing out lookout there make way, make way, and occasionally some one would halloo lookout for that nigger and let him pass, and so far as Mr. Glennon is concerned I do not remember coming into contact with him in any shape." "I am frequently exposed to insults," he added. "They seem to have a disposition to insult me in such a way that I cannot make a report of it or get any clear of it."

The board concluded that Baker did say "son of a bitch," but to no one in particular, and that his classmates often provoked and insulted him. "The general deportment of Mr. Baker toward his classmates is reprehensible at times, and yet the Board is of the opinion that these cases would not occur were Mr. Baker not incited so to act by the bearing of the other cadets." The members of the board recommended no punishment and Rodgers let the matter drop.[23]

Trouble returned in less than a fortnight. At seamanship drill on 11 November, Baker went to his usual station on board the practice ship. He received several conflicting orders, leaving him standing on the deck not knowing what to do. Finally James Thorn Smith said to fellow first classman George M. Stoney, "Can't you find something for this darkey to do?" Stoney gave Baker an order that conflicted with a previous one, so Baker stood still for the rest of the exercise. The first classmen reported Baker for disobedience. Admiral Rodgers ordered a board of inquiry. The board declared the whole thing a misunderstanding. Again Baker escaped punishment.[24]

Nevertheless, Baker seemed destined to repeat the experience of his predecessors. In January 1875, he failed the math and French portions of his first semiannual exam. The Academic Board recommended dismissing him.[25] While he awaited Robeson's ruling, two of his classmates attacked him. Born and raised in Florence, Alabama, John Hood received his appointment from Representative Joseph H. Sloss, a former Confederate soldier. Hood had passed the semiannual exam comfortably in all subjects. Lawson Melton, a South Carolina native, had been appointed by none other than Robert B. Elliott. Like Baker, Melton had been found deficient at the exam.[26]

While the midshipmen were returning to quarters after supper on 7 February, someone marching behind Baker hit him with a snowball. Baker turned around and shouted, "Take care at whom you throw snow balls." "Who in hell are you talking to?" said Hood. "You," answered Baker. Hood punched Baker in the face. "Kill the damned nigger!" he yelled. Melton joined in the attack. Baker broke free and ran back to quarters. Melton pursued him for a short distance, shouting, "I'll kill you if I catch you." Baker reported the assault to the officer in charge. Afterward, another pair of plebes told Hood and Melton that they heard Baker mutter "cowardly sons of bitches" as he returned to his room.

The next morning Melton followed Baker to the gymnasium. Baker spotted him, smelled trouble, and started back to quarters. "Hold on Mr. Baker," said Melton, "I want to talk to you a minute." Baker refused, wondering aloud whether Melton intended to strike him again. "Oh, no," said Melton, "I just want to speak with you." Baker stopped. "Come on Hood!" Melton shouted. Hood jumped out from behind the building, accused Baker of insulting him, grabbed his arm, and began beating his head with a club. Melton grabbed Baker's other arm and also laid into him with a club. Baker broke free and reported the attack to the officer in charge.

Detailed letters of explanation written by Hood and Melton obviated the need for a board of investigation. Hood expressed no regret and freely admitted attacking Baker. In fact he seemed proud of it. He told the officer in charge that he had long intended to strike Baker if the black cadet ever spoke to him. He said that he "was only carrying out that threat."[27]

Melton was equally unrepentant. He too freely admitted attacking Baker. "My only regret," he wrote in his letter of explanation,

is that I did not hurt him worse for this reason. He has often been known to curse several of us, in the vilest language, and lately his manner has been so insulting, that we could not endure it. I know that if I had not struck him then I would have struck him some other time. I assure you, Sir, it is humiliating enough to a Southern boy to be placed on a level with a negro; and it is something he will indure when he is obliged to, but to indure an insult after such humiliation is more than he can do. I have been taught never to receive an insult, and now when it was offered by a negro, I could not help striking him. I also admit, that it was ungentlemanly, thus to strike a negro, and I deeply regret having lowered myself thus. I think Sir, that I would repeat it, on the slightest provocation.[28]

Admiral Rodgers suggested that Robeson dismiss Hood and Melton "for wantonly assaulting Cadet Midshipman Baker." Baker "lives in a state of entire isolation," noted the superintendent,

and so far as I can observe and learn, conducts himself inoffensively, and with much discretion. I have observed on the part of some of the other Cadets, a disposition to treat him unfairly, but he has hitherto been protected from personal violence. The excuses submitted by Messrs. Hood and Melton, the manner in which they renewed their assault this morning, and in which they justify it, and indicate their readiness to repeat it, prove how gross was their misconduct, and how grave their disregard of the rights of Cadet Baker, who is here under the same law by which they themselves hold their Cadetships. The excuse of Mr. Melton is the more extraordinary, as he owes his Cadetship to the appointment of a colored member of the House of Representatives.

Robeson immediately dismissed Hood and Melton.[29]

An article in the *Army and Navy Journal* said that Hood's and Melton's dismissal "ought to have a beneficial effect. It is difficult to get these young men to appreciate the fact that the Department and the Superintendent of the Academy are determined as long as the law authorizes the appointment of colored cadets, and they are sent to the institution, to protect them in their rights—as much so as if they were white."[30]

Whether Hood got the message or not, he almost immediately sought reinstatement. On 26 February, one of his relatives, Kentucky banker L. M. Longshaw, fired a letter to Robeson. "I acknowledge with grief that the boy acted shamefully," he wrote, "and the more especially so, as he had been taught to respect the rights of others, *no matter what their walk in life."* Hood's mother told Congressman Goldsmith W. Hewitt, Sloss's successor, that her son had come to regret attacking Baker and implored Hewitt to reappoint him. Hewitt did so. "When we take into consideration [Hood's] tender years," Hewitt wrote Robeson, "and the fact that he was reared in the South, imbibing of course the Southern feeling or prejudice against the negro *socially* and the fact that the colored cadet gave the first offence I think that he ought to have been excused upon his promise of better conduct for the future." Hood graduated second in the Class of 1879. His career was distinguished by the fact that he was on board the famous Civil War ship *Kearsarge* when she wrecked in the Caribbean in February 1894 and on board the *Maine* when she exploded in Havana harbor four years later. Hood ultimately rose to the rank of rear admiral.[31]

To punish the fourth class for its ill treatment of Baker and to prevent further violence, Admiral Rodgers issued an order on 9 February making the fourth classmen march to and from quarters at all meal and drill formations, assigning them extra infantry drill on Wednesday and Saturday afternoons, and restricting them to quarters on Saturday evenings.[32]

Later that month, Rodgers dismissed a cadet engineer who refused to fence with Baker. The cadet's father defended his son's action, telling Rodgers that "his son was raised as a Southerner, and not on social equality with a negro, and he could not advise his son to do what he would not do himself."[33]

Nevertheless, the punishments that Rodgers had meted out to Baker's classmates produced the intended result. Most of the plebes subsequently pledged to stop mistreating Baker.[34]

In the annual exam the following June Baker made passing grades in all subjects. In a class of ninety-four cadet midshipmen, he stood seventy-fifth in mathematics, fifty-fourth in grammar, thirty-ninth in history and composition, and seventy-second in French. The Academic Board rated his study habits and aptitude for study as "fair." Nevertheless, the board inexplicably recommended that Baker be turned back along with twenty classmates. Robeson approved. Powerless to do anything about it because he was a plebe, Baker accepted his fate.[35]

At the same time, the Academic Board recommended dropping Baker's classmate Charles Renwick Breck, a Mississippi native. While Robeson deliberated on the matter, Breck attacked Baker. After the assault Breck explained to Rodgers that Baker had looked at him with an expression Breck found offensive and had said "oh Lord" to him "in a very insulting tone." "I knocked him down for it," admitted Breck, "and struck him a few blows."[36] Rodgers saw no need for an inquiry and recommended dismissing Breck summarily. Robeson had already approved dropping Breck on academic grounds. Breck left Annapolis without further ado.[37]

For Admiral Rodgers, the incident confirmed doubts about Baker that had recently entered his mind. Scuttlebutt had it that the black cadet's "manner and language have been provoking and offensive in the extreme to other cadets." The Breck affair led Rodgers to think that Baker's problems resulted as much from his attitude as his race. On several occasions in the following months the superintendent counseled Baker "of the necessity for prudence" and "of carefully abstaining from giving offense." No doubt Baker's change in attitude stemmed from resentment at being shunned, but Rodgers was getting fed up with him. Baker's defiance flew in the face of the submissiveness that Rodgers seemed to want and that Worden had seen in Conyers but not McClennan.[38]

Rodgers's patience ran out with the next imbroglio. One evening in late October 1875 as the naval cadets sat down to supper, the midshipman who usually sat on Baker's right was absent. Because of crowding in the mess hall, midshipmen customarily removed empty seats from the table. Baker started to push the chair away and called for the steward to remove it. Frederick P. Meares, the plebe seated on the other side of the empty chair, pushed it back into place. Meares, a North Carolinian, did not wish to sit beside Baker. The chair fell under the table. Other classmates kept pushing it into Baker's leg. Blaming Meares, Baker said that if he did not stop, he would throw both Meares and the chair "far away from the table." Baker was subsequently reported for "using obscene and vulgar language" during the incident.

Rodgers immediately ordered an investigation. A board convened on the 22nd and heard testimony from Baker, Meares, and five other midshipmen who had been seated at the table. Meares testified that Baker said, "You think you are hell on a stick." The naval cadet who had been seated on Baker's left testified that Baker had mumbled something, but he could not make it out. Others said that they heard Baker call Meares a "God damned son of a bitch." Baker testified that Meares and another cadet had "assumed an attitude in this affair which was very provoking." He denied using foul language. The board determined that Baker had been provoked, yet found him guilty of calling Meares a "God damned son of a bitch."

In his report to Robeson, Rodgers said that Baker had "applied to Cadet Midn. F. P. Meares . . . epithets so gross and indecent . . . that I am compelled to ask that he may be dropped from the rolls of the Naval Academy." He added that Meares was "one of the most correct, inoffensive, and prudent of our Cadets." "I have hitherto taken great pains to encourage and protect Cadet Midn. Baker," he concluded, "but I now feel it my duty to ask for his dismissal."[39]

Robeson asked Rodgers whether he would dismiss a white cadet midshipman for swearing as Baker had done. Rodgers replied that he would

> unhesitatingly do so. When any one wearing the uniform of a Naval Officer, shall at the mess-table, call a messmate a "God damned son of a bitch," the scandal is so vile, that it seems in my opinion, to stamp the utterer of such foulness as unfit for the association of gentlemen. But, in the case of Mr. Baker, the circumstances were peculiarly discreditable, for a large part of his old classmates are under a pledge, not to molest him in any way, and under the severe discipline applied to cadets last winter, for troubling Mr. Baker, his old classmates carefully abstain from every act towards him, that might displease the authorities of the Naval Academy. I have dealt so severely with those who have annoyed him, that I must seriously urge my request that he may be dismissed.

After pondering the matter for a few days, Robeson decided to follow Rodgers's advice.[40]

Baker returned to Columbus, Mississippi, studied law, and became a superintendent of public education. He later moved to Washington, D.C., where he became an assistant patent examiner for the U.S. Patent Office and a prominent member of the black community. After the turn of the century he published several books and articles on African American inventors and scientists. He died on 27 April 1928.[41]

African Americans nearly broke the color barrier at the Naval Academy during Reconstruction. The political climate of the Republican Congress enabled blacks to attend service academies for the first time. Robert Elliott, Richard Cain, and Henry Barry sent black midshipmen to Annapolis as part of a quest to reshape America into a place where race did not limit a person's opportunities. There is both irony and poetic justice in the fact that South Carolina and Mississippi, which had fought for an independent racial slavocracy during the Civil War, became the first states to send black midshipmen to the Academy. Unfortunately, the freshman congressmen who appointed Conyers, McClennan, and Baker lacked the political clout to persuade anyone to intervene on their behalf. The window of opportunity for blacks to break the color barrier slammed shut with the compromise of 1877, when, as Robert Elliott put it, the Republican Party in the South crumbled "like a rope of sand."[42]

The political climate in President Grant's cabinet favored African American attendance at the Academy. For all his faults, Secretary Robeson tried to ensure that the black cadet midshipmen got a fair chance to succeed or fail on their own merit. Robeson even went so far as to overrule Academic Board recommendations to dismiss Conyers and McClennan for things that would have done in a white midshipman. Although political considerations motivated Robeson's actions, the fact that he took them at all marked him a racial reformer.

President Grant, however, remained ambivalent about African American midshipmen. Although he reportedly once expressed interest in their plight, he did nothing to help them.

Superintendents Worden and Rodgers attempted to level the playing field for black naval cadets. The admirals were no fire-breathing abolitionists, but they sent a clear message to the battalion that they would not tolerate physical mistreatment of African American midshipmen.

Still, they condoned their silencing, reasoning that white naval cadets had the right to choose their own friends. Like most white Americans, Worden and Rodgers believed that the right to social equality did not accompany the right to equal professional opportunity. And when the black midshipmen responded to the discrimination with defiance instead of deference, the superintendents recommended their dismissal.

Admiral Worden treated the abuse of Conyers and McClennan as part of the larger hazing problem at the Academy, not as a separate racial issue. While Schley and other Academy officers believed that only "stringent" measures would accord the black midshipmen equal rights and freedom from molestation, Worden considered the offense and not the victim in determining punishments for Conyers's and McClennan's tormentors. Worden's policy curbed but failed to eliminate attacks on the black midshipmen.

Admiral Rodgers treated the abuse of Baker as a racial problem, not as hazing. Rodgers strove mightily to ensure that Baker got a fair chance, meting out severe punishment to those who mistreated Baker and ultimately extracting a pledge from the fourth class to leave him alone. Rodgers's policy also curbed but failed to eliminate attacks on Baker. Nor could Rodgers make anyone befriend Henry Baker. Neither he nor any other element of the Naval Academy's culture proved strong enough to overcome the racism inherent in American society during this era.

The biggest social problems facing the black midshipmen came from their own classmates, fellow plebes. Regardless of their geographical or social origins or whether their families had ties to Massachusetts radicals or Mississippi planters, all of the black naval cadets' classmates shunned them for racist reasons. Each fourth class seems to have made a tacit agreement to silence Conyers, McClennan, and Baker. The upper classes might also have reached a similar agreement. What George L. Andrews, a Military Academy graduate and professor, wrote about "West Point and the colored cadets" also applied to the Naval Academy:

> That Southern cadets, with their opinion of the colored race, would kindly welcome such new-comers was not to be expected; but most, if not all, of even the Northern cadets had similar and almost equally strong feelings. The Northern cadet might, it is true, be more ready than his Southern comrade to admit the legal rights of the colored race, yet he was but little, if at all, more inclined to admit them to social equality. The fact that this feeling was exhibited by the candidates before admission, and before the Academy could exercise any influence, shows that it was brought by the white cadets from their respective homes scattered throughout the country, and was undoubtedly shared by their relatives, friends and neighbors.[43]

Some cadet midshipmen might have befriended Conyers, McClennan, or Baker under other circumstances, but behind the Academy's walls, the fear of ostracism prevented them from doing so. The white naval cadet who made social contact with an African American midshipman did so only at the behest of his mother and only under cover of night. Having no help from friends worsened the odds for surviving a weeding-out process as intense as plebe year.

Those who physically assaulted the black cadets constituted a minority. Most of the perpetrators launched their attacks after failing examinations. On the verge of being dismissed from the Academy, they lost whatever inhibitions they might have had about venting their racist impulses.

The fact that some of them secured reinstatement to the Academy must have dampened the superintendent's message that abuse of black naval cadets would not be tolerated. That people like Duer and Hood were reappointed, while people like Collamore and Goodfellow were not, must be chalked up to politics. But whether they got back in or not, their justifications for the assaults echoed the words of Mrs. Goodfellow's appeal to Julia Grant: "We can not blame boys for not looking upon colored cadets as their equals *socially.*"[44] Whatever their stance on equal opportunity for African Americans, white midshipmen refused to accord them social equality.

Racism prevented upperclassmen from offering support or guidance to Conyers, McClennan, and Baker. Although there is no evidence that upperclassmen abused them, they largely condoned the ill treatment accorded them by their own classmates, despite the fact that some of the upperclassmen and cadet officers treated Conyers with civility.

The decisive blow to Conyers's chances came from academic problems. Born under slavery at a time when it was illegal to educate black people in the South, and despite hard study before entering the Academy and during the summer after his plebe year, Conyers never acquired the necessary skills to succeed academically at the Academy. Had he been able to do so he might have graduated, for his classmates stopped harassing him after plebe year. Had his classmates accepted him socially, one or more of them might have given him the tutoring he needed.

McClennan was never fully motivated to succeed at Annapolis. He had entered the Naval Academy for an education rather than to become a naval officer. The abuse he suffered at the hands of his peers quickly soured him on any notion he might have entertained about breaking the color barrier. When the opportunity arose to get an education elsewhere, he readily abandoned Annapolis and took it.

Baker did better academically than either Conyers or McClennan; his downfall resulted instead from ill treatment at the hands of his peers and from his refusal to respond to their torments submissively. At first, Baker tried to find humor in his peers' behavior toward him. Eventually, however, their silence and attacks angered and embittered him to the point that he was ready to explode over the slightest provocation. Had he not been continuously annoyed or ignored, he might not have lost his temper in the mess hall incident that proved to be the last straw in his case. But given Baker's temperament and the racial climate at the Academy, some other racial slight would have sent him over the edge and administered the coup de grâce to his naval aspirations.

Rodgers dealt with five major incidents concerning Baker. In the first Baker was charged with calling another cadet midshipman a "son of a bitch." Rodgers let Baker go unpunished because he believed that the racism Baker encountered among his classmates had provoked him into behaving improperly. In the final incident, Baker was again charged with calling another cadet midshipman a "son of a bitch." Although Rodgers believed that racism had provoked Baker this time as well, he used the swearing as grounds for dismissal. The admiral wanted the black midshipman to accept passively the way his white peers were treating him, but Baker's pride and temperament did not allow it. Because Rodgers disliked Baker's attitude, the admiral used the swearing as a pretext for dismissing him.

The fact that McClennan and Baker were black, proud, and defiant not only put off Worden and Rodgers; it might even have scared them a little. Perhaps the notion of black anger reminded them on some level of violent antebellum slave revolts. It certainly threatened the status quo, demonstrating that black people wanted far more sweeping change at a much faster rate than most white people would tolerate during Reconstruction. After all, pride, outrage against injustice, and defiance against authority constitute the prime ingredients of revolution. As members of the naval and American establishments, the superintendents doubtless found contrary thoughts and actions disquieting. Although Conyers felt pride and outrage too, he appeared more willing to conform than McClennan and Baker did and was therefore better able to evoke sympathy from the Academy leadership.

While Conyers's fate after leaving Annapolis remains unknown, the fact that McClennan and Baker subsequently rose to prominence in the black community marks them as survivors. That they gained admission to the Academy at all, survived their ordeal, and went on to succeed also marks them as winners. Their success in life demonstrates that racism deprived good men of a fair chance to obtain commissions, and that racism deprived the Navy of the services of potentially fine officers.

If there was any glory for the Navy in the Academy's failure to graduate a black midshipman during Reconstruction, it resided in the fact that those in charge at least made an attempt to provide an equal professional opportunity for African American naval cadets.

PART II

Persona Non Grata

*Jim Crow and the
Naval Academy, 1877–1941*

3

Segregation by Occupation

After Reconstruction, segregation became the predominant pattern of race relations in the United States, and it sustained the doctrine of white supremacy well into the twentieth century. By World War I, so-called Jim Crow[1] statutes effectively separated the races and disfranchised black people throughout the South. By the Depression, racial separatism had penetrated all corners of American life, north and south. Jim Crow also pervaded the fleet. White sailors brought to the service the same attitudes toward race that had given birth to racial separatism back home, so the Navy adopted a policy of segregation by occupation to facilitate recruitment and retention. As time went on, the Navy assigned black sailors to a narrowing range of occupations, effectively separating them from their shipmates by duty and living accommodations. As a result, opportunities for African Americans in the Navy plummeted to their nadir.

But even as Jim Crow reigned supreme, black people sought to overthrow the racial caste system. Ever increasing numbers of blacks and sympathetic whites joined the National Association for the Advancement of Colored People (NAACP), the National Urban League, and similar organizations. The discontent that later fueled the modern civil rights movement began to ferment as African Americans campaigned for greater employment opportunities, sought equal representation in government, and called for the elimination of segregation.

The fledgling civil rights movement early identified America's armed services as a target in its antidiscrimination campaign. Black leaders argued that since black taxpayers helped pay for the Navy and Army, black people ought to have equal opportunities within their ranks. They focused on issues such as segregation in the enlisted forces of both services, the dearth of black officers in the Army, and the absence of black officers in the Navy. As was the case during Reconstruction, black leaders sought to integrate the Navy's officer corps by striking at its very source, the

United States Naval Academy. Between Reconstruction and World War II, perhaps two dozen African Americans received appointments to the Naval Academy, but only two of them became midshipmen.[2]

The state of race relations in America accounted for the low number of blacks appointed to the Academy during this period. Segregation appeared below the Mason-Dixon Line after Reconstruction as southern whites used racial discrimination to regain and maintain their status as a superior caste. The new system of race relations imposed upon black people included segregation of public facilities, disfranchisement, inequality before the law, limitations on economic opportunity, and demeaning rules for social interaction.

After Reconstruction crumbled in the late 1870s, southern Democrats created legal barriers to black suffrage that stripped them of political power, such as poll taxes, literacy requirements, property requirements, and the white-only primary. For all practical purposes, the South became a one-party region, and the party was all white. In the wake of disfranchisement, the few civil rights that African Americans had gained during Reconstruction evaporated. At first, discriminatory ordinances, rules, and regulations trickled onto southern law books. Then, in 1896, the Supreme Court opened the floodgates. In *Plessy v. Ferguson,* the Court decided that "legislation is powerless to eradicate racial instincts" and laid down the "separate but equal" rule that legalized many forms of discrimination. During the next quarter-century segregation laws mushroomed in the South. Signs reading "white only" or "colored" appeared over entrances and exits, theaters and boarding houses, toilets and water fountains, waiting rooms and ticket windows. Jim Crow laws in various southern states mandated segregation in parks, circuses, saloons, ice cream parlors, hospitals, public transportation, and homes for the aged, indigent, blind, and deaf. South Carolina codes prohibited textile factories from allowing whites and blacks to work together in the same room or to use the same lavatories and drinking water buckets. Public facilities reserved for African Americans, such as schools and hospitals, received less funding than those for whites and were markedly inferior. In 1930, for every two dollars spent for black education in the South, seven dollars was spent for whites. Black people also had shabbier housing and poorer recreational facilities. "Separate but equal" was not simply a non sequitur; it was a lie.

Jim Crow etiquette accompanied the legal strictures. It included taboos against blacks and whites dancing, swimming, eating, or drinking together. The biggest taboo was interracial sex or marriage, particularly for black males. Some states passed miscegenation laws, outlawing interracial sex and marriage. In the South, whites expected blacks to behave deferentially during conversations and business transactions. Clarence Mitchell, later the director of the Washington, D.C., branch of the National Association for the Advancement of Colored People, called segregation a "constant corroding experience" because of the humiliation it caused and its implication of racial inferiority.[3]

White southerners sometimes evinced paternalistic attitudes toward individual African Americans who followed Jim Crow etiquette but almost always regarded black businessmen, professionals, landowners, and educated blacks as "uppity," "smart," or "out of place." Southern whites often resorted to violence to keep African Americans "in their place." Below the Mason-Dixon Line, whites could strike or beat "uppity" blacks, steal or destroy their property, and cheat them in transactions with legal impunity.

Lynching was the ultimate price for defying the doctrine of white supremacy. Lynch mobs sometimes tortured their victims before killing them, slicing off their fingers, ears, noses, tongues, toes, or genitals; gouging out their eyes; or roasting them alive over open fires. In one instance a pregnant black woman allegedly said something offensive to a white woman and a lynch mob slit open her womb, murdering her and her unborn child. Black males suspected of sexual liaisons with white women stood the greatest chance of meeting a violent and painful death. Other victims included mentally retarded individuals, transients, and known felons. But many were respectable citizens in the African American community who displayed too much talent, ambition, or independence to suit white racists. From the 1880s through World War I lynching "was not merely a spontaneous, sporadic, 'redneck' affair," as historian Joel Williamson put it, but "an established institution in a whole and ongoing cultural complex shared by several million white southerners."[4] As a result, white juries routinely acquitted people accused of lynching and many perpetrators never went to trial. At least 2,868 African Americans died at the hands of lynch mobs between 1882 and 1917.[5]

White racism also relegated blacks to an inferior economic condition. Before World War I, 90 percent of African Americans lived in the South, mostly in rural areas. Except for small upper- and middle-class minorities, most black people teetered on the brink of poverty. The majority worked as sharecroppers or menial wage laborers. In the South, the "peonage" labor system trapped black sharecroppers in the shadow of slavery. It forced African Americans who became indebted to their employers to remain on the farm until the debt was paid off, a process that high interest rates often delayed for years. Racism also ensnared African American wage earners, as many trades excluded black people. Factory and shop owners often prohibited blacks from doing skilled work. African Americans usually received lower wages for the same work. When hard times hit, black people tended to be the first to lose their jobs. While black workers served the white community, black white-collar workers, business persons, and professionals were restricted to the black community or to black schools, hospitals, or other public institutions.

Above the Mason-Dixon Line, restrictive housing covenants, zoning ordinances, or neighborhood associations excluded black people from many white neighborhoods. African Americans were expected to use different beaches and not to patronize certain dance halls, hotels, and restaurants. Although black people had the right to vote and enjoyed better living conditions and economic opportunities, more equal protection under the law, and greater freedom as human beings up north than down south, by no means did they have the same rights and opportunities as white people.[6]

During the Spanish-American War and World War I, debate raged in the black community about whether African Americans should serve in the U.S. armed forces. The positive argument ran that African Americans could win equal rights on the battlefield. Opponents declared that blacks should not sacrifice themselves to further the interests of their white oppressors.

During World War I, scholar and civil rights activist W. E. B. Du Bois urged fellow African Americans "to forget our special grievances" for the duration and to "close our ranks shoulder to shoulder with our own white fellow citizens and the allied nations that are fighting for democracy."[7] A. Philip Randolph, one of the twentieth century's most prominent black labor leaders and spokesmen, pointed out that black sailors and soldiers had fought in all previous American wars, but their collective sacrifices had never earned equal rights for their race. Many African Americans decided to "close ranks" anyway. Significant numbers volunteered during both the Spanish-American War and World War I and many distinguished themselves in combat. For example, the all-black 369th United States Infantry Regiment serving in France spent more time under fire than any other American unit and became the first Allied outfit to cross the Rhine River. The Germans nicknamed the 369th "Hell Fighters" and the French awarded the Légion d'Honneur, the French equivalent of the Medal of Honor, to 171 of its officers and enlisted men.

But in neither the Spanish-American War nor World War I did military service alter African Americans' status among their countrymen. Black servicemen found that Jim Crow followed the flag as white Americans carried their prejudice overseas. During World War I, black soldiers who volunteered to "help make the world safe for democracy" endured discrimination at boot camp, received inferior training and equipment, and served in segregated units. Four out of five black soldiers sent to France served as laborers rather than as combat troops. In many French towns the Army forbade black soldiers from visiting cafes or civilian homes. White American servicemen counseled French soldiers and civilians to maintain complete separation of the races, lest black soldiers assault and rape white women. Even the headquarters of the American Expeditionary Force suggested that French officers treat blacks as second-class soldiers.

After the war, the welcome home that black soldiers and sailors received dashed any remaining hope that their service record would advance the struggle for civil rights. Race riots and mob violence erupted in cities across the country during what came to be called the "Red Summer" of 1919. Mobs lynched more than seventy blacks, several of whom were veterans in uniform. A revived Ku Klux Klan demanded that African Americans "respect the rights of the white race in whose country they are permitted to reside." A wave of violence swept across the South and Southwest as Klan terrorists flogged their victims, branded them with acid, tarred and feathered them, and burned them alive in public.[8]

The picture remained bleak during the "Roaring Twenties." Persistent labor union discrimination, a decline in the number of semiskilled jobs, and the general fluctuation of American industry severely constricted the African American wage earner's share in that decade's prosperity. Agricultural problems exacerbated the already tenuous existence of the black sharecropper and tenant farmer. Republican presidents did not have to rely upon the small black vote to assure their political power. Jim Crow continued to flourish. A Birmingham law of 1930 even prohibited whites and blacks from playing checkers together.

The Depression made things even worse. A report published in 1933 revealed that more than 17 percent of the black population was on relief, a proportion roughly double their presence in the population. During the early thirties the jobless rate for black males in major industrial cities like

New York, Chicago, Detroit, and Philadelphia ran between 40 percent and 60 percent, much higher than the overall jobless rate of 25 percent.[9]

By World War II, segregation had become firmly embedded in America's cultural landscape. Although black and white Americans gazed up at the same sky, they lived in two separate and very different worlds on the earth below.

Segregation also descended on the Navy after Reconstruction. The late nineteenth century witnessed the birth of the "New Navy" as wooden men-of-war gave way to steam-powered, armored warships built of steel and armed with rifled breech-loading guns and self-propelled torpedoes. The new ships demanded a new type of sailor, with more differentiated and specialized skills. As the fleet expanded after the war with Spain, the Navy needed more sailors than ever before during peacetime. To meet these demands, the Navy totally revamped its personnel policy. Instead of looking for experienced mariners in port towns, the Navy turned inland for raw recruits, spent good money to train them, and improved service life and benefits to retain them.[10]

At first the New Navy employed the same racial policy used during the Civil War. Black sailors accounted for 10 percent of all enlistees in 1870, 14 percent in 1880, and 9.5 percent in 1890. Although increasingly more likely than whites to be cooks, stewards, and landsmen, black sailors still served at sea as firemen, storekeepers, carpenters, water tenders, oilers, and in other specialized billets, and they messed and berthed with their white shipmates. Individual officers could advance or restrict the careers of black sailors according to their personnel needs or the whims of their own prejudice. Although no African American sailor seems to have made petty officer first class during this period, a handful became second- and third-class petty officers. Still, no African American became a commissioned officer.[11]

As the nineteenth century turned into the twentieth, white recruits from rural areas in the South, East, and Midwest brought into the New Navy the same attitudes toward race that had produced Jim Crow laws and customs back home. An officer noted in the U.S. Naval Institute *Proceedings* that some white sailors had a "prejudice" against "working alongside, messing with or billeting near the negro." A former sailor wrote the editor of the *Army and Navy Journal* that he and most other white enlisted men considered serving with black sailors "one of the most disagreeable features of naval service." "I will not go so far as to say that every white man in the Navy was opposed to negroes," he added, "but I will say that the overwhelming majority were, and that it was not confined to men from the South." A white chief petty officer agreed. "Voicing the sentiments of the majority of enlisted men," he wrote to the *Army and Navy Journal,*

> I desire to state that the enlistment of negroes for general service should not be encouraged, but rather discouraged, as the presence of negroes on board ship in a crew composed of white men is not only objectionable to the enlisted man, but is a cause of dissension as well. I personally know of instances where much confusion and dissension have arisen, caused by the placing of negro petty officers over white men.[12]

Naval policy gradually began to reflect such sentiments. Officers increasingly believed that white sailors would take orders only from a member of their own race, so they withheld promotions from African Americans. As a result, fewer and fewer black sailors became petty officers. In 1904, a New Orleans recruiter refused even to enlist blacks, claiming that doing so would make it impossible to recruit whites. In 1905, receiving ships in Norfolk set aside separate mess tables for African Americans. Throughout this period, the Navy increasingly concentrated black sailors in specialties that isolated them from the rest of the crew, particularly as messmen and coal heavers. Segregation by occupation soon became the norm.[13]

Jim Crow steered the Navy's racial policy through World War I and into the Depression. During the Spanish-American War, one in ten sailors was black. During World War I, African Americans constituted less than 3 percent of the enlisted force. In April 1917, Secretary of the Navy Josephus Daniels wrote New Jersey Senator Joseph S. Frelinghuysen that "as a matter of policy . . . it has been customary to enlist colored men in the various ratings of the messman branch . . . and in the lower ratings of the fireroom; thus permitting colored men to sleep and eat by themselves."[14] The Navy suspended first enlistments of African Americans altogether on 4 August 1919 because officers believed Filipinos made better messmen than blacks. Filipinos seemed neater, quieter, less sullen, and less threatening. By 1932, blacks constituted just over one-half of 1 percent of the enlisted force. When naval officials sensed that the Philippines were moving toward independence and that the supply of Filipino messmen was dwindling, they reopened the steward's branch to African Americans on 4 January 1933.

Although blacks could serve with whites on board large warships, their duties were limited to preparing food or waiting on officers, and they lived apart from the rest of the crew in separate compartments. The Navy forbade petty officers in the steward's branch from exercising authority over general service enlistees. Stewards wore distinctive uniforms that resembled waiters' attire. Most black sailors seethed with resentment at their status as "messboys" or "chambermaids of the braid."

In June 1940, the Navy's 4,007 black sailors accounted for 2.3 percent of its total strength of 170,000. At the beginning of World War II, only twenty-nine African American sailors in the regular service were not messmen. Historian Frederick Harrod believed that the primary motive for the Navy's Jim Crow policy was to prevent blacks from achieving positions of authority over whites.[15]

Although the same motive shaped the experience of black officers in the Army, African Americans broke the color barrier at the United States Military Academy during the Jim Crow era. The black experience at West Point provided the impetus for the black community's effort to send African Americans to Annapolis.

Between 1870 and 1889, twenty-seven African Americans received appointments to the Military Academy, twelve became cadets, and three graduated.[16] Each of the three black Military Academy graduates suffered social ostracism while cadets. West Point's first black graduate became a plebe in 1873, the same year that Alonzo McClennan entered the Naval Academy. Born into slavery in Georgia on 31 March 1856, Henry Ossian Flipper arrived at West Point with an appointment from Congressman James C. Freeman (R-GA). Flipper was the seventh black to receive a nomination and the fourth to be admitted. James Webster Smith, the first black cadet, advised Flipper not to "thrust himself on the white boys" if he wished to avoid unpleasant consequences. Flipper took the advice. He remained dignified, aloof, and polite and refrained from forward conduct with the white cadets. His classmates ignored or ostracized him in public, but a handful offered encouragement in private. After enduring four years in "Coventry," with no one speaking to him openly outside the line of duty, he graduated fiftieth in a class of seventy-six cadets in June 1877. New York newspapers hailed the event as a landmark in race relations. In a book he wrote after leaving West Point, Flipper maintained that the upperclassmen, officers, and instructors had always treated him courteously and fairly.[17]

Six years after Flipper graduated, John Hanks Alexander became a plebe. Born to free black parents in Helena, Arkansas, on 6 January 1864, Alexander spent two years at Oberlin College in Ohio before entering the competition sponsored by Democratic Congressman George W. Geddes of Mansfield, Ohio, for an appointment to the Military Academy. Inspired by Flipper's success at West Point, Alexander won the appointment and became a cadet in 1883. The officers, instructors, upperclassmen, and even his classmates treated him as an equal, but none of them socialized with him. Alexander was not totally isolated, however, for four African Americans became cadets during his years at the Military Academy, including Charles Denton Young, the third black West Point graduate. Still, Alexander came to view Academy life as something to be endured rather than enjoyed. Endure he did, and in June 1887, he graduated thirty-second in a class of sixty-four, to thunderous applause.[18]

Charles Denton Young entered the Military Academy in 1884, one year after Alexander. Born in Mayslick, Kentucky, on 12 March 1864 and raised in Ohio, Young entered the Military Academy in 1884, was dismissed for academic deficiency at the end of his plebe year, and reentered in 1885. Young also got the silent treatment, but many of his white classmates secretly pulled for him. "We esteem [him] highly," wrote one classmate, "for his patient perseverance in the face of discouraging conditions." Young did make it, but graduated with the dubious distinction of being the Class of 1889's "anchor man," the cadet with the lowest academic standing.[19]

As a rule, the African American cadets who did not graduate were dismissed for academic deficiency and suffered social ostracism or worse at the Military Academy. Easily the most bizarre case was that of Johnson Chestnut Whittaker. Whittaker entered the Military Academy three years after Flipper. As was customary with black cadets, no white cadet spoke to Whittaker except on official business. On 7 April 1880, Whittaker failed to appear for morning roll call. The cadet officer of the day went to Whittaker's room to investigate. When nobody answered the door, the cadet officer stepped inside and found Whittaker lying motionless on the floor in his underwear, with his wrists bound, legs trussed to the side rail of the bed, and blood on the floor from slashes in his ears and left hand. Throughout repeated questioning by the authorities, Whittaker maintained that three masked men had broken into his room and attacked him in the middle of the night. The superintendent believed instead that

Whittaker had slashed his own ears and tied himself up in order to spend time in the hospital and thereby avoid final exams two months later. Although President Chester A. Arthur ultimately exonerated Whittaker, the Army dismissed him for academic deficiency.[20]

Racial discrimination plagued the Army careers of the first three black Military Academy alumni. In 1866, Congress decreed the formation of two black cavalry regiments, the Ninth and Tenth Cavalry, and four black infantry regiments, which, three years later, were consolidated into the Twenty-fourth and Twenty-fifth Infantry. The Army soon stationed all of them on the western frontier. Nicknamed "Buffalo Soldiers," the Ninth and Tenth Cavalry earned a degree of fame for their exploits in the wars against Native Americans. At first, all the commissioned officers in the black regiments were white, with the exception of a few chaplains. Upon being commissioned, Flipper joined the Tenth Cavalry Regiment at Fort Sill, Oklahoma. His career ended abruptly in 1882 when the Army dismissed him for conduct unbecoming an officer, a charge that arose from an accusation that he had mishandled government funds. Flipper's punishment did not fit the crime, and had he been white, the Army would not have cashiered him. After leaving the Army Flipper carved out a successful career as an engineer and surveyor for various mining companies. He died on 3 May 1940. Nearly sixty years later, President William J. Clinton acknowledged the Army's mistake and, on 19 February 1999, pardoned Flipper.

Alexander served in the Ninth Cavalry for seven years, then received an assignment as professor of military science and tactics at Wilberforce University, a black institution in Ohio that the War Department had designated as "a school for military training." Alexander died of heart disease there on 26 March 1894.[21]

Charles Young became the most famous black officer of his day. After receiving his commission, Young served in the Ninth and Tenth Cavalry and as professor of military science and tactics at Wilberforce until May 1898, when he left the Regular Army to command the Ninth Ohio Volunteer Colored Infantry. Corporal Henry O. Atwood, who served with Young in that outfit, described him as a "staunch disciplinarian, an effectual, impetuous leader, and a capable tactician."[22] Major General J. C. Breckinridge, Young's commanding officer, declared, "Certainly we should have the best obtainable officers for our volunteers and therefore some such men as [Major] Young . . . , whether black or white, must be sought for."[23] Young rejoined the Tenth Cavalry on 28 January 1899.

After two years spent in helping put down the Philippine Insurrection, he served as superintendent of Sequoia and Grant National Parks in California and military attaché to Haiti and Liberia. In 1916, Young distinguished himself leading troops of horsemen in combat under Brigadier General John J. "Black Jack" Pershing during the so-called Punitive Expedition against Pancho Villa in northern Mexico.

During World War I, it seemed natural that Young, then a lieutenant colonel, should receive command of the Tenth Cavalry. But it was not to be. Several white officers in the Tenth who feared that they would have to serve under Young complained to their senators, who, in turn, pressured Secretary of War Newton D. Baker into preventing Young's advancement. Baker dodged any flak that might have arisen from the racial question by concocting a phony excuse for ousting Young from the Army. Alleging that Young's blood pressure was too high, the War Department retired him with the rank of colonel on the grounds of medical disability in July 1917. Shocked at the news, Young demonstrated his good health by riding a horse from Chillicothe, Ohio, to Washington, D.C. In late 1917 the Army recalled Young to active duty with the Ohio National Guard. After the war he returned to Liberia as the U.S. military attaché. He asked Henry Atwood to be his aide and to serve with him on a commission to militarize Liberia's constabulary. Atwood assented.

While in Africa Young determined to study the history of the black race "to stir in the colored American a pride of ancestry," as Atwood put it. Young took several extended trips into the interior of Africa to meet local leaders and visit places of historical interest. He contracted a malignant strain of malaria on the last of these trips and died in a hospital in Lagos, Nigeria, on 8 January 1922. Young's remains were interred in Arlington National Cemetery. His funeral was a major event in Washington's black community. Young's example would later inspire Henry Atwood to launch a concerted effort to break the color barrier at the Naval Academy.[24]

Between Young's graduation in 1889 and 1930, only two African Americans received appointments to the Military Academy. Both became cadets, but neither one lasted more than six months. With black disfranchisement in the South, only a small proportion of black voters in northern cities, and the widespread racism that gave rise to segregation, it had become politically inexpedient for congressmen to appoint blacks to West Point.[25]

Thus, despite the pioneering and heroic efforts of the first black cadets, the situation for African Americans at the Military Academy remained unchanged between the Civil War and the Depression. Flipper, Alexander, and Young graduated only after demonstrating the extraordinary ability to endure years of silence and ostracism from their peers. Their graduation neither made life at the Military Academy easier for the black cadets who followed nor fostered the acceptance of blacks among white cadets. While many white cadets probably silently rooted for them, none had the courage to risk ostracism themselves by offering overt support. Each African American cadet who followed in Flipper's footsteps essentially had to relive Flipper's experience. This is not to criticize those first black cadets, for their efforts and their goals cannot be faulted. American society had not yet matured enough to accept African American Military Academy graduates, for as Young's case demonstrates, they embodied one of racists' worst fears: the possibility of a white man being subordinated to a black man. For many people who later strove to break the color barrier at the Naval Academy, Young's case provided inspiration, particularly to Henry O. Atwood.

A situation parallel to that in West Point existed in Annapolis. Between Reconstruction and 1928, three African Americans received appointments to the Naval Academy. In April 1896, Congressman George E. White, a Massachusetts native, former Union soldier, and representative of the Fifth Illinois District, nominated Robert Foster Wheeler, a Chicago native. Wheeler never reported for the entrance exam, however, and never entered the Academy.[26]

A year later, White appointed another black Chicagoan, John William Smith, who had graduated from Chicago High School at the head of his class, winning a gold medal for excellence in his studies. Smith's teachers and "many influential men" from the Fifth District had recommended him to Congressman White for the appointment. In May, when the time came for Smith to report to the Naval Academy to take the entrance exam, more than one hundred of his high school classmates escorted him to the railroad station. Smith passed the mathematics portions of the exam but failed in grammar, geography, and history. Academy rules permitted him to retake the exam the following September. Although Smith admitted to being unprepared in May, Congressman White believed that Academy officials had deliberately undergraded his papers to keep him from becoming a midshipman. White threatened to demand a congressional investigation if he suspected discrimination during the September exam, and vowed to continue reappointing Smith and nobody else as long as he remained in Congress. In the end, Smith never appeared for the re-examination and White never reappointed him after all.[27]

That same year (1897), Congressman W. B. Shattuc, a former Union cavalry officer and representative of the First Ohio District, appointed Richard C. Bundy, an African American from Cincinnati. Due to graduate in June from Cincinnati High School, Bundy was slated to take the Academy entrance exam in September. Several other congressmen urged Shattuc to withdraw Bundy's name, declaring that "it was an unwritten law not to allow a colored boy at Annapolis." "They told me if I persisted it would break up the school and that other students would resign," Shattuc told a reporter for the *New York Times*. "Let them resign," Shattuc replied. He pointed out that Bundy had won the appointment in a competitive exam, outscoring all the white candidates. "I'm going to see that he goes to Annapolis and receives fair treatment if it is in my power to do so," he declared.[28]

African Americans welcomed the news of Bundy's appointment. Richard E. King, a prominent black lawyer in Annapolis, congratulated Bundy and advised him to be courteous and studious and thereby "elevate his race in the eyes of respectable people." Other leading black citizens of Annapolis viewed Bundy's nomination within the larger context of the struggle for equal rights. "The time has come when the colored race must demand every political and official privilege that belongs to them as American citizens," they told a reporter for the *New York Times*. Bundy promised to do his best.[29]

Bundy's impending arrival at the Naval Academy created a stir akin to that caused by James Conyers's matriculation. Captain Philip H. Cooper, the superintendent, assured Secretary of the Navy John D. Long that Bundy would "not be discriminated against." But he predicted that Bundy would face the same sort of bleak existence at Annapolis that Flipper, Alexander, and Young had endured at West Point. "I can foresee the life he will lead at the academy in part," Cooper noted.

> He will not of course be *persona grata* with other cadets; he will lead a
> solitary and forlorn existence in social relations; in official matters he
> will be as the others are and have the countenance of the authorities.
> Within the walls of the academy he will have no associates of his color,

for he can not look to the servants and messengers for companionship
and if he can stand four years of such a life he will be rewarded with a
certificate of proficiency.[30]

Lyman A. Cotten, a second classman from North Carolina, wrote his
girlfriend that the "chief excitement" at the Academy at that time was
"the negro candidate appointed from Ohio." Cotten noted that the black
candidate appointed in 1896 had "backed out and did not come on to
take his exams, but this one says he is going to enter and get in the service. . . . It will be awful if he does get in. Just think of eating at the same
mess with a negro. It goes rather hard for a southerner." Other upperclassmen also objected to the presence of a black naval cadet, but most
intended to accord Bundy the respect due his uniform. White candidates
preparing to enter as Bundy's classmates generally opposed "forced association with a colored cadet." A few made threats.[31]

Bundy arrived in Annapolis in late August and stayed at the home of
Dr. William Bishop of the same family that had taken Conyers under their
wing. Bundy and eighty-four other candidates reported to the Academy
for the entrance exam on 1 September. Although nothing untoward happened to Bundy, none of the other candidates spoke a word to him.
Rumor had it that if Bundy passed the scholastic exam, Academy physicians would prevent him from becoming a midshipman by concocting
some basis for failing him on the physical exam. The whole question became moot when he failed the scholastic exam. He never entered the
Academy.[32]

No African American received an appointment to the Naval Academy
in 1898. The brief fin de siècle ferment to break the color barrier ended
abruptly because, as President William McKinley's staff explained to Benjamin O. Davis, Sr., in turning down his first request for a nomination to
West Point, appointing a black man to a service academy had become politically infeasible.[33]

In 1911, African American Civil War hero Robert Smalls wrote to
President William Howard Taft and asked for an appointment for his son
to either the Military or the Naval Academy.[34] On 13 May 1862, Smalls,
then an enslaved mariner and helmsman, had taken the Confederate side-
wheeler *Planter,* its black crew, and their families, and steamed right past
the Confederate batteries in Charleston harbor. After turning the vessel
over to the Navy, he served both the Union army and the Union navy as
a pilot until December 1863. That month, the skipper of the *Planter* de-

serted his post when the ship came under fire. Smalls took over and conned the ship safely to the wharf. For this act he received command of the *Planter*. Nevertheless, Smalls's request to President Taft must have fallen on deaf ears because his son never entered either academy. Jim Crow had become so powerful that even a hero of Smalls's stature lacked the clout to secure an appointment. No African American would become a midshipman until the Depression.

Despite this bleak outlook, African Americans kept trying to break the color barrier at the Naval Academy as part of the larger campaign to secure equal rights. During World War I, boll weevils, storms, floods, and tightening credit made farm life increasingly more tenuous in the South. When a wartime labor shortage opened up jobs previously unavailable to them up north, African Americans began the "Great Migration." Increasing opportunities in the North coupled with deteriorating economic conditions, discrimination, disfranchisement, poor education, and the daily humiliation of Jim Crow etiquette below the Mason-Dixon Line drove hundreds of thousands of black people from the rural South. "Northern fever" gripped southern blacks as word spread of better treatment and higher wages up North. Some 1,373,000 black people moved out of Dixie during the first three decades of the twentieth century, mostly to cities in the North and Midwest, where they hoped to find a better life. The percentage of blacks living in cities jumped from 22 percent in 1900 to 40 percent in 1930. In 1940, 77 percent of African Americans still lived below the Mason-Dixon Line, but the great migration was well underway.

At the same time, African American intellectuals and leaders like Colonel Young began to take pride in their culture and heritage in order to help them cope with the horrors of Jim Crow. In 1915, this movement fostered the organization of the Association for the Study of Negro Life and History. Its chief publication, *The Journal of Negro History*, sought to enhance self-respect and instill black pride by substituting a record of achievement for traditional notions of racial inferiority. In Harlem in the 1920s, the "New Negro" movement stimulated a growing racial consciousness and fostered a group identification among black intellectuals and literati. Marcus Garvey's "Back-to-Africa" movement also fostered black pride, and it attracted the largest mass following among black Americans in the nation's history.

Black pride fueled protest movements as ever increasing numbers of African Americans took up the fight against Jim Crow. In 1909, a group of black activists led by W. E. B. Du Bois met with white educators, publicists, clergymen, judges, and social workers to lay the foundation for what became the NAACP, an organization dedicated to ending segregation, obtaining equal education for black children, reenfranchising African Americans, and enforcing the Fourteenth and Fifteenth Amendments. The NAACP carried on in the spirit of the abolitionists and became the central organization of black protest and a power to be reckoned with in national politics. Between World War I and World War II, the number of local chapters skyrocketed from fifty to more than five hundred. The NAACP employed legal, educational, and informational means to secure equal rights for African Americans. It fought segregation in the courts, discrimination in education, lynching, and Jim Crow in the armed forces.

In 1911, three organizations dedicated to improving economic and social opportunities for blacks merged to form the National League on Urban Conditions for Negroes, commonly known as the National Urban League. By World War II, branches of the National Urban League had sprung up in forty-eight cities. The National Urban League struggled to obtain equal employment for African Americans, to win admission of blacks into labor unions, and to convince white employers to hire blacks. The most significant step towards the unionization of blacks was the organization of the Brotherhood of Sleeping Car Porters and Maids by A. Philip Randolph in 1925. When the brotherhood took steps to secure better work conditions and higher wages, the Pullman Company condemned it as a dangerous organization and denounced Randolph as a professional agitator. The Pullman Company made wage concessions during the 1920s and fully recognized the brotherhood in 1937 with a major wage increase.

Black protest emerged at the grass roots level as well. The "Don't-Buy-Where-You-Can't-Work" movement originated in Chicago in 1929 and quickly spread to other black communities, primarily in the North. Through picketing and boycotting, the movement aimed to force business establishments located in black neighborhoods to hire black employees.[35]

Politicians began to pay closer attention to black protest, for the mass migration of African Americans to northern cities led to a political resurgence that placed blacks once more in the thick of American politics and gave them the kind of strength that they had not exercised since Reconstruction. The concentration of blacks in places like Chicago and New York began to alter the structure of key political districts, making the black vote increasingly crucial to success in local elections. During the thirties and forties, growing numbers of black politicians secured seats in the state legislatures of California, Illinois, Indiana, Kansas, Kentucky, New Jersey, New York, Ohio, Pennsylvania, and West Virginia.

African Americans also made inroads into national politics. In 1928, Chicagoans elected Oscar Stanton DePriest to the House of Representatives. Born the son of ex-slaves in Alabama and raised in Kansas, DePriest had moved to Chicago in 1899 as a house painter and almost immediately entered politics, serving first as ward committeeman and then as the city's first black alderman. DePriest was the first African American elected to Congress in twenty-eight years, the first black congressman elected from the North, and the only African American in Congress during his three terms in office. Throughout his tenure in Washington, DePriest remained a friend to the NAACP and an opponent of southern Democrats. Black people all across America considered DePriest their representative; many considered him the realization of their fondest dreams.

DePriest, in turn, viewed himself as the representative of America's twelve million black people and devoted himself to civil rights issues. In speeches he suggested that blacks patronize only those businesses that hired blacks. In Congress he introduced an antilynching measure, constitutional amendments to enforce the Fourteenth and Fifteenth Amendments, a bill to provide pensions for aged former slaves, and antidiscrimination legislation regarding the Civilian Conservation Corps (only the last became law).[36]

DePriest also targeted discrimination at the service academies. He had campaigned on the promise to appoint African Americans to Annapolis and West Point. In the spring of 1929 he nominated four young black men to the Naval Academy and one to the Military Academy. The law now allowed each congressman, senator, or territorial delegate to have five midshipmen at the Naval Academy at any one time.

DePriest selected his nominees on the basis of their performance in a competitive exam; politics did not factor into the equation. Nor did he limit his appointments to candidates from his own congressional district. Three of his Naval Academy appointees hailed from Chicago. The fourth, Charles Edward Weir, was a native of Washington, D.C. Regulations specified that "candidates allowed for congressional districts . . . must be actual residents of the districts . . . from which they are nominated." Furthermore, appointments from D.C. were to be made by the president, based on the results of a competitive exam. But because DePriest considered himself the representative for black America and had committed himself to breaking the color barrier, he nominated candidates who seemed best prepared to cope with the academic ordeal that they would face at the Academy, regardless of where they came from. Charles Weir had graduated first in his class at Dunbar High School in Washington. To maintain an air of legality, DePriest created a fictitious Chicago address for him on the appointment form. In appointing a Dunbar alumnus to the Naval Academy, DePriest launched a tradition that would last a quarter-century.[37]

Dunbar was the first public high school for black people in the United States and the nation's best black academic high school. The school traced its lineage back to 1870, when it was founded as the Preparatory High School for Colored Youth in the basement of the Fifteenth Street Presbyterian Church, between I and K Streets, Northwest. Its founders intended it to be an institution devoted solely to preparing black students for college, and so it remained until 1955, when desegregation changed its character. In 1916, the school moved to a newer and larger building on First and N Streets Northwest and was renamed for the famous African American poet Paul Laurence Dunbar.

Dunbar set its academic standards so high that only the best and brightest could meet them. It instilled in its students a sense of individual and racial pride and taught them to value intellectual accomplishment. Dunbar students regularly placed first in citywide tests given in white schools as well as black schools. Alumni who continued their education at Ivy League institutions found themselves as well prepared as white students who had attended the best prep schools. Because of Dunbar's reputation as America's premier black prep school, African American families were known to move to Washington just so their children could attend. One such family was that of Alonzo Clifton McClennan, who remained in Charleston by himself to continue his successful medical practice but rented a house in Washington for his wife and children so that the kids could attend Dunbar.[38]

DePriest was obviously aware of Dunbar's national reputation, so it must have seemed to him a sure bet to appoint the school's number one student to the Naval Academy. Indeed, Charles Weir was the only one of the congressman's 1929 Naval Academy appointees who passed the entrance exam. Two of the Chicagoans failed; the other was disqualified because he exceeded the maximum age limit. Weir, however, did not pass the eye test. He wrote DePriest that the doctors and officers at the Academy had treated him kindly and courteously during the examination. The congressman believed that the results were fair. He had known that Weir had borderline eyesight but had hoped it was good enough to see him through the exam.[39]

Meanwhile, a rumor began circulating among Navy people that upperclassmen had taken two black midshipmen out in the Chesapeake Bay and tied them to a buoy, where they drowned. It is unclear how or where the rumor started, but by the winter it had made its way into naval circles in northern New Jersey. The rumor outraged Eleanor D. Wiltsie, a member of the Plainfield New Jersey Women's Republican Club whose son was a Navy lieutenant and alumnus of the Academy's Class of 1921. "I have asked for the proof of this terrible assertion," she wrote the Navy Department, "and have been told that the Naval authorities quietly 'hushed it up.'" Acting Secretary of the Navy Ernest Lee Jahncke promptly denied the rumor. "There have been no colored midshipmen at the Naval Academy for several years," he assured Mrs. Wiltsie. Evidently word of mouth had transformed Weir's peaceful if disappointing denouement at Annapolis into something ugly and sinister.[40]

A classic urban legend, this rumor persisted in one form or another at the Naval Academy for the next twenty years. The most common version had it that upperclassmen tied a black plebe to a buoy out in the bay. Accounts varied as to the identity of the black plebe, the date the incident was to have occurred, and whether the story was true or a myth. Accounts of the outcome also varied. Some had it that the victim died; others said that he was rescued, but promptly resigned.[41] Nothing in the documentary record substantiates any version of the story, but its prevalence foreshadowed the racial attitude among white midshipmen that the next several African American midshipmen would face at the Academy.

Whether DePriest ever heard the rumor or not, he announced that he intended to persist in nominating African Americans to the service academies. "Only in one respect will I insist [upon] favoring Negroes," he declared, "and that is in my recommendations for appointments to West Point and Annapolis. As long as I am in Congress, I'll appoint only Negroes to those two schools, or until some white Congressman appoints a Negro." Incidentally, DePriest's 1929 Military Academy appointee, Alonzo S. Parham, passed the entrance exams, became a cadet, got the silent treatment, and after six months was dismissed for academic deficiency along with the usual one-third of the plebe class.[42]

African American newspapers followed DePriest's effort to appoint young black men to the service academies. In those days the black press served as a forum for protest against discrimination. The *Pittsburgh Courier,* edited by Robert L. Vann, was a leading black newspaper with a national circulation. During the 1920s Vann had supported A. Philip Randolph's struggle to win recognition for the Brotherhood of Sleeping Car Porters and had published Marcus Garvey's nationalist ideology. In the 1930s the *Pittsburgh Courier* reported regularly on racial injustice and instances of breaking barriers in business and society. Articles on discrimination, lynchings, beatings, murders, and police brutality filled its pages.[43]

Vann early identified discrimination in the armed services as a target for his editorial ire. On 5 August 1926, a commentary entitled "A National Disgrace" appeared in the *Courier.* "It is exceedingly doubtful whether in all modern history there has been a single instance of more studied insult and discrimination than that of the War and Navy Departments toward the Negroes in the two services," it said. "In the Navy, Negroes have been relegated to the position of mess attendant and coal passer. They are kept out of sight when a parade is held ashore. To the expensive workshops erected with public monies for the instruction of enlisted men in the skilled trades, the black sailors are not admitted." The editorial marked the opening of a protracted campaign for equal opportunity for blacks in the Navy and Army and eventual racial integration of the armed services that Vann would wage until his death in 1940 and that the *Pittsburgh Courier* would carry on beyond World War II.[44]

Vann incorporated racial integration of the service academies into his campaign for equal opportunity in the armed forces. A few weeks after Parham left West Point, Vann wrote an editorial on the racial policies of the services. "If segregation is to continue to be a policy of the United States government in its defense organizations," it said,

> then there ought to be several battleships, cruisers, destroyers and submarines completely manned by Negroes, and battalions or regiments of black field artillery, coast artillery, engineer and signal troops, to say nothing of aviation detachments. We must not stop at sending a few Negroes to Annapolis and West Point, but demand that they be given something to command when they graduate.

Vann called on "the 500,000 Negro war veterans" to "organize themselves into a strong body independent of any white organization and pledge themselves to work definitely for a squarer deal for the Negro in the army and navy through intelligent propaganda and political action." If something was not done, he warned, "the next war will find the Negro in an unenviable position."[45]

In the spring of 1930, DePriest appointed two "carefully selected" black Chicagoans to the Naval Academy, as the *Pittsburgh Courier* put it. In an effort not to repeat the previous year's gaffe of appointing one candidate who was too old and another with poor eyesight, DePriest took special pains to ensure that the new appointees were scholastically and physically qualified. The extra effort proved inadequate. One candidate never reported for the entrance exam; the other failed the "substantiating exam," a condensed version of the regular exam administered to those candidates who presented an acceptable "certificate" from an accredited secondary school. DePriest also appointed black Chicagoans to the Military Academy in 1930, but they fared no better. Undaunted, the congressman vowed at a series of meetings held in Philadelphia that fall that he would "keep bombarding Annapolis and West Point with Negro applicants." "Thousands of our race fought and died in the World War, proving once and for all their patriotism, yet Negro boys I sent to those two schools were eased out," he declared. "I'll keep on sending boys of my race up to those schools till they'll have to let them stay, because it is my right to do so."[46]

That same year, Joseph A. Gavagan, a white congressman from New York City, joined the fray. A lifelong Tammany Democrat, Gavagan attended public and parochial schools in the city, served in the Army during World War I, and earned a law degree from Fordham University in 1920. After years as a member of the state assembly, on 5 November 1929 he was elected to Congress to fill the vacancy left by the death of Royal H. Weller, the representative of the Twenty-first District. This district encompassed the Washington Heights and Inwood sections of Manhattan, including a small piece of Harlem, which in those days was divided geographically among three congressional districts, none of which had a black majority.

In the House, Gavagan staunchly supported Franklin D. Roosevelt's New Deal and championed legislation opposing racial discrimination and religious intolerance. Throughout his time in office he struggled in vain to get an antilynching bill through Congress.[47]

In March 1930, Gavagan appointed William Myers Chisolm, an African American from Harlem, and three white New Yorkers to the

Naval Academy. Like DePriest, Gavagan selected his appointees on the basis of their performance in competitive exams. "The chances that one or more Negro youths will enter the United States Naval Academy at Annapolis," exclaimed the *Pittsburgh Courier*, "appear greater than any time since 1874, when Henry E. Baker was there." The *Courier* expressed pride that Chisolm had beaten out a number of whites in the competitive exam and predicted that Gavagan's action would certainly gain him "more race followers in the Harlem district." Chisolm, a 17-year-old freshman at Columbia University, felt confident that he could pass the entrance exam. He did not.[48]

DePriest's effort to send African Americans to the service academies finally bore fruit in the spring of 1932, when Benjamin Oliver Davis, Jr., entered the Military Academy. Davis was born on 18 December 1912 to an Army family. His father had entered military service in 1898 and on 2 February 1901 received a commission as a second lieutenant in the Regular Army. He served in the Tenth Cavalry during the Philippine Insurrection, as military attaché to Liberia, on the Mexican Border Patrol, and as professor of military science and tactics at Wilberforce University and Tuskegee Institute, rising to the rank of colonel by 1932. In 1940 he became the Regular Army's first black general. Throughout his career the Army studiously tried to avoid placing him in positions in which he would command whites. Nevertheless, Davis Sr. clung to the belief that only through full integration of blacks into society could America live up to the principles enunciated in the Constitution.

Davis Jr. grew up fully aware of racism. One night in 1923, the Ku Klux Klan paraded through Tuskegee Institute to protest the Veterans Administration's plan to establish a veterans hospital staffed by African American doctors and nurses nearby. The Davis house stood on the route of the march. Although black families had been advised to remain indoors with their lights off, the Davis family witnessed the march from their front porch with the lights on, with Davis Sr. wearing his white dress uniform. Davis Jr. never forgot "the night of the Klan."

Benjamin O. Davis, Jr., entered the Military Academy with an appointment from DePriest on 1 July 1932, determined to succeed in hopes of making it easier for black cadets who followed. He received "special attention" from the start. Davis roomed alone in a room designed for two cadets. At first, a few fellow plebes and two upperclassmen were friendly toward him. Then one day early in plebe year he was approaching an assembly area where a cadet meeting was in progress when he heard someone ask, "What are we going to do about the nigger?" Thereafter nobody spoke to him outside the line of duty.

Davis endured four years of silence. He roomed alone the entire time. Whenever the cadets traveled to football games on buses or trains, nobody sat next to him. His messing assignment changed frequently because many white cadets objected to eating at the same table with him. This kind of treatment filled Davis with a mixture of embarrassment, anger, hate, and pity. He survived by remaining impassive when others ignored or maltreated him, and by telling himself that he was superior in character to those who silenced him. He even felt sorry for them, wondering how people devoted to "Duty, Honor, Country" could rationalize treating him so.

During his first class year he applied for the Army Air Corps but was rejected because the Army had no plans for black pilots. The superintendent told Davis that this was "only the beginning" of what he would encounter in the Army because of his race and because it was not "logical" for a black officer to command white troops. In June 1936, Davis graduated thirty-fifth in a class of 276, becoming West Point's first black graduate of the twentieth century. Newspapers around the country carried the story and Davis received a pile of congratulatory telegrams and letters. Benjamin O. Davis, Jr., did become a pilot, commanded the 332d Fighter Group during World War II, and in 1954 became the first black general of the U.S. Air Force.[49]

Neither Oscar DePriest nor Joseph Gavagan had similar luck with the Navy. Although both congressmen kept appointing African Americans to the Naval Academy, none of their candidates passed the entrance exams. Two more DePriest appointees succeeded in entering the Military Academy, but neither of them graduated. One was dismissed for academic deficiency. The other, Felix Kirkpatrick, fell victim to a deliberate and successful campaign on the part of white upperclassmen to "skin" him out on demerits. Gavagan remained in Congress until 30 December 1943, when he resigned to serve as a justice on the New York Supreme Court. DePriest was defeated in the 1934 election by Arthur Wergs Mitchell, the first African American Democrat elected to Congress.[50]

Mitchell's election symbolized a momentous shift in political allegiance among black people. During the first three decades of the twentieth century, African Americans had become increasingly disaffected with the party of Lincoln. In 1924, when the Democratic and Progressive candidates for president promised, if elected, to make no distinctions on the basis of race, African Americans began to desert the Republican Party. Republican President Herbert Hoover alienated black voters with his support for the movement to resurrect a strong Republican Party in the South with white leadership, and for his appointment to the U.S. Supreme Court of John J. Parker, who reportedly said that the "participation of the Negro in politics is a source of evil and danger to both races."[51] Walter White, executive secretary of the NAACP from 1931 to 1955, described Hoover as "the man in the lily-White House."[52] In 1932, Robert L. Vann castigated "the eating cancer of Hooverism" and declared that black people should turn the portrait of Abraham Lincoln "to the wall," declare their debt to Republicans paid, and join the party of Roosevelt.[53]

Soon after taking office in 1933, President Franklin Delano Roosevelt gained a large following among black people. Under the New Deal, the federal government became an instrument of social change. Its relief and recovery programs promised to benefit African Americans. Roosevelt regularly received black visitors and in turn paid visits to black organizations and institutions. The president's programs and attitude heightened his popularity among black voters.

During the New Deal, the Democratic Party, once the party of white supremacy, became the champion of black rights, largely through the efforts of white liberal reformers like Harold L. Ickes. A former president of the Chicago branch of the NAACP and secretary of the interior from 1933 to 1946, Ickes supported contralto Marian Anderson in her imbroglio with the Daughters of the American Revolution over that organization's refusal to permit her to perform in Constitution Hall and introduced her to the seventy-five thousand people gathered at the base of the Lincoln Memorial to hear her sing on Easter Sunday 1939. Ickes spurred the Roosevelt administration into bringing in a number of prominent blacks during the thirties and forties to serve as race relations advisers in New Deal departments and agencies. The members of Roosevelt's socalled Black Cabinet did not often have access to the president, and they worked as civil servants rather than as policy makers, but they helped increase employment opportunities for African Americans in industry and government. The number of black employees on the federal payroll increased from fifty thousand in 1933 to some two hundred thousand by the end of 1946. Although most of them occupied lower-skilled and -paying jobs, it was progress.

The New Deal's most prominent black rights advocate was Eleanor Roosevelt. She championed equal justice before the law, equal educational opportunity, equal employment opportunity, and equal participation in politics. She was known to have a close relationship with Mary McLeod Bethune, and she invited the National Council of Negro Women, of which Bethune was president, to have tea at the White House. She regularly visited black schools and federal projects and spoke to African American groups. When the Daughters of the American Revolution barred Marian Anderson from Constitution Hall, Eleanor Roosevelt resigned from that organization. Black people revered her as a symbol of hope for a better tomorrow.[54]

Similarly, Arthur Mitchell embodied the hopes and dreams of African Americans, just as Oscar DePriest had. Mitchell rode into Congress on the wave of black support for the New Deal and on a current of strife in Chicago's second ward. Soon after taking office, this African American Democrat became the point man of the black community's efforts to break the color barrier at the Naval Academy.[55]

Arthur Wergs Mitchell was nothing if not controversial. "He is a man of considerable ability," noted an anonymous Associated Negro Press (ANP) writer in 1942. His distinguished appearance, clear diction, and luxurious Packard automobile impressed people. His education, financial success, and election to Congress in the face of Jim Crow symbolized African American hopes for a better life. While he never launched significant legislation during his eight-year tenure in the House, he tried to defend individual African Americans and to push through several meaningful civil rights measures.[56]

But Mitchell's faults far exceeded his virtues. Although he made history as the pioneering black Democratic congressman, represented Chicago's Bronzeville district on Capitol Hill from 1935 to 1943, and was once nearly as famous as Jesse Owens and Joe Louis, Chicago bears no monument to him nor street named for him. His biographer described him as a man of "dubious character," a "scoundrel," a "huckster," a "cog in the Chicago Machine," and a "tool of the white political structure." Claude Barnett, founder and head of the Associated Negro Press, branded him a "four-flusher" and an "Uncle Tom." Many who knew him well found him imperious, egotistical, and self-serving.[57]

Born on 22 December 1883 to former slaves in a one-room cabin on a farm near Roanoke, in east central Alabama, Mitchell received a rudimentary education from a white tutor. At age seventeen, he entered Tuskegee Institute, where he absorbed Booker T. Washington's precepts and methods and developed respect for his status and reputation.

Mitchell later attended Columbia and Harvard. He then returned to Alabama, where he operated in succession four schools in different rural areas. He raised significant funds from white northern philanthropists by promising to improve the status of blacks through education, but used much of the money to line his own pockets. In one scheme, he falsely promoted the West Alabama Institute, a school of dubious merit, as an authorized offshoot of Tuskegee Institute. When Booker T. Washington caught wind of this fabrication, he denounced the school to northern philanthropists. Although Mitchell admired his former teacher, he had no compunction about obtaining secret information about Washington's personal life and blackmailing him into issuing a favorable reevaluation of himself and the school to the philanthropists.

During World War I, Mitchell involved himself in preparedness drives and urged young men to enlist. In 1919, he moved to Washington, D.C., when legal problems arising from disgraceful dealings with illiterate landowners forced him to flee from Alabama. In the capital he started a real estate company, engaged in "loan sharking," studied law, and gained admission to the bar. He also joined Phi Beta Sigma, a social fraternity for black professional men, and served for nine years as its president.

Phi Beta Sigma provided Mitchell's entree into politics. Through fraternity contacts, he landed a job in 1928 as a Republican campaign organizer for Herbert Hoover in Chicago. Mitchell became enthralled with politics in the Windy City, particularly after Oscar DePriest's election in 1928. He concluded that Chicago's Democratic Party offered blacks greater opportunities for political power than were available either in Washington or with the Grand Old Party, so in 1929, he moved to Chicago and became a Democrat.

In Chicago, Mitchell devoted much time and energy to the party's Second Ward. Local Democratic Party committeeman and ward heeler Joseph E. Tittinger soon realized that Mitchell was content to follow the party's white leadership and adroit at showing empathy to whites with "Negro problems." With Bronzeville's black residents demanding support for African American nominees and Mitchell's ability to reassure whites that he would not neglect their interests, Tittinger saw him as the perfect token black candidate to run against DePriest in 1934. Tittinger's backing and white distaste for DePriest sealed Mitchell's victory in the First District, which had a white majority.

For the sake of party harmony, Chicago and Washington Democratic bosses warned Mitchell not to meddle in southern affairs or to criticize

New Deal policies as had DePriest, whose strong civil rights stance had alienated many white voters. Having no desire to jeopardize his congressional career in an independent course, Mitchell consistently voted with Democratic majorities according to the Chicago political machine's instructions. He voiced strong support for Franklin Delano Roosevelt and the New Deal and, during his first term, eschewed stumping for civil rights measures.

Mitchell soon emerged as Roosevelt's best-known African American defender. In return, the White House maintained an open line of communication with the congressman. Roosevelt granted almost all of Mitchell's requests for private audiences. In general, both men enjoyed these meetings, finding them cordial and useful. In deference to the president, Mitchell usually minimized complaints and refrained from questioning Roosevelt or criticizing New Deal policies. Nevertheless, Mitchell lacked clout with FDR. For example, he proved unable to forge a role for himself in the selection of appointees to the Fair Employment Practices Committee established on the eve of World War II.[58]

Mitchell's view of fellow African Americans also shaped the course of his civil rights record in Congress. He harbored a degree of genuine contempt for members of his own race, and when angry with a black person, would hurl the epithet "darky." A proponent of Booker T. Washington's accommodationist philosophy, he detested "troublemakers," particularly protesters and activists. During his campaign he had denied that he would become the representative at large for black America as DePriest had been. "I am not here to represent the colored man," he told reporters shortly after taking office. "I am here to represent my constituents."

In Washington, he willingly subordinated racial issues to other political matters when his Chicago bosses so demanded. He distrusted organizations like the National Negro Congress, which aimed at uniting African Americans; demonstrated no interest in helping black-dominated unions like the Brotherhood of Sleeping Car Porters; and soon after taking office alienated the NAACP by opposing an association-sponsored antilynching bill and generally neglecting civil rights issues. In fact, his relationship with NAACP leaders quickly degenerated into a shouting match in the black press, with Mitchell denouncing association leaders as "self centered" and "a bunch of Communists" and the NAACP branding Mitchell "a menace to the Negro race." Nevertheless, Mitchell did not advocate racial submission, declared himself an opponent of all forms of segregation, and believed that gifted blacks should have full access to the rights of citizenship, including the right to an education at the Naval Academy.[59]

Like many of his white colleagues, Mitchell determined whom to appoint to the service academies largely on the basis of political expediency. After winning the 1934 election, Mitchell declared that while DePriest had been in office, "no white boys [from the First District] have had an opportunity to enter Annapolis or West Point, but that will be altered now. There will be no discrimination."[60]

Mitchell's public declaration of color blindness hid the political machinations behind many of his service academy appointments. On several occasions, Chicago's Mayor Edward J. Kelly sought Mitchell's help in securing nominations for the sons of friends. Mitchell delivered them without fail. In June 1936, for example, he nominated Joseph Tittinger's son George to West Point. Mitchell also made appointments as favors to fellow Illinois House Democrats.[61]

Politics even dictated the timing of Mitchell's nomination of black candidates to the service academies. "I have been very much moved by the tone of your letters seeking the appointment of your son to a cadetship at the Military Academy at West Point," he wrote a white friend in July 1935,

> but owing to the fact that this is my first appointment the members of the organization in Chicago who have much to do with matters of this kind in the district, thought it imperative that the first appointment go to a member of my own Race to meet an argument that has been made against me to the effect that I am neglecting the interest of the Negroes wholly in my official appointments. . . . This has now been settled and my next appointment will go to a white boy.[62]

Mitchell's principal and two alternate appointees to the Military Academy in 1935 were black Chicagoans sponsored by Tittinger, but the congressman promised to appoint his friend's son when his next Military Academy vacancy became available. Mitchell's first appointment to the Naval Academy, made on 18 July 1935, was of a white Chicagoan who failed to pass the entrance examinations. To the press Mitchell announced that future service academy appointments would reflect a "50-50 colored and white" ratio. This policy so upset Chicago NAACP members that some of them considered making it an issue in the 1936 campaign.[63]

But politics did not always determine who Mitchell appointed. In fact, he had great difficulty in finding young black men willing to try to break the color barrier at the Naval Academy. While there was no shortage of qualified black males approaching him for a nomination to West Point, precious few sought an appointment to Annapolis.[64] With the black press trumpeting both Benjamin O. Davis, Jr.'s progress at the Military Academy and the Navy's relegation of black sailors to the steward's branch, African Americans believed that they stood at least some chance of getting through the Military Academy but no chance at all at the Naval Academy. Consequently, Mitchell had to seek out black candidates for Annapolis. "The appointments that I have made to the Naval Academy of colored boys were not made because the boys themselves sought the appointment," he lamented to NAACP attorney Charles Houston in 1938. "In each and every case, I have sought out the boys at much trouble and have encouraged and persuaded them to enter."[65]

Mitchell launched his campaign to break the color barrier at the Naval Academy in October 1935, when he received a letter from the Navy Department informing him that he had two vacancies. Initially, he relied on his secretary, Claude Holman, to find qualified black candidates. But when Holman failed to turn up anybody worth appointing, Mitchell conducted the search himself. In December he wrote to pastors of black churches throughout his district, asking them to inform their congregations that he was sponsoring a competitive examination for appointments to the service academies. "I am very desirous of having at least 10 Colored Boys take and pass this examination," he said. Ten white and five black boys took the exam on 4 January 1936.[66]

Mitchell also looked for candidates outside his congressional district, particularly among Dunbar High School alumni who had excelled both academically and in the Cadet Corps. The Washington High School Cadet Corps had begun in the white schools in 1882 when a chemistry teacher organized two companies of students to give them basic military training and to inculcate principles of good citizenship. By the 1930s the Cadet Corps had become interwoven into the fabric of the school system, with thirty companies and seven bands distributed among the District's seven high schools. A faculty member who was either an Army reserve officer or had had military training ran the cadet organization in each school, with a retired Army officer serving as professor of miliary science and tactics to supervise the entire corps. District regulations made "drill" compulsory for boys over fourteen years of age, and cadets received credit for physical education. Only participation in varsity athletics, physical unfitness, or parental objection excused a boy from serving. Administrators found that the best cadets were also the best students, so they supported the corps and emphasized its physical and social benefits.

The Cadet Corps taught fundamentals of military discipline, with training based on the U.S. infantry drill manual. The cadets drilled twice a week for an hour and a half at the school athletic field or on a nearby street. Students became cadet officers on the basis of their scholarship and citizenship. Three years in the Cadet Corps gave the boys knowledge of military drill equivalent to what soldiers acquired during basic training.[67]

Like the other components of the D.C. school system, the Washington High School Cadet Corps was segregated. Largely through the efforts of Christian Fleetwood, the Cadet Corps was established in the Preparatory High School for Colored Youth in 1888, six years after its founding in the white schools. Fleetwood had joined the Union army in 1863 and served as a sergeant major with the Fourth U.S. Colored Infantry until May 1866. For saving his regimental colors at the battle of Chaffin's Farm, Virginia, on 29 September 1864, he received the Medal of Honor. After the war he organized and commanded units in the District of Columbia Militia and D.C. National Guard. He also became a leading citizen in Washington's black community, particularly its churches. On one occasion he received a letter of thanks for his "many kindly services" on behalf of the Berean Baptist Church from none other than Henry E. Baker. Fleetwood helped establish cadet training for blacks primarily to benefit African American aspirants to West Point, who, by and large, were not admitted to military prep schools.[68]

By the 1930s, each of Washington's black high schools, Dunbar, Armstrong, and Cardoza, had several cadet companies that together formed the Twenty-fourth Regiment. The black units had black instructors and a separate professor of military science and tactics. African American cadets did not participate in the annual competitive drills with whites but, beginning in 1902, held their own annual competitive drill at the District's Griffith Stadium. The annual drill was a major event in the black community, drawing thousands of spectators, including black leaders like Mary McLeod Bethune. Dunbar units usually dominated the competition, and distinguished members of Washington's black community presented the awards.[69]

When Arthur Mitchell took his seat in the House in January 1935, Henry O. Atwood, the same man who had served with Charles Young in the Ninth Ohio Volunteer Colored Infantry and in Liberia, was Dunbar's Cadet Corps instructor. Born in Washington, D.C., on 8 May 1881, Atwood received his education at the M Street High School and Lincoln University, Pennsylvania, and did graduate work at Howard University. Atwood joined the Army during the Spanish-American War and, during World War I, served as captain in the 368th Infantry in France. After serving with Young in Liberia, Atwood in 1925 received a commission in the Army Reserve and became an instructor of military science and tactics in the Cadet Corps, assigned first to Armstrong High School, then to Dunbar in 1933. The following year he rose to the rank of lieutenant colonel in the Army Reserve. His colleagues in the D.C. school system praised his frankness, integrity, loyalty, and devotion to work. He handled cadets with kindness, not severity. Dunbar alumni who drilled under Atwood remembered him as a pleasant man with an uncanny memory who took a strong interest in his students and encouraged them to develop a broad range of career options. Atwood was well regarded in black Washington's military and social circles and had many friends. He belonged to the Associated Charities, the 12th Street Branch of the Young Men's Christian Association (YMCA), the Sons of Union Veterans, and the Mu-So-Lit Club, a musical, social, and literary society of elite black men that met in a handsome row house at 1327 R Street Northwest. The society's members were exclusively Republican; its annual Lincoln-Douglass birthday celebration in February was the social highlight of the year; and its programs, featuring distinguished speakers, were far more political than cultural.[70]

Atwood had long revered the memory of Charles Young. Once a year Atwood and several other African American veterans who had served under Young visited their leader's grave at Arlington National Cemetery to hold a memorial service. "[Colonel Young] was particularly understanding of the young and ambitious, whether a struggling student, or one who was trying to follow an inner urge toward artistic expression," Atwood recalled.

He had faith in the elements of greatness within the black man and with his all but divine enthusiasm came nearer than he knew to stirring a like faith in others. He never lost his determination to go to the sources in

Africa where he believed he would find the truth about the black man which would stir in the colored American a pride of ancestry.[71]

Throughout his affiliation with the Cadet Corps, Atwood remained on the lookout for a successor to Young to send to West Point. In a nutshell, Atwood sought to maintain the flow of black cadets through the Military Academy and to break the color barrier at the Naval Academy. He undoubtedly believed that successful African American graduates of Annapolis and West Point would become symbols of black pride and inspire other African Americans as Young had inspired him.[72]

It is unknown whether Atwood had ever made contact with Oscar De-Priest, but he developed a relationship with Arthur Mitchell, and the two men quickly joined forces to send African Americans to the service academies. From the start, Atwood played an integral role in Mitchell's search for appointees. As with Mitchell, potential candidates did not approach Atwood; the colonel had to seek them out. From among his charges in the Cadet Corps, Atwood sought individuals with the right combination of brains, discipline, leadership, athletic ability, and social grace to survive at the service academies.[73]

4

"Railroaded Out of Navy"

The first group of young men whom Colonel Atwood recommended for the Naval Academy included George E. Burke, James D. Fowler, Paul P. Cooke, and James Lee Johnson, Jr., all outstanding Dunbar alumni from the Class of 1933. George Burke had been a member of the honor society and captain of E Company in the Cadet Corps. After graduating from Dunbar, he enrolled at Miner Teachers College in Washington, D.C. James Fowler had been president of the honor society, commander of the Second Battalion of the Cadet Corps, vice president of the Cadet Corps Officers' Club, and manager of the swimming team. After high school, he entered Howard University and studied premedicine, intent on becoming a neurosurgeon.[1]

Paul Cooke had been an honor student, commander of F Company in the Cadet Corps, and first baseman on the varsity baseball team. After high school, Cooke enrolled at Miner Teachers College, where he majored in English. Early in 1936, Colonel Atwood approached him with the idea of going to the Naval Academy. Atwood said that there hadn't been a black midshipman in more than fifty years, that it was high time for a black to go to Annapolis, and that he thought Cooke could make it. He promised Cooke that if he would accept an appointment, Congressman Mitchell would give him one.

Although Cooke had never before considered a naval career, he had no qualms about joining the Navy. His father and two uncles had been enlisted men. His father had sailed around the world with the Great White Fleet, received an honorable discharge in 1908, and worked as a machinist at the Brooklyn Navy Yard until he lost his job after World War I as a result of demobilization. The elder uncle had been a petty officer. Because of family tradition, Cooke never saw the Navy as a place where blacks were limited to preparing food or waiting on officers. He immediately accepted.[2]

James Lee Johnson, Jr., was so smart that his friends nicknamed him "Socks," short for Socrates, the Greek philosopher. Johnson was born on 26 August 1916 at Freedman's Hospital (now Howard University Hospital) in Washington. His father held a federal job as a clerk for the Railway Mail Service, working on the trains that ran between Washington and Rocky Mount, North Carolina. His mother, Gertrude Bacchus Johnson, owned a card and gift shop, "Gertrude's," on U Street in northwest D.C.

The Johnsons lived at 1737 S Street, Northwest, about three blocks from DuPont Circle. "The whole area was sprinkled with people of unusual accomplishments," recalled James Jr.'s younger brother Frank. Next door lived Dr. Norman Harris, chief of the clinics at Freedman's Hospital. Down the street lived NAACP attorney Charles Houston. African American physicians, educators, lawyers, D.C. government officials, and Howard University professors populated the neighborhood.

The Johnson brothers loved science and were always building model airplanes, launching model rockets, and working on various projects. Fascinated by aviation, James built a working wind tunnel in the basement. Frank set up a chemistry lab. "Please move your lab to the back of the house," his mother told him. "I don't want the front of the house blown up." Nevertheless, Gertrude and her husband encouraged their children in all their activities.

The Depression had little impact on the family. James Sr.'s secure federal job and Gertrude's thriving business shielded them from it. James Sr. worked on the train on alternate weeks. He spent the off weeks in the card shop. Gertrude traveled regularly to big distributors in New York and Chicago to select the cards she sold. James and Frank had paper routes, delivering the Washington *Evening Star.*

James Sr. and Gertrude Johnson also shielded their boys from racism. Although Washington existed below the Mason-Dixon Line, it afforded African Americans more cultural opportunities than other southern cities. Museums, libraries, government buildings, and the zoo were open to everyone. On weekends there was always something to do, and the Johnsons did "not have to worry about this matter of segregation," Frank recalled. When movies opened downtown, Gertrude took the boys to see them, despite the theaters being closed to blacks. Gertrude, James Jr., and Frank were all very light skinned, so they were taken for white and never had any problem.

Nevertheless, the Johnsons could not escape the fact that they lived in a separate society. Businesses on nearby Connecticut Avenue discriminated against blacks. White people remained outside of James Sr. and Gertrude's social circle. And with no white families living in the neighborhood, James Jr. and Frank grew up without white friends.

The Johnsons coped by ignoring Jim Crow as best they could. James and Gertrude never talked to their boys about racial matters. "The feeling was that we were just as good as anybody," recalled Frank. "There was no need to discuss it, really." The boys heard little about racial pride outside of Dunbar High School. "It was just a matter of being proud of yourself and trying to accomplish something," Frank said. As a result of their upbringing, the boys seldom encountered prejudice.

After graduating from Dunbar with honors, James Jr. entered the Case School of Applied Science, now Case Institute of Technology at Case Western Reserve University, in Cleveland, Ohio. He spent three pleasant years among Case's mostly white student body and faculty. Popular with classmates and staff, he encountered no racial problems. He fenced, ran track, and made mostly Bs and Cs. During his junior year at Case, Johnson received a letter from his mother, who said that Colonel Atwood had recommended him to Mitchell as a potential appointee to the Naval Academy. She asked whether he would accept an appointment if Mitchell offered him one.

For James Lee Johnson, Jr., ships had been a lifelong hobby and passion. As a boy he had designed and built many a model boat. He dreamed of becoming a line officer in the Navy, commanding ships, working his way into the field of naval architecture, and, ultimately, designing ships. He figured that the Naval Academy would be an ideal first step toward this goal, so he told his mother that he was very much interested in going to Annapolis. "I knew that the United States Navy [was] considered the most arrogant, the most prejudiced, and the most overbearing of all the Government groups," Gertrude recalled, "and I did not fail to tell my son." Other relatives, friends, and acquaintances who read about the Navy in the black press or who knew black Navy veterans plainly told James about the hardships he would face at the Academy because of his race. James, however, believed that taking advantage of the opportunity would do justice to his race. Proud of her son's positive attitude and courage, Gertrude told Atwood that James would accept an appointment.[3]

Mitchell was looking for candidates whose scholastic training would permit them to skip the regular academic examination and who would easily pass the physical examination. The young men that Atwood suggested had been honor students, athletes, and Cadet Corps leaders in high school, and they all had three years of college. They certainly seemed qualified, scholastically. To ensure that they would meet the physical standards, Atwood had each candidate get a physical examination before taking the Academy physical.

In March, Mitchell appointed Burke, Cooke, Fowler, Johnson, Gilbert Reed, and James Gilbride to the Naval Academy. Cooke, Johnson, and Reed were principals, the others alternates. Reed and Gilbride were white Chicagoans. At the same time Mitchell nominated three whites and two blacks to the Military Academy. "I am doing what I set out to do, fight for the things that I believe are right," he declared in a speech at Dunbar High School. "I have struck out in an effort to smash the tradition at the Naval Academy, where, for some reason or other, our people have not been accepted." For the benefit of his white constituents and party bosses, he pointed out in a press release that the nominations were "evenly divided between the races."[4]

A candidate for admission to the Naval Academy seeking to avoid taking the regular "mental examination"[5] (as the scholastic entrance exam was called to distinguish it from the physical exam) had two alternatives. If he submitted an acceptable college "certificate" attesting that he had satisfactorily completed a minimum amount of work in specified subjects, he did not have to take a mental exam. A candidate who lacked the proper college education but submitted an acceptable certificate from an accredited secondary school took the "substantiating examination" in mathematics and English instead of the regular mental exam. Either way, the Academic Board had the final say in determining whether a certificate was satisfactory.[6]

The Academic Board issued Fowler a permit for examination on 7 March but revoked it on the 31st because Fowler was a few days too old for admittance. Burke withdrew his nomination when the death of his father left him responsible for the support of his family. Paul Cooke was weak in mathematics, so he enrolled in a college math course and hired a tutor to prepare for the substantiating exam in April. Unfortunately, these measures proved inadequate, for he failed the mathematics portion and did not become a midshipman.[7]

"Socks" Johnson fared better. The Academic Board accepted both his secondary school and college certificates, enabling him to skip both the regular and substantiating exams. On 15 June 1936, Johnson reported to the Naval Academy for the physical exam and passed with flying colors. Later that day James Lee Johnson, Jr., was sworn in, becoming the twentieth century's first African American midshipman.[8]

The black community celebrated the event. "No Negro has ever graduated from the U.S. Naval Academy," noted an editorial in the *Pittsburgh Courier,*

> Young Mr. Johnson of Chicago [sic], we hope, will be the first but not the last.
>
> Both schools of the services have fought in every possible way to remain lily-white, for, so far as the Negro is concerned, both services are simply glorified versions of the Ku Klux Klan, dedicated to the proposition that, first, the Negro must never command troops; secondly, that he must never serve except in the very lowest branches of the service: the infantry, the cavalry, the engineering department and the mess rooms, and thirdly, that he must never serve except in a segregated capacity, as far as possible from the seat of glory until the need for his aid is too great to no longer deny him consideration.
>
> West Point and Annapolis are the fountain heads of this stream of race prejudice, color discrimination and segregation, that keeps alive interracial hatred and strife in this country. If the stream is to be purified, we must start with the source.
>
> Lt. Davis and young Mr. Johnson are a good start. We must send dozens of young colored men like them to these two schools.[9]

Numerous African American newspapers approached the Academy for photos of the twentieth century's first black midshipman and for interviews with him. Johnson, however, wanted no publicity and turned them all down. Nevertheless, particularly at the beginning and end of his stay in Annapolis, Johnson had a celebrity status in the black community comparable to that of Olympic athlete Jesse Owens, in terms of the amount of ink the press gave the story.[10]

The administration of the Naval Academy had changed between Henry Baker's departure in 1875 and "Socks" Johnson's arrival in 1936. Throughout the first half of the twentieth century naval officers considered the office of superintendent "one of the prize positions in the Navy," according to naval historian and former Academy faculty member Richard S. West. "As a shore station of considerable dignity and social standing it has often attracted officers at the peak of their careers." The superintendent remained the Academy's highest-ranking officer, but instead of reporting directly to the Secretary of the Navy, he now reported to the Bureau of Navigation, the organization then responsible for the administration of naval personnel. The superintendent still handled the overall administration of the Naval Academy, commanded the officers assigned there, and supervised all the civilian employees. But with nearly 2,280 midshipmen enrolled at the Academy in July 1936, almost a tenfold increase in the student body since the 1870s, he was far less involved in the midshipmen's daily lives than his Reconstruction-era predecessors had been.[11]

The commandant of midshipmen, who remained the Academy's second-ranking officer, had assumed this role. Responsible for command and administration of the Regiment of Midshipmen, the commandant also saw to the midshipmen's discipline and professional training. He enforced the regulations, maintained order in Bancroft Hall, and directed all the midshipmen's drills and tactical instruction. He was responsible for their mess, laundry, and quarters. And he reported daily, monthly, semiannually, and annually to the superintendent on their conduct and aptitude for the service.[12]

Rear Admiral David Foote Sellers was superintendent when James Lee Johnson, Jr., entered the Naval Academy. Admiral Sellers's career epitomized the dreams of officers who regarded the battleship as the ultimate expression of naval power. Born at an Army post at Austin, Texas, on 4 February 1874, Sellers became a midshipman in 1890. After graduating fifth in the Class of 1894, he spent much of the next quarter-century in battleships. During World War I he commanded successively the battleship *Wisconsin* (Battleship No. 9), the Atlantic Fleet transport *Agamemnon* (No. 3004), and District Forces Afloat, Fifth Naval District, receiving the Navy Cross for his wartime service. After the war he filled a series of command and staff billets and rose to the rank of rear admiral. In July 1927, he assumed command of the Special Service Squadron and helped put down an uprising in Nicaragua, for which President Herbert Hoover awarded him the Distinguished Service Medal. Thereafter Sellers served as judge advocate general of the Navy; commander Battleship Division

One; commander Battleships, Battle Force; and commander in chief, U.S. Fleet, in the accompanying rank of admiral. In June 1934, he reported to Annapolis for his sunset tour as superintendent.[13]

Sellers believed strongly in conformity. "The average youth who enters the service is more or less irresponsible and an essential individualist," the admiral wrote in the United States Naval Institute *Proceedings,* one of the Navy's principal professional journals. Midshipmen, he argued, must learn to subordinate themselves "to the plan of the whole." "So far as is humanly possible, they must think and act alike under a given set of conditions."[14] Emphasis on conformity was not unique to Sellers but integral to the Academy's culture. "The midshipman should stow his information away in an orderly manner so that it can be easily drawn upon," advised Captain W. D. Puleston. "His mind should be neatly and completely furnished like his locker."[15] "This is not an environment which favors original thought or act, or even any material departure from beaten tracks," noted Academy historian Park Benjamin. "It is particularly one that calls for conservatism of action."[16] Conformity applied to a midshipman's social life as well as his professional life, including following the prevailing attitude toward race.

Like Sellers, Captain Forde Anderson Todd, the commandant when Johnson came on board, adhered to the principle of conformity. Born in Anderson, South Carolina, on 20 February 1881, Todd attended Richmond Academy in Augusta, Georgia, and spent a year at Charleston College in Charleston, South Carolina, before entering the Naval Academy in September 1900. After graduating in the middle of the Class of 1904, Todd spent most of the early part of his naval career at sea in battleships and cruisers. During World War I, he served as gunnery officer of the battleship *Idaho* (BB-42) and executive officer of the battleship *Utah* (BB-31). After the war he filled a variety of command and staff billets, culminating in a tour as skipper of the *Idaho*. He left the battleship to begin his tour as commandant in April 1935. For most of his career, Todd and his wife maintained their "official" residence in Charleston.[17]

The commandant headed the Executive Department, which supported him in quartering, messing, and disciplining the midshipmen and administering their daily routine. The Executive Department staff included the regimental officer and executive officer of Bancroft Hall, the first lieutenant, four battalion officers, and eight company officers corresponding to the eight companies and four battalions constituting the Regiment of

Midshipmen. Executive Department officers were responsible not only for administration and discipline, but also for counseling and guidance of the midshipmen.

Seniors assumed many responsibilities in enforcing discipline and during drill. The superintendent appointed midshipman officers from the first class to train them in the exercise of military authority and to provide military and administrative leadership for the regiment. Three sets of midshipman officers, called "stripers" for the stripes worn on their sleeves, served as regimental, battalion, and company officers during the academic year. The superintendent selected the "Fall Set" and "Winter Set" from the first class on the basis of their previous records and the "Spring Set" from the best of the midshipman officers in the first two sets. Midshipmen also served as watch officers in Bancroft Hall. All upperclassmen shared responsibility for enforcing discipline.[18]

Regulations governed almost every aspect of a midshipman's life. Infractions fell into two categories. Class "A" or "honor" offenses involved serious breaches of discipline. They included, among other things, lying, cheating, stealing, intoxication, marrying, hazing, and offenses indicative of "moral turpitude." Midshipmen guilty of Class "A" offenses were generally dismissed, or "separated," from the Academy. Class "B" or "conduct" offenses involved comparatively minor infractions such as unauthorized use of chewing gum; untidiness in dress or person; improper haircut, shave, or shoe shine; arriving late to formation; bedding not properly turned back; unmilitary conduct; and room in disorder. "Violations of the innumerable rules and regulations that govern the Naval Academy are numerous, inevitable and expected," wrote Kendall Banning in a primer for prospective midshipmen.

To report a midshipman for an infraction, in Academy slang, was to "fry" him. Any officer or upperclassman could fry a plebe for a Class "B" infraction by submitting a "delinquency report," as it was formally called, to the battalion office. One of the commissioned Navy officers posted there investigated the charge, then either canceled the report or approved it and forwarded it to the commandant. The commandant also either canceled or approved the report. If the latter, he assigned the appropriate number of demerits and forwarded the report to the superintendent, for his information. Demerits served both as a record of misconduct and as a basis for determining punishment.

A midshipman could challenge a delinquency report, but this was a perilous course of action, since it was a Class "A" offense to file a false report. Such situations generally boiled down to one person's word against another's.

Punishments for Class "B" offenses included restriction; reprimand; deprivation of leave, recreation, or privileges; suspension; or reduction in midshipman rank. The usual punishment was extra duty, which generally consisted of rowing a heavy boat or marching back and forth in a prescribed area. Plebes who accumulated more than three hundred demerits were subject to dismissal.[19]

Demerits also served as an indication of a midshipman's "aptitude for the Naval Service." Officers and first classmen evaluated not only a plebe's conduct but also his "officerlike qualities," defined by the regulation book as "those qualities which reflect his ability as a leader, his sense of duty, his military attitude and bearing, and his desirability in time of war." The resulting performance grade, called "grease," was derived according to procedures established by the commandant. Upperclassmen received grease marks as well, but theirs were determined by different procedures than those used for plebes.[20]

James Lee Johnson and his shipmates in the Class of 1940 soon learned that they occupied the lowest position in the hierarchy of naval officers, a status reflected in their nickname, "plebes." Having been outstanding in their previous lives, plebes were reduced to near nothingness upon entering the Academy. They enjoyed precious few privileges and no prestige whatsoever, and their egos were subjected to systematic indignities.[21]

In addition to the regulations that all midshipmen had to follow, plebes were also required to observe a series of "rates" as part of their indoctrination. "Rates" included information that plebes had to know, things they had to do, and privileges accorded to upperclassmen but denied to them. For example, plebes "rated" giving up their seats to upperclassmen, double-timing it to all formations, keeping to the center of corridors, and memorizing the menu for the next meal.

Plebes also rated learning every bit of information and trivia in *Reef Points*, the "plebe bible," for upperclassmen regularly quizzed them on it. The book described the various buildings and monuments in the Yard (as the campus was called), extracurricular activities available to midshipmen, and Academy sports. It included information about ships, aircraft, organization of the fleet, and Navy traditions; lyrics to songs such as "Anchors Aweigh"; and the names of all the Academy's athletic coaches. Its glossary introduced plebes to officially approved jargon, such as "anchor man," the midshipman with the lowest standing in his class; "bull," the nickname for English and history; and "crab," a girl from "Crabtown" (Annapolis). There were also poems given as answers to stock questions, such as, "How long have you been in the Navy?" Plebes were expected to sing the songs, name the names, recite the poetry, or answer the questions on demand. At any time, an upperclassman could stop a plebe to ask him questions or give him a spot inspection.

Admiral Sellers declared that the Naval Academy's student body represented "a cross-section of the United States," with representatives from "every shade and degree of political, economic, and social background." It is true that midshipmen came from every state in the Union, but Sellers's statement is misleading. While the different American socioeconomic classes and ethnic groups had representatives at the Academy, they were not proportionally represented. James Lee Johnson, Jr., for example, was the only African American midshipman in 1936, and most of his classmates came from native-born, Anglo-Saxon, and upper- or middle-class families.[22]

Young Americans entered the Naval Academy for a variety of reasons. Motivations included family tradition, desire for education and social enhancement, experience in a military setting, and boyhood ambition. Some wanted to pursue a relatively secure and promising career; others had a "calling" to the naval profession. Whatever their particular motivation, at bottom, those who entered the Academy during the midthirties did so to pursue careers as naval officers.[23]

Regional diversity sometimes caused mild friction. Midshipmen from the North and the West Coast were surprised to find that the Civil War had never ended. Many southern midshipmen still retained a great deal of antagonism toward Yankees. "I thought the Civil War was something I'd read about in the history books and it was settled," recalled a Class of 1940 alumnus from the Midwest, "but not in their heads."[24]

Attitudes towards race and ethnicity among the midshipmen and Executive Department officers and in the Naval Academy's culture mirrored those in society. In addition to racism, Depression-era Americans harbored varying degrees of prejudice against certain ethnic and religious groups, such as Irish, Italians, Jews, and Catholics, and considered ethnic jokes and slurs harmless and socially acceptable. The glossary of officially approved Naval Academy slang in *Reef Points* reflected these attitudes. It defined "Chico" as a Filipino "mess boy." "Dago" referred to any foreign language. To "French out" was to take unauthorized leave. A "Spanish athlete" was a nonathlete.[25]

Many of the Navy songs that midshipmen learned also contained derogatory ethnic references. The song "Colombo" referred to Christopher Columbus as "a Dago from Italy." The song "There's Many a Man Been Murdered in Luzon" included the word "Gu-Gu," which *The Book of Navy Songs* defined as "the soldiers' and sailors' nickname for the little brown [Filipino] insurrecto." "Gu-Gu" was a Filipino reference to evil demons.[26]

The institutionalized slurs toward African Americans had a decidedly sharper edge. *Reef Points* defined "moke" as a "colored corridor boy or mess attendant." The Navy song "Bible Stories" included the word "darkys" in the chorus. Another Navy song declared that the solution to the "vexing Chinese question" was to send "a hundred negro reg'ments" to China to "start a Coon Republic." Such institutionalized racism both reflected and reinforced negative attitudes that midshipmen brought into the Academy from their hometowns.[27]

For midshipmen like Connecticut native Harvey Bryant Seim, Class of 1940, who had gone to high school with African Americans, the presence of a black midshipman at the Naval Academy didn't seem unusual. But others, particularly southerners, "were not disposed to welcome blacks." Seymour Einstein, Class of 1941, recalled that "any minority entering the sanctity of the closed officer class of the Navy was destined to endure hardships, and a black person even more so. . . . A black American at the Naval Academy had one chance in a million of surviving the first (plebe) year. Perhaps if he were a black Nigerian he might have survived because of diplomatic pressures . . . but a black American, that was unheard of!" Before returning to Annapolis from their summer practice cruise, a group of first classmen discussed James Lee Johnson, Jr. The majority opposed his receiving a commission.[28]

Perhaps the most ominous portent of how Johnson would fare was the commandant of midshipmen's racial attitude. "At this state of society," Captain Todd later noted in a letter to Admiral Sellers, a black midshipman "rubbing elbow to elbow" with white midshipmen "all day long offers infinite opportunities for serious friction." Such was the culture of the Naval Academy when James Lee Johnson, Jr., began plebe summer.[29]

From the start, Johnson and the 735 other newly minted plebes faced tremendous pressure to learn the ropes and to conform. Naval customs and language quickly supplanted the folkways that they had grown up with. For example, Bancroft Hall had no walls, floors, or stairs, but rather bulkheads, decks, and ladders. And while civilians might regard "yes" as a polite response, in the Navy only "Aye, aye, sir!" would do.

Plebes spent the summer undergoing military indoctrination and physical training. Marching, shooting on the rifle range, sailing, rowing, tying knots, keeping their rooms and persons scrupulously neat and clean, memorizing the countless rules, regulations, and plebe rates, and a boatload of similar activities absorbed literally every waking moment. In addition to the drills and exercises, plebe summer included a lecture and reading course under the Department of English and History. In September plebes began classwork to familiarize themselves with Academy methods of recitation and study before the academic year began in October. If there was any consolation, it was that the upper classes were away on their summer practice cruise; only two-thirds of the second class remained at the Academy at any one time in the summer, and only a few of them were involved in indoctrinating plebes. Until the return of the regiment, plebes enjoyed relatively peaceful meals and went about in Bancroft Hall with minimal hassle.[30]

Johnson faced an additional, unique pressure. While every other plebe had at least one roommate, Johnson roomed alone throughout his stay in Annapolis. This made him solely responsible for the cleanliness and order of his room, a vitally important aspect of plebe life. And he had no roommate to doublecheck his appearance, help with plebe rates, or do the thousand other things that roommates do for each other.[31]

Many midshipmen disliked Johnson's presence. "This institute is filled with southerners who, I am sorry to say, are prejudiced against Mr. Johnson," wrote Gilbert Reed, Mitchell's white appointee, in a letter to the congressman. "I have found them to be very narrow minded on the subject of attending school with a colored boy."[32]

On Johnson's very first night in Bancroft Hall, a junior told the black plebe that "upperclassmen from the South" would use "every means" to ensure that his stay at the Academy "would be short and unpleasant." He tried to persuade Johnson to resign. Johnson refused.[33]

In the coming weeks, Johnson found that certain midshipmen were trying to bury him in delinquency reports, some legitimate, others not. "There are some in the second class (mostly southerners) who are quite antagonistic towards the presence of a Negro in the Naval Academy," he wrote Mitchell on 6 August, "and who would do all they could, even to the telling of lies about me, in order to cause my departure." For example, two second classmen had charged him with telling a falsehood, but the battalion officer let him off with a warning. Some of his fellow plebes joined in the act by cracking jokes in ranks, hoping to get him to smile and thereby draw demerits for smiling in ranks. By the end of plebe summer, Johnson had amassed 102 demerits for "room not in proper order," being "out of uniform" or "untidy in dress," and a host of other minor infractions.[34]

Even commissioned officers openly discriminated against Johnson. When Admiral Sellers gave a reception at his home for the plebes in August, Johnson, like the rest of his classmates, attended. Shocked at the black plebe's breach of southern etiquette, some of the commissioned officers greeted his arrival with stares and raised eyebrows. Many of Johnson's classmates turned their backs on him. Johnson persevered, went through the reception line, and followed all the protocol prescribed for midshipmen. But the scandalous appearance of a black man at a white officer's home for a social function caused many midshipmen and a few commissioned officers, including Johnson's own battalion officer, Lieutenant Commander Lemuel P. Padgett, Jr., to complain to Admiral Sellers. Padgett, a Tennessee native, afterwards lectured Johnson on protocol and the Negro's "place." The dressing down appalled the black plebe, for his parents had shielded him from racism as a child and he had never encountered such attitudes at Case.[35]

Somehow, Johnson remained optimistic. That same month, he wrote Mitchell that he had not "experienced as much trouble as I had expected." He believed that the senior commissioned officers were "fair minded" and willing to give him "an even chance." He believed that his engineering studies at Case would enable him "to stand well up in scholastic work." While the demerits had come thick and fast at first, they were tapering off. Besides, the slate would be wiped clean on 1 September, when summer demerits were removed from the conduct records of the fourth class. "I have no intention of quitting now," resolved Johnson, "or at any time in the future." Doing so would be "tantamount to an admission of weakness or of incompetency."[36]

On 4 August, Mitchell wrote Johnson to give him a pep talk. He reminded his appointee that an Academy education cost more than thirty thousand dollars and that among twelve million African Americans, he was the only one "to enjoy that kind of distinction." He urged Johnson never to give up, no matter how difficult things became. "Remember that you have thousands pulling for you," he said. "I shall never be too busy to come to your rescue if it is necessary. I am profoundly interested in your success." The congressman suggested that Johnson adopt the motto of his own high school class: "Bend to the oar though the tide be against you."[37]

That same day, the congressman wrote Gilbert Reed. "Please remember me most cordially to Johnson and tell him that I am depending upon him to deliver," Mitchell said. "He is the first colored boy to be admitted to the Academy for nearly seventy years. Tell him he must not fail. I expect you to help him in every possible way." Reed did, in fact, contact Johnson, despite the risk. Johnson thought him "a fine fellow." Reed, in turn, found Johnson to have "a fine spirit and plenty of fight."[38]

Other midshipmen supported Johnson as well. Many silently admired his courage for trying to survive in a hostile environment. Most plebes who knew him seemed to respect him. Many treated him cordially; some, even a few southerners, to his surprise, went out of their way to help him. Johnson was never universally silenced at the Naval Academy as Benjamin O. Davis, Jr., had been at West Point.

By and large, however, most of Johnson's classmates, even if they harbored no racial prejudice or were indifferent to the presence of an African American at the Naval Academy, minimized contact with him, fearing that upperclassmen would make their lives miserable if they interacted with him normally. It was easier to conform to the prevailing racial etiquette.[39]

Life for any plebe became harder when the first and third classes returned from their summer activities and the academic year began. For all the difficulties fourth classmen experienced in making the transition from civilian life during plebe summer, they did not have to contend with a full academic program. "Throughout the academic year the daily events in the life of a midshipman are governed by a rigid schedule," noted a pamphlet describing the Academy. Reveille sounded at 6:20. Forty seconds after the first note, room inspection began. Midshipmen had twenty-five minutes to shave, shower, and dress before reporting at 6:45 to breakfast formation, where they underwent personal inspection. Afterwards they marched to breakfast, ate, and marched back to clean their rooms. Classes started at 7:45. From Monday through Friday, the academic day was divided into six hour-long periods, with two morning periods reserved for study. Lunch formation and another inspection took place at 12:20. Fifth period began at 1:10, followed by either a long afternoon drill or the sixth period and a short drill. The drills ended at 4:10 or 4:30, and from then until the dinner formation (and inspection) at 6:40, midshipmen engaged in athletics or extra duty. The evening study period lasted from 8:00 until 9:50, with taps blown at 10:05. Plebes caught not studying during study period or out of bed after taps went on report. Saturday mornings were split between recitation and drill and afternoons were free for those who had no extra duty. On Sundays reveille sounded at 7:15, followed by mandatory church attendance. Sunday afternoons were free.[40] "Only the utilization of every precious minute of the sixteen waking hours will enable midshipmen to take part in the extracurricular activities without detriment to their academic work," cautioned one alumnus.[41]

In addition to a full academic schedule, plebes had to deal with the full complement of upperclassmen. During the summer, relatively few upperclassmen had been around to give them a hard time. Now many eyes watched their every move. All upperclassmen shared responsibility for plebe indoctrination, which began in earnest in October. Mealtimes were particularly difficult, for the mess hall was the principal forum in which upperclassmen tested them on *Reef Points* and other "plebe knowledge." A fourth classman had to answer questions while sitting rigidly on the edge of his chair, "keeping his eyes in the boat" (gazing steadily ahead unless responding to an upperclassman), and "eating a square meal" (raising the food perpendicularly from the plate until level with his mouth, then conveying it horizontally to its destination). A plebe who screwed up might have to "shove out," which meant having to remain in a seated position without actually touching the chair.[42]

To enforce plebe rates and minor infractions of the regulations without filing delinquency reports, the Academy condoned a method known as "coming around." If a plebe made a faux pas in the mess hall, answered a question improperly in a corridor, or chuckled while in ranks, an upperclassman could order him to "come around" to his room that night for what *Reef Points* called "a fitting reprimand."[43]

This system of discipline permitted an upperclassman a great deal of latitude. Sometimes he might have a plebe come around for arbitrary or personal reasons. It might be that he disapproved of the plebe's attitude, hometown, education, ethnic group, or religion. It might also be that he simply disliked him. A plebe often had no way of knowing the real reason behind an invitation to come around.

Some of the punishments were rather mild, such as making a fourth classman learn a Frank Sinatra tune, or having a southern plebe sing "Marching through Georgia." Typically, the plebe had to do the number of pushups corresponding to his class year. James Lee Johnson's class had to do forty. Although hazing was a Class "A" offense, the Academy condoned paddling, commonly called "beating ass." "Some upperclassmen would require us to bend over and then hit us with brooms, heavy aluminum bread pans or—worst of all—the long-handled serving spoons," recalled former President Jimmy Carter, a graduate of the Class of 1947. Many upperclassmen made paddling into a game, something light and fun; a small minority used it to indulge sadistic impulses. A plebe could refuse to submit to paddling and certain other "punishments" but could not refuse to run the obstacle course in the dark before reveille.[44]

Some midshipmen, particularly those with military service before entering the Academy, considered plebe rates, plebe knowledge, and other aspects of the Naval Academy's systems of indoctrination and discipline to be petty, silly, demeaning, or downright juvenile. Others later came to see value in them as effective means of preparing officers for combat. Whatever their view, the system left a lasting impression on Naval Academy alumni. "These punishments for infractions of official or unofficial rules were frequent," recalled Carter. "There was no way to escape, not even for the best behaved of midshipmen. It was sometimes a brutal form of training and testing. If one ever showed any weakness, he was assaulted from all sides with punishment and harassment, and forced out of the academy." Essentially, Naval Academy officials had been unable to eliminate hazing, so they institutionalized it in an effort to control it. As a result, it was almost impossible never to break a rule, and an upperclassman out to "get" a plebe could easily find a pretext for making his life difficult.[45]

With the return of the upper classes for the fall 1936 semester, James Lee Johnson's situation, which had improved toward the end of plebe summer, plummeted. As he later told reporters, life at the Academy became "almost unbearable." Both upperclassmen and fellow plebes in his battalion (First Battalion) launched verbal attacks with sickening regularity. Plebes shouted vulgar insults at him without incurring punishment. In particular, a group of Arkansans who lived a few doors away in Bancroft Hall habitually and loudly referred to him as "that nigger son of a bitch." Others occasionally made more threatening comments, such as "let's treat him like we treat the nigger down our way" and "let's string him up." Nevertheless, Johnson never believed that the others would do him physical harm.[46]

Prejudiced midshipmen expressed their racism in deed as well as in word. At meals, they saw to it that the seats on either side of Johnson remained empty. This outraged the African American mess steward who served Johnson's table; he believed that the white midshipmen were treating Johnson like a "leper." Racists in the upper classes instructed white plebes to "leave [Johnson] alone; don't bother with him." A first classman from Kansas wrote his congressman that he intended to take action that would result in Johnson's dismissal. The senior had nothing personal against Johnson but was prejudiced against all African Americans because a black man had allegedly killed his father.[47]

A group of upperclassmen from Johnson's own battalion renewed with a vengeance the campaign to fry him out on demerits. It was a concerted, deliberate effort. Those involved, largely southerners, went out of their way to find a basis for putting him on report. They routinely fried him for things that they let other plebes get away with or that they only issued warnings for. Johnson challenged the reports when he believed himself innocent. In many such instances, his battalion officer, Commander Padgett, agreed and tore up the report. But these were pyrrhic victories, for they only made the upperclassmen try harder to make subsequent charges stick.[48]

And many did stick. While in ranks on one occasion, a first classman made a humorous remark. Johnson and everyone around him grinned openly, but only Johnson got fried for smiling in ranks. Whenever one particular first classman from Florida had duty as "Taps Inspector," he would wait outside Johnson's room for taps and then burst inside, hoping to catch him out of bed. Although the ploy worked only once, the Floridian kept trying. On several occasions, upperclassmen hid parts of Johnson's uniform and did other things to make him late for formation. As a result he was reported "late to formation" at least eight times, racking up thirty-six demerits in the process. Upperclassmen inspected Johnson's room daily, sometimes several times a day, looking hard for a speck of dust or something slightly askew. Johnson went on report six times for "room not in proper order," thereby tallying forty demerits. To present the illusion that they were not discriminating against Johnson, the upperclassmen always filed reports on one or more other hapless plebes at the same time.[49]

No upperclassman did Johnson the favor of having him "come around" instead of frying him. Upperclassmen routinely punished plebes for minor infractions of the regulations with "come arounds" instead of delinquency reports. Punishment by delinquency report meant that the plebe would receive demerits and might have to perform extra duty to work them off. But if the upperclassman had the plebe come around to his room for a paddling or a set of pushups, the punishment ended right then and there, with no lingering repercussions. In Johnson's case, however, the upperclassmen went strictly by the book, writing him up for every minor infraction, so that the black plebe received demerits for things that his white classmates could work off simply by doing pushups. By not hazing him at come arounds, the upperclassmen were discriminating against him.[50]

Their reason for doing so did not in all cases stem from prejudice. Just before classes started that fall, the seniors from the First Battalion attended a briefing given by Lieutenant Commander Padgett. Padgett explicitly ordered "that there would be no hazing of Johnson," as Class of 1937 alum Robert Erly recalled. "This meant no physical contact (i.e., swatting with broom or other implements)." The battalion officer's order inhibited upperclassmen from having Johnson come around.[51]

Johnson took the abuse with quiet dignity. A senior from Nebraska, a junior from Missouri, and others told him flat out that most upperclassmen opposed his receiving a commission. Johnson soon realized that the demerits he was getting were the result of a deliberate effort to bring about his dismissal. Still, he strove to fit in. Adhering to the axiom "never bilge a shipmate," he never tried to take official action against his tormenters. In letters to his parents and aunt, he focused on things that he genuinely enjoyed, such as doing well at the shooting range, being in a winning drill company, and attending Navy football games, particularly the away games at Princeton and Notre Dame and the annual showdown with the Army. Only rarely did he hint at the hell of his existence. He determined to stick it out.[52]

What was happening to Johnson was also obvious to those living nearby in Bancroft Hall. One plebe wrote his father that Johnson was being "crucified." "Everyone in the school almost has been laying for him," he said.

His conduct record would be a lot clearer than mine and many others here if he were subjected to the same treatment and the same breaks as the rest of us. . . . The upper classmen are apparently sitting up nights studying the rules for technicalities on which they can trip up the colored boy. They are loading demerits on him every time he turns around, but he takes it like a man.

Even plebes who were not in Johnson's battalion heard that the first classmen "were determined to make life at the Naval Academy unbearable for Johnson."[53]

Some who sympathized with Johnson succumbed to pressure not to socialize with him or help him, even though remaining mute tore them up inside. "I was, and still am, ashamed of my own reaction to all of this at the time it was happening," recalled Bruce P. Hayden, a Michigan native who lived across the hall from Johnson and who occasionally stood watch with him.

> I didn't like it and took no part in it, but as a second classman intent on graduation a year and a half hence, I lacked the courage to stick my own neck out or say anything to anybody. I believe I was one of the few to give Johnson an occasional smile or word of encouragement, but even this was rare, since it seemed to me that he was always under observation, and I certainly did not want to attract attention to myself. . . . He had lots more guts than the 200 or 300 of us who well knew what was going on but who didn't speak out.

Hayden believed that the commissioned officers intended to prevent Johnson from graduating. Consequently he deliberately limited his contact with Johnson to avoid being labeled a "nigger lover," afraid that such a reputation would follow him into the fleet and adversely affect his career.[54]

Despite such fears, a handful of midshipmen, mostly New Englanders, risked the ostracism of their peers or the wrath of upperclassmen and played handball with Johnson or otherwise befriended him. Most of his company mates maintained at least cordial if not friendly relationships with him. And black stewards gave him first-class treatment in the mess hall.[55]

Johnson's sympathizers genuinely admired him. One fellow plebe found him "bright and gentlemanly" and "just as good as any of us." Another recalled him as a "great athlete" and "brilliant" student. An upperclassman who lived across the hall found him "a very decent guy" and "a thoroughly patient one who well knew exactly what was happening to him, but who did his best to survive nonetheless."[56]

Executive Department officers kept close tabs on the black plebe. Ever since Johnson had become a midshipman, Admiral Sellers and Captain Todd had held "frequent and serious conferences about him." Both men paid particularly close attention to his conduct record.[57]

Serious trouble started brewing near the end of the first semester. By 15 January 1937, Johnson had amassed 181 demerits, more than half of the three hundred permitted plebes. Accordingly, he had to spend an enormous amount time marching them off. The extra duty deprived him of time he could have spent studying.[58]

Nevertheless, his grades had been good enough to allow him to attend away football games, to go home for Christmas leave, and to attend President Roosevelt's second inauguration. Midshipmen in dire academic straits received no such liberty. Johnson made 3.00 or above in all of his subjects during the first semester (with 4.00 being the highest grade and 2.50, passing), except in English.

Although Johnson had maintained passing weekly and monthly grades in English, he did poorly on two examinations, bringing his final mark down to 2.41. "Socks" Johnson was a classic left-brained individual: highly capable in mathematics but not so good with words. A friend once compared the process by which he wrote letters to woodcarving. It took Johnson a long time to organize his thoughts and several drafts before the product satisfied him.

Johnson knew that English was the most subjectively graded course at the Academy. He suspected that prejudice might have contributed to his low exam scores. At least one first classman shared this opinion and told him so. Curiously, as soon as the faculty posted the first term's grades and Johnson's failing English mark became common knowledge, upperclassmen stopped putting him on report.[59]

Nevertheless, things began to snowball. On 27 January, Admiral Sellers wrote James Lee Johnson, Sr., that his son had accrued an extraordinarily high number of demerits, exceeded by only one other classmate. Sellers said that the average midshipman received less than one-third of the maximum. He added that during a recent ten-year period, only 113 midshipmen were found deficient in conduct, while 1,735 were found academically deficient. "This will show the relative ease with which a midshipman possessing the normal qualifications as officer material can remain here if he makes any sort of effort at all," concluded Sellers. He urged Mr. Johnson to "use your influence in calling to your son's attention the seriousness of his present situation and the importance of over-

coming such habits of carelessness or indifference which he may have."
Mr. Johnson passed the letter along to Mitchell.[60]

Three days later, James Sr. visited his son at the Academy. They had a
long talk. James Jr. knew he was in trouble and regretted his conduct
record. Mr. Johnson concluded that his son was "overanxious" to comply with the rules and that racism lay at the root of his woes. "If it were
possible for each person to think of him as another midshipman instead
of a negro," he wrote Sellers, "I feel he would [lose] a little of his tense-
ness and work with greater ease and accomplish more."[61]

Admiral Sellers's letter to Mr. Johnson alarmed Mitchell. The congressman immediately wrote President Roosevelt a forceful letter, with
none of the usual fawning. He asserted that most of Johnson's demerits
had resulted from delinquency reports filed "by persons who object to his
presence in the Academy." "Johnson is entitled to a degree of protection,"
he declared, "which . . . he is not getting." He demanded "that something
should be done to guarantee him a square and fair deal." He asked for a
conference to discuss the matter.[62]

That same day (29 January) Mitchell also fired off a letter to Admiral
Sellers. "Having kept in close touch with Midshipman Johnson and
knowing his eagerness to make good, and his ability as a student," he
wrote, "I am at a loss to know why these demerits have piled up in such
an incredibly short time." He suggested that racism was to blame and
asked Sellers "to look into the manner in which this young man is being
treated." Mitchell said that he wanted to talk to Sellers about the matter.[63]

Instead of investigating Mitchell's implication that Johnson was being
discriminated against, Sellers and Todd reviewed the plebe's conduct
record yet again. "As regards the contingency of the dismissal of Midshipman Johnson for unsatisfactory conduct," Sellers wrote Mitchell, "I
can assure you that no summary action will be taken nor is any contemplated in this case."[64]

On 2 February, while doing business in Washington, Admiral Sellers
dropped by Mitchell's office to discuss Johnson. Mitchell told the admiral that he was convinced that Johnson had not received fair treatment.
Sellers reiterated that he had examined Johnson's conduct record in detail
but had found no evidence of discrimination. "In so far as an ingrained
prejudice against associating with the negro race on the part of certain individual midshipmen, notably those from the Southern States, [is] concerned," Sellers said, neither he "nor anyone else could overcome it." On

the other hand, the admiral could "prevent any individual from allowing his racial prejudice to be used to persecute or treat the colored midshipmen unfairly." Mitchell went on at length about the treatment African Americans had received in civilian colleges and at West Point. Sellers replied rather coldly that he was responsible only for what went on at the Naval Academy. Mitchell asked if he could visit Johnson at the Academy. Sellers assented.[65]

Mitchell and Colonel Atwood went out to Annapolis two days later. After an upbeat chat with Johnson, the congressman and colonel spoke with the First Battalion officer about the black plebe's conduct record. Commander Padgett admitted that Johnson's relative social isolation had probably contributed to his demerit total. He said that midshipmen often received posted schedule changes and other information by word of mouth. Without a roommate or "the same associations that some others might have," Johnson simply did not always get the information he needed to avoid getting fried. Nevertheless, Padgett declared that he and the other commissioned officers in the battalion had "leaned over backward" to see that Johnson "got more than justice." He claimed to have canceled delinquency reports on Johnson that he would have approved on others. He also admitted canceling several reports that "might be considered as *not entirely just.*" He said that Johnson was doing well academically, except in English. "He may run into difficulty in that," he said.[66]

Mitchell and Atwood then met with Captain Todd. The congressman reiterated his concern that Johnson had not been treated fairly. The commandant assured him that Johnson "had received more consideration than any other midshipman." Mitchell and Todd chatted for two hours. Even though the commandant said that he "did not believe that Johnson would make a good naval officer," the congressman felt reassured. He concluded that the Executive Department had not discriminated against his appointee and that Johnson was in no immediate danger of dismissal.[67]

In fact, Johnson's naval career was sinking fast. On 8 February, four days after Mitchell's visit, the Academy marched the fourth class into the sick bay for an eye test. The doctor noted Johnson's vision at 17-17, diagnosed him with "myopia," and marked him unqualified. Although Johnson's eyes had been fine at Case and he had come to Annapolis with 20-20 vision, he figured that the close work at the Academy must have temporarily affected his eyesight. Indeed, vision problems had plagued midshipmen for years. One-ninth of the Class of 1934 failed the eye test during their senior year and did not graduate. The deterioration of midshipmen's vision had become so pervasive that it prompted an investigation by a House Naval Affairs subcommittee. But according to one of Johnson's classmates, eye tests were normally given in the summer; the timing of this one resulted from the administration's desire not to have to commission a black officer.[68]

The Academic Board convened the next morning. After discussing changes in textbooks, the board spent rest of the day and most of the next on the deficiency sheet for the first term, reviewing each case individually. The fifth case they examined on 10 February was that of James Lee Johnson, Jr. "Having in view his unsatisfactory mark for the term in English," noted the minutes, "his unsatisfactory conduct record which indicates his inability to adjust himself to the military life, his failure to meet the required standard as regards eyesight on the annual physical examination, and the further fact that he is not considered officer material, the board unanimously decided to recommend that he be dropped." Thus Johnson, along with 144 other midshipmen, was slated for dismissal.[69]

The next morning (11 February), Lieutenant (j.g.) Carl G. Christie, the Third Company officer, handed Johnson a resignation form. The Academy still gave midshipmen found deficient the opportunity to save face by resigning without suffering the ignominy of dismissal. But Christie did not explain this to Johnson; he simply handed him the form and told him to sign it. The plebe hesitated. He said that he did not want to sign without advice. Christie ordered him to sign immediately. Johnson asked permission to telegram Mitchell and await a reply. Christie sent him to the battalion officer. In a friendlier tone, Padgett explained to the plebe that signing the resignation was merely a formality. The Academic Board could tear it up later. Refusing to sign would only create hard feelings with the commandant. But if he did sign, he would receive the greatest consideration. Thus pressured, rushed, and cajoled, Johnson signed.

As the day wore on, the black plebe became increasingly apprehensive about what he had done. He tried to find Padgett, but the commander had left Bancroft Hall. He asked the officer of the watch why the Executive Department was in such a hurry to get the resignations signed. "The Department had planned—" the officer began to say, but stopped himself red-faced in midsentence as though his tongue had slipped. He then explained that to save the government money, the Academy wanted to terminate as soon as possible the pay of those who would be leaving.

Secretary of the Navy Claude A. Swanson accepted Johnson's resignation on 12 February.

The next day Johnson was summoned to the superintendent's office. Admiral Sellers spoke briefly about Johnson's failure to meet the requirements, then handed him Swanson's acceptance of his resignation, effective on 15 February. Johnson suddenly realized that he had been duped into resigning against his will. It dawned on him with crystal clarity that Padgett's "friendliness" and "fairness" had been affected. The real reason the officer had pressured him into signing the form was that the Executive Department wanted to be rid of him. Frustrated and enraged, Johnson burst into tears.[70]

Shortly thereafter, James Johnson Sr., fired off a telegram to Captain Todd. He explained that he had kept in close touch with his son since James had entered the Academy. He knew that his son had borne insults, threats, and gibes with little complaint. James Jr. had believed that if he tended his business and worked hard, he would receive fair treatment. But he had not. James Sr. declared that "bitter race prejudice" had undone his son and demanded that the commandant provide "detailed information." Todd wired back a brief, cold message stating that the Academic Board had found Johnson deficient in conduct, English, and eyesight, and had recommended his dismissal. This became the Naval Academy's official explanation of Johnson's denouement from that point on.[71]

Word of Johnson's forced resignation reached Mitchell on 13 February. The congressman immediately launched a campaign to have his appointee reinstated. He fired off a telegram to Admiral Sellers, expressing surprise at the Academic Board's action. "After the conversation I had with you at my office last week and the conference I had with other officers at the Academy, I was practically assured that no such steps . . . would be taken," he said. "To say the least I am disappointed in you." He then wired President Roosevelt, reporting Johnson's dismissal and reiterating his request for a conference. The White House scheduled a meeting with Mitchell for the sixteenth.[72]

The congressman also told the press about Johnson's forced resignation. He released selected documents to the *Pittsburgh Courier,* declaring that Sellers was "guilty of assisting in the railroading of this boy out of the School" and that the admiral was "deeply prejudiced and has been absolutely unfair to Johnson." He promised to request a congressional investigation and vowed "to ring no backing bells on this matter."[73]

The story broke in the *Baltimore Sun* on 14 February and in the *Washington Times* two days later. The *Sun* reported that naval officials attributed Johnson's resignation to his deficiencies in conduct, English, and eyesight. In both papers, Mitchell expressed surprise at Johnson's dismissal and declared that his appointee had been "railroaded" out of the Academy.[74]

Mitchell met with President Roosevelt on the sixteenth as scheduled. The congressman spoke more forcefully than he had in past meetings with the president. Roosevelt promised to investigate Johnson's case. After the meeting, Mitchell told reporters outside the White House that "we will get fair play" from an executive inquiry. He vowed to continue his campaign to break the color barrier at the Naval Academy.[75]

The president directed that Johnson's resignation "be held in abeyance" pending an investigation of the case. Roosevelt had Secretary Swanson handle the inquiry. Swanson, a native Virginian with a litany of "darky" jokes, compiled a memorandum to the president containing Johnson's conduct and English marks and the Academic Board's original reasoning behind the decision to dismiss him. "Where a midshipman leaves the Academy for any reason," he concluded, "it is not possible to reinstate him except by an act of Congress. In view of the fact that Midshipman Johnson is only one of a large number of midshipmen required to leave the Academy because of deficiencies, it is considered that it would be a discrimination in his favor to undertake any action of this kind." Swanson's "investigation" amounted to nothing more than an effort to uphold the Academic Board's ruling.[76]

On the morning of 17 February, President Roosevelt held a conference at the White House with Swanson and Rear Admiral Aldolphus Andrews, chief of the Bureau of Navigation, to discuss Johnson's case. Admiral Andrews told Roosevelt that according to the attorney general, "the action of the Academic Board in the case of academic deficiencies of midshipmen is final." Roosevelt said that dropping Johnson was not in the Navy's best interests and that Johnson "should be carried over provisionally during the rest of the academic year."

That afternoon, Swanson summoned Sellers to Washington. He told the superintendent about the morning meeting and ordered him to reconvene the Academic Board, acquaint them with the president's views, and report back to him.[77]

The Academic Board met at 9:32 A.M. on 18 February. The members reviewed the cases of the 145 midshipmen they had recommended to be dropped. In each case, they adhered to their initial recommendation. Johnson's case came last. Sellers informed the others of Roosevelt's opinion. After a "full and free" discussion, the board voted unanimously to stick to its original position. Later that day Admiral Andrews reported the board's findings to the president. Roosevelt tended to shy away from civil rights issues unless it was politically inexpedient to do so, because he feared that activism would alienate southern Democrats. He upheld the board's decision. That same day, James Lee Johnson, Sr., drove out to Annapolis, picked up his son, and brought him home.[78]

Secretary Swanson told reporters that Johnson's dismissal was final. "I am satisfied from the evidence presented me by the Chief of the Bureau of Navigation that there was no railroading of the colored midshipman," he said.[79]

Mitchell considered Secretary Swanson's "investigation" to be nothing more than a "white washing." After all, neither Johnson nor any other midshipman was ever called upon to testify before naval officials. He concluded that upperclassmen and Academy officials had deliberately forced Johnson to resign for racist reasons.[80]

Mitchell wasted no time in airing this view to reporters. The headline on the front page of the 20 February *Pittsburgh Courier* blared, "Railroaded Out of Navy." The article included Mitchell's opinion that the superintendent's prejudice played a large role in Johnson's dismissal. Under the heading "The Same Old Story," the article briefly recounted what had happened to James Conyers, Alonzo McClennan, and Henry Baker. The *Afro-American* reported that two first classmen "engineered, with the aid of academy officials, the campaign to 'get' the Washington boy." *Newsweek* magazine ran a story rebuking the Academy for its prejudice. It pointed out that Sellers had forbidden midshipmen from talking to the press about the Johnson case and had refused to talk to reporters himself.[81]

The Johnsons, however, did speak to the press. On 21 February, James Jr. returned to Case. Shortly after arriving in Cleveland, he told reporters that the Naval Academy had discriminated against him. He said that he had been duped into signing his resignation, that upperclassmen had conspired to bury him in demerits, and that his English papers had been undergraded. He pointed out that while several classmates deficient in *two* subjects had been given reexaminations, he had not. He concluded that the Academy had indeed railroaded him out.[82]

Gertrude Johnson issued a statement to the *Washington Tribune* and *Afro-American*. She said that several people had told her and her husband that they should never have permitted their son to enter the Academy. She disagreed. "My son feels, within himself, that he made a great effort," she declared. "He accepted humiliations, insults, prejudices, and discriminations, but I can say he took it like a man, for he believed that he was representing, not just James L. Johnson Jr., but the colored race."[83]

President Roosevelt's approval of Secretary Swanson's closing of the Johnson case limited Mitchell's options. The congressman could not simply reappoint Johnson, for the young man had passed the age limit for incoming midshipmen. He figured that the only way that Johnson could get back into the Academy was for the president to reappoint him on the grounds that he had been unfairly ousted.[84]

Mitchell concluded that there was little to gain by pressing the fight. He drafted a resolution directing Swanson to turn over to the House all records pertaining to Johnson and the other recent resignees, but never submitted it. He searched for information that would incriminate the first classmen whom he suspected were the ringleaders in burying Johnson in demerits, but he never obtained enough evidence to reopen the case. He launched similar fruitless inquiries into the backgrounds of Commander Padgett, Captain Todd, and Admiral Sellers. As he had feared, these efforts came to naught. Still, he kept the issue in the public eye by talking to reporters.[85]

Mitchell's fight for Johnson elicited a wide variety of responses. "I read about the Negro middy being so hazed that he was forced to quit your academy," wrote one woman to the superintendent. "Allow me, through you, to heartily congratulate your upperclassmen who did the hazing in having the brains to have selected white parents to be born to. And as far as you are concerned, you are a disgrace to the traditions of Farragut, Porter and Cushing, all of whom fought together with Negro sailors."[86]

African American newspapers, political organizations, and individuals deluged Mitchell with praise. James and Gertrude Johnson wrote to express their gratitude. The American Society for Race Tolerance and the National Negro Congress commended him and offered their support. "We need more men of your type," declared a member of Mitchell's old fraternity, Phi Beta Sigma. "I write to express my profound admiration to you for your patriotic efforts on behalf of young Johnson at the Naval

Academy," wrote West A. Hamilton, owner of a Washington printing company.

> You are indeed a fighter. I believe much good is going to result from your efforts not alone for the Negroes of America but for all the youth, who may in the future be students of Annapolis. Of course there always have and always will be dismissals from the Academy for failure. How convenient to simply throw in the unwanted Negro cadet. Carry on. The generations yet unborn will rise and call you blessed.

Even an elderly pastor who had known Henry Baker wrote to wish Mitchell well. "Right must prevail," he declared.[87]

White people also praised Mitchell. Stephen M. Young, a former Democratic representative from Ohio and member of the House Naval Affairs Committee, urged Mitchell to insist upon a complete investigation. "If you cannot accomplish the reinstatement of this midshipman," he reasoned, "you at least may, by your efforts, insure that young men in training to be officers in the United States Navy and Army must not be discriminated against because of race or color." The father of one of Johnson's classmates wrote Mitchell an anonymous letter outlining some of the mistreatment that the black plebe had endured. He agreed that the "powers-that-be" had "white-washed" the whole matter.[88]

Mitchell received anonymous hate mail as well. "You yellow nigger," wrote one racist, "you have a lot of gall to try to force a nigger through the Naval Academy." Another racist, signing his letter "A Hint to the Wise," wrote, "If you niggers don't quit pushing yourselves where you have no business, you are going to heed a lot of trouble for yourselves. You know there is no place in the Navy for Nigger officers." A third letter contained a clipping related to Johnson's dismissal across which were scrawled racial epithets linking Mitchell with Abraham Lincoln. The sender had addressed the letter to "Mitchell, Nigger Department, House of Representatives."[89]

Such threats and insults only increased the congressman's desire to get an African American through the Naval Academy. His original motivation for doing so had been mainly political, but now it was becoming personal. He did not like the hate mail and the way Admiral Sellers and others in the Executive Department had said one thing and done another. But he did enjoy basking in the limelight. "I am the only congressman in the United States who will appoint a colored boy to this Academy," he wrote to Mrs. L. L. O'Connell, a white woman who had approached Mitchell for an appointment for her son. "This being true, I must with fairness to my people supplant Johnson by another colored boy." To another supporter, he wrote, "I expect to continue the fight until we break down the barriers."[90]

James Lee Johnson, Jr., rebounded from his Annapolis agonies and achieved his dreams. With his family's help, he returned to the trajectory he had been on before going to the Academy. In 1938 he graduated from Case with a bachelor's degree in mechanical engineering. After that he worked for a year in the blueprint department of the Cleveland Waterworks, then took a job as a junior engineer at the Picatinny Arsenal in Dover, New Jersey. In 1941 he was commissioned in the U.S. Army Air Corps; trained as a technical officer at Chanute Field, outside Rantoul, Illinois; became one of the first five officers selected for the Ninety-ninth Pursuit Squadron (the famed and highly decorated Tuskegee Airmen); and served in North Africa and Italy during World War II. Before going overseas, he married Madeline Beatrice Murray. Together they raised two daughters and a son. Johnson received an honorable discharge in 1945, then got his master's degree at the Massachusetts Institute of Technology on the G.I. Bill. Ironically, Johnson spent the bulk of his professional career working for the Navy as a civilian. After MIT and a stint as a physicist with the Bureau of Standards, he landed a job in 1948 as a naval architect at the Naval Ship Research and Development Center (later called the David Taylor Model Basin) in Carderock, Maryland. After retiring from David Taylor in 1973, he continued studying fluid mechanics and developed a design for a high-speed sailing craft that he patented in 1990. He died three years later.[91]

Gertrude and James Johnson noticed a change in their son's personality after he returned home from Annapolis. He became more introverted. The viciousness of the racism he encountered at the Academy had been so traumatic that it made him wary of other human beings. Earlier, Colonel Atwood had talked about getting Frank appointed to the Military Academy, but after James Sr. and Gertrude saw what the Naval Academy had done to James Jr., they wouldn't hear of it. Elmer Jones, who served with James Jr. in the Tuskegee Airmen during World War II, found Johnson a private person who had trouble relating to peers. In 1974, Johnson spoke at length about his Naval Academy experience to historian Dennis Nordin. He had never before or since discussed it with his children, brother, or friends.[92]

In 1990, the Class of 1940 published a book commemorating the fifti-eth anniversary of their graduation. The book dedicated one page to each graduate and nongraduate. The compilers had searched for Johnson in Chicago but, of course, never found him there, so the book appeared without a page on their black shipmate. Later, two Class of 1940 alumni happened to see Johnson's obituary in the *Washington Post,* contacted his family, and with their help, put together a page on Johnson that the class president then sent to everyone who had received the book. Although the page lacks details on Johnson's Academy agonies, several of his class-mates remember what happened and believe that he was indeed forced out because he was black.[93]

5

"They Shall Not Pass"

On the day that James Lee Johnson, Jr., left Annapolis, the Bureau of Navigation wrote Arthur Mitchell that he now had a vacancy at the Naval Academy and was entitled to nominate one principal and three alternates. After news of Johnson's forced resignation hit the street, the congressman received letters from more than a dozen young men, black and white, seeking nominations to the Academy. But Mitchell had already made other plans.[1]

The congressman intended to send only African Americans to the Naval Academy in 1937 and to rely exclusively on Colonel Atwood for candidates. Even before Johnson's ouster had become final, Mitchell had solicited Atwood for recommendations. Again the congressman wanted safe bets: individuals qualified to enter by the college certificate method, sure to pass the physical examination, and possessing the right stuff to survive. Atwood selected seven Dunbar graduates and, on 13 February 1937, marched them into Mitchell's office, where the congressman announced that he was considering them for service academy appointments. Eventually Mitchell narrowed the Naval Academy list to two: James Irving Minor, Jr., and George Joseph Trivers. The congressman gave them both fictitious Chicago addresses and forwarded their nominations to the Bureau of Navigation on 10 March. That same day, he released their names to the press.[2]

The news thrilled eighteen-year-old James Minor. Son of the principal of the Monroe Laboratory School, a teaching school connected with Miner Teachers College, Minor was a major in the High School Cadet Corps and worked as a newsboy for the *Washington Tribune*. His classmates voted him as having the "best disposition." After graduating from Dunbar in 1933, Minor entered Howard University and was in his junior year in premedicine when Atwood approached him with the idea of going to the Naval Academy. "I feel very happy over my appointment," Minor told reporters. "I intend to do my very best there."[3]

George Trivers was mystified by his appointment. He was born in Philadelphia on 24 April 1917. His father had walked out on the family when he was four. His mother, Claudine T. Trivers, took George and his sister to Washington and settled down in a house in Anacostia, the section of the District south of the Anacostia River.

In his new home Trivers developed a lifelong love of nature and the outdoors. Anacostia still retained much of the rural flavor from the days when the government had given the land to freed slaves and Frederick Douglass was the most prominent inhabitant. In the 1930s, the area featured small residential communities nestled in among farmland. The fertile soil covering the gently rolling hills supported a variety of crops and wild fruits, nuts, and animals. "To go to the swimming hole," Trivers recalled, "you went through the woods, and you wore a straw hat and a minimum of clothes. You could eat blackberries all the way down to the swimming hole and all the way back."

The 1930s were hard times for the Trivers family. Jim Crow, the Depression, and single motherhood weighed heavily upon Claudine as she struggled to feed her children. She acquired an education at Miner Normal School, predecessor to Miner Teachers College, substitute taught at Birney Elementary School when she could, and worked as a maid in Washington's Wardman Park Hotel. George had to go to work as soon as possible to supplement his mother's meager income. He picked string beans on a farm by the riverbank during the summer, worked at the post office at Christmastime, and delivered newspapers year round. He became one of the leading newsboys for the *Washington Tribune* and later directed several other newsboys in distributing the paper throughout Anacostia.

Despite hard times, Claudine never lost faith in education and instilled this value in her son. In those days African Americans accorded teachers a high social status, and teaching was one of the few professions open to them. All his life, George aspired to be a teacher. Toward that end he made the trek by trolley and on foot to northwest D.C. every day to attend Dunbar High School, where he drilled under Colonel Atwood. After graduating from Dunbar in 1933, he attended Miner Teachers College. Although tuition cost only six dollars per semester, Trivers held down jobs while in college to help support his family. He worked variously in the registrar's office, delivering newspapers, and running an elevator, but still managed to make As and Bs and to become the valedictorian of his class.

Trivers despised segregation and all the injustices that went with it. African Americans could buy hot dogs and sodas at lunch counters in drug stores or five and tens. "You could stand at the end of the counter and eat all you wanted" or "walk around the store with your hot dog and soda in your hands," he recalled years later, "but you couldn't sit there and eat." Department stores allowed African Americans to hold only menial jobs, but welcomed their money. "There were no milkmen of color, or bus drivers, or meter readers. They were all white." Trivers found economic discrimination particularly loathsome, so on occasion he joined in local "don't buy where you can't work" protests aimed at opening more jobs to black people.[4]

Trivers had never given a thought to a career in the Navy until the meeting in Mitchell's office on 13 February 1937. Neither Mitchell nor Atwood had approached him with the idea of going to the Naval Academy before then, so when the congressman announced that he was considering him for an appointment, it came like a bolt from the blue. It also posed a dilemma. The idea of doing something significant for his people by breaking a color barrier appealed to him, but his family depended on his income. "I was very concerned about how my mother and sister would fare, since I was the breadwinner," Trivers recalled. "I was torn between doing something important to our group of people . . . and staying with mother and sister. . . . To go to the Naval Academy to help destroy this barrier was important to me. I would have been selfish to refuse, yet I wasn't totally at ease physically or mentally, because I [didn't know] what to expect." After mulling it over, he decided to go to the Academy. On 30 March the Academic Board accepted Trivers's secondary school and college certificates and declared him mentally qualified for admission to the Academy.[5]

Things did not work out for James Minor. He had maintained a B-plus average at Howard until his junior year, when his grades suddenly plummeted and the dean placed him on academic probation. Strangely, Mitchell seemed to be unaware of this fact when he appointed Minor to the Academy. The Academic Board rejected Minor's college certificate and the lad failed the substantiating exam given in April. It also seems strange that a student with Minor's background would fail the substantiating exam, despite his latent academic troubles.[6]

To Mitchell's chagrin, Trivers spent the spring of 1937 studying for the teachers' examination slated for June. Since eligibility for a teaching appointment in the D.C. school system depended upon passing that exam, it was crucial that aspiring teachers be well prepared, so Trivers spent many a late night studying. Mitchell tried to persuade Claudine Trivers to pressure her son into withdrawing from Miner and focusing exclusively on preparing for the Naval Academy. But how could the congressman expect George Trivers simply to abandon his studies at the end of his senior year? From Trivers's perspective, the opportunity to break the color barrier at the Naval Academy had popped out of thin air four months before a test that represented the culmination of four years of college and an entree into a profession that promised greater social status and material comfort than he had ever known. Trivers refused to throw it all away to pursue a brand-new goal and one not of his own devising. While Claudine Trivers was explaining on the telephone the reasoning behind her son's decision, Mitchell grew angry and slammed down the receiver. Although the congressman surely saw the logic behind the decision, he perceived it as a slight. Trivers studied for the teachers' exam almost to the point of exhaustion, but the effort paid off. He passed and graduated one point shy of cum laude at Miner. Now it was time to go to Annapolis.[7]

Trivers reported to the Naval Academy for the physical examination on 16 June 1937. During the exam, an upperclassman asked him if he was afraid. Trivers had grown up in a section of Washington where his only contact with nonblack people occurred in neighborhood shops owned by Asians or Jews. He had had no white friends as a child and no social interaction with white people as a young adult. He had read about things that had happened to black people in the South. And he really had no idea about what to expect at the Academy, other than what he could glean from newspaper articles about Johnson. Nevertheless, he turned to answer the upperclassman and said, "No." Trivers truly believed that his education at Dunbar High School and Miner Teachers College had prepared him for the Academy. He passed the physical and was sworn in as a midshipman later that day.[8]

News of Trivers's admittance into the Academy drew mixed responses. It pleased African Americans from Mitchell's district in Chicago, even though Trivers was obviously a Washingtonian. The *Pittsburgh Courier* reported that "the Illinois congressman is keeping his promise to keep on appointing colored youths to the Naval Academy made after James Lee

Johnson, Jr., was railroaded out." "I note that you have just succeeded in appointing another negro to the Naval Academy," began an anonymous letter.

Such an effort is not surprising, coming from Ill., as that state is willing to be represented itself by a negro. It's easy to understand that living in that environment, you wouldn't have any proper appreciation of the impossibility of making people in the East or people with proper self respect *any* where, live in such close daily contact with negroes. There is no place for one at the Academy and less than no place . . . for one in the service. The situation of white men taking orders from a negro is so outrageous, that even you should know it wont be allowed. . . . The only pity is, that *you* can't take the punishment your appointee will get.[9]

For someone who loved nature like Trivers, the Naval Academy had a definite appeal. Rowing the big cutters on the Severn River thrilled him, and he truly enjoyed sailing. He also liked playing basketball and working out with the punching bag in the gym.[10]

Otherwise Trivers had a miserable time at Annapolis. Like Johnson, Trivers had no roommate and had to go it alone. None of the second classmen helped him get oriented as they did for white plebes. Their attitude reflected that of the larger service: black people shouldn't be officers and therefore they don't belong at the Naval Academy.

Right from the start, a group of second classmen went out of their way to put him on report. They searched his room high and low for dirt, even if it meant poking a white-gloved finger into the overflow hole in the sink to find some. Trivers got fried for not having his shade rolled "two blocks" even before he knew that "two blocks" meant fully rolled up. As a result, he piled up thirteen demerits in the first two days. To avoid getting more, he rose an hour before reveille each morning to clean his room, using a piece of cardboard to dig out dirt and dust from between cracks in the window sills, closets, and floors, and he spent every spare moment pouring over *Reef Points* and the Naval Academy regulations book.[11]

Some upperclassmen expressed their racism toward Trivers openly. "Come here, nigger," they would say. As a plebe, Trivers had to respond with, "Aye, aye, sir!" After his first gym class, Trivers joined other plebes in a game of basketball. The next day after gym class, two upperclassmen grabbed the ball and announced that there would be no more games until Trivers left. Thereafter he played basketball by himself.[12]

Several fellow plebes also displayed their racism openly. "Nigger, stay away from us," they hissed. They stepped on Trivers's toes or kicked his heels while marching in ranks. Sometimes they spat on him. Once somebody even spat on Trivers's plate in the mess hall. In social settings they shunned or avoided him. If anyone ever felt any sympathy for him, Trivers remained unaware of it.[13]

The situation soon worsened. Ever since Trivers had entered the Academy, Captain Todd had been "anxious for an opportunity to come in contact with him in a natural manner." About two weeks after being sworn in, Trivers put in a request to attend Episcopal services in town, giving the commandant his pretext. He summoned Trivers to his office. To plebes, into whom fear of upperclassmen was literally pounded, the commandant of midshipmen seemed like an all-powerful being. Trivers must have approached this meeting with much trepidation.

After a brief discussion about church, Todd came to the point. With a cold, detached manner, he asked Trivers "about himself and his ultimate desires in regard to staying in the Navy." Trivers said that he was getting along all right but that he was lonely. He bilged none of his shipmates. The commandant said that Executive Department officers would do everything they could "officially" to see that Trivers got a "square deal and sympathetic treatment" at the Academy. But how he would fare after graduation was problematic. "A successful life for a man must necessarily primarily depend on his having a congenial occupation," Todd explained, but Trivers had not chosen one. "At this stage of amalgamation of [your] race into general society, [you are] rendering a disservice to [your] people by forcing [yourself] on other young men who as yet [do] not have themselves under control, and thus [you are] stirring up antagonism in [your] work and play." The commandant of midshipmen told the black plebe that he ought to resign from the Academy because there was no place in the Navy for a black officer.[14]

Trivers began to doubt that he could remain at the Academy. The extremely unsettling chat with the commandant compounded the loneliness of being shunned by the other midshipmen. He discussed the situation with his mother. Afterward Claudine dashed off a short note. "Now listen George," she wrote. "I am asking you to do this and hope you will attend to it. Please send in your resignation as soon as possible. I need you here."[15]

Trivers considered his mother's plea. He knew that he could better serve his family outside the Academy than inside. He was already well on the way to a teaching career when Mitchell had approached him with the notion of breaking the color barrier. Unused to the kind of open, ugly prejudice that the other midshipmen had displayed toward him and never really committed to a naval career in the first place, he decided to leave. On 3 July he submitted his resignation. "In the short period in which I have been a midshipman," he wrote, "I have come to realize that I am out of place in the Naval Service."[16]

Three days later (6 July), Mitchell received word of Trivers's resignation from a member of the Associated Press. Exactly how the reporter got the story is unclear. In any case, Mitchell immediately telephoned Claudine Trivers for confirmation. Claudine told the congressman that her son was dissatisfied with the Academy and that he had indeed submitted his resignation.

The next morning, Mitchell went down to Annapolis with attorney Emory B. Smith. They had an hour-long chat with Captain Todd. Mitchell went on at length about discrimination toward African American midshipmen, then asked Todd what he had to say about Trivers. Todd recounted parts of his recent meeting with Mitchell's appointee. He said that Trivers had decided to resign because he "had discovered since entering the Academy that he . . . was unfit for Naval service" and maintained that Trivers had mentioned "no unpleasantness of any kind." Mitchell then spent five minutes with his appointee. Trivers verified the gist of Todd's statement and added that he had no desire to remain at the Academy.[17]

On 7 July acting Secretary of the Navy Admiral William D. Leahy accepted Trivers's resignation. The letter of acceptance dripped with unintentional irony. "I wish for you a successful career in civil life," it said, "and that you will remember with pleasure your experience at the Naval Academy." Trivers went home the next day.[18]

In Mitchell's mind, Trivers had betrayed him. Mitchell feared that Trivers's failure to persevere might somehow reflect poorly on him. To stave off any potential bad publicity, the congressman denounced the twenty-year-old in a press release:

> I [am] convinced that Midshipman Trivers is not the type that would make good in the Navy. I do not believe that he is the fighting type. I am impressed rather strongly that he does not wish any position that requires strenuous effort; that he is like many other young men I have known—he wishes to move along the line of least resistance. I am only

too sorry that I did not discover this weakness in him before he was named as a candidate for a scholarship at the Academy. Unlike Midshipman Johnson, an appointee of mine who resigned several months ago, Trivers does not measure up to what I regard as the standard required in military life.[19]

"I am very much disappointed in Trivers," Mitchell wrote to the editor of the Norfolk *Journal and Guide,* "and would never have appointed him had I not been led to believe that he had in him a great deal more ambition, courage, and real fight than he has shown." Mitchell emphasized that there was no truth to rumors that Trivers had been railroaded out like Johnson.[20]

News of Trivers's resignation hit the street almost immediately. The 9 July *Washington Post* printed a brief article stating that Trivers quit "because he found he could not do a midshipman's work" and that there had been no "unpleasantness" behind his resignation.[21]

Trivers resented such statements, so he told his side of the story to a reporter from the *Washington Tribune.* He denied being unfit for naval service. What really lay behind his resignation were the "insults" and "studied punishment" heaped upon him by other midshipmen and condoned by the officers. Trivers's statement made the front page of the 10 July edition.[22]

Subsequent accounts of his resignation varied; some were sympathetic, others neutral, and still others reflected Mitchell's point of view. In a letter printed in the *Boston Herald,* one African American decried the fact that no member of his race had ever graduated from the Naval Academy. "It has been estimated that the education of a single midshipman or cadet over a period of four years costs the government $19,000 (approximately)," he argued. "Colored Americans must not be denied this opportunity to share in common with all Americans, the rights guaranteed under the constitution of the United States." The *Pittsburgh Courier* and *Washington Tribune* printed Mitchell's nasty press release without comment. An article in the *Philadelphia Tribune,* describing itself as a "portrait in the unmaking of a martyr," suggested that in picking subsequent candidates for the Naval Academy, sponsors should "give them tests on courage." *Time* magazine outlined Trivers's mistreatment at the Academy and expressed both Mitchell's and Trivers's points of view about the plebe's decision to resign. "Weak or strong," it concluded, "George Trivers decided enough was enough."[23]

The stories outraged many people. Edward Strong, national youth chairman of the National Negro Congress, wrote Secretary Swanson, charging that Trivers had been "forced out" because of the Academy's "discriminatory policies." He demanded a full investigation. "Negro young people throughout the United States are greatly alarmed over this situation," he declared. Similarly, Joan Stauffer, a Massachusetts resident, in a letter to the superintendent condemned the Academy for condoning prejudice. "I feel this is an outrageous example of unfairness," she wrote. "Annapolis is subsidized by U.S. taxes paid by negroes as well as whites. In time of war the negroes are called upon equally with the whites to sacrifice their lives."[24]

Captain Todd responded to such letters by stating that the Academy had been more than fair to Trivers and that Trivers had "voluntarily submitted his resignation" like others in his class who believed that "strict adherence to a routine would not suit them." But since Mitchell had denounced Trivers and had not called the Academy to account for how Trivers had been treated, the young man's resignation generated nothing like the firestorm that Johnson's ouster had ignited. Accordingly, Todd had few such replies to send.[25]

Mitchell might have acted the gentleman and offered his condolences or made some other gesture of kindness to Trivers for at least trying to break the color barrier at the Naval Academy. But the congressman didn't have it in him. Instead of seeing his appointee as a target of discrimination, all he could see was a traitor and a failure. So in public and to the press, Mitchell essentially called the twenty-year-old a coward. His private ranting topped even that. On a paper to which he had pasted an article entitled "Negro Quits Annapolis," Mitchell scrawled, "Can't make a silk purse out of a pig's ear."[26]

As much as Trivers's resignation enraged Arthur Mitchell and highlighted his lack of character, it pleased Executive Department officers and revealed their true feelings about black midshipmen. In a letter to Admiral Sellers, who was out of town for the summer, Captain Todd declared Trivers's departure from the Academy a "miracle." The commandant noted that his meeting with the black plebe had had the intended effect. "The following Saturday he appeared in my office and to my utter amazement said that he had talked over the matter with his mother and that they both thought he should resign, and he had his resignation in his hand," he wrote. "I forwarded it immediately. . . . As it stands we are very fortunate in being rid of Trivers."[27]

Nine months later, Captain Milo F. Draemel, Todd's successor as commandant, spelled out the Academy's policy toward black midshipmen in a memorandum to the superintendent:

> If colored candidates for the Naval Academy pass the required mental and physical requirements, they are admitted. Upon admission, and when they become midshipmen, the regulations of the Naval Academy apply to them in the same manner as they apply to all midshipmen, and efforts are made to avoid any discrimination against them because of color. In the Naval Academy, as in every locality, institution, or gathering of people, there are individuals who prefer not to associate with members of the colored race, just as some others prefer not to associate with members of their own race. This problem is a national one, and can not be eliminated at the Naval Academy any more than it can be in civilian life. It will continue to be a condition and problem at the Naval Academy in every instance when the situation arises. The question of the equality of races regardless of color is one that is answered differently by individuals, and until this individual difference of thought and opinion is eliminated there can be no answer to the problem of discrimination.
>
> In each instance where a colored midshipman had been in the Naval Academy within the last three years the discrimination which has existed has been that of individuals. In no case had there been any concerted discrimination on the part of the regiment or the officers attached to the Academy.[28]

This memorandum represents the first admission in writing by an Academy official that James Lee Johnson and George Trivers had encountered discrimination, albeit by "individuals." It also demonstrates that the Naval Academy's racial policy had not changed since the end of Reconstruction. The leadership intended to continue to condone social discrimination. African American midshipmen remained persona non grata.

Like James Lee Johnson, Jr., George Trivers rebounded from his Annapolis agonies and achieved his dreams. After resigning from the Naval Academy, Trivers joined the District of Columbia Branch of the NAACP and worked for almost two years as an elevator operator in northwest D.C., earning a dollar a day. In March 1939, he received a teaching appointment to Shaw Junior High School in Washington. The following September he received a transfer to Banneker Junior High School, where he taught math and science to seventh, eighth, and ninth graders. During World War II he spent the summers earning a master's degree in math and science at New York University. After the war he married Meta Lewis and together they raised three sons. George Trivers remained at Banneker until he retired in 1972. In retirement he returned to the joy of being on the water that he had experienced at the Naval Academy. For several years he and his sons raced outboard motorboats, traveling a circuit that stretched from New Jersey to Florida. Instead of prejudice on the circuit, the Triverses found camaraderie. George Trivers lived out the rest of his life in southeast Washington, only a few miles from the house in Anacostia where he grew up. He died in 2000.[29]

Despite Trivers's difficulties at the Academy, a few congressmen continued trying to send African Americans to Annapolis. In January 1938, Congressman Joe Gavagan asked Walter White to "try and find a suitable candidate for appointment to the U.S. Naval Academy." Perhaps at White's suggestion, Elliotte Johnson Williams, one of the congressman's black constituents, approached Gavagan for an appointment to the Academy after graduating from high school later that year. Williams had tailored his high school curriculum toward an Academy education, concentrating on mathematics, physics, and history. Impressed by the young man's enthusiasm and determination, Gavagan nominated him that August.[30]

A reporter for the *Pittsburgh Courier* asked Williams whether he would go through with the appointment. Brimming with confidence, Williams said that he had no doubt that he could graduate from the Academy. "It has been my ambition to become a naval officer ever since I donned my first sailor suit and carried my first rifle at the age of eight," he told the reporter. "I haven't just been picked for this assignment . . . I picked the assignment. . . . I have dreamed of being a naval officer ever since I was a child." The reporter reminded Williams of what had happened to James Lee Johnson and George Trivers at Annapolis and to Alonzo Parham and Benjamin O. Davis, Jr., at West Point. "Hasn't the experience of these young men had any discouraging effect on you?" he asked. "I made the decision that I would not let my Negro blood prevent me from even attempting a career that I felt should be mine if I worked diligently," Williams replied, adding naively that his success at the Academy would depend on his personality. He planned to respond to the inevitable racially motivated hazing by remaining courteous, unassuming, and oblivious to any low tactics directed against him. "Congressman Gavagan is helping me, not as one Negro," he concluded, "but helping me to help my people. I shall always remember him as a real man, a good fellow who wanted to help a black boy feel like an American."[31]

Williams passed the scholastic entrance exam in February 1939 and reported to the Naval Academy for his physical exam the following June. The doctors rejected him "by reason of defective vision, recurrent albumin and occasional granular casts in urine, and persistent hypertension." The Board of Medical Review reexamined Williams and confirmed these findings. Gavagan took another swing and reappointed him in 1940. Williams reported to the Academy for the physical that June. Again, the doctors rejected him "by reason of defective vision (mixed astigmatism), and Albumin in urine." Gavagan did not need a third strike to realize that Williams was out.[32]

This outcome did not surprise Arthur Mitchell. He knew that racism was firmly embedded in the Naval Academy's culture. Even so, he did not entirely blame the Academy for the failure of his own efforts to break the color barrier there. He lamented to one correspondent that he had "very little support from the colored people themselves" in trying to find blacks willing to go to Annapolis. "While there is much to be said in condemnation of the prejudice that exists against Negroes at the Military and Naval Academies," he told another correspondent, "there is also much to be said about the Negroes' short comings in connection with our experience at these Academies. . . . [The Naval Academy is not] wholly at fault as to what has happened either in the Johnson case or the Trivers case. It is my opinion that the right type of boy could have held on in both cases."[33]

In March 1938 Mitchell complained to NAACP attorney Charles Houston that he had "not been able to find a colored boy during the past twelve months who wanted to be appointed as midshipman. . . . I am beginning to believe that our people are simply not interested." Houston suggested Mitchell contact black colleges, youth councils, and other youth groups in search of prospective black midshipmen. A year later, Mitchell told journalists Olive Diggs and Metz Lochard that he had been searching for the past six months for a black candidate to fill one of his vacancies at the Naval Academy but had been unable to find one.[34]

Nevertheless, Mitchell remained committed to breaking the color barrier at Annapolis and having one of his own appointees graduate from

West Point. He had better luck with West Point. His first few nominees to the Military Academy had failed the entrance exam. Then, James D. Fowler, the same fellow whom the Naval Academy had rejected for being too old, graduated magna cum laude from Howard University in June 1937. Although Fowler still intended to pursue a medical career, Mitchell persuaded him to abandon this aspiration and serve his race by following in Benjamin O. Davis, Jr.'s footsteps at West Point. Although Fowler knew he would have a hostile reception there, he accepted the nomination, passed the entrance exam, and entered the Military Academy on 1 July 1937.[35]

Fowler had a hard time indeed. Upperclassmen abused him and classmates shunned him. He received more demerits during plebe year than any other member of his class, walked more punishment tours than 95 percent of his fellow cadets, and nearly failed academically. "At each formation," a classmate recalled,

five or six upperclass cadets would descend on "Mister Fowler," who was lucky if he received only five demerits per appearance. Dirty cap visor, stubble on chin, lint on braid, cuffs not pinned properly, dirt in fingernails, spot on trousers, and un-shined shoes would fill half a page of the delinquency report for [him] almost every day that summer and fall, and much of this was accompanied by cruel and unwarranted verbal abuse. Those of us who were his classmates at this time, of course, suffered the usual indignities of new cadets, but even we could distinguish between our treatment and that reserved for "Mister Fowler." For four years at West Point, Jim Fowler shared a room with no one. He was not welcome on Corps squads, at hops or at the Boodler [convenience store]. During plebe year, he was awakened during the night and kept awake to induce drowsiness in class the next day. Regular tours on the area and frequent special attention also reduced his time for study. We, his classmates, were advised to refrain from speaking to him and were threatened with ostracism ourselves if in any way we tried to give Jim support or encouragement. . . . A few may have whispered words of encouragement now and then, but there never was any overt action to separate ourselves, either as a class or as individuals, from the policy and practices of the institution.[36]

Mitchell appealed directly to the president. He told FDR that "there has been a most determined effort on the part of some of the cadets to make it absolutely impossible for Fowler to remain at the Academy," simply "because of the fact that he is colored." After reviewing Fowler's records, Roosevelt sent the superintendent of the Military Academy an unambiguous message: "I want the colored boy, James Fowler, Jr., to graduate." It is unclear why FDR intervened so forcefully, but his action had a decisive impact. Fowler graduated in 1941.[37]

During the graduation ceremony, the audience clapped louder for Fowler than they did for the anchor man, even though tradition dictated that the anchor man receive the loudest applause. Many of Fowler's classmates congratulated him, even some who had originally objected to his presence.[38] Three more black Mitchell appointees would graduate from the Military Academy.[39]

Fowler's success reinforced Mitchell's conviction that "the right kind of boy can and will stick it out" at the Naval Academy.[40] The congressman found two promising candidates in 1941. That January, Charles Toussaint Gadsden, Jr., a black Chicagoan who lived outside of the First District, informed Mitchell that he wanted to become a midshipman. Mitchell was intrigued. Gadsden had graduated eighth in a class of 585 from Tilden Technical High School, was currently enrolled at Armour Institute of Technology (later the Illinois Institute of Technology), and hoped to become a submarine commander. Two clergymen, the Reverend Dr. Harold M. Kingsley and the Reverend Dr. William S. Braddan, the pastor of Gadsden's church, sent Mitchell letters of recommendation on Gadsden's behalf. Kingsley declared that "it is absolutely necessary for us to break the bottle neck both in military defences and in entrances to the Military and Naval Academies." Mitchell told the reverend that his other black appointees to the Naval Academy "were boys that I had to run down and persuade to go to the school. Gadsden is the first young colored lad in the United States to appeal to me for an appointment. I have an opening which I have been holding for just such a call."

Mitchell interviewed Gadsden in person while on business in Chicago at the end of the month. The young man impressed him, so he gave Gadsden the appointment on 3 February. Reverend Braddan had a flier printed to celebrate the event. With pictures of the American flag and words to the song "God Bless America" as a backdrop, the flier announced that Gadsden was "on his way to the U.S. Naval Academy, the toughest spot, for a Negro, in the world."[41]

That same month, Mitchell nominated another black candidate to the Naval Academy, Alvin Jerome Thompson, a native Washingtonian. It is unclear precisely how Mitchell arrived at that decision, but it is likely that Colonel Atwood had something to do with it. In any event, an article on the front page of the 15 February *Pittsburgh Courier* carried the headline "Mitchell Names Two to Annapolis." "I will continue to make these appointments as long as I have power to," the article quoted Mitchell as saying, "and I believe we will eventually break down the barriers and establish the Negro in the United States Navy to positions of ensigns and officers."[42]

Unfortunately for Mitchell, the outcome had a nauseatingly familiar ring. Toussaint Gadsden sailed through the scholastic portion of the entrance exam in May, scoring nearly perfect marks. He then passed the three-day preliminary physical exam given at the Ninth Naval Armory in Chicago. On 8 July he reported to the Academy for his official physical exam. Although the Chicago Navy doctors indicated that Gadsden had perfect vision, Academy Navy doctors declared his right eye "five points off" and disqualified him. Alvin Thompson qualified scholastically by the college certificate method but also failed the July physical "by reason of defective vision." The Board of Medical Review reexamined him and upheld the original finding. Neither Gadsden nor Thompson became a midshipman. The Associated Negro Press implied that Academy doctors had used the eye test as a "weapon" to exclude blacks. "'They Shall Not Pass' seems to be the motto of the U.S. Naval Academy," declared the organization.[43]

That same spring, another initiative to break the Naval Academy's color barrier emerged in Detroit. This effort was rooted in the 1936 election, when Democratic congressman George D. O'Brien won a seat in the House, representing Michigan's Thirteenth District. Ernest Mitchell, an African American attorney, had helped O'Brien get elected as secretary of Detroit's George D. O'Brien for Congress Club. After his victory, O'Brien asked Mitchell what he wanted in return. Mitchell said that he would like to see an African American enter one of the service academies. O'Brien authorized Mitchell to form a committee to find a suitable candidate.[44]

In 1939, Congressman O'Brien did, in fact, appoint an African American to the Military Academy: Detroit native Clarence M. Davenport. Ernest Mitchell, however, was not the one who discovered Davenport. Instead, O'Brien credited Mable E. Flack, "an outstanding woman in civic and political affairs," as the *Pittsburgh Courier* put it. "Without the aid of any political organization," the congressmen told the *Courier*, Mrs. Flack "found a young man with the right qualifications" and prevailed upon O'Brien to appoint him. In a letter to Walter White, however,

Mitchell implied that it was he who had found Davenport. In any case, Davenport made it through the Military Academy, graduating on 19 January 1943.[45]

In April 1941, Ernest Mitchell launched "a movement in the hope that the other Michigan members of Congress will follow [O'Brien's] example en masse" in appointing African Americans to the service academies, as he put it in a letter to Walter White. He hoped that if Michigan congressmen began sending blacks to West Point and Annapolis, "other states would follow suit." On 18 April, Mitchell sent letters to Senator Prentiss Brown and Representatives Louis Rabaut, Rudolf Tenerowicz, John Dingell, John Lesinski, and George Dondero, urging them to assist O'Brien in "whipping the other Michigan congressmen into line." "It would be a highly commendable thing for the State of Michigan if our representatives in Congress blazoned a trail that may be followed by representatives from other States in recognition of the Negro," he added. The letters implied that O'Brien was a party to the "movement," but O'Brien found out about it no sooner than his colleagues did. Mitchell attempted to recruit O'Brien with a flattering letter that praised him for being a trailblazer. He then outlined his strategy: "I am sending a copy of this letter to Mr. Walter White of the NAACP, to whom I will send copies of all answers which I receive from the Michigan congressmen and Senator. Where I fail to receive replies I will also inform him." It was a crude attempt at subtle coercion.[46]

O'Brien responded positively to Ernest Mitchell's appeal. "I shall do my best toward persuading the other members here," he said. Rabaut, Lesinski, and Brown promised to consider the matter. Dondero informed Mitchell that he nominated candidates to the service academies on the basis of their performance in competitive exams and their physical qualifications.[47]

Congressman Dingell rebuked Ernest Mitchell for what he considered crude tactics. "It is not within my province to in any way 'whip the other Michigan congressmen into line,'" he said. "I have . . . no right nor control over any other Member of Congress." He said that the "question of proportionate representation" was "fundamental and fair" and opined that other congressmen would respond positively if approached "properly." He expressed disapproval of Mitchell's tactic of sharing his correspondence with the NAACP. "Implied or veiled threats might in some instances be resented," he said. "Honey is more palatable than vinegar." He added, "We in Washington do not look upon Mr. Walter White as a 'bogy man' nor as an individual who might be induced to punish those who fail to respond to such proposals." He pointed out that he had already appointed an African American to West Point.[48]

Dingell's appointee, Ambrose B. Nutt, never made it to West Point. For reasons that remain unclear, the Military Academy rejected him. Dingell appealed to President Roosevelt for a waiver for Nutt, but the appeal came to naught, for FDR felt that the War Department had good reason for rejecting him. Dingell vowed "to recognize a Negro" with an appointment.[49]

Congressman Tenerowicz informed Ernest Mitchell that he had already nominated an African American to the Naval Academy, a fellow named Charles Edwin Smith. After receiving the appointment, however, Smith turned it down, asking for a nomination to West Point instead. Since this occurred after the 10 April closing date for the receipt of appointments, Tenerowicz was unable to appoint another African American in his place.[50]

It must have dawned on Ernest Mitchell after receiving Tenerowicz's reply that his initiative to send an African American to the Naval Academy in 1941 was doomed from the start, since he had launched it after the deadline. Nonetheless, he followed through on sending copies of the congressmen's replies to Walter White. White thanked him for the copies and the effort. Unfortunately, Mitchell's effort also came to naught, in terms of getting a black appointed to a service academy in 1941.[51]

However, Mitchell's attention did spur Walter White to give greater consideration to the color barriers at the service academies. He suggested to the various branches of the NAACP that they insist that their congressmen nominate qualified African Americans to the Naval Academy and the Military Academy, "particularly in those states where the Negro vote is decisive."[52]

Politics played crucial roles in shaping the Navy's racial policy as well as in African Americans' efforts to change it. After Reconstruction, naval policy and practices toward blacks mirrored those of the American South. As legalized discrimination outside the Navy increased, opportunities for African Americans inside the Navy decreased. By the Depression, the Navy had relegated blacks to the role of "chambermaids to the braid" to prevent them from acquiring billets that would put them in command of white sailors.

Black people fought back. The Great Migration, black pride movements, and increasing African American participation in civil rights organizations like the NAACP symbolized black people's loathing of segregation and represented concrete steps toward overthrowing Jim Crow. African Americans' growing population in cities outside the South and shift in allegiance to the Democratic Party gradually increased their political power. The nascent civil rights movement early targeted color barriers in the Navy as a step toward ending segregation in society. African American leaders sought both greater opportunities for black sailors in the fleet and berths for black midshipmen at the Naval Academy.

Individual efforts rather than any sort of grassroots or mass movement resulted in the appointment of blacks to the Naval Academy during the Jim Crow era. Because of political inexpediency or personal prejudice, most congressmen never thought of appointing an African American to the Naval Academy. Those few who did nominate blacks as midshipmen did so because of idealism and because African Americans constituted a significant proportion of their constituency.

Idealism in particular motivated Oscar DePriest to break the Naval Academy's color barrier. He viewed the appointment of African American midshipmen as an assertion of black people's civil rights. In keeping with his role as representative to all African Americans, he considered candidates from both inside and outside his district, and he made appointments on the basis of individual performance in competitive exams. Young men interested in going to the Naval Academy approached him for an appointment; he did not seek them out. This strategy enabled him to appoint the nation's best and brightest African Americans who wanted to be naval officers. Given Dunbar High School's place as the nation's top black academic high school and a pillar of black pride, it was only natural that DePriest and successive black congressmen nominated Dunbar alumni.

Initially, DePriest seemed to lack basic information about the Academy and its admission requirements. During his first opportunity to nominate midshipmen in 1929, he selected one candidate who was too old and another whose eyesight wasn't good enough. Thereafter, none of DePriest's appointees passed the Academy's entrance exams.

Similarly, Joseph Gavagan nominated African Americans to the Naval Academy because he opposed racial discrimination and because he represented black New Yorkers in Congress. But none of Gavagan's black Naval Academy nominees ever passed the entrance exams either.

Political pragmatism shaped Arthur Mitchell's course in trying to break the Naval Academy's color barrier during his first two terms in office. Like most congressmen, he made many appointments as political favors or to pay political debts. At first, he appointed black candidates to the Naval Academy to appease critics who had charged him with neglecting civil rights issues. Appointing both blacks and whites to the Academy made good political sense throughout his career. He could tell a black audience that he was smashing a color barrier and a white audience that he was color blind.

Mitchell developed a good strategy for identifying black candidates to send to Annapolis. His reliance on the head of Dunbar High School's Cadet Corps made perfect sense because of Dunbar's reputation and Colonel Atwood's personal acquaintance with the strengths and weaknesses of each potential nominee.

Henry O. Atwood sought to break the color barrier at the Naval Academy for idealistic reasons. He hoped that African American midshipmen would become symbols of black pride in the tradition of Charles Denton Young. Atwood's strategy for finding candidates for the Naval Academy involved identifying individuals possessing the brains, brawn, and intestinal fortitude to survive four years in a lily-white institution, then persuading them to give it a try.

More African American appointees would have become midshipmen during the 1930s had they passed the Academy's entrance exams. Congressmen DePriest, Mitchell, Gavagan, and Rudolf Tenerowicz appointed at least seventeen and probably more young black men to the Academy between 1929 and 1941. It is difficult to believe that only two of these appointees were capable of passing the scholastic and physical examinations, particularly since DePriest and Mitchell were so intent on nominating safe bets. Why would Gavagan have reappointed Elliotte Johnson Williams if he thought he would fail the eye test a second time? Why would Navy doctors at the Academy have disqualified Toussaint Gadsden for defective vision when Navy doctors at the Ninth Naval Armory in Chicago had found no defects in Gadsden's vision just weeks earlier? How could William Chisolm, a freshman at Columbia University, fail the Academy's scholastic entrance examination? How could so many graduates of the famous Dunbar High School have failed to meet the Academy's scholastic entrance requirements? The fact that the Academy rejected so many well-educated African Americans on the basis of scholastic deficiency, and the fact that it rejected on the basis of defective vision so many nominees whose eyesight non-Academy physicians had declared normal suggests that during the Depression Academy officials falsified examination results to prevent African Americans from entering.

It is not surprising that certain Academy officials and midshipmen took action to enforce the racial status quo. The Academy served as gatekeeper for the Navy's officer corps. Although the Academy was no longer the sole source of line officers, only Academy graduates could hope to attain the Navy's highest ranks. Keeping the regiment of midshipmen lily white conformed to the Navy's racial policy of limiting African American sailors to servant duties and excluding them from the officer corps. The behavior of Academy officers and white midshipmen toward black midshipmen reflected the policy of the leadership—"They Shall Not Pass," as the Associated Negro Press put it.

Nevertheless, some white midshipmen's attitudes about black people being midshipmen had progressed since Reconstruction. A minority of plebes and upperclassmen, largely New Englanders and a sprinkling of southerners, risked the ostracism of their peers or the ire of their superiors by helping or befriending James Johnson. Johnson was never isolated to the extent that Conyers, McClennan, Baker, or black Military Academy cadets had been.

Unfortunately for Johnson and George Trivers, racism still flourished at the Naval Academy. Racism was embedded in the Academy's culture, and evidenced by the slurs against blacks in Navy songs and in *Reef Points*. It was also embedded in the behavior of midshipmen who called Johnson "nigger," spat on Trivers, instructed plebes to ignore black shipmates, and otherwise expressed their racism overtly. Covert expressions of racism proved more sinister. Evidence suggests that a small group of largely southern-born upperclassmen planned and conducted a campaign to fry Johnson out on demerits. Although Johnson and Trivers never suffered physical assaults on the scale of their Reconstruction predecessors, they encountered a similar degree of prejudice.

The pervasiveness of racism at the Academy coupled with the pressure to conform caused midshipmen like Bruce Hayden to ignore Johnson. Such midshipmen had no qualms about interacting socially with black people outside the Academy, but avoided doing so on the inside for fear that they would be ostracized or that their careers would be jeopardized. Accordingly, most white midshipmen simply snubbed their black shipmates.

The behavior of Executive Department officers in the 1930s toward black midshipmen had regressed since Reconstruction. Although Admirals Worden and Rodgers had condoned the silencing of James Conyers, Alonzo McClennan, and Henry Baker, they had at least made some attempt to level the playing field for black midshipmen. They not only provided counseling, but the boards of inquiry they convened to investigate the assaults on the black cadets and other actions sent a message to the white cadet midshipmen that they would not tolerate physical assaults on black naval cadets. Although their actions failed to eliminate racially motivated hazing, they at least tried to do so.

The actions of Admiral Sellers, Captain Todd, and Commander Padgett in the cases of James Johnson and George Trivers indicate that they considered black midshipmen persona non grata. Sellers, Todd, and Padgett were all southerners whose attitude toward African Americans reflected the racial caste system in which they had been raised. This attitude surfaced in Padgett's dressing down of Johnson for attending the plebe summer reception at Admiral Sellers's home as well as in Captain Todd's assessment of Johnson's "grease." According to this view, a black man should not command white men; therefore, Johnson was not good officer material.

Executive Department officers were derelict in their duty toward Johnson and Trivers. Although their responsibilities included providing guidance and counseling to midshipmen, there is no evidence that they ever offered advice to their black charges. Admiral Sellers told James Lee Johnson, Sr., that *he* ought to counsel his son, instead of having an Executive Department officer do so. The only advice offered to Trivers was Captain Todd's suggestion that he resign.

Commander Padgett behaved even more badly. He told Congressman Mitchell and Colonel Atwood the he had canceled several conduct reports on Johnson that "might be considered as not entirely just." Although filing a false delinquency report was a Class "A" offense punishable by separation from the Academy, there is no evidence that Padgett ever prosecuted the midshipmen who had filed the false reports on Johnson. Worse, given the procedures for reappointing midshipmen, Padgett's explanation to Johnson about the significance of signing the resignation was an outright lie.

The degree of complicity of Executive Department officers in the racist midshipmen's campaign to fry Johnson out on demerits is difficult to assess. Although there is no direct evidence linking Executive Department officers with specific delinquency reports or acts of racially motivated hazing, Mitchell, Johnson, and several other midshipmen were certain that officers were involved somehow.

Given the procedure for filing delinquency reports, Commander Padgett, Captain Todd, and Admiral Sellers were well aware that an unusually high number of reports were coming in on Johnson. Although Padgett knew that some of the reports were unjust, the Executive Department never convened a board to investigate whether Johnson was being discriminated against. Rather than query possible wrongdoers, Sellers and Todd simply reviewed Johnson's conduct record over and over again. Had the Executive Department convened a board of inquiry or somehow spread the word that it would not tolerate unjust treatment of black midshipmen, people like Bruce Hayden, who knew what was going on but were afraid to say anything, might have tried to stop it.

Executive Department officers sent no such signal. Padgett claimed to have canceled reports on Johnson that he would have approved for others, and he did rule in Johnson's favor on several occasions when the black plebe challenged a report. But the Executive Department never took *decisive* action to stop or prevent upperclassmen from filing false reports against Johnson, despite Admiral Sellers's pronouncement to Mitchell that he had the power to do just that. Whatever their ultimate degree of complicity might have been, they certainly condoned the racist midshipmen's campaign to fry Johnson out. Indeed, Johnson's demerit total was one of the three main criteria used by the Academic Board to recommend dropping him.

It is also difficult to assess the other two criteria—Johnson's English grades and eyesight. Certainly Johnson's English grades suffered because marching off demerits robbed him of time to study. Johnson himself admitted that he found writing to be difficult. But at least one first classman told Johnson, in effect, that his English papers had been deliberately undergraded. Johnson and Mitchell agreed with this assessment. If Academy officials had deliberately undergraded entrance examinations to prevent black appointees from matriculating, it stands to reason that they would deliberately undergrade an English exam to prevent a black midshipman from graduating. Similarly, it is unclear whether the eye examination that Johnson failed had been administered within the context of the vision problems then plaguing many other midshipmen, or to create another pretext for ousting Johnson. What is true is that Johnson never had eye trouble after he left the Academy.[53] Again, if Academy officials had deliberately disqualified black appointees on the basis of falsified eye exam results, it stands to reason that they would disqualify a black midshipman on the same basis.

Mitchell was right when he called Secretary Swanson's investigation of Johnson's resignation a "white washing." Swanson did no more than Sellers and Todd had done to find out what had really happened to Johnson. The secretary simply reviewed the records with an eye toward upholding the Academic Board's dismissal recommendation.

President Roosevelt's involvement in the Johnson case had virtually no effect on its outcome. Although he gave Mitchell a chance to vent, he followed the advice of Admirals Andrews and Sellers and closed the case. Since Roosevelt had never put much stock in Mitchell to begin with, he was less likely to respond to pressure from the Illinois representative than he might have been had it come from some other congressman.

Had a different group of officers been in charge at the Academy during the mid-1930s, Johnson and Trivers might have received fair treatment. Large organizations like the Navy and institutions like the Naval Academy were not monolithic in attitudes or policies on any given subject. Such organizations and institutions tend to reflect the personalities of their leaders. Not every naval officer harbored racial prejudice; it just so happened that in 1936 and 1937, the secretary of the Navy, the superintendent, the commandant, and the first battalion officer all hailed from a section of the country that had legalized discrimination. While it is certainly true that not all southerners were racists, the actions of Swanson, Sellers, Todd, and Padgett indicated that they embraced the mores of the southern racial caste system. They believed that there was no place in the Navy for black officers; therefore, African American midshipmen did not belong at the Naval Academy. Had the superintendent's or commandant's attitudes resembled those of Admirals Worden and Rodgers, they might have taken decisive action to stop the unjust treatment of Johnson and Trivers. As it was, Sellers and Todd condoned it. These attitudes indicate that the institution was clearly not ready for African American midshipmen before World War II.

James Lee Johnson, Jr., had entered the Academy both to pursue a career as a naval officer and to do something for his race. Given a level playing field, he would have had an excellent chance of becoming the Naval Academy's first African American graduate. He certainly had the necessary intelligence and athletic ability. Even if the other midshipmen had given him the silent treatment instead of hazing him and heaping demerits on him, Johnson could have endured. His private nature and strength of character would have enabled him to find solace within himself as Benjamin O. Davis, Jr., had done at West Point. It is impossible to know how his vision would have fared had his experience been less stressful.

As it was, the racist midshipmen's campaign to fry him out, coupled with the Executive Department's malign neglect, ensured that he would fail. No African American could have graduated from the Naval Academy under the circumstances that Johnson had faced. His case, along with Trivers's, reinforced the black community's perception of the Navy as a racist institution.

PART III

Breaking the Color Barrier

World War II and the First
Black Graduate, 1942–1949

6

Racial Policy "Revolution"

World War II ended the Great Depression, propelled unparalleled numbers of women into the work force, launched an era of sustained economic growth, and marked the rise of the United States to global preeminence. The war also reshaped the contours of the black community. It accelerated the migration of black people from the South to the North and from rural to urban areas. It increased the number and clout of urban black voters in the North. In some places it created unprecedented economic opportunities for African Americans. And it contributed decisively to the rise of black consciousness and mobilization of dissent that later culminated in the mass civil rights movement of the 1960s.

World War II also had a profound impact on the Navy. During the war, the Navy fielded the largest force of men and women in its history. On 1 July 1940, the active-duty personnel strength of the Navy, Marine Corps, and Coast Guard totaled 203,127 officers and enlisted men. After the Japanese attack on Pearl Harbor, the Navy and the other services deluged the media with calls for volunteers. Americans answered in unprecedented numbers. Between 30 November 1941 and 30 June 1945, the Navy enlisted an average of sixty-five thousand recruits per month. The high point came during fiscal year 1944 when some twenty-five thousand men and women entered the Navy each week. The number of new recruits who joined the Navy each month during that period exceeded the total number of enlisted men in the Navy in 1934. Many had never set foot on a boat in their lives. The Navy had to train them for service on board thirty different types of combat vessels, fifty different types of auxiliaries, and thirty-five types of landing craft. The Navy needed people not only in unprecedented numbers but also with an unprecedented range of specialized skills, for ships and weapons systems were more technologically complex than ever before. By 1 July 1945, the sea services had

137

ballooned to 4,031,097 uniformed men and women, 3,388,556 of whom served in the Navy. Despite this dizzying growth, there seldom came a period during the war that did not find the Navy wanting for personnel.[1]

Because of this need to tap all of America's human resources for war and because of political pressure on the Roosevelt and Truman administrations from civil rights advocates, the Navy revolutionized its racial policy. By the end of the war black sailors were no longer restricted to the messman's branch, but found most enlisted billets open to them, at least in writing. In reality, decades would pass before actual practice caught up with policy. Most significantly, the Navy was forced to take the unprecedented step of commissioning African American officers. In this atmosphere of fundamental changes in American society and the Navy's racial policy, the push to integrate the Naval Academy held greater promise of success than ever before.

During the World War II era, ferment in black communities pushed civil rights advocacy to the fore in a manner not seen since Reconstruction. African Americans assumed increasingly important roles in organizations such as the United Steel Workers, United Automobile Workers, and other labor unions. The Congress of Industrial Organizations (CIO), one of two major groupings of American labor unions, fought for equal employment opportunity for black workers. Many Americans became convinced that the government should guarantee employment without discrimination. New York, Massachusetts, and other states set up agencies analogous to the Fair Employment Practices Committee.[2] Black activism and the need for labor power resulted in dramatic increases in the quantity and quality of jobs open to African Americans, as well as in their average income. By the war's end, most major industries had at least some black workers in their plants. The number of black people employed in manufacturing more than doubled while the number of unemployed blacks fell from 937,562 in 1940 to 151,000 in 1944.

Yet employers still tended to give black workers the hottest, heaviest, and dirtiest jobs. Many of the 5.5 million black people who moved to urban areas between 1941 and 1945 to seek jobs in the defense industry encountered housing shortages, restrictive covenants, substandard dwellings, inadequate medical care, deficiencies in education, poor recreational facilities, and other problems. With black people living in overcrowded ghettos and still facing discrimination amidst rising expectations of gaining equal rights, it is no surprise that NAACP leader Walter White could describe an area like Harlem as a "cauldron of brooding misery and frustration."[3]

Consequently, discontent with the racial status quo rose, the fight against discrimination escalated, and black protesters adopted more militant tactics during the war. Leaders such as Mary McCleod Bethune, Ralph Bunche, W. E. B. Du Bois, Rayford Logan, A. Philip Randolph, and Roy Wilkins recognized that the war had heightened racial issues and demanded—not begged for, as black leaders had done in the past, but demanded—first-class citizenship and full economic, political, and social equality for black people. Walter White praised the increasing militancy and unity of African Americans in making these demands. Membership in established civil rights organizations soared; the membership of the NAACP increased nearly tenfold. New civil rights organizations sprang up. The Congress of Racial Equality (CORE), destined to play a major role in the civil rights struggle during the fifties and sixties, emerged in 1942 from a Christian-pacifist organization. Influenced by the militant but nonviolent tactics and philosophy of Mohandas Karamchand Gandhi in India, its members staged pickets, boycotts, and sit-ins to attack segregation in drugstores and department stores in northern cities. Blacks also engaged in acts of civil disobedience. Hundreds of followers of the Temple of Islam, the separatist-nationalist movement whose members were commonly known as Black Muslims, refused to register for the draft. Black individuals and small groups staged "stool sittings" to force eateries to serve African Americans. Many viewed the war as a white man's fight or simply had no desire to serve in the armed services. One draftee remarked that his epitaph should read, "Here lies a black man killed fighting a yellow man for the protection of a white man."[4]

Black rage sometimes exploded during the war. In June 1943, a fistfight between several black and white youths in Detroit sparked the worst American race riot of World War II. It lasted more than thirty hours, claimed nine white and twenty-five black lives, destroyed hundreds of thousands of dollars worth of property, and ended only when President Roosevelt sent in six thousand federal troops. Race riots also broke out in Los Angeles, Chicago, and Harlem.

At the same time, racism diminished in some places in the United States during World War II. "No greater hope for the eventual solution of the tangled race issue can be found," wrote Walter White in 1945, "than in those instances where some white Americans have shown that their democracy rises above prejudice and ignorance." In 1944 Gunnar

Myrdal identified "the gradual destruction of the popular theory behind race prejudice" as "the most important of all social trends in the field of interracial relations" and declared that "the popular beliefs rationalizing caste in America are no longer intellectually respectable." He noted that even some segregationists considered racial prejudice "irrational." Psychology, education, anthropology, and social science were all explaining differences among groups in terms of "environmentalism" instead of race. During the war America proclaimed racial equality and universal brotherhood in battling Nazi Germany and its "master race" dogma. White opposition to integration in housing, transportation, and education decreased slowly during the 1940s. Prominent white men and women like novelist Pearl Buck and unsuccessful Republican presidential contender Wendell L. Willkie advocated equal rights for African Americans. In a wartime survey of 12,622 students in sixty-three colleges throughout the country, more than 73 percent believed that America needed to end discrimination against blacks in order to implement the Four Freedoms worldwide. Blacks and whites together formed the Southern Regional Council to work toward abolition of disfranchisement.[5]

This is not to say that white people and black people across America embraced each other as social equals. In fact, the racism of many white people intensified during the war, especially as blacks moved to urban areas in search of more lucrative jobs in war industries. But it is safe to say that under pressure from both black people and white people, Jim Crow's throne began to crack.

Amid this ferment, voices decrying the racial situation at Annapolis were drowned out by a chorus calling for broader opportunities throughout the armed services. By 1937, abolition of discrimination in the Army and Navy had become one of the NAACP's primary objectives. At its annual conference held that July, the NAACP passed a resolution condemning discrimination in the armed services. In October, the organization urged President Roosevelt to end discrimination and open all branches of the Army and Navy to African Americans. That same month, in response to a speech by the president warning of the threat to the United States posed by "aggressor nations," NAACP attorney Charles Houston urged the secretary of the Navy to end discrimination "in all branches and services of the Navy" and to give black citizens "the same right to enlist [and to] qualify for commissions and promotions as other citizens." In 1938, the NAACP passed a resolution calling upon FDR to issue an executive order to end discrimination in the armed services and denouncing any legislation that proposed creating segregated units in the Army and Navy. That same resolution urged African American voters "to support candidates for Congress who will pledge themselves to appoint Negro youth to Annapolis and West Point." In September 1939, Walter White petitioned Roosevelt to appoint a biracial commission that would investigate discrimination in the Army and Navy and recommend removal of color barriers.[6]

President Roosevelt moved cautiously on civil rights issues. Although sympathetic toward the plight of black people, FDR had done little for them during his first years in office, arguing that he could not afford to offend southern Democrats, who controlled the major committees in Congress, and thereby jeopardize his New Deal legislation. Although he had formed a "black cabinet" of advisers on racial issues in 1934 and supported an antilynching bill in 1938, he remained wary of political fallout from civil rights measures. Instead of granting White's requests, Roosevelt had his secretary refer the NAACP leader to a War Department report on new black units being created under presidential authorization.[7]

In preparing a reply to this communication, White and Roy Wilkins, assistant secretary of the NAACP and editor of *The Crisis,* agreed to incorporate the idea of admitting more blacks into the Military and Naval Academies into future NAACP initiatives to desegregate the armed forces.[8]

Wilkins returned to the subject of the Naval Academy's color barrier in May 1940 during the debate over the conscription bill, but the policy limiting blacks to the messman's branch overshadowed Annapolis. On 26 July, Thurgood Marshall, head of the NAACP's legal department, wrote Secretary of the Navy Frank Knox, arguing that the Navy's racial policy would undermine the "unity" of the American people in carrying out the defense program. Marshall urged Knox to remove color barriers throughout the Navy.[9]

Knox, however, believed that it was "no kindness to negroes to thrust them upon men of the white race."[10] Born on the first day of 1874—while Alonzo McClennan was fighting his losing battle at the Naval Academy— Frank Knox grew up in Boston, Massachusetts, and Grand Rapids, Michigan. During the Spanish-American War he embarked on a brilliant 42-year-long journalistic career, pausing only to serve as an officer in the Army during World War I. Although Knox was a Republican and had lashed out at the New Deal, his support of the administration's foreign policy attracted the attention of President Roosevelt, who sought to include him in a coalition cabinet. Knox became secretary of the Navy on 11 July 1940.

Knox both trusted and depended upon his uniformed advisers. He routinely delegated responsibilities to them, allowed them to operate freely, and stood by them when necessary. "Any layman would be a damn fool to get himself mixed up in the professional business of trying to fight a naval war," he once told friends. "My job is to find out what the top admirals want to put across, talk it over with them and then do my damnedest to see that the job gets done as economically and efficiently as possible." His early pronouncements on racial policy echoed the views of most of the Navy's senior officers. Since Knox supported their opposition to altering the racial composition of the fleet, change in the Navy's racial policy moved at a snail's pace while he remained secretary.[11]

Knox had the Bureau of Navigation prepare a reply to Thurgood Marshall. "After many years of experience," noted the bureau, "the policy of not enlisting men of the colored race for any branch of the naval service except the messman branch, was adopted to meet the best interests of general ship efficiency."[12]

In the wake of the Japanese attack on Pearl Harbor, the pressure on Knox to broaden opportunities for African American sailors increased dramatically. On 9 December 1941, Walter White wired Knox, asking whether, in light of the intensive recruiting drive then underway, the Navy would accept black recruits for duty outside the messman's branch. The telegram declared that the Navy's present racial policy was "doing more than almost any other single thing to dampen the enthusiasm of Negroes for all-out aid to their country." The Bureau of Navigation sent White an unequivocal reply: "There has been no change in the Navy's policy regarding enlistment of men in the colored race and for the time being no change is contemplated." White protested this fact to the president and demanded that he order the Navy "to abandon its jim crow policy."[13]

Articles denouncing specific instances of naval discrimination peppered the pages of African American newspapers in the following weeks. The office of Assistant Secretary of the Navy Ralph A. Bard, which monitored the way the black press portrayed the Navy, described these articles as "resentful with occasional vitriolic outbursts" and predicted that protests against the Navy's racial policy "will grow in number if not in intensity."[14]

Charles Houston wrote Knox that "the Pearl Harbor attack has left many Negro citizens wondering about this pure-white 'battle efficiency.'"

He called upon the secretary to "enlist and promote sailors on the principle of the best man for each rating regardless of race, creed, or color, and let it be known that the Navy belongs to a democracy."[15]

Two months after Pearl Harbor, the *Pittsburgh Courier* coined a slogan that symbolized the African American campaign against discrimination during the war, "Double V" or "Double Victory." The newspaper declared that "in our fight for freedom we wage a two-pronged attack against our enslavers at home and those abroad who would enslave us." Although the *Courier* trumpeted the "Double V" as a departure from the "Close Ranks" slogan of World War I, it was really a continuation of Robert Vann's prewar effort to open the services to blacks.[16]

Vann had stepped up the *Courier's* ongoing campaign against color lines in the Army and Navy in 1938. Nearly every issue of the *Courier* printed that year included an article or editorial about discriminatory military practices. African American leaders, organizations, and other black newspapers supported the campaign. The *Courier's* "Campaign for Army and Navy Equality" rested upon familiar logic. Since African American tax dollars helped pay for the armed services, black people should have equal opportunities for education and jobs in the armed forces. If African Americans were allowed to prove that they could compete on an equal basis with whites in the Army and Navy, it would demonstrate their value as citizens and validate their demand to end discrimination. Essentially the same argument that Vann had been printing since 1926, it embodied fairness, patriotism, and the traditional African American aim of gaining civil rights through military service.[17]

One *Courier* article suggested a prescient solution to the problem of breaking the Naval Academy's color barrier. It discussed the color barrier in the context of the secretary of the Navy's report for 1940. The Bureau of Navigation section stated that the Navy was short of officers and declared this deficiency "a matter of grave concern." Nevertheless, the *Courier* lamented, the Navy adhered rigidly to the color line.

The problem of . . . getting colored commissioned personnel in the Navy is twofold. First, the appointment of colored youths as midshipmen must be secured. If such appointments can be obtained, it will be necessary for the President, the Secretary of the Navy, or the Chief of the Bureau of Navigation to take precautions to see that such appointees are given a fair opportunity to graduate.

The writer implied that a black midshipman couldn't graduate without some sort of official intervention.[18]

The *Courier*'s wartime "Double V" rhetoric built upon that of its pre-war "Campaign for Army and Navy Equality." Other black newspapers and most black leaders adopted the "Double V" slogan. Defeat of fascism abroad and racism at home became the African American battle cry during World War II. At the heart of "Double V" rhetoric lay the belief that African Americans would have to serve as equals in the armed forces in order to gain equal rights at home. The press urged blacks to insist on serving in all branches of the Army and Navy, even if doing so meant confronting discrimination or even violence. Whatever the price of their insistence, African Americans were never to abandon their patriotism. Accordingly, black newspapers continued to decry discrimination in the armed services while encouraging their readers to support the war effort and fight to participate equally in combat against the foreign enemy.[19]

President Roosevelt sought a middle course between Knox's exclusion policy and African American demands for equal opportunity. While he did not advocate integrating the crews of warships, he believed that broadening opportunities for black sailors made good political sense. He suggested to Knox that "the Bureau of Navigation might invent something that colored enlistees could do in addition to the rating of messmen."[20]

This kind of pressure exasperated Knox. He lamented to a friend that he was "seriously embarrassed by the effort among a small class of negroes against the Navy" because of its racial policy. "During the progress of the most dangerous war in which we have ever engaged is not the time to take up a problem so filled with dynamite as this one," he added.[21]

Nevertheless, further pressure from the president compelled Knox to address the problem. At the secretary's request, the naval leadership developed a plan for enlisting five thousand African Americans for billets outside the messman branch. The plan entailed forming black service units in the shore establishment, black crews for naval district small craft and selected Coast Guard cutters, black construction regiments, and black composite battalions in the Marine Corps. These recommendations were based on the assumption that black enlisted men would be segregated and that black petty officers would not be given authority over white sailors. On 7 April 1942, Knox announced that the Navy was planning to accept African American volunteers in the naval reserve for general service, limited to these duties.[22]

Many African Americans wondered how the new policy would apply to the question of black officers. While announcing the new policy to the press, Secretary Knox said that the Navy had no plans to "to use Negroes in commissioned grades." The *Pittsburgh Courier* declared, "We intend to require him to formulate some plans." Dozens of African Americans sent Knox postcards demanding that "officer schools must be opened up to the colored people as well."[23]

Some observers expressed optimism that blacks would be admitted to the Naval Academy. "If internal and external pressure can open one door," declared the Cleveland *Call and Post,* "then, by the same method, we can use it to open all the others that bar our entrance into every department in these services including the Naval Academy." One observer hoped that the new policy would enable blacks to "look forward with reasonable objectivity to Annapolis in the same basis as their white brothers."[24]

Others expressed doubt or criticism. The Norfolk *Journal and Guide* pointed out that the new policy made "no mention that the doors of the academy would be opened to Negroes." "Annapolis is completely closed to negroes, nor can they obtain commissions in any other way," declared one citizen. "Men who are perfectly qualified to receive a commission, even to enter the service, are refused on trumped up charges." The *Washington Tribune* decried the new policy's lack of provisions to commission blacks and asserted that "it is the Navy's fault that we have no Academy graduates among us."[25]

At first, Secretary Knox categorically opposed commissioning black naval officers. In early February, he told Senator William H. Smathers, who was slated to serve on the Academy's Board of Visitors, why. Knox wrote,

> The experience of many years, has demonstrated that [Negro petty officers] can not maintain discipline among men of the white race over whom they may be placed for the purpose of advancement. It is to be expected, therefore, that members of the negro race serving as officers in the Navy would face the same difficulties. It is impracticable to so assign officers to particular duties which would make it possible that, in the case of negro citizens appointed as officers, they would command only members of their own race.

The Board of Visitors was a group of distinguished citizens appointed annually by the president to evaluate the Academy's curriculum, management, and physical plant and report their findings and recommendations to the secretary. Vice President Henry A. Wallace formally appointed Smathers to the board that spring.[26]

Smathers made the issue of blacks at the Naval Academy a special interest. Although born and raised on a North Carolina plantation, he served as a U.S. senator from New Jersey from 1937 to 1943. A lifelong Democrat, he backed the New Deal and endorsed the Zionist cause in Palestine. A month before the Board of Visitors meeting, scheduled for 20 to 23 April, he told Rear Admiral John R. Beardall, the superintendent, that he intended to spend most of his visit investigating whether black midshipmen had been discriminated against. "It is my opinion that if we are to live as a nation and succeed in this war," he said, "we must do it as one people united." He asked Admiral Beardall to provide him with "all the information on the Negro appointments, and why none of them completed his course there and was made an officer." The black press picked up the story of Smathers's "probe" of the Academy.[27]

Beardall sent Smathers a two-page letter including a few lines each about James Conyers, James Johnson, and George Trivers. The letter attributed Conyers's resignation to "scholastic deficiencies"; Johnson's to deficiencies in conduct, English, and eyesight; and Trivers's to personal reasons. It included quotes from the minutes of the Academic Board meetings concerning Conyers and Johnson and a sentence from Trivers's letter of resignation. Beardall's letter bore no hint of the ill treatment that these three had suffered at the hands of their fellow midshipmen. The superintendent promised to supply Smathers with further information upon his arrival in Annapolis, if he so desired. Smathers's inquiry apparently went no further. Although nothing significant resulted from it, the inquiry signaled a growing congressional interest in the Navy's racial policy, including the question of black officers.[28]

With the opening of the enlisted general service to African Americans, it seemed inevitable that the Navy would have to commission black officers. Still, Knox opposed doing so too early. As he told Senate Naval Affairs Committee Chairman David I. Walsh, "we will have to develop a considerable body of Negro sailors before we can even approach the problem of the Negro commissioned officer."[29]

African Americans enjoined the Navy to address the problem sooner rather than later, particularly in the case of a black sailor who had distinguished himself at Pearl Harbor. Just before 8:00 A.M. on 7 December 1941, Mess Attendant 2d Class Doris Miller was collecting junior officers' laundry on board the battleship *West Virginia* (BB-48) when general quarters sounded. The 22-year-old, six-foot three-inch, 225-pound share-cropper's son from Waco, Texas, sprinted for his battle station at the an-tiaircraft battery magazine amidships, only to find it a twisted shambles. He then scrambled to the well deck, where an ensign ordered him to the signal bridge to help with the wounded. Amid bombing and strafing from Japanese planes, clouds of smoke and walls of flame from the burning ship, and the smell and noise and terror of it all, Miller and the ensign soon reached the bridge, itself on fire. While another officer and several enlisted men struggled to improvise a stretcher to carry the mortally wounded skipper somewhere safer, Miller manned a .50-caliber machine gun on the starboard wing of the bridge. Although he had never fired a machine gun before, he started shooting at Japanese aircraft. A few of the planes at which he and other gunners were firing went down. Miller ran out of ammunition after fifteen minutes. Meanwhile, the others had been unable to fashion a stretcher, so Miller helped them carry the skipper down to a more sheltered place under an antiaircraft gun on the port side. There the skipper ordered, "Abandon ship!" With the normal escape routes blocked by fire, Miller and the others reached shore by descending hand over hand down ropes dangling from a crane.[30]

An article based on eyewitness accounts of Pearl Harbor appeared in the *New York Times* fifteen days later. One sentence mentioned Miller's action, but not his name: "A Negro mess attendant who never before had fired a gun manned a machine gun on the bridge until his ammunition was exhausted." Inquiries about the identity of the mess attendant and demands that he be rewarded soon flooded the Navy Department. Walter White implored President Roosevelt to award the unnamed sailor the distinguished service cross. "The heroism of this Negro mess attendant merits special consideration," he argued, because "the policy of the United States Navy in limiting Negro volunteers to service as mess attendants caused this and other Negroes to go into situations of extreme danger in a far more vulnerable manner because they had been denied the opportunity to learn how to operate . . . weapons." Knox promised to investigate.[31]

Two months later, the Navy Department released Doris Miller's name in a letter to White. Miller quickly became one of the most famous black people in the United States, achieving a celebrity stature akin to that of boxer Joe Louis. Various individuals and groups used Miller as a platform for launching attacks on the Navy's racial policy. Others reiterated demands that the Navy reward him for his action. The *Pittsburgh Courier* hailed him as "the first Negro hero of World War No. 2." The NAACP declared that "the greatest honor" the Navy could pay Miller would be to grant African Americans equal opportunity. The *Chicago Sunday Bee* also called upon the Navy to abolish the color bar. Senator James M. Mead (D-NY) and Representative John Dingell introduced bills to award Miller the Medal of Honor.[32]

The *Amsterdam Star News*, an African American newspaper published in New York City, campaigned to have Miller appointed to the Naval Academy. "There is perhaps no better time than now to crack the un-Democratic policy of the U.S. Navy," declared a story on the front page of the 21 March edition. A coupon for mailing to the president accompanied the article. "As a token of national appreciation," it said, "Colored America urges you to send Dorie Miller, messman hero of Pearl Harbor, to the Naval Academy for training." More than five dozen readers clipped the coupon, signed it, and sent it to FDR. One of them included a clipping of the *Pittsburgh Courier*'s "Double V" emblem.[33]

Knox ignored all of these suggestions. He gave no consideration to broadening opportunities for blacks beyond the steps he had already taken. He opposed giving Miller the Medal of Honor; Senator Mead and Representative Dingell's bills soon faded from view. To each person who sent in a coupon from the *Amsterdam Star News*, Knox's office sent a brief letter stating that Miller, born on 12 October 1919, was too old for appointment to the Academy. Instead of recognizing Miller in a meaningful way, on 1 April Knox awarded him a letter of commendation, thereby damning him with faint praise.[34]

Black newspapers expressed outrage at the slight, pronouncing it yet another example of the Navy's bigotry. Attorney General Francis Biddle believed that the Navy should have decorated Miller. "You may wish to urge the award of a medal," he suggested to President Roosevelt.[35]

FDR did just that. He ordered Knox to award Miller the Navy Cross, the Navy's second-highest honor. Miller became the first African American to receive the medal. Admiral (later Fleet Admiral) Chester W. Nimitz, commander-in-chief, Pacific Fleet and Pacific Ocean Areas and fellow Texan, pinned the medal on Miller's chest during a ceremony on 27 May 1942 at Pearl Harbor. The Navy promoted Miller to petty officer (ship's cook third class), sent him on a tour of the country to promote war bonds, featured him on a recruiting poster, and reassigned him to the escort carrier *Liscome Bay* (CVE-56). African American organizations and individuals praised FDR for honoring Miller. On 24 November 1943 a Japanese submarine torpedoed the ship, which carried Miller to the bottom. Black people across America mourned his death.[36]

While the *Amsterdam Star News* was campaigning for Dorie Miller to break the color barrier at the Naval Academy, Arthur Mitchell made one last attempt to do so as well. Although only fifty-nine and in good health, the congressman decided not to run for reelection in 1942. Because he had pressed litigation against three Chicago-based railroad corporations in defiance of secret orders to stop, the Chicago political machine decided to dump him. Mitchell was slated to leave Congress in January 1943.

In April 1942, Mitchell announced to the black press that he was seeking "the right kind of colored youngsters" to fill one or two of his three available vacancies at the Naval Academy. A month later, the congressman announced the appointment of two black candidates to the Academy, Joseph Banks Williams, a student at Hampton Institute, and Leeland N. Jones, Jr., from Buffalo, New York. It is not clear how Mitchell found these two youths. In any case, the congressman expected their high academic standing to exempt them from the scholastic entrance examination. He told reporters that Williams and Jones were "capable and worthy and have the courage to fight it out and remain at the school." If they met all the admission requirements, they would enter on 1 July. "With the newly adopted naval policy many believe there is a good chance of the appointees making good," reported the *Pittsburgh Courier*.[37]

Mitchell's appointment of Williams and Jones drew praise from the black community. "We are all hopeful that this . . . is the most epoch-making appointment that has yet been made to the Naval Academy because of the lowering of the bars for the enlistment of colored men in the Navy," wrote Ira Lewis, who had replaced Robert Vann as editor of the *Pittsburgh Courier* after Vann's death in 1940. "It is just possible that not only . . . the officials at Annapolis, but the student body as well, will look upon these appointees in a different light." David Apter, director of public relations at Hampton Institute, offered his services in publicizing Williams's nomination. Russell Service, program director of the Buffalo Young Men's Christian Association, hailed Jones's appointment as "one of the high spots in the civic history of our community. Those of us close to young people here know of no one more deserving or better qualified morally, physically and mentally—and are confident that he 'has the stuff' to succeed at this point where many have failed."[38]

Meanwhile, Walter White received an anonymous letter alleging that "the two Negro boys who are entering Annapolis this year will be deliberately got rid of in one way or another." The informant implied that Academy "authorities" were plotting to foster an effort by the midshipmen to oust Jones and Williams. The informant obtained this information from another person who supposedly heard it from an Academy staff member. White forwarded the letter to the superintendent, who emphatically denied the allegation. "The Naval Academy's policy is one of meticulously fair and equal treatment for all midshipmen regardless of race, creed or color," he declared.[39]

Neither Williams nor Jones got the chance to test this policy. In mid-July, the Bureau of Naval Personnel (on 13 May 1942, the Navy renamed the Bureau of Navigation the Bureau of Naval Personnel, a title more befitting its duties) informed Mitchell that the Academic Board had rejected both of their college certificates. Since Mitchell had nominated Jones and Williams after the 1942 entrance examinations had been held, the rejection of their certificates precluded them from entering the Academy that year.[40]

Although Mitchell had once told reporters that it was one of his "most cherished ambitions to see colored men make good and graduate from the United States Naval Academy," Jones and Williams were the last straw. On 19 November the chief of Naval Personnel informed the congressman that he had five vacancies at the Academy. Mitchell submitted candidates for all five. None was black. Instead of taking one final shot at breaking the color barrier, Mitchell went out of office as he had gone in, placing other political concerns above race. One of his last appointees was the son of a friend of Chicago mayor Edward Kelly. No African American entered the Naval Academy while Knox remained secretary of the Navy.[41]

Meanwhile, the Navy began enlisting African Americans for general service on 1 June 1942. Black recruits received boot training at Camp Robert Smalls, an isolated section of the Great Lakes Training Center on Lake Michigan north of Chicago. Thirty-one percent of those who graduated from boot camp went on to advanced training, which took place at Camp Robert Smalls or at Hampton Institute in Hampton, Virginia. The rest received assignments to naval stations and local defense craft or to naval ammunition depots as unskilled workers.[42]

Naval personnel planners, who had expected black volunteers to flood recruitment offices after the new policy went into effect, were surprised when they only trickled in. Ten times as many black volunteers signed up for the Army as did for the Navy, owing to the Navy's lily-white image. Although the number of black enlisted men in the Navy climbed from 5,026 to 26,909 between 30 June 1942 and 1 February 1943, their proportion actually fell from 2.5 percent to 2 percent. At the latter date, over two-thirds of black sailors were stewards and all Navy stewards were black.

As this reality became apparent, the *Pittsburgh Courier* grew entirely critical of the Navy's new policy. In the fall of 1942, it polled readers with the question, "Do you believe the Navy offers the American Negro greater opportunity to serve his country than the Army?" More than 75 percent of the respondents said no. The newspaper declared that little had been done to alter the black sailor's situation as the Navy's "domestic servant." While African Americans could take pride in the Army's black commissioned officers, ranging from Brigadier General Benjamin O. Davis, Sr., to hundreds of young lieutenants graduating from the Officers' Training Schools each month, the highest rank a black man could achieve in the Navy remained chief petty officer. Several respondents raised the question of black midshipmen: "When will our government open the doors of Annapolis to the Negro lads?" Black educators also protested the exclusion of African Americans from the Naval Enlisted Reserve (V-1) officers' college training program.[43]

Many white naval officers objected to the Navy's racial policy, too. One ensign, the son of wealthy New Yorkers, was so shocked by the attitudes he encountered in the service that he donated a full month's pay to the NAACP. "I always intended to contribute to your organization," he said in his cover letter, "but never felt so strongly about the matter as since I came in contact with the attitude of the officers of our Navy."[44]

The Navy revisited its recruitment policy for African Americans when broader manpower issues led FDR to end volunteer enlistments in the armed forces in February 1943. Thereafter the Navy could no longer rely upon volunteers, but had to obtain recruits in the eighteen to thirty-eight age bracket exclusively through the Selective Service System. The new imperative required the Navy to accept a proportional share of black draftees, in an amount up to 10 percent of its authorized enlisted strength. Paul V. McNutt, chairman of the War Manpower Commission, insisted that the Navy draft at least 125,000 blacks before January 1944. Accordingly, the Bureau of Naval Personnel raised the Navy's monthly quota of blacks from twenty-seven hundred at the beginning of 1943 to 14,150 by the end of the year.[45]

On 25 February Knox forwarded to Roosevelt a Bureau of Naval Personnel plan for utilizing the larger numbers of black sailors that the draft would bring into the Navy. To avoid "mixing white and colored personnel of general service ratings aboard larger combatant ships," the bureau sought "to send a somewhat higher percentage to Naval Districts and to certain other activities." The plan called for creating more all-black units—construction battalions; local defense, district, and small-craft crews; and service companies—and increasing the number of black cooks, bakers, ammunition handlers, stevedores, and laborers at naval bases and shore stations. Roosevelt approved, for he still did not favor integrating combatant crews.[46]

Retaining segregation and a limited range of occupations for black sailors, the Navy's policy for black draftees differed little from its policy for black volunteers. It restricted most black sailors to shore duty; concentrated them in large groups; assigned them to jobs with little prestige and few chances of promotion; excluded them from the WAVES (Women Accepted for Volunteer Emergency Service) and the Nurse Corps; and denied them commissions. The *Pittsburgh Courier* denounced the "functional segregation" of this policy and lamented it as a "tragic affair." Articles in the 23 October 1943 edition, printed on the occasion of Navy Day, summarized the evolution of the Navy's racial policy since 1938 and concluded that "some progress has been made." Still, the Navy was a long way from "full and complete integration." For example, "no Negro attends the Naval Academy at Annapolis, although the cadet enrollment at this institution has been doubled."[47]

On 29 December, the Negro Newspaper Publishers Association, headed by John Sengstacke, editor of the *Chicago Defender,* wrote President Roosevelt, declaring that "the Navy has chosen to put into practice policies which set the Negro apart as a different and inferior type of citizen. This is not only unjust, illegal and arbitrary, so far as the Negro is concerned, but, as you can easily see, the practice establishes a dangerous and insidious precedent respecting the status of any distinguishable type or class of citizenship" and "spreads the 'master race' theory among Americans." FDR referred this letter to the Navy Department, where an officer in the Bureau of Naval Personnel rightly concluded that the black press sought nothing short of "complete integration."

Asked to comment on Sengstacke's letter, Rear Admiral Randall Jacobs, chief of the Bureau of Naval Personnel, declared,

It has been found that the complete integration of the training and assignment of negroes with whites, from their first induction in the Navy,
regardless of the higher qualifications of some individual negroes, is not
to the best interests of the Navy nor to the individual himself. The individual negro finds it difficult to sublimate his race consciousness and
become an integral part of the established Navy program. The Navy
will continue to effect integration only to the extent that the attitude of
both negroes and whites indicates that integration is practicable. To do
otherwise would ignore the fact that racial prejudices on the part of
both negroes and whites do exist on a national scale—and it is believed
that the attitude of the negro press in deliberately developing race consciousness and *undue sensitivity to discrimination* [!] on the part of the
negro in the Navy is retarding national progress in this direction—the
Navy cannot undertake in time of war any program which will be
detrimental to its war effort and serve only to further the interests of a
racial minority."[48]

Jim Crow practices added insult to injury. The officer in charge of the
black recruits at the Great Lakes Naval Training Center believed that
African Americans needed "special treatment," so he employed unusual
disciplinary methods and issued demeaning orders designed to ensure
that blacks retained "their own culture," such as directing recruits to sing
spirituals en masse on Sunday evenings. Black sailors with specialized
training often found themselves assigned to billets that underutilized their
skills and housed in separate and unequal accommodations. Black shore
patrolmen at naval stations and bases were told not to police whites and,
in case of interracial fights, to handle only the black participants. Black
sailors also encountered Jim Crow abroad. In one instance, a white officer kicked a black Seabee for drinking from a "white" fountain on an island in the Pacific. In another, a group of African American sailors heard
that a Red Cross canteen in Plymouth, England, was serving Coca-Cola
and hot dogs with mustard. "We hadn't had Coca-Cola and hot dogs and
mustard since we'd left the States," recalled Steward's Mate Lorenzo A.
DuFau. He and several shipmates entered the canteen, "excited about getting hot dogs. This lady told us *it wasn't our canteen,* that our canteen
was a few blocks down. It was such a slap in the face."[49]
Jim Crow in the Navy brought discontent among black sailors to a
boil. "It made me angrier than hell," recalled Steward's Mate Ray Carter.

Here I am spoiling for a fight with the enemy and the question begins to arise, just who the hell is the enemy. . . ? If I had to do it all over again, or if I had to do it today for what "they" call "our democracy," I would not go in. I would go to jail first.[50]

The boiling racial tension spilled over into discipline problems and violence. Like black civilians, black sailors became increasingly more inclined to protest against discrimination. Sometimes they refused to do work not usually performed in their ratings, equating deviation from the norm with diminution of status. In June 1943, some 350 black sailors in an ordnance battalion at Naval Ammunition Depot, St. Juliens Creek, Virginia, rioted when they learned that they would be seated Jim Crow style at a radio broadcast. The next month, 744 black Seabees staged a protest over segregation on a transport in the Caribbean.[51]

During the final months of Knox's tenure, the Navy took several more steps toward solving its "Negro problem." In August 1943 the Bureau of Naval Personnel set up a "Special Programs Unit" to oversee black enlistment. Disgusted by segregation, members of the unit sought to reform the Navy's racial policy out of a genuine sense of fairness. They convinced the bureau to open more overseas billets to black sailors, invent new billets for them in the general service, and assign more black specialists to billets that would utilize their training.

The Special Programs Unit also lobbied to have all-black crews assigned to combatants. If applied broadly, this idea would dissolve concentrations of black sailors in naval stations and create billets for those with specialized training. With the blessing of Admiral (later Fleet Admiral) Ernest J. King, who, as Chief of Naval Operations and commander-in-chief, U.S. Fleet, was the Navy's top officer, the Bureau of Naval Personnel devised plans to man the destroyer escort *Mason* (DE-529) and the patrol craft *PC 1264* exclusively with black enlisted men. Although both ships experienced teething troubles, no racial friction developed between the white officers and black sailors and the crews of both ships served capably on active duty. Eventually, both skippers replaced their white petty officers and some of their commissioned officers with African Americans. One of the officers, Samuel Gravely, became the first black naval officer to achieve flag rank.[52]

The commissioning of African Americans constituted the most radical change in the Navy's racial policy during World War II. On the eve of America's entry into the war, Chester Nimitz, then a rear admiral and chief of the Bureau of Navigation, rationalized the Navy's bigoted policy toward commissioning blacks in a letter to a member of a Michigan draft board:

> The Navy Department had, for some time past, refused to accept applications for enlistment from negroes in any but the messman branch. This policy was instituted in the interest of harmony and efficiency aboard ship after many years of experience. The principles which dictated the adoption of that policy apply equally to the appointment of negroes as officers, either in the Regular Navy or the Naval Reserve. This is no reflection upon the negroes, either as a race or individually. It is simply a matter of practicability. One does not install a part in a machine, no matter how excellent that part may be in itself, unless it will fit and work smoothly with the other parts. That, frankly, covers the Navy Department's attitude on this question. Negro officers aboard ship would form a small unassimilable minority which, despite anything we could do, would inevitably form a source of discord that would be harmful to the service.[53]

Before 1944, African Americans became naval officers only by accident. On 8 June 1942 the Navy inadvertently commissioned Bernard Whitfield Robinson, a black medical student at Harvard, because the officer who signed him up had apparently not seen him first and had assumed he was white. Robinson did not begin active duty until 1944. Similarly, on 28 September 1942, the Navy commissioned Oscar Wayman Holmes an ensign in the Civil Aeronautics Administration–War Training Service Program before realizing that Holmes, a light-skinned man, was an African American. Holmes finished the program and then completed flight instructor training, but the Navy did not allow him to train aviators. "I don't think they wanted old Oscar Holmes to be teaching those white boys [to fly]," he recalled. Instead, he eventually served during the war as a lead pilot in the Naval Air Transport Service. Neither Robinson nor Holmes received official publicity. It is possible that the Navy inadvertently commissioned other African Americans as well.[54]

During the war the Navy obtained officers from three basic sources: the enlisted ranks, civilians, and college training programs. The Naval Academy produced only about 1 percent of the officers who served in the Navy during the war; the rest were commissioned in the Naval Reserve.

A college education was a prerequisite for all naval officers, except aviation cadets.

Officers procured directly from civilian life began naval service with minimal indoctrination training, if not immediately. To be eligible, civilians needed at least some college or "good business experience." Roughly 48 percent of the officers procured between Pearl Harbor and the end of 1944 came directly from civilian life. The Navy virtually ceased procuring officers this way early in 1945 because it expected a flood of ensigns to pour out of its college-training-program pipeline that year.

Although the Bureau of Naval Personnel had no formal policy for procuring officers from the enlisted ranks, a sailor had to meet certain age, educational, and other requirements. Most important, he had to have a recommendation from his commanding officer. The enlisted service provided some 22 percent of the officers procured between 7 December 1941 and 31 December 1944. Selectees received an education at the Naval Academy or in a college training program.

The V-12 program was the preeminent navy college training program of World War II.[55] The 131 private undergraduate institutions that participated produced some sixty thousand naval officers during the war. Trainees with no prior college work spent nearly two years in the program, while those with at least seven semesters could finish in as little as eight months. Graduates received their commissions immediately or underwent further training, depending on the needs of the service.

In December 1942, the Navy Department announced that the V-12 program would begin on 1 July 1943. Although the department never barred African Americans from the program, it never trumpeted this fact outside the fleet. In the absence of a publicized racial policy statement, many African Americans assumed that the V-12 program was closed to them and only a handful applied. Since the application had no place for prospective candidates to indicate their race, the Navy never knew exactly how many blacks it accepted into the program. At least two African Americans came on board in July 1943 and nine others the following November. Six of the eleven were civilians; the other five were enlisted men.[56]

The minuscule number of black V-12s seemed unlikely to satisfy demands for an African American presence in the Navy's officer corps. Adlai Stevenson, Secretary Knox's special assistant, realized that something more ought to be done. "Obviously this cannot go on indefinitely without making some officers or trying to explain why we don't," he told Knox. Stevenson recommended commissioning ten to twelve blacks directly from civilian life, adding a few more from the ranks, and assigning them administrative duties "with the negro program."[57]

After prodding by the Special Programs Unit to follow through on Stevenson's advice, the Bureau of Naval Personnel finally acted. On 2 December 1943, Admiral Jacobs proposed to Knox that the Navy commission twelve black line officers from the enlisted service and ten black staff officers from civilian life and post them in training and staff billets at Great Lakes and Hampton Institute. This plan reflected the prewar Army's tendency to use black officers to train black enlisted men and, in the short run, it avoided the Navy's age-old phobia of placing blacks in positions of authority over whites. It also kept the Naval Academy lily white.

Both Knox and King approved the plan. Knox, however, told Jacobs that "after you have commissioned the twenty-two officers you suggest, I think this matter should again be reviewed before any additional colored officers are commissioned."[58]

The Bureau of Naval Personnel carefully screened the black enlisted ranks for line officer candidates with "character" and "self respect" but without "extreme" attitudes. After the FBI completed a background check on each potential trainee, the officer in charge of the Naval Training School at Hampton Institute chose eight candidates, the officer in charge of black training at Great Lakes chose seven, and the commandant of the Eighth Naval District chose one.

The sixteen black officer candidates began a segregated training program on 1 January 1944 at Great Lakes. All sixteen passed, but the bureau returned three to the enlisted ranks for reasons it never explained. Twelve entered the U.S. Naval Reserve as line officers on 17 March 1944; the last became a warrant officer. They were later dubbed the "Golden Thirteen." The black press hailed the event as a step toward democracy.

The Bureau of Naval Personnel assigned two of the twelve new ensigns to the faculty of Hampton Institute, four to yard and harbor craft duty, and the rest to training duty at Great Lakes. The bureau labeled them "Deck Officers Limited—only," a designation usually reserved for those with physical or educational deficiencies that prevented them from performing all the normal duties of a line officer. This designation constituted discrimination, since all twelve had been businessmen or professionals in civilian life and none had any physical problems. Tardiness in finding candidates delayed the commissioning of staff officers as per Jacobs's plan until the summer of 1944.[59]

The pace and direction of the Navy's racial policy changed dramatically when James Vincent Forrestal became secretary of the Navy after Frank Knox died of heart failure on 28 April 1944. Born on 15 February 1892 in Matteawan, New York, some sixty miles up the Hudson River from New York City, Forrestal grew up in a lower-middle-class, Irish Catholic family that imbued him with the values of hard work and self-reliance. His biographers considered him able, noble, patriotic, dedicated, and selfless. Forrestal attended Dartmouth and Princeton but never graduated, spent three years as a naval aviator, then left the Navy in 1920 and began climbing the corporate ladder as an investment banker. By 1932, his net worth exceeded five million dollars.

On the eve of World War II, President Roosevelt recruited bankers, industrialists, businessmen, and lawyers to take part in America's rearmament. On 22 August 1940, FDR appointed Forrestal the first undersecretary of the Navy, a new position created the previous spring. In this job Forrestal organized and directed the entire Navy procurement effort, and thus played a pivotal role in creating the most powerful fleet the world had ever seen.

When Forrestal assumed the office of secretary of the Navy on 9 May 1944, the press, the public, and the Navy cheered his appointment. He remained in that position until the summer of 1947, when he became the nation's first secretary of defense.[60]

Forrestal had had black friends at Dartmouth and was a longtime member of the National Urban League. He considered racial prejudice "an irrational thing, rooted in ignorance." "Bigotry damages the spirit of the bigot more than it injures its object," he once said at a National Urban League dinner, "but it is destructive and corroding for both." He perceived the problem of prejudice in terms of efficiency as well as fairness.[61]

As secretary of the Navy, Forrestal knew he needed the support of senior officers to change the Navy's racial policy, so he enlisted the aid of Admiral King during a meeting in the summer of 1944. "I'm not satisfied with the situation here," he told King. "I don't think that our Navy Negro personnel are getting a square break. I want to do something about it, but I can't do anything about it unless the officers are behind me. I want your help. What do you say?" King gazed out a window for a moment, then spoke. "You know, we say that we are a democracy and a democracy ought to have a democratic Navy," he said. "I don't think you can do it, but if you want to try, I'm behind you all the way."[62]

Forrestal had already begun experimenting with the Navy's racial pol-icy. On 20 May 1944 he proposed to President Roosevelt a plan for inte-grating black sailors into the crews of large auxiliaries, not to exceed 10 percent of a ship's complement. Knox had strongly opposed the radical step of integrating the crews of warships. "It is simply impossible in the midst of a war to mix the races on the same ship," he had written in the spring of 1942. "I can only fight one war at a time and the one on our hands is now big enough without introducing a race war besides." For-restal, however, took the opposite tack, arguing that black sailors re-sented not being assigned to general service billets at sea, while white sailors resented blacks because they didn't have to go in harm's way. For-restal argued that integration would not only boost morale but also "[ef-fect] economies of manpower" by breaking up large concentrations of black sailors in shore billets and facilitate interchange of white sailors be-tween the United States and forward combat areas. If no trouble resulted from this experiment, he intended to put black sailors on board other types of ships. Both Roosevelt and King approved.

Forrestal's plan worked. After several months of having black sailors on board, the skippers of the integrated auxiliaries reported no racial dif-ficulties. This success led Admiral King to approve a plan submitted by Admiral Jacobs on 6 March 1945 for the gradual assignment of black sailors to all auxiliaries, again not to exceed 10 percent of the crew.[63]

Forrestal advanced the Navy's racial policy on other fronts as well. On 28 July 1944 he submitted a plan to the president for integrating the WAVES. Knox had said African Americans would enter the WAVES only over his dead body. Roosevelt delayed approving Forrestal's plan until Thomas E. Dewey made it a campaign issue, charging that FDR was dis-criminating against black women. By November 1944 the Navy was not only enlisting black WAVES but also training them on an integrated basis. Forrestal also ended segregation in the enlisted specialist training pro-gram and took further steps to break up the large concentrations of black sailors in ammunition depots and base companies. The Bureau of Naval Personnel offered training programs to prepare officers for integration.[64]

In February 1945, nine months after Forrestal became secretary of the Navy, the Bureau of Naval Personnel released a publication entitled *Guide to Command of Negro Naval Personnel.* The guide symbolized how much the Navy's attitude had changed since Pearl Harbor. "Racial theories waste manpower," declared a section that renounced the doctrine of white supremacy. "The Navy accepts no theories of racial differences in inborn ability, but expects that every man wearing its uniform be trained and used in accordance with his maximum individual capacity determined on the basis of individual performance." The guide acknowledged that previous racial policies had probably deterred many capable and skilled African Americans from joining the Navy, thereby depriving the service of valuable manpower. It also acknowledged that "separate but equal facilities" for black sailors usually meant inferior facilities.[65]

These steps proved too little too late to defuse the racial time bomb that the Navy's segregationist policy had planted. Riots, mutinies, and other racial incidents plagued the Navy in 1944 and 1945. Three gained national prominence. On 17 July 1944, an explosion destroyed two ammunition ships loading out at Port Chicago in San Francisco Bay and killed over three hundred people, including 250 black sailors. All of the men who loaded ships there were black; all of the officers were white. When some of the black survivors refused to return to work, the Navy court-martialed fifty of them, found them guilty of mutiny, and sentenced them to varying terms of hard labor followed by a dishonorable discharge. Through the efforts of the black press, Lester Granger, NAACP attorney Thurgood Marshall, and others, the Navy overturned the convictions and returned the men to active duty. In December 1944, a riot on Guam capped months of harassment of black sailors by white Marines. The Navy sent forty-three black sailors to prison for rioting and related offenses. Efforts by Walter White and other civil rights advocates resulted in the release of the black sailors early in 1946. In March 1945, a thousand black Seabees in a construction battalion at Port Hueneme, California, refused to eat for two days in protest against discrimination at the base. The hunger strike enabled the men to avoid arrest for mutiny while they publicized their grievances. No violence erupted and the hunger strike resulted in the dismissal of the commanding officer.[66]

Such incidents convinced senior naval officers that further reforms were necessary and hardened Forrestal's resolve to see them through. Before the war, Fleet Admiral Nimitz believed that shipboard integration "wasn't practicable." Wartime experience changed his mind. "If you put all the Negroes together," he explained to an auxiliary skipper who berthed his mixed crew in segregated compartments, "they'll have a chance to share grievances and to plot among themselves, and this will damage discipline and morale. If they are distributed among other members of the crew, there will be less chance of trouble."[67]

Nimitz, King, and other uniformed observers had seen integration work on small patrol craft, large auxiliary vessels, and in the WAVES. In the weeks following the riot on Guam, Forrestal and King hammered out a plan for gradual but total integration of the enlisted general service. The plan rested on the premise that segregation wasted manpower and resources, while integration promoted efficiency. Segregation had impeded the Navy in putting black sailors to work in jobs that fully utilized their training or expertise, and it had squandered funds in building separate duplicate facilities for black sailors instead of simply using existing facilities. The idea that segregation was wasteful and integration efficient turned the rationale for the Navy's prewar racial policy upside down.

As the end of the war approached, the Navy continued breaking down racial barriers. The surgeon general accepted African American women into the Nurse Corps in March 1945. That same month, Forrestal appointed Lester Granger as a civilian aide on racial affairs, the first such position in American naval history. The following June, the Bureau of Naval Personnel integrated recruit training.[68]

Granger facilitated implementation of the new policy by visiting naval installations and bases and selling naval commanders on the pragmatism of integration. He also interviewed black sailors about their living and working conditions and eventually reported to Forrestal on the progress of the new policy and offered recommendations.[69] In July he released a statement listing some of the "gains" that African Americans had made in the Navy over the past two years:

(1) Admission of Negroes to general service.

(2) Rating of Negroes in practically every category and training of Negroes as commissioned officers.

(3) Assignment of Negro personnel to auxiliary craft up to ten per cent of a ship's complement.

(4) Assignment of Negro commissioned and petty officers to these vessels to serve in their duties without regard to rank.

(5) Important elimination of racial segregation in mess and in recreational facilities.

(6) A beginning of assigning Negro personnel to combat duties on warships.[70]

Several years later, a group of African American leaders met in Washington to discuss the racial policies of the armed services. "Regarding the

Navy," recalled Granger, who had attended the meeting, "we felt that during the closing years of the war . . . a serious and, in general, successful effort was made completely to revise Navy policy and practice in the use of Negro personnel."[71] The Navy had indeed revolutionized its racial policy during World War II, at least in writing.

The Navy's racial practices, however, lagged far behind the new policy. Like African Americans after Reconstruction, black sailors would have to wait for decades and for another upheaval to force actual practice in line with written policy.

The wartime strength of blacks in the Navy peaked on 31 August 1945. On that date, the Navy had 166,915 African American enlisted men and women out of a total enlisted strength of 3,009,380, a proportion of 5.5 percent. While this figure more than doubled the prewar proportion of blacks in the Navy, it was only half of the proportion of blacks in the United States. Approximately 50.2 percent of black sailors were cooks and stewards and all stewards were black. Some fifty-nine thousand of the rest were ordinary seamen, assigned largely to all-black labor units and base companies. Only sixty-eight of the Navy's 73,685 enlisted WAVES were black, a percentage of less than 0.09.[72]

The African American presence in the officer corps was even more negligible. On 31 August 1945, the Navy had sixty-four black officers, including two WAVES and four nurses. These sixty-four men and women accounted for less than 0.02 percent of the Navy's total of 325,074 warrant and commissioned officers, and none of the black naval officers was a regular. "The Navy has come a long way," noted one black sailor, "but has a hell of a long way yet to go."[73]

While the Army had made only minimal changes to its racial policy during World War II, it had commissioned more African Americans. In August 1945, black Army officers numbered 7,768, accounting for roughly .88 percent of all Army officers. Of these, 6,140 were male commissioned officers, up from 462 in December 1941.[74]

The Military Academy had produced only a handful of these officers. Between James Fowler's matriculation in 1937 and mid-July 1945, eleven African Americans entered West Point, many of them Mitchell appointees. Eight of the eleven graduated, five during the war.[75] As plebes, these black cadets received the same sort of treatment as had Fowler. Henry Minton Francis, a Dunbar alumnus whom Mitchell appointed in 1941, endured incessant harassment and a campaign to skin him out on demerits. On one occasion, he found human excrement in his shoes just before formation. Only having time to dump out the shoes, he put them on and made formation, where the inspecting cadet asked, "Why do the nigger stink?" Francis stuck it out and graduated on 6 June 1944. He later recalled that he would have preferred the isolation that Benjamin O. Davis, Jr., had suffered rather than the extra attention.[76]

Ernest J. Davis, Jr., another Dunbar alumnus and Mitchell appointee (no relation to Benjamin O. Davis, Jr.), entered the Military Academy in July 1942. During "Beast Barracks," equivalent to plebe summer, Davis suffered more hazing and harassment than did his white classmates, including night visits to induce fatigue. Unlike his white classmates, Davis never received an invitation to officers' quarters during his stay at West Point. Davis, too, persevered, graduating in June 1945.

Nevertheless, the situation for black cadets at West Point improved during the war. Francis became the first African American to earn the rank of cadet sergeant. Davis received help from several white upper-classmen, including, to his surprise, an individual from Louisiana.[77]

No African American had yet graduated from the Naval Academy. While Forrestal was breaking color barriers in the fleet during the spring of 1945, Congressman Adam Clayton Powell, Jr., joined the ranks of those who sought to break the color barrier at Annapolis.

Born in New Haven, Connecticut, on 29 November 1908 and raised in New York City, Adam Clayton Powell, Jr., was ordained to the ministry in 1931. During the next decade he was senior pastor at the Abyssinian Baptist Church in Harlem and a New York City councilman. In 1942, he founded and became editor of the *People's Voice,* a black weekly newspaper. Playing to a national audience in these roles, Powell engaged in protest activities, fought racial discrimination in employment, demanded abolition of the poll tax, and advocated making lynching a federal crime. Tall, well educated, elegant, and eloquent, Powell earned a national reputation as an outspoken, flamboyant, and energetic activist and spokesman for the black community.

After the New York state legislature passed a reapportionment bill that carved out a new congressional district in Harlem with a black majority (the Twenty-second), Powell won a seat in the House in 1944, becoming the first black congressman from the eastern seaboard since Reconstruction. In Washington, Powell stood on Capitol Hill and shouted against America's racial dilemma, and pundits dubbed him "Mr. Civil Rights." Asserting a religious brand of moral superiority over white segregationists, Powell expressed outrage that a country founded on the ideals of equality and freedom would sanction discrimination. Having no patience for those who advocated doing away with segregation gradually, he sought an immediate end to it.

A go-for-broke politician, Powell clashed early with President Harry S. Truman, who succeeded Roosevelt after his death on 12 April 1945. Later that year the Daughters of the American Revolution, a group that had just barred Powell's wife, Hazel Scott, from performing at Constitution Hall because of her race, invited Bess Truman to a tea. Powell urged the First Lady not to go. When she did, Powell angrily pronounced her the "last lady of the land." Truman never spoke to him again.

Unlike Arthur Mitchell, Adam Powell neither depended upon nor tried to curry favor with white political bosses. But he was no antiwhite demagogue. He believed in and practiced racial equality, nondiscrimination, nonsegregation, and interracial organization, and he strove to achieve mutually respectful relations among America's various ethnic and racial groups.

During World War II Powell fully embraced the "Double V" rhetoric. In speeches he equated the struggle against Hitler with that against Theodore G. Bilbo, the racist governor of Mississippi, and delighted in Mississippi congressman John Rankin's refusal to sit beside him in the House chamber. "I am happy that Rankin will not sit by me because that makes it mutual," he said. "The only people with whom he is qualified to sit are Hitler and Mussolini."

Ending segregation in the Navy and Army had long numbered among Powell's special interests. Early editions of the *People's Voice* devoted considerable space to "Jim Crowism" in the armed forces. Powell was particularly disturbed by the fact that very few African Americans had graduated from West Point, and none had ever gotten beyond the first year at the Naval Academy. Shortly after taking his seat in the House in January 1945, Powell began looking for potential nominees.

Phoebe Nelson, Powell's secretary, had a friend in Washington whose nephew had distinguished himself at Dunbar High School. The lad was currently enrolled in the Army Specialized Training Program at Howard University and was interested in attending the Military Academy. Nelson told the congressman all about this young man, whose name was Wesley Anthony Brown.[78]

World War II had profoundly changed the political and economic status of African Americans. During the war black people moved north in ever increasing numbers to seek better jobs and living conditions. The concentration of African Americans in northern cities increased their political clout, making the black vote in certain districts key to winning elections and enabling black politicians like William Dawson and Adam Clayton Powell, Jr., to take seats in Congress.

Black people wielded their newfound political power in an effort to win full civil rights. Not content to postpone the fight against discrimination until after the war, African Americans sought a simultaneous victory over fascism abroad and racism at home. The federal government and the armed forces were the principal arenas in which the fight against discrimination occurred during World War II. Black leaders continued to keep breaking the color barrier at the Naval Academy on their national agenda.

Political pressure coupled with the need to utilize all available sources of personnel had forced the Navy to revolutionize its racial policy during the war. Under Secretary of the Navy Frank Knox, the Navy opened only a narrow range of enlisted ratings to black sailors, commissioned a mere handful of black officers, and hamstrung both officers and men with a policy of segregation. No African American entered the Naval Academy while Knox remained in office.

Far more sweeping change came after James Forrestal took the helm in 1944. Unlike Knox, Forrestal believed that segregation of the fleet impaired the Navy's fighting efficiency. In a stepwise fashion he integrated the crews of naval auxiliaries, the WAVES, specialist training, recruit training, and the enlisted general service. Also during his tenure, the Navy's first African American officers went to sea. Ultimately, he declared the Navy's policy toward African Americans to be one of equal opportunity. This revolution in the Navy's written racial policy, along with the national political impulses that sparked it, laid the groundwork necessary for breaking the Naval Academy's color barrier.

7

The Greater Challenge

Adam Clayton Powell could not have found a better candidate to break the color barrier at the Naval Academy than Wesley Brown.[1] A descendent of Virginia slaves, Brown was born on 3 April 1927, the only child of William and Rosetta Brown. The family lived with Rosetta's mother, Katie Shepherd, in her house in Washington at 1305 Q Street Northwest, just off Logan Circle. With employment so uncertain during the Depression, people often lived with relatives. Sharing a house reduced the cost of living and provided a safety net if someone lost a job. Harriet Tyler, Wesley's aunt, as well as Granville Johnson, Hattie Cofer, and Bessie Carter, Katie's foster children, also lived at 1305 Q Street. Although Katie had taken in the foster children for the income, she treated them as her own.

Katie's late husband, John Shepherd, had bought the house shortly before his death in 1930, paying cash. John's father had been born in slavery and had instilled in him the idea that a family should own its own home. In hard times the family members would have a place to live, and they could grow food, rent a room, run a business, or use the property in some other way to get by. Katie's house was a four-story, five-bedroom, two-bathroom row home. The property included a backyard and garage, but since the family didn't own a car, the garage was used for storage.

Wesley never spent much time with his father. William, who was born in Washington in 1909 and never finished high school, drove a truck for John Kalivretenos and Sons, a fruit and vegetable wholesaler in the Florida Avenue market on the 1200 block of Fifth Street Northeast. William delivered produce to restaurants and hotels and was one of the few men on the block who held a job throughout the Depression. He did so by almost never taking a day off, working from the crack of dawn till about six in the evening. But the job had its perks. John Kalivretenos, a Greek immigrant who founded the business in 1913, had a big heart, put people above profit, and treated employees like family.[2] He allowed William to take home whatever food was left on the truck at the end of the day. William, in turn, gave most of it away, so there was usually a group of neighbors waiting for him to get home. Together they distributed the food to the man who had just lost his job, to the mother with the new baby—to whomever needed it most. William's generosity earned him the respect and gratitude of his neighbors.

Rosetta was born in Washington in 1912 and did finish high school. She pressed clothes at the Elite Laundry on Fourteenth and W Streets Northwest. Wesley saw more of her than he did his father because Rosetta got home from work earlier, and she and Wesley spent many a Saturday together at the zoo, the Smithsonian, or other cultural spots in Washington.

With both parents working, Wesley was raised by his grandmother. Katie Shepherd was the matriarch of the family. She ruled the roost with a mixture of love and iron. She instilled in the children a strong work ethic and sense of morality, saw to it that they went to church, and insisted that they do well in school. She also drilled into them her belief that each succeeding generation should strive to do better than the last, frequently reminding the family that her own mother had been born in slavery and that her late husband's parents had been slaves.

Although Katie never had a job, she worked hard all her life. After her husband died, she got by on rent from family members, the money the District paid her to support the foster children, and, later, rent from boarders. She considered it her duty to run her house properly and raise the children to be good citizens. She taught them to respect old folks and to say "sir" and "ma'am." She never allowed Wesley to do what she considered women's work—washing dishes and laundry, house cleaning, cooking, sewing, and so forth. She regarded women who did not bake their own bread as lazy and believed that they were shortchanging their families. Wesley thought that she was one of the oldest people in the world and loved her dearly.

Katie was a devout Christian. The John Wesley African Methodist Episcopal (AME) Zion Church, at Fourteenth and Corcoran Streets Northwest was the center of her life. Under the leadership of Pastor Stephen Gill Spottswood, who was also president of the D.C. branch of the NAACP, the church was an important center for civil rights activities. Reverend Spottswood later became a bishop and chairman of the board of the national NAACP. Katie spent every Sunday at church until about

2:00 in the afternoon, attending services and meetings and socializing. Occasionally Paul Robeson and Roland Hayes sang there. During the week Katie went to church for Bible study classes, board meetings, and other events. Accordingly, the church loomed large in Wesley's youth. He attended Sunday school regularly and learned to read there in classes taught by Aunt Harriet's close friend Marie Smith. As a result he could read the newspaper by the time he entered kindergarten.

Education also figured prominently in Wesley's youth. Katie valued education as a means to a better life and as a measure of prestige. Although she never finished high school, she saw to it that all of her children and foster children did. At school, kids like Wesley who made good grades were respected. "There was a general peer pressure, acceptance, and reward for good scholarship," he recalled. Teachers maintained tight control in the classroom and rarely had to deal with discipline problems. Wesley went to Garrison Elementary School, named after abolitionist William Lloyd Garrison, and Shaw Junior High School, named for Colonel Robert Gould Shaw, who commanded the famous Fifty-fourth Massachusetts Volunteers during the Civil War. In 1941 he entered Dunbar High School.

Although the military did not rank with religion and education in shaping Wesley Brown's character, it had a strong influence. The superintendent of his Sunday school, Victor J. Tulane, had a Ph.D. in chemistry and taught at Howard University. He had joined the Army during World War I and had served as a lieutenant in the infantry. Tulane was much prouder of his rank than his degree. Wesley's godfather, Hewlett Smith, had joined the Army during the Spanish-American War. He had served as a sergeant under Charles Young and was part of the group that made the annual pilgrimage to Young's grave in Arlington National Cemetery. Smith didn't talk much about the Army, but when he did he praised his comrades and condemned the Army's treatment of black soldiers. Wesley could not help noticing that veterans like Tulane and Smith were treated with an extra measure of respect within the community because they had served.

In Wesley's youth, Logan Circle and the surrounding neighborhood was an intellectual and social center of residential black Washington. Duke Ellington had grown up in a house at Thirteenth and T Streets Northwest. Distinguished attorneys Belford V. and Marjorie M. Lawson lived at 8 Logan Circle. Belford Lawson often stood in the forefront of landmark civil rights decisions. Marjorie Lawson was later appointed

D.C. juvenile court judge by John F. Kennedy. Adam Clayton Powell, Jr., and singer Hazel Scott Powell rented the Lawsons' upstairs when they first came to Washington in 1945. Stephen Gill Spottswood lived across the street on Q Street. Arthur Mitchell lived on the 1300 block of R Street close to Fourteenth Street and occasionally attended church at John Wesley. Todd Duncan, who sang the lead in *Porgy and Bess* on Broadway during the 1930s, lived at Sixteenth and T Streets Northwest, only a few streets away.[3]

Wesley felt a tremendous sense of community while growing up. Neighbors were friends. "We never locked our door," he recalled. For about a quarter, an adult could buy a trolley pass that enabled him or her to take along any number of children. On many a Saturday or Sunday one of the adults would use one of these passes to take all the neighborhood kids sightseeing in Washington.

Most of the other children in the neighborhood also lived with their grandparents, who looked after them while the parents worked. The grandmothers kept their eye on all the children, not just their own. Most grandmothers had no qualms about spanking somebody else's child they caught doing something wrong. They also liked to needle each other. "Katie, I know you have taught that young man how to do things properly," a neighbor would tell Wesley's grandmother, "but for some reason . . ." Such needling tended to worsen the punishment received from one's own grandmother. Kids caught in the act would often say, "You're not going to tell my grandmother, are you?" If so, as Brown recalled, "you'd get it again."

Despite this rich community life, the same cloud of segregation that hung over Washington during James Johnson's boyhood still polluted the cultural atmosphere. Black civil servants worked separately from whites. In 1938, 90 percent of the 9,717 regular black federal employees held custodial jobs. White property owners excluded blacks from their neighborhoods by means of legally binding restrictive covenants. Black Washingtonians were barred from the city's public tennis courts, playgrounds, and swimming pools. African Americans could watch spectator sports in Uline Arena, Washington's largest indoor sports facility, but they were not permitted to ice skate there. Most restaurants and theaters refused to serve African Americans. Downtown nightclubs employed blacks, but did not cater to them. Even barber shops and eateries on Capitol Hill were segregated. African Americans who commuted by bus between Washington and Virginia could sit anywhere they wanted to while in the city, but when the bus reached the Virginia state line, the driver stopped and black people moved to the back.[4]

Whereas James Johnson's family tried to ignore prejudice, Wesley Brown's family acknowledged its existence. Wesley became aware of segregation in kindergarten. He would ask his parents to take him to a movie. "You can't go there," they would reply. Jim Crow laws prohibited black kids from playing in white playgrounds, so Wesley and his friends played in the streets and alleys, even when the nearby white playground was empty. Sometimes they played on the lawn in Logan Circle until the park police drove them off. When Wesley grew old enough to take the trolley by himself, he would go exploring. On one occasion he disembarked in a white neighborhood. A policeman approached him. "Get back on the trolley," he said. "Go back to where you belong." Segregation remained so pervasive that Brown had little contact with white people. Any interaction he did have stemmed from school, church, or community activities and, later, government jobs, but it was formal and circumscribed by events. Black Washingtonians simply didn't socialize naturally or informally with whites. "We more or less lived in our own world," he recalled.

Brown acquired a deeper understanding of his culture and heritage by devouring books and articles on African American history. As soon as he could read, he joined the Association for the Study of Negro Life and History, founded by black historian Carter G. Woodson to ensure that African Americans received their proper place in history. Brown regularly perused *The Journal of Negro History* and the *Negro History Bulletin,* which the association launched in 1937. For the black community, these journals contradicted the false and belittling image of blacks portrayed in white publications and served as forums for black protest. For Brown, the journals helped instill self-respect, pride in accomplishment, and distaste for discrimination. History also helped him acquire a firm grasp of the African American experience in the armed services. Reading history, particularly African American military history, became a lifelong passion.

On the whole, Wesley had a pleasant childhood. He played chess, checkers, and cards with his aunts and uncle. Katie allowed the children to listen to the radio before dinner during the week and to family programs like *Seth Parker* on Sunday. At the local YMCA Wesley boxed, played table tennis, and learned to swim.

Katie beamed with pride when Wesley joined the Boy Scout troop sponsored by the church. He spent many a Saturday morning at the

Carnegie Library on Ninth and K, where there were fewer distractions than at home. He finished the Harvard Classics by the end of ninth grade. One Easter, while rolling eggs on the White House lawn with other young Washingtonians, he met Eleanor Roosevelt. In 1941, he saw Joe Louis fight Billy Conn.

Of all Wesley's boyhood experiences, hearing Marian Anderson sing at the Lincoln Memorial on Easter Sunday in 1939 was the most moving. He recalled that despite the presence of seventy-five thousand people, "you could hear a pin drop" just before her opening number. Then, standing on the steps with the statue of Lincoln looming behind her, she began singing "My Country 'Tis of Thee." Although Wesley stood way out in the throng by the reflecting pool, her voice came in loud and clear over the speakers set up for the performance. Even at twelve, the irony of her opening number struck him, for he had read about how the Daughters of the American Revolution had barred her from performing at Constitution Hall.

After racial prejudice, the Depression ranked as the strongest influence on Brown's boyhood outside of home and church. Like most Americans in those days, people in the neighborhood worked hard, suffered, and helped each other out. Jobs were hard to get and hard to keep. Those with jobs often went in an hour early on Monday to prevent others from coming by and offering to work for less money. Wesley's most vivid recollection of the Depression was of the beggars who appeared at the back door. The family kept a loaf of store-bought bread on hand for them. Each beggar received one slice and repaid the kindness by washing windows or shoveling coal.

As soon as he was old enough, Wesley Brown went to work. When he was about eleven, he sold the *Pittsburgh Courier,* the *Afro-American,* and *Liberty* magazine. He later had paper routes, delivering the *Daily News,* the *Washington Post,* the *Evening Star,* and the *Times Herald.* When he was fourteen, he landed a job at the Elite Laundry with his mother. He emptied the pockets of coats and trousers and was allowed to keep any coins he found. After the clothes were cleaned and pressed, he bagged them and hung them on the rack. To make it easier for the drivers, he also sorted the clothes by route, even though he was not expected to do so. The drivers expressed their appreciation by tipping him on payday. With both parents working, Wesley was able to save much of his earnings.

After the Japanese attack on Pearl Harbor, World War II assumed the place occupied by the Depression in the backdrop of Wesley Brown's youth. Like most Americans, Brown and his family regarded Franklin Roosevelt and Winston Churchill as heroes and the Japanese and Germans as threats to humanity. The war changed the family's perception of Russians from bomb-throwing terrorists to embattled foes of Hitler. They'd always considered Mussolini a joke and had harbored antifascist feelings since the Italian invasion of Ethiopia in 1935. The war permeated the fabric of their everyday lives. Blue-starred flags in neighbors' windows meant that a friend or acquaintance had gone to war. A gold star meant that a service member had died. Rationing reduced the availability of basic commodities like sugar, butter, and meat. As the war progressed, rumors spread around the community that Jews were disappearing from their homes in Europe and were never being heard from again.

Brown's family shared in the increased economic opportunities that World War II brought to the black community. With the Navy, Army, and industry gobbling up traditional sources of labor power, jobs opened to black Washingtonians on an unprecedented scale, albeit in the lower-paid categories. Rosetta Brown left the laundry for a better job as a filing clerk in the War Department's Munitions Building on Constitution Avenue.

During the summer of 1942, Wesley Brown landed a full-time job, working days in the mailroom at the Navy Bureau of Medicine on Twenty-third Street Northwest. Although he was only fifteen years old, the Navy paid him an adult salary. As September approached, he went to the personnel office and asked for night-shift work. The woman behind the desk was incredulous. Why in the world did he want to do that? He said that he planned to finish high school and go on to college. The personnel officer's jaw dropped. Surely this fellow knew that a black kid would never get a better job, even with a college degree. She told him so, adding that if he did go to college, he would lose all the pay, retirement, and other benefits that he would accrue if he continued working. Brown had heard it all before, but his mind was set on the greater challenge—getting a good education. He remained quietly insistent. The personnel officer acceded and found him a night job. For the next several years Brown worked in various mailrooms in Navy Department activities on Constitution Avenue. Ultimately he worked from four to midnight, six nights a week, a schedule that allowed him to stay in school. With time and a half for the sixth night, he made nearly two thousand dollars a year, quite a respectable sum for that time. Brown wedged in his homework between mail deliveries. Since he lived at home and had little time to spend his money, he managed to save a large portion of it.

Alonzo Clifton McClennan
as a young man. Courtesy
of his granddaughter, Mrs.
Maude T. Jenkins.

Rear Admiral John Lorimer
Worden, Superintendent of
the Naval Academy,
1869–1874, April 1873.
Naval Historical Center.

Left to right, Colonel Henry O. Atwood, Cadet James D. Fowler, and Represen-tative Arthur W. Mitchell (D-IL), 1939. Chicago Historical Society ICHi-26233.

James Lee Johnson, Jr., c. 1936. Photographer Addison N. Scurlock. Chicago Historical Society ICHi-27232.

George Joseph Trivers, c. 1937. Courtesy of George Joseph Trivers.

Captain Forde A. Todd, Commandant of Midshipmen, 1936–1937. *Lucky Bag,* 1937, Nimitz Library, United States Naval Academy.

Sixteenth Company, Class of 1949, plebe year, c. 1946. Wesley A. Brown stands in the third row, far left. *Lucky Bag,* 1947, Nimitz Library, United States Naval Academy.

Midshipman 1/C Wesley Anthony Brown. *Lucky Bag,* 1949, Nimitz Library, United States Naval Academy.

Mishipman 1/C Donald Boone Whitmire. *Lucky Bag,* 1947, Nimitz Library, United States Naval Academy.

Midshipman 1/C Joseph Patrick Flanagan. *Lucky Bag*, 1947, Nimitz Library, United States Naval Academy.

Midshipman 1/C Howard Allen Weiss. *Lucky Bag*, 1947, Nimitz Library, United States Naval Academy.

Midshipman 1/C Edward Joseph McCormack, Jr. *Lucky Bag,* 1947, Nimitz Library, United States Naval Academy.

Midshipman 1/C James Earl Carter, Jr. *Lucky Bag,* 1947, Nimitz Library, United States Naval Academy.

Wesley Brown and his mother Rosetta Brown with Naval Academy diploma, 3 June 1949. Copyright *Washington Post*; reprinted with permission of D.C. Public Library.

Wesley Brown in first-class midshipman's uniform holding diploma. *Saturday Evening Post*, 25 June 1949. Reprinted with permission of The Saturday Evening Post Society, © 1949 (renewed).

Wesley Brown received the usual excellent prep-school-equivalent education at Dunbar High. He did well academically, making mostly As and Bs. His work schedule prevented him from participating extensively in sports, but he did find time to play tennis, run cross country and track, and join the debating club. He took annual leave from work in order to compete in track meets and tennis matches. He also found time to sing in the choir and compete in interscholastic Americana Quizzes. During his junior year he took a course in pre-engineering math at Howard University. Dunbar instilled a sense of confidence that he could handle any challenge; that if someone else could do something, he could do it too.

Brown also took an aviation course during his junior year. With the Ninety-ninth Pursuit Squadron—the soon-to-be-legendary Tuskegee Airmen—training for combat, several of Brown's classmates had decided to try to join the Army Air Corps. Brown told his mother that he was interested, too. Rosetta talked him out of it. "The first thing you should do is finish high school," she said. If he didn't, she argued, he would be at a disadvantage if flying for the Army didn't work out. Brown took aviation classes throughout his junior year but remained in school. Nevertheless, the military had seized his imagination.

Like most of his classmates, Brown joined Dunbar's Cadet Corps. Participation in the corps became mandatory in May 1943, owing to the war. Colonel Henry O. Atwood was now professor of military science and tactics, Senior High Schools, Divisions 10–13—the overall head of the Cadet Corps for all of Washington's black high schools, a position he had attained in 1939. Captain Elijah A. Reynolds became head of Dunbar's battalion in 1942. The cadets drilled twice a week from 7:30 to 9:00 in the morning. As the annual competitive drill approached, the cadets drilled three times a week. Brown's performance impressed Colonel Atwood. During Brown's senior year Atwood selected him to head the Dunbar battalion. Brown led the battalion to first place in the annual competitive drill in March 1944. Atwood then appointed Brown head of the regiment of cadets for Washington's black high schools, with the rank of cadet colonel.[5]

That same year, Brown began developing an ambition to enter West Point. No single individual can be credited with pointing him in that direction, nor did a vivid image of himself as a cadet suddenly pop into his mind, precipitating a shout of "Eureka!" Rather, a number of subtler themes that resonated throughout his life had coalesced: the rise up from slavery; the duty of each generation to do a little better than the last; the emphasis on education; the Depression-inspired appeal of a "free" education; the respect garnered by military men such as Hewlett Smith and Victor Tulane; and the portrayal of military service as the means to a double victory—a portrayal he had encountered in the *Pittsburgh Courier*s he had sold in the neighborhood. He admired neighbors who had gone to the Military Academy and regarded them as role models. Ernest J. Davis, Henry Minton Francis, and James D. Fowler had grown up in the neighborhood and had attended Dunbar High School. Brown had once seen Fowler, dressed in his cadet uniform, speak at Shaw, and had gone up to him afterwards and expressed an interest in West Point. Colonel Atwood remained committed to getting young African Americans appointed to the Military Academy, and he and Captain Reynolds had talked to Brown about becoming a cadet. And Brown had a family friend in Congress, Representative William Levi Dawson.

Dawson filled the seat in the House vacated by Arthur Mitchell. Born the grandson of a slave in Albany, Georgia, on 26 April 1886, Dawson received his education in Albany public schools, Fisk University, and Northwestern University Law School. During World War I he was gassed and wounded while serving as a lieutenant in the 365th Infantry in France. For the rest of his life, shrapnel embedded in his left shoulder prevented him from raising his left arm past shoulder level without the other hand. Still, he felt lucky to have survived. To the men under his command who had not, he dedicated his life to ensuring that their deaths had not been in vain. From 1933 to 1939, Dawson served on the Chicago City Council. In 1942 he was elected to Congress and seven years later became chairman of the House Committee on Expenditures in the Executive Departments, the first black chairman of a major committee.

Although William Dawson's mentor was Oscar DePriest, he resembled Arthur Mitchell in several respects. A quintessential machine man, Dawson had risen to power because it served the needs of the Windy City's political elite. He maintained an iron grip on his South Side fiefdom, allowing no other political entity access without his blessing. He even hired Mitchell's former secretary, Christine Ray Davis, as his own secretary. Soon after taking office on 6 January 1943, Dawson introduced anti-lynching legislation, anti–poll tax legislation, and a bill to establish a permanent Fair Employment Practices Commission. Later, however, his "public silence on the race issue reached legendary heights," according to historian William Grimshaw. Unlike Mitchell, Dawson remained soft-spoken and unpretentious and avoided fanfare and headlines throughout his tenure in Congress (3 January 1943–9 November 1970).

One of Dawson's early efforts to serve his race was an initiative he launched soon after taking office to desegregate the armed forces. In 1943, he asked Metz T. P. Lochard, editor of the *Chicago Defender,* Olive M. Diggs, editor of the *Chicago Bee,* and A. N. Fields, editor of the Chicago edition of the *Pittsburgh Courier,* to serve on a committee for selecting suitable candidates for him to appoint to the Military Academy. In 1944, Dawson nominated an African American to West Point.[6]

When in Washington, Dawson attended services at the John Wesley AME Zion Church. Harriet Tyler, Wesley's aunt, was a good friend of Dawson's secretary, Christine Davis, and soon became friends with the congressman. It was at church that Wesley Brown first met Dawson. The youth wasted no time in expressing his interest in West Point. Brown later met Dawson through Colonel Atwood and reiterated his inclination toward cadethood.

Brown also harbored an ambition to become a civil engineer. He always had what he called an "edifice complex." As a boy, he had taken several trips to Virginia to watch the Pentagon being built. Bridges, tunnels, and skyscrapers fascinated him. His aspirations toward engineering and cadethood were certainly not incompatible. After all, the Military Academy was America's first engineering school.

But Brown was not yet old enough for West Point when he graduated from high school in June 1944. He would have to wait until 1945 to apply. He decided to spend the interim in college. Always one to create as many options for himself as possible, he applied to Cornell for a scholarship and at the same time took the nationwide exam for the Army's Specialized Training Reserve Program, equivalent to the Navy's V-12 Program.

Brown heard from the Army first. His exam scores had qualified him to enter the Specialized Training Reserve Program at Iowa State, Penn State, New York University, and Howard University. He decided to stay close to home, so he picked Howard. He enlisted in the U.S. Army Reserve as a private on 2 May 1944 and started classes on 10 July, only a few days after graduating from Dunbar. Thus he became the first of his family to enter college. This was a significant achievement, for in 1940, only 15 percent of all nineteen-year-old Americans were in college, and the proportion for African Americans was much lower.[7] Brown lived on campus in a room with four other trainees. He majored in electrical engineering and made good grades except for chemistry, which he had never taken before. He also took military science courses and drilled.[8]

Brown intended to seek an appointment to West Point during his freshman year at Howard, confident that he could secure one from Congressman Dawson. But when an opportunity arose for a nomination to the Naval Academy, Brown considered changing course. Aunt Harriet had impressive connections in Congress. She was good friends not only with William Dawson's secretary but also with Adam Powell's secretary, Phoebe Nelson. Early in 1945, Phoebe told Harriet that Powell wanted to break the color barrier at the Naval Academy. Phoebe asked whether Harriet's nephew Wesley was interested in an appointment. If so, she said, he should take the competitive Civil Service examination that Powell was sponsoring to finalize his list of nominees.

Harriet passed the word to her nephew, who decided to take the exam. Both service schools offered an engineering curriculum, but Brown figured that the Naval Academy's course would serve him better in the civilian world if his military career didn't work out. "I was covering my bets," he later recalled. After Brown took the exam, the Civil Service Commission forwarded the results to Powell's office. Brown had done well. Phoebe Nelson told her boss about Brown and asked if she could include him on the list of appointees. Powell agreed to put him down as third alternate.

Nelson then telephoned Brown. If the principal nominees and first two alternates failed to meet the Academy's entrance requirements, Brown would have a shot at the Naval Academy. Would he accept the nomination if it came to that?

Brown pondered the offer. Did he really want to go to the Naval Academy? He had never really thought about a naval career before. He had certainly never considered becoming a naval officer. Since several African Americans had already graduated from the Military Academy, West Point seemed a safer bet. But the possibility of breaking the color barrier at the Naval Academy intrigued him. It awakened a yearning to emulate the African American military heroes he so admired, had read about, and had grown up with. He decided that if the opportunity to become a midshipman arose, he would seize it. Fully aware of the pioneering role he would play and the difficulties he would face, he made a conscious decision to try to break the color barrier at the Naval Academy. Once again, he chose the greater challenge. Brown told his aunt's friend that if Congressman Powell offered him the nomination, he would accept.[9]

That spring witnessed an unprecedented effort to enroll African Americans in the Naval Academy. For his part, Adam Powell adopted a new tactic. Instead of appointing one or two or three or four African Americans, he blanketed the Academy with ten black nominees. The list included Wesley Brown, one other Howard University student, and eight native New Yorkers. The attrition rate proved to be 90 percent, with the Academic Board rejecting the certificates of nine of Powell's nominees. Four of them failed the regular entrance exam, two failed the substantiating exam, and three never took either exam. Only Wesley Brown made it past the scholastic hurdle. The Academic Board accepted his certificates from both Dunbar and Howard, enabling him to skip the entrance exams. The only remaining hurdle was the Academy's physical examination, slated for June.[10]

Two other African Americans received appointments to the Naval Academy that spring: Elmer J. Taylor, Jr., and Eugene C. Harter, Jr. Taylor's nomination came from Democratic congressman John E. Sheridan, representative of the Fourth District of Pennsylvania. Taylor was Sheridan's second black appointee to the Naval Academy. Sheridan had appointed black Philadelphia native Joseph Donald Johnson to the Academy in January 1944, but Johnson never entered. Harter's nomination came from Congressman Clarence James Brown, Representative of Ohio's Seventh District. Brown voted with the Republican majority for the abolition of poll taxes and unsuccessfully sponsored an amendment that would have prohibited discrimination in the recruitment of nurses for the armed services. Although no further information about the whys and wherefores of these cases has been found, the outcomes are clear. The Academic Board accepted Taylor's secondary certificate but not his college certificate, and Taylor failed the substantiating exam. The Academic Board rejected both of Harter's certificates, and Harter failed the regular exam. Of the unprecedented number of twelve African Americans appointed to the Naval Academy that year, Wesley Brown remained the sole survivor.[11]

Adam Powell telephoned to offer Brown the principal nomination. Struck speechless for a moment, Brown recovered and accepted it. Powell congratulated him. To comply with the regulation that a candidate reside in the congressional district from which he was appointed, Powell listed a New York address for Brown on the nomination form. It was not a serious attempt at fiction, however; the address was for a vacant lot. Brown received his appointment on 10 April.

Wesley Brown's mother, father, aunts, and uncle were proud of him. Katie Shepherd was particularly proud. Her grandson had already reached a milestone by being the first of his family to enter college. The appointment to the Naval Academy afforded him the opportunity to reach even higher. An avid newspaper reader, Katie knew what had happened to James Johnson and George Trivers. Yet the possibility that her grandson might not make it never entered her mind. Sadly, she would not see him enter the Naval Academy. Two weeks after he received the appointment, she passed away in her sleep. Since she was only sixty-five and had not been ill, her death came as a shock.

In the remaining weeks before his physical exam, Brown read everything he could get his hands on about the Academy. He paid particularly close attention to Kendall Banning's *Annapolis Today,* Leland Lovette's *School of the Sea,* and *A Guide to the United States Naval Academy.* He must have looked askance at Lovette's assertion that "in the five or six cases where young men of African descent have entered Annapolis, it must be said in all fairness to the authorities that no racial discrimination was shown." He wrote to the superintendent and acquired a copy of Academy regulations. He talked to several Dunbar graduates who had gone to West Point about what to expect at a service academy. He also spoke with George Trivers, who told him about some of the Academy's customs as well as his own experience there. Trivers said that he had been unable to stand the isolation that the others had imposed on him. He said that Brown might have to be a loner to succeed. Teachers, neighbors, and family members offered advice, too. Some said that because he was black, going to the Academy would be a dehumanizing experience. They implored him not to go. One teacher told him what had happened to James Johnson. The teacher said that Johnson had never been the same; the ordeal at the Academy had impaired his personality, snuffed his sparkle, and dulled his ambition. Colonel Atwood and Captain Reynolds told Brown that if he forgot about race and concentrated on doing well, he would get along fine.[12]

Characteristically, Brown found inspiration in African American military history. James Fowler loaned him his personal copy of Henry O. Flipper's autobiography, a first edition. Holding the dog-eared book thrilled Brown and reading it heartened him. "If a guy born in slavery could enter the Military Academy in 1873 and graduate on time in the top half of his class," he thought, "I can handle the Naval Academy."[13]

Brown also found inspiration in the John Wesley AME Zion Church, whose congregation heard sermons not only about the word of God but about civil rights as well. The NAACP held many events there to keep black Washingtonians involved in the movement. For example, on Sunday, 8 April 1945, the NAACP sponsored a mass rally at the John Wesley Church, featuring an address by Roy Wilkins. Later that year, the District of Columbia Branch of the NAACP held its annual meeting there. Like Reverend Spottswood, Sunday school superintendent Victor Tulane was a member of the NAACP, as was Brown's neighbor Marjorie Lawson. Thus the NAACP, through the church, joined Wesley Brown's family, high school, and love of history as a source of positive self-image to help him weather the coming storm.[14]

Brown had already passed an Army physical before entering the Specialized Training Reserve Program, so he figured he would have no trouble with the Naval Academy's regular physical exam. Congressman Powell was not so sanguine. He insisted that Brown get an unofficial preliminary examination at the Naval Dispensary in the old Navy Annex on Constitution Avenue. Brown received the exam on 8 May. A dentist looked at his teeth and reported him "not physically qualified for the Naval Academy" owing to "marked malocclusion." The Navy's surgeon general forwarded a copy of the report to Powell. Brown visited the father of one of his Howard roommates, a civilian dentist on the staff at Fort Myer, James Bowman. Dr. Bowman examined Brown, did some research on malocclusions in Navy and Army regulation books, and concluded that the gap in Brown's teeth was not so large as to unfit him for the Academy. Thereafter "the telephones between Washington and Annapolis hummed for a few days over just how much tolerance there is in a malocclusion case," Brown later recalled. No doubt Powell got involved in the buzz.

Brown reported to the Naval Academy for the regular physical examination on 25 June 1945 dressed in Army khakis, with orders in one hand and overnight bag in the other. The physical lasted three days. The Academy dentist checked Brown's teeth and had him bite on a probe. Brown clamped down hard, trying his best to close the gap. The dentist tugged on the probe and pronounced Brown's "slight open bite" "not disqualifying." The Medical Examining Board declared him "physically qualified."[15]

On 30 June 1945, Brown and the others who were slated for induction that day donned their "white works"—Academy uniforms resembling sailors' uniforms—and reported to Memorial Hall. (With the war on, plebes entered the Academy in small groups throughout the summer rather than all at once.) There they took the midshipman's oath, surrounded by battle flags, war trophies, and busts and paintings of naval heroes. As Brown held his right hand aloft and recited the words, he gazed at the flag that Oliver Hazard Perry had flown on 10 September 1813 during his great victory on Lake Erie, a large blue flag featuring James Lawrence's dying words, "Don't give up the ship." After administering the oath, Captain Stuart Howe Ingersoll, commandant of midshipmen, delivered a stirring talk on naval tradition. He told the newly minted plebes that he expected them to uphold and enlarge these traditions, just as the men in the fleet were doing that very moment fighting the Japanese. To Brown, the distinguished and elegant-looking gentleman seemed to epitomize the ideals of the institution he had just become a part of. While listening at attention to the commandant's remarks, Brown reflected on everything he had gone through to get there and pondered what was to come. The whole experience moved him deeply. Although aware of how African American midshipmen had fared in the past, he pledged to himself then and there to stick it out, come what may.[16]

Wesley A. Brown was fully qualified to do so. He possessed the right combination of intelligence, social graces, and athleticism to make it. His grandmother, parents, aunts, uncle, and teachers had instilled in him self-reliance, self-discipline, self-esteem, and self-confidence. Dunbar and Howard had given him a fine academic grounding. Having attended high school, played sports, led the Cadet Corps, held a full-time job, and taken a college course all at the same time, Brown was accustomed to working hard, working smart, and budgeting his time. His Cadet Corps experience, talks with West Point cadets, voracious appetite for history and other reading material, and stint in the Army had familiarized him with military regimentation, steeped him in African American military tradition, and given him an inkling of what to expect at the Naval Academy.

Perhaps most important, Brown believed in himself; he honestly believed he could break the color barrier. In light of the cold, hard reality facing African Americans of his generation, the personnel officer's advice to keep his day job at the Bureau of Medicine had been utterly sound. But Wesley Brown was a bit of a dreamer. He refused to accept the limitations that prejudice tried to impose on his race. His family, teachers, and books had freed his mind to conceive of things like getting a college education, becoming an engineer, and becoming the first black graduate of the Naval Academy—aspirations that other African Americans might never even have considered. The mechanics by which he set about fulfilling his dreams—exploiting family connections, maximizing his options, working hard—demonstrated that he had a firm grasp of reality. Wesley Brown's head might have been up in the clouds when he accepted the appointment to the Naval Academy, but his feet were planted firmly on the ground.

The Naval Academy that Brown entered bore a striking nonresemblance to the one that George Trivers had left eight years before. Although its general appearance remained essentially the same, the population had changed dramatically. The Classes of 1930 to 1939 averaged 421 graduates, while the Classes of 1940 to 1949 averaged 728 graduates, an increase of about 72 percent. Class size for the era peaked with the Class of 1946 at 1,046 graduates. Altogether, between February 1941 and June 1945, 4,304 midshipmen graduated from the Academy, while 3,319 young men graduated from the Naval Reserve Midshipmen's School at Annapolis. In 1945, the organization of the midshipmen caught up to their larger numbers, changing from a regiment of four battalions to a brigade of six battalions.[17]

More striking than the increase in the Academy's population were the changes in its nature. By 1945, many of the officers assigned to the Academy's Executive or Academic Departments had come to Annapolis straight from combat duty.[18]

The commandant had seen action in both strategic arenas of the two-ocean war. Born on 3 June 1898 in Massachusetts and raised in Maine, Stuart Ingersoll had graduated with the Class of 1920, spent a year on a battleship, then served for four years in destroyers on the China Station. After a year of flight instruction, he was designated a naval aviator in June 1926. For the next several years he flew in various torpedo, fighting, and patrol squadrons, helped develop arresting gear for aircraft carriers, and worked in the Bureau of Aeronautics. Early in the war he became operations officer on the staff of Commander Task Force 24, where he helped coordinate air and surface units against German U-boats during the Battle of the Atlantic, for which he received the Legion of Merit. He then did a tour in charge of the Naval Air Station, Anacostia.

On 10 April 1944, Captain Ingersoll took command of the light aircraft carrier *Monterey* (CVL-26) and spent the next ten months in the western Pacific. Steaming with Task Forces 58 and 38, the carrier launched air strikes against Japanese shipping and installations in New Guinea, Truk, the Marianas, the Bonins, the Ryukyus, and the Philippines. The *Monterey* took part in the two largest naval engagements in history, the Battle of the Philippine Sea (popularly known as the Great Marianas Turkey Shoot) and the Battle of Leyte Gulf. Under Ingersoll the carrier fought off Japanese air attacks and weathered the infamous typhoon that struck the Third Fleet in December 1944. For his conduct during these actions he received the Navy Cross. A few months later, in March 1945, he became commandant of midshipman.

Tall and intelligent, Captain Ingersoll treated subordinates with the right mix of friendliness and firmness. "Our chief job," the 47-year-old New Englander told a reporter shortly after arriving in Annapolis, "is to mold character."[19]

Several of Ingersoll's subordinates in the Executive Department had also seen combat in the Pacific. Commander Eugene Alexander Barham, for example, had had a ship shot out from under him. "Slim" Barham graduated from the Naval Academy in 1935. After a year on a battleship, he served on a succession of four-pipers until February 1942, when he was assigned duty in fitting out the new destroyer *Laffey* (DD-459). He became the ship's engineer officer at her commissioning on 31 March.

The *Laffey* spent the next 228 days in the Pacific. First she steamed with Task Force 18 escorting carriers; then she operated with Task Forces 64 and 67, trying to stop the "Tokyo Express" from delivering reinforcements down "the Slot" to Guadalcanal. On Friday, 13 November 1942, the *Laffey* and seven other American destroyers and five cruisers fought eleven Japanese destroyers, one cruiser, and two battleships in a naval melee that one skipper likened to "a barroom brawl after the lights had been shot out." The *Laffey* nearly got sliced in two by the Japanese battleship *Hiei* when she crossed the *Hiei*'s "T." Her stern cleared the battleship's overhanging stem by less than 20 feet. As the *Laffey* moved off she poured fire from every available gun into the *Hiei*'s tall, pagodalike superstructure, which collapsed like a house of cards.

A few minutes later, shells from three Japanese destroyers and the battleship *Kirishima* ripped into the *Laffey* while a torpedo blew off her stern. In an instant the once taut ship became a blazing, sinking wreck, with most of her crew killed or wounded. One young sailor, still conscious, lay on the deck, his broken legs pinned under twisted steel. Fires raged in the space below, heating the deck plates and scorching his flesh. Two torpedomen worked frantically to free him before he was cooked, blown away by incoming shells, or drowned by rising water. The torpedomen successfully extricated the sailor, but neither the torpedomen nor the sailor were ever seen again. The skipper ordered abandon ship. As Barham struggled to put as much distance between himself and the *Laffey* as he could, the destroyer exploded and sank. Barham organized the survivors into a train of liferafts and boats and led them toward Guadalcanal until some Higgins boats picked them up. All told, twenty-two of *Laffey*'s crew died, 102 were wounded, and seventy-five received minor injuries. None escaped unhurt. For his conduct during this action Barham received the Bronze Star. Although wounded, he didn't put in for a Purple Heart for fear of worrying his family.

Afterward Barham became skipper of the destroyer *Dashiell* (DD-659), which he commanded until July 1944. He joined the Naval Academy Executive Department the following September. A shipmate from the *Laffey* described him as "a highly intelligent and remarkably resourceful man whose courage and maturity substantially exceeded the usual allowance of these virtues to his peers."[20]

For officers fresh from combat like Barham and Ingersoll, shepherding midshipmen through the Naval Academy was a walk in the park.

When the 1945–1946 academic year began, the classes of 1947 through 1949 were present at the Naval Academy. The first class, the Class of 1947, had entered in 1943. Owing to the crushing demand for naval officers during World War II, their curriculum had been compressed into three years. They were slated to graduate in June 1946. Many individuals in '47 would go on to make outstanding contributions to the Navy and to their country, including future President Jimmy Carter, Chief of Naval Operations Admiral William J. Crowe, Jr., Central Intelligence Agency Director Stansfield Turner, noted Vietnam War POW James B. Stockdale, and Medal of Honor recipient Thomas J. Hudner, Jr.[21]

The Class of 1948 was originally slated to graduate in June of 1947 on the compressed wartime program. But with the end of the war and demobilization, the Class of 1948 was split in two. The top half, designated 1948A, remained on schedule to graduate in three years. The bottom half, designated 1948B, would stay for a fourth year, to their great chagrin.

The Class of 1949 would be the first postwar group to have a normal, four-year curriculum from the beginning. Initially, the Class of 1949 consisted of 1,105 midshipmen, with some 63 percent having had prior military service. A number of them had received combat decorations and eleven had been officers in the Naval Reserve.[22] "Our class was very heterogeneous," recalled one Class of '49 alum. "We had classmates who had been Ensigns in the fleet; we had some who had been Marine sergeants; we had some who were entitled to wear the Army's Combat Infantry Badge."[23]

Prior military service set the Classes of 1947 through 1949 apart from pre– and post–World War II classes. More than 50 percent of each class consisted of midshipmen who had served in the military before entering the Academy. Most had been enlisted men in the Naval Reserve who had joined up for the V-12 program. A large proportion of these classes entered the Academy with a year or two or more of college under their belts.[24]

The Classes of 1947 through 1949 shared an equally important distinguishing characteristic: many of them might not have entered the Academy if not for the war. "Every patriotic youth was expected to join up or be drafted," recalled one '48A alum. "Upon graduation from high school," noted one of Brown's classmates, "I had three choices: Army, Navy, Marines." Many draft-age American men chose the Navy because "going to sea was preferable to slogging around in the mud," said another '49 alum. A graduate of '48A put it more graphically: "I chose the Navy over the Marine Corps because . . . I preferred fish eating at my corpse rather than jungle maggots and worms." Many who entered the Academy during the war wanted to serve their country for the duration but had no intention of remaining in the Navy afterwards. A few became midshipmen to avoid combat, hoping the war would end before their graduation. "Because of the method of selecting candidates," noted Bureau of Personnel Chief Vice Admiral Randall Jacobs in a postwar plan for training naval officers,

> the Academy has trained large numbers of men who had no burning desire or outstanding qualifications for the Naval service as a life-long career. Very few young men form fixed ideas in high school as to the careers for which they are best suited, and those who do frequently discover later that they have made mistakes. It has been inevitable, therefore, that many candidates for the Naval Academy have been motivated by the desire to obtain an education at minimum expense, to please their parents or friends, or to follow a profession about which they knew practically nothing and which they later found to be uncongenial. Consequently, a large proportion of Naval Academy graduates

have returned to civilian life, and have repaid the Navy for their education, if at all, by service of limited duration in the Naval Reserve.

Jacobs's lament pertained to the prewar period as well, but the war magnified the problem. To be sure, many midshipmen entered the Academy during World War II for the traditional reason—to fulfill a lifelong dream of becoming a commissioned officer. But whatever their motive for entering, those who had no plans for a naval career could afford to be less concerned about fitting into the Academy mold than those who did.[25]

Of the 3,216 midshipmen present at the beginning of the 1945–1946 academic year, 4 percent were Jewish, 20 percent were Catholic, and the rest were Protestants. Virtually every ethnic group in America had at least a few representatives among them. Wesley Brown was the only African American.[26]

The impending arrival of a black plebe caused a buzz at the Academy, although nothing like the uproar that had accompanied James Conyers's matriculation in 1872. At a meeting just before Brown's swearing in, Commander William S. Estabrook, Jr., the executive officer, told the officers assigned to "plebe detail" that a black youth was about to be sworn in. Estabrook noted that the last black midshipman "had been unable to take the treatment he received." He told the other officers "to make certain" that this new black midshipman "was not harassed or treated unfairly." He indicated that this order had originated in the Navy Department and had reached him as a "pass-down-the-line" instruction via the superintendent and commandant. The Navy Department, it seemed, had assumed that other midshipmen were going to give Brown a hard time because of his race and wanted it stopped before it started.[27]

Nevertheless, from the outset, Executive Department officers treated Brown differently from his classmates, in one respect. They did not assign him a roommate. Naval Academy officials from the 1940s must have harbored the same apprehensions that their predecessors from the 1870s and 1930s had had about blacks and whites rooming together. Instead of fretting, however, Brown reveled in the privacy after having had four roommates at Howard.

With stories about Brown's appointment appearing in national newspapers, virtually all of the incoming plebes were aware that they had a black classmate.[28] For the vast majority, Brown's presence mattered little. Many wondered whether he would make it, but with everything they had to do to get by themselves, they seldom thought about him.[29]

A small group of plebes felt that Brown deserved a fair shake. Several offered to room with him. Brown declined. Given what he had learned about the experiences of black midshipmen and cadets in the past, he figured that sooner or later, someone would give him a hard time because of his race. When that happened, he did not want a roommate to have to share the burden, nor did he want the guilt of someone being harassed because of him.[30]

Another small minority of plebes strongly resented having an African American in their midst. A group of southern-born plebes habitually referred to Brown as "that damned nigger" when talking among themselves, although not within Brown's earshot. Of course, not all southerners resented the presence of a black midshipman and not all those who did were southerners. But wherever these prejudiced plebes hailed from, they expressed their feelings by refusing to sit beside Brown at meals or in chapel, by occasionally whispering nasty comments anonymously in ranks, or by simply ignoring him. "I am ashamed of how I treated Wesley," noted a classmate from St. Louis, Missouri. "I never purposely offended him, but like others in my class, I never offered my hand or a tinge of friendship to him." It

> was not personal; no matter who had been in his place, if black, I would have given him the same treatment. . . . I brought my prejudice with me to the U.S. Naval Academy. We were not tested for prejudice as a prerequisite for entry. I had learned prejudice in my neighborhood over an 18-year period. Those of us who were brought up in my locale were schooled in judging everything and everybody without examination. We majored in Prejudice. . . . My mother never had a positive statement to make about the black race. No disrespect meant towards her; she was born in 1902 and was indoctrinated with the mores of that time—no white person associated freely with blacks.[31]

While some classmates ignored Brown because of prejudice, others did so out of fear. One plebe recalled that a recently graduated junior commissioned officer assigned to plebe detail unofficially but emphatically instructed a group of fourth classmen that they "must by no means permit Brown to last the summer." The plebes "would be considered 'gutless' if we let 'that nigger' stay." Such naked prejudice angered this plebe, whose well-educated parents had taught him that prejudice "is a foolish business at best." He responded by sitting next to Brown at the mess table and talking to him. Nothing happened to him for doing so, and no one treated him any differently than they had before.[32]

Graham Leonard, also in '49, recalled that just before Brown was sworn in, an officer from the Executive Department mustered all the plebes who had already taken the midshipman's oath in a room in the basement of Bancroft Hall. According to Leonard, the officer ordered the group to silence Brown—not to talk to him outside of official business. Virtually from the beginning of the Naval Academy's history, the silent treatment existed as a method for classmates to ostracize an individual because of who he was or something he had done. During Reconstruction, white midshipmen had almost universally silenced their black classmates. While most of James Lee Johnson's classmates avoided talking to him, a few risked ostracism themselves and tried to befriend him. Whether Leonard's memory was accurate or not with regard to a commissioned officer giving an order to silence Brown, it wouldn't have been out of the ordinary for an upperclassman to do so.[33]

Leonard and several classmates responded to the alleged admonition to silence Brown by going out of their way to help him. Leonard had become a midshipman because his father, a wealthy businessman, had wanted him to, and because Leonard didn't want to become a businessman like his father. Later in life Leonard described himself as obnoxious, vain, energetic, and rebellious. His battalion officer described him as "below average officer material." Leonard piled up so many demerits that the Academy dismissed him for "unsatisfactory conduct not involving moral turpitude" about two months before the end of plebe year. Leonard knew from the start that he "didn't fit in very well." He was "enraged by the fact that other people could get away with something just because they'd been there a year." A native of Kingsport, a small town in the mountains of eastern Tennessee, Leonard grew up amidst segregationist values but "bent over backwards" to treat African Americans as equals, often to the point of making them "uncomfortable." Leonard perceived that one small minority of his Academy classmates strongly opposed Brown's presence and wanted him out while another small minority had a strong desire to help him and to see him through. Individuals in both groups seemed willing to risk their naval careers to further their respective ends. The rest sat on the fence. Leonard and four or five other plebes started a rumor that Congress had passed an "injunction" stating that anyone caught trying to harm Brown would be severely punished. Although Leonard knew that there was no such thing as a "congressional injunction," he hoped that the rumor would inhibit fence-sitting class-mates from falling in with those who opposed Brown's being there. There is no evidence as to how widely the rumor circulated or what effect it might have had.[34]

Reactions to the presence of a black midshipman from the few upper-classmen remaining in Annapolis that summer likewise fell across a broad spectrum. With the Academy still running on the compressed wartime schedule, upperclassmen spent roughly one-third of the summer on leave, one-third taking classes, and one-third on the "practice cruise" designed to familiarize midshipmen with life at sea and the different branches of the service. Each class was split into two groups that alternated between academics and cruising. As a result, more upperclassmen remained on the Yard during the summer than had been the case before the war. Even so, since the plebes were living in a separate section of Bancroft Hall, they still had relatively little contact with upperclassmen during the summer as compared with the academic year.[35]

A handful of first classmen from each group was assigned administra-tive duties and stood watches in the plebe section of Bancroft Hall during their summer academic period, including Midshipman 1/c Joseph Patrick Flanagan, Jr. Following summer leave, Flanagan returned to the Academy in early July, then took classes until 18 August, when he embarked on his first class cruise. Soon after returning to the Yard after leave, Flanagan heard talk that a black kid had just become a plebe and that other plebes were giving him a hard time.

Joe Flanagan was nothing short of outstanding. Born and raised in an upper-middle-class family in Wilkes Barre, Pennsylvania, he had never considered military service until the wave of American patriotism created by the attack on Pearl Harbor swept across Pennsylvania's coal region. Before entering the Academy in 1943, Joe had gone to prep school at Wyoming Seminary and had spent three terms in the V-12 program at Princeton. He had played football, edited the school newspaper, and wrestled at the collegiate level even at Wyoming Seminary. He continued to shine on the varsity wrestling team at Navy. It was while wrestling for Wyoming Seminary that Flanagan developed the ambition to enter the Academy. During a match against Navy at Annapolis, Joe became en-chanted with the Yard. He obtained a congressional appointment, en-tered by the certificate method, and breezed through plebe year. Joe ex-celled not only in sports but also in his studies; he stood near the top of his class for most of his time at the Academy. On the eve of his graduation, the superintendent praised him for demonstrating "outstanding of-ficerlike qualities" and contributing "by precept and example to the de-velopment of these qualities within the Brigade," and commended him for his "leadership" and "high ideals of duty, honor, and loyalty."[36]

Flanagan's devout Irish Catholic parents had taught him that everyone was equal in God's eyes and that prejudice was therefore sinful. Joe had heard a rumor that previous black midshipmen had been hazed out of the Academy. The news that Brown was already having a hard time infuri-ated him. He decided to act. He went over to the plebe's room on the Sev-ern side of Bancroft Hall and walked in. The room was bright and airy and neat as a pin. Brown stood bolt upright. After exchanging a few pleasantries, Flanagan offered to help Brown if any problem arose.[37]

A problem arose almost immediately. A few days after Brown was sworn in, Brown asked a fellow plebe down the hall, William H. Sword, to go running with him. "Sure," said Sword. The two quickly discovered their mutual interest in tennis and began playing tennis together.

Bill Sword was good friends with Joe Flanagan. They had grown up in Wilkes Barre together and had been classmates at Wyoming Seminary and at Princeton. But when Joe Flanagan went to the Naval Academy, Bill Sword went to war. Sword had joined the Army ROTC at Princeton and was called to active duty in the spring of 1943. He served as an enlisted man in the Army Air Forces in an air evacuation unit, which flew badly wounded soldiers from continental Europe to hospitals in England. He ended up at Annapolis because soon after he went on active duty, a supe-rior officer had ordered him to take the national competitive exam for the service academies. Sword did so because he was told to, not because he wanted to attend Annapolis or West Point. Literally as the result of a coin toss, he selected the Naval Academy on the exam form, then promptly forgot about the whole thing. The orders to Annapolis a year and a half later took him completely by surprise. Shortly after Sword arrived on the Yard, his old friend Joe Flanagan "spooned" him, dropping the formal distance between plebe and upperclassman with a handshake. Like Joe Flanagan, Bill Sword believed racial prejudice was wrong. Sword's par-ents had taught him that it wasted time and resources. So he thought nothing about running or playing tennis with Wesley Brown.[38]

But Midshipman 1/c Donald Boone Whitmire, another good friend of Joe Flanagan, didn't like it, not one bit. Don Whitmire was nothing short of outstanding, too. Raised in Decatur, a small town in north central Al-abama, Whitmire entered the University of Alabama at Tuscaloosa in

January 1940. An indifferent student, he made mostly Bs, Cs, and Ds. But while he fumbled in the classroom, he excelled on the gridiron. Standing five feet, eleven inches tall and weighing 215 pounds, he played both offensive and defensive tackle for the Crimson Tide on teams that won the 1941 Cotton Bowl and the 1942 Orange Bowl. In 1942 he made All American and was selected for Alabama's all-time squad. Confronted with the choice of being drafted or entering an officer training program in 1943, Whitmire enlisted in the Marines and enrolled in the V-12 program at the University of North Carolina, Chapel Hill. There he could play football until his officer training ended, perhaps one season at best. Then he would go on active duty.

During the war the military academies offered athletes the option of playing for three full seasons. This enabled the Academy to attract some of the greatest players in its history, including halfback Bobby Tom Jenkins, guard John "Bo" Coppege, and running back Bill Barron. For three seasons, beginning in 1943, Navy contended for the national championship.

One day that summer, head coach John Whelchel and line coach Edgar "Rip" Miller were in an office at the Academy discussing the upcoming season and poring over a football yearbook. They spotted a picture of Whitmire dressed in a Crimson Tide uniform, looking tough and mean. At that moment, Miller looked up to see former Alabama star Bobby Tom Jenkins in the hallway. Miller called Jenkins into the office and asked him if he knew Whitmire. Jenkins said yes; in fact, "Whit" had been his roommate at Alabama. Coach Whelchel had Jenkins telephone Whitmire to sound him out about playing for Navy. Whitmire soon appeared in Whelchel's office. The coach asked what made him such a good tackle. Whitmire got down into a three-point stance. "When the ball is snapped," he said, gazing up at Whelchel, "I look across the line at the guy in front of me, and then I knock his goddamn head off."

Whitmire's appointment to the Academy came from none other than Chicago Congressman William L. Dawson. Whitmire was sworn in on 24 September 1943, well into the football season. Although he got off to a late start, he played with unmatched intensity. He never tried just to block opponents but to bury them. He made All American at Navy in 1943 and 1944 (the last two years of his eligibility for college football), received the Knute Rockne Memorial Trophy as college football's best lineman in 1944, and went on to enter the College Football Hall of Fame. He is considered the greatest Navy lineman ever. Football was virtually a religion at the Naval Academy, standing almost as high on the totem pole as Neptune and John Paul Jones. Football heroes like Whitmire enjoyed a status well above that of the average midshipman.

Whitmire distinguished himself off the gridiron, too, by making outstanding marks in "aptitude for the service." Along with Joe Flanagan, Stansfield Turner, and a dozen other '47 classmates, Whitmire received a letter of commendation from the superintendent. While most athletes skedaddled from the Academy as soon as possible after the war ended, Whitmire decided to make a career in the Navy and ultimately rose to the rank of rear admiral. "When I went back home," he said, "I found I was held in high esteem by the town folks. My parents and four brothers and sisters were proud seeing me in uniform. It made me realize there was more to life than football."[39]

Joe Flanagan had met Don Whitmire during their second year at Navy, when wrestling coach Ray Schwartz prevailed upon the big tackle to try out as a heavyweight wrestler. When Whit appeared at the wrestling loft, Schwartz asked Flanagan to introduce him to some holds. Flanagan recalled that although Whit outweighed him by some sixty pounds, "he was a sucker for 'take downs' and other maneuvers and he became very annoyed that a stripling like myself could practically turn him around and upside down at will. After a few sessions he told Ray Schwartz that he was no longer interested in wrestling. However, Whit and I stayed close friends."[40]

Flanagan found Whitmire, with his deep southern drawl, a bit rough around the edges at first. "But he was a classmate who wanted to be well regarded by his peers. And he worked at it, graduated, and became an admiral. Now that's a perfect example of the Naval Academy taking somebody who anywhere else would have been a terrible redneck and converting him into a paragon of public service."[41]

Don Whitmire, whose father was Decatur's chief of police,[42] came to the Academy with a deeply ingrained prejudice against African Americans. He believed that there was no place for black officers in the Navy nor black midshipmen at the Naval Academy. Seeing Bill Sword and other plebes running with Wesley Brown, playing tennis with Brown, and otherwise treating Brown as an equal infuriated Whitmire. He decided to act. One day early in July, just before the beginning of the first upperclass summer academic period, Whitmire and a small group of southern-born classmates confronted Bill Sword and several other plebes in Sword's room in Bancroft Hall. Whitmire stood nose to nose with Sword and glared down at him. He told Sword to stop playing tennis with Brown, to have nothing to do with him, to silence him. In the course of the confrontation Whitmire called Sword the racist's ultimate epithet, "nigger lover."[43]

Bill Sword didn't like it, not one bit. He had no intention of following Whitmire's instructions. He immediately visited his old friend Joe Flanagan and told him what had happened.

Joe dropped everything to have a talk with Don. "Whit, put yourself in Brown's position," he said. "It's hard enough being a plebe around here without a lot of extraneous hazing." It was an appeal to Whitmire's reason. Flanagan persuaded the big tackle that it was wrong to pressure plebes into silencing Brown simply because of his race. It was not something that an officer and gentleman would do. If the Navy had seen fit to make Brown a midshipman, then Brown deserved to be treated with the respect due the uniform. Whitmire agreed. He stopped trying to silence Brown. This elevated Whitmire in Flanagan's eyes. Although Whit still didn't like the idea of a black midshipman and was never particularly nice to Brown, he proved open minded enough to see past his prejudice to the logic of Flanagan's appeal.[44]

What effect Whitmire's reversal had on the classmates who had backed him up during the confrontation with Sword and the other plebes is unknown. It seems certain, however, that the removal of a player of Whitmire's stature adversely affected the game the racist minority in the first class was playing.

Wesley Brown remained unaware of Whitmire's aborted effort to have him silenced. With the formal distance between plebes and the upper classes deeply embedded in the Academy's culture, plebes simply weren't privy to what upperclassmen said or did when the plebes weren't around. Nor did any of the plebes talk to Brown about the tension between the small minority of their classmates who wanted him out and the small minority who wanted him in. To be sure, Brown heard the occasional muttered remark and knew well the feeling behind the dirty looks that a few people gave him now and then. But there were no verbal threats. He wasn't being shunned. He played lots of tennis that summer. And he was making friends.

On the whole Brown was more concerned with learning how to survive as a plebe than with being the only African American in a lily-white environment. While the nature of the population at the Academy had changed significantly since James Lee Johnson's time, the regimen and everyday lives of plebes and upperclassmen had not, despite the war. "During those first few weeks we had more to do than there were hours in the day," Brown recalled. "We ran to formation, learned customs and regulations, memorized 'can's and can't's' until our eyes popped." The plebes took refresher courses in basic math, English and history; learned how to tie knots, row cutters, and sail; and studied naval tradition. Brown had no trouble with the academics, but the absence of African Americans from the naval tradition course struck him as a glaring omission. Brown's greatest concerns included losing the Army slang he had picked up in the Specialized Training Reserve Program in favor of Navy jargon ("head" instead of "latrine" and so forth) and making sure he put on the proper uniform. A few turn-backs from the last class gave him tips on stowing his locker and shining his shoes. Having been cadet colonel at Dunbar, he had no trouble with drill. "Things were much easier than I had expected," he recalled.

Nevertheless, Brown realized that he would be under close scrutiny, so he adhered to the regulations and plebe rates as closely as possible and kept his room and his person tidy. Despite his gregarious and outgoing nature, he also kept a low profile and generally kept to himself. Not "imposing" himself on his classmates had been a key part of Henry O. Flipper's strategy for survival at West Point and, after reading Flipper's autobiography, Brown decided to apply the same strategy at Annapolis. He wanted others to think of him as just another plebe.[45]

Brown's status as a celebrity in the black community sometimes prevented him from blending inconspicuously into the background. On 14 August 1945, news of the cease-fire in the Pacific hit Annapolis. The Executive Department relaxed disciplinary regulations and a riotous V-J Day celebration broke out. Midshipmen snake danced through "T-Court," smeared paint on the statue of Tecumseh, banged on drums, blew horns, and flung rolls of toilet paper into the air. The Japanese bell clanged incessantly. Although it was usually rung only after a victory in the Army-Navy game, the superintendent had it moved to Tecumseh Court just for this occasion. A "voluntary" service at the chapel capped the celebration and a parade through Annapolis was slated for the sixteenth.[46]

Like Washington in those days, Annapolis was a segregated southern town. African Americans accounted for about a third of the city's population. Jim Crow laws and customs confined them to separate sections of town. Black Annapolitans attended separate schools, attended separate churches, ate in separate restaurants, patronized separate movie theaters and taverns, and were buried in separate cemeteries. Most black Annapolitans depended on the Naval Academy for their livelihood. Their jobs entailed maintenance of buildings and grounds and cooking and cleaning in Bancroft Hall. Many black Annapolitans considered the news about a black midshipman entering the Academy to be almost as significant as the end of the war.[47]

Indeed, Wesley Brown was something of a celebrity among African Americans across the country. After the newspapers had picked up the story of his entrance into the Academy, he received numerous letters from women he had never met before, including a New York fashion model. Many women enclosed photographs and some even proposed marriage![48]

Wesley Brown's dark complexion stood out in stark relief against his white uniform as the midshipmen formed up for the parade. The middies received instructions not to talk and to look straight ahead while marching. Crowds cheered them as they wound through the streets. When they marched through the Fourth Ward, where most black Annapolitans lived, attention focused on Wesley Brown. Shouts of encouragement—"Hang in there!" "Don't let 'em get you down!" "We're with you!"—came from everywhere. "There he is!" cried one old black woman sitting in a rocking chair on her porch. "Oh Wesley boy! You show 'em! You set the pace for them, Wesley boy! You set the pace for them! You show them white boys, Wesley! You show them white boys!" Sweat poured down the back of Brown's neck. The cheers both heartened and embarrassed him. He worried whether this attention in the streets of Annapolis would make things tougher for him in Bancroft Hall. No one said anything to him during the parade, nor did anyone comment when the midshipmen returned to Dahlgren Hall to store their rifles, nor did anybody give him any extra grief later on because of his reception in town.[49]

That same day, Vice Admiral Aubrey Wray Fitch relieved Rear Admiral John R. Beardall as superintendent. Admiral Beardall had occupied the post since January 1942. According to Richard S. West, Jr., an associate professor in the Academy's Department of English, History, and Government, Beardall's primary task had been "to turn out as great a number as possible of *adequately* trained young officers . . . in the shortest possible time." Eugene Barham considered Beardall a competent officer but believed that he had relaxed standards too much to accomplish this task. When Admiral Fitch became superintendent, morale in the Executive Department soared. Barham likened the transformation to that which had occurred in the South Pacific when Vice Admiral William F. Halsey relieved Vice Admiral Robert L. Ghormley in October 1942. Fitch "let it be known that we were there to train officers for the Navy."[50]

Like Commander Barham, Admiral Fitch had had a ship shot out from under him in the Pacific. Born on 11 June 1883 and raised in St. Ignace, Michigan, Fitch graduated from the Naval Academy in 1906. In 1929 he risked his career by beginning aviation training at the Naval Air Station, Pensacola, where, as a 46-year-old commander, he trained with officers half his age and a third his rank. In March 1942, he became Commander Air Task Force in the Pacific, flying his flag in the carrier *Lexington* (CV-2). In May his task force defeated the Japanese in the battle of the Coral Sea, the first naval battle in history fought entirely from the air, in which opposing surface forces never made contact. The victory saved the sea line of communication between Australia and New Zealand, but Fitch lost the *Lexington* to Japanese bombs and torpedoes. In September 1942 he began a tour of duty as Commander Aircraft, South Pacific Fleet, during which American and New Zealand aviators under his command shot down 3,031 Japanese planes. For his wartime service he received the Distinguished Service Medal, the Distinguished Flying Cross, the Legion of Merit, and other decorations. On 1 August 1944 he reported to the Navy Department for duty as Deputy Chief of Naval Operations for Air and remained in that position until becoming superintendent, the first naval aviator in the billet.

During the war Admiral Fitch landed on territories taken by American forces shortly after their seizure to monitor air activities and select bases for future operations. Admiral Halsey said that Fitch "flew everywhere he had no business being." Popular with naval officers, Fitch rarely if ever had publicity officers or newspaper correspondents at his headquarters, so he remained largely unknown to the American public. Those who did know him found him a kindly, quiet, and unpretentious officer with a good sense of humor and a steely determination to see that every man under his command received fair treatment.[51]

Plebe summer ended about six weeks after Fitch took the helm. With classes scheduled to begin on 29 September, the plebes were divided among the companies of the Brigade according to their foreign language preference. Wesley Brown took German and was assigned to the Sixteenth Company, Fourth Battalion.[52]

Brown's preparation had paid off, so far. He had adjusted quickly to the discipline of Academy life. He was aware that some individuals disliked the idea of his being there, but they had not made his life any more difficult than it had to be. He remained unaware that some had tried to silence him and that others had tried to stop them. Plebe summer academics, indoctrination, and physical training had posed no problems. To be sure he had had to hustle and work hard, but on the whole, plebe summer had not been terribly difficult. The greater challenge was yet to come.

8

Demerits by the Bucketful

The event that many plebes had dreaded all summer—the return of the upperclassmen from their summer activities—took place on Friday, 28 September 1945. First-semester recitations began promptly the next day. All midshipmen now faced the grim prospect of four months of academic grind, relieved only by ten days of Christmas leave, provided that they earned passing grades. Fourth classmen faced not only a full academic schedule at the Academy for the first time but also the scrutiny of the entire complement of upperclassmen, many of whom loved to "run" plebes—that is, to participate actively in quizzing them, correcting their behavior, and administering "plebe punishment."[1]

Commander Earle K. McLaren and Commander Eugene Barham were the battalion officers assigned to the Fourth Battalion. McLaren and other Executive Department officers figured that Brown was in for a hard time. Because of what had happened to black midshipmen before, McLaren recalled, "we all anticipated he might encounter difficulties because of his race."[2]

Eugene Barham often wondered why Brown had been assigned to his battalion. Commander Barham was the only officer in the Executive Department from the deep South. Born in Oak Ridge, Louisiana, he grew up in the South's social and economic aristocracy. His ancestors came to America from England in the seventeenth century. Successive generations migrated west and south across Virginia, North Carolina, Kentucky, Tennessee, Mississippi, and into Louisiana. Barham's great-grandfather was one of the first sheriffs of Ouachita Parish. His grandfather served in the Confederate army and thereafter started a huge mercantile business, selling everything and anything related to farming. His father owned and operated one of the largest cotton plantations in northeast Louisiana. As a boy Barham spent countless hours hunting, fishing, and roaming about the family holdings on horseback. His parents taught him to trust in God, to strive to succeed, and to behave honorably and charitably toward others as befitted his privileged birth.

Barham grew up in the top echelon of the southern racial caste system. All the African Americans he knew as a boy were tenant farmers, many of whom worked his family's land. On Saturdays the farmers would go to town in horse-drawn wagons or buggies. Whenever Barham's father's car overtook a tenant's buggy or wagon, the black driver would pull over and tip his hat as the car passed by. Barham recalled that a friendly feeling existed between the races, but nobody dared to cross caste lines. "Our cook had a boy about my age," he said. "We played together every day, wrestled and talked. He was my friend, my buddy. Yet we didn't intermingle socially."

At first, Barham had mixed feelings about Brown's presence at the Academy. "I can't say I was enthusiastic about him being there," he admitted. Still, his family had taught him to treat others with respect, regardless of their race or color.

Moreover, commanding men in battle had amplified Barham's sense of noblesse oblige. Between surviving the destruction of the *Laffey* and joining the Executive Department, he had served as executive officer and then skipper of the destroyer *Dashiell*. The ship saw action at Tarawa, Kavieng, Saipan, and Guam. She provided close-in support to the Marines, frequently came under fire from Japanese artillery and machine guns ashore, and rescued survivors of landing craft hit during amphibious operations. Once the *Dashiell* picked up a Marine who had been shot through the head but was still alive. The bullet had passed just behind the man's eyes, severing his optic nerves. "Imagine floating around out there blind, abandoned," Barham said. During combat, Barham usually remained on the bridge, went for long periods without sleep, and lived on coffee and cigarettes. It was a hard life. Barham felt it was his duty to make it as easy as possible for his men to get their jobs done. Lives depended on it.

Barham carried this philosophy from the bridge of the *Dashiell* into the Fourth Battalion office in Bancroft Hall. After going through war, he wasn't about to let racism interfere with the ability of a man under his command to carry out his mission. Wesley Brown "was to get a fair shake," he recalled. "I was going to see that he was treated the same way any other midshipman was. I wasn't going to let him be imposed upon."[3]

Every upperclassman knew that the Class of 1949 included an African American. Most had already heard of Wesley Brown through newspapers or scuttlebutt. Any that remained in the dark about his presence became enlightened soon after classes began when the Executive Department passed word on how Brown was to be treated. Precisely how this was done remains unclear. Some midshipmen recalled the word coming down at a meeting or meetings of the first class; others recall it spreading informally, as would a rumor. However it was transmitted, the message was clear: Brown was to be treated no better and no worse than any other plebe. Anyone who discriminated against him would be punished.[4]

Feelings among upperclassmen about the phenomenon of a black midshipman varied from one individual to the next. To the vast majority, Wesley Brown's presence at the Naval Academy was an insignificant issue, nothing more than a curiosity. A few first classmen wondered what his "drags" would look like ("dragging" was midshipman slang for dating; "drags" were dates). But by and large, most upperclassmen were too concerned with their studies, sports, or girlfriends to worry about Brown or what implications a black Academy graduate might have for the Navy.[5]

As was the case in the 1930s, however, racist upperclassmen who wanted the Academy to remain lily white resented threats to the racial status quo. Most such midshipmen hoped Brown wouldn't graduate. Some realized that "the time had arrived" for the Academy to accept blacks. "It was a bitter pill for many of us," recalled a first classman from Illinois, "and I can't say I welcomed the change." Many southerners felt they could tolerate an African American as a classmate but had difficulty with the idea of a black officer commanding white enlisted men. "A few midshipmen, mostly Southern, were emphatic that a black had no place in a wardroom—so why send him to the Academy?" recalled a third classman. "But their emotion was more disgust than anger, and not so much personally directed at Brown as at whoever had arranged such an 'experiment.'"[6]

In at least one instance, a faculty member aired racist views in public. Midshipman 1/c Thomas J. Hudner, Jr., recalled hearing a southern-born civilian professor from the Department of English, History, and Government say, in class, that the "nigger" would "never get through." A native of Fall River, Massachusetts, Hudner would earn renown and receive the Medal of Honor during the Korean War for his heroic attempt to save the life of another Brown, his squadron mate Jesse L. Brown, the first African American naval aviator to fly in combat. Hudner, whose parents had never uttered a prejudiced word in his presence, was appalled at the professor's bigotry. The man dwelt at least two or three minutes on the subject of blacks at the Academy. He said that "the last nigger . . . never made it beyond plebe year" and that it would be the same for Brown. One wonders whether it was this same professor who had lowballed James Lee Johnson's English grades.[7]

If any other faculty members shared this professor's views, they kept it to themselves. No professor ever treated Wesley Brown with anything but fairness and propriety. "All through my years at the Naval Academy," he recalled, "my instructors treated me impartially. I never received special attention, either positive or negative."[8]

A few upperclassmen, however, discussed ways to ensure Brown's failure. "Most of the midshipmen from the southern states were overtly opposed to having any blacks at the Naval Academy," recalled a third classman from upstate New York. "There were certain southerners I knew of who were very anxious to rid the Academy of Wesley Brown."[9]

Other upperclassmen perceived the opposite attitude among southerners. "The general sentiment of my classmates from the South at that time was not to perpetuate what many considered an attitude repugnant to their intelligence," recalled a first classman in Sixteenth Company. "Having been removed from the environment where the attitude held sway [their hometowns], they were not as required to follow it as before, and could let reason govern." Joe Flanagan made a similar observation. "Southerners got more accepting of Wes than the Northerners did," he recalled. "Northerners had no relationship to blacks, really. The Southerners had grown up with them. . . . Northerners really didn't quite know how to handle him. I think they were, perhaps, more of a problem than the Southerners." A plebe in the Sixteenth Company best summarized the situation: "Attitudes toward Wesley among those in classes above him varied with individuals; prejudice obviously existed in some quarters. Not unexpectedly, southern midshipmen tended to be least supportive of him. But prejudice was not limited to southerners."[10]

Most upperclassmen did not discriminate against Brown. In fact, in stark contrast to the way James Lee Johnson was treated, many upperclassmen in the Sixteenth Company helped Brown. "I remember inspecting his appearance during one of our first meal formations," noted John J. Dempsey, a native New Yorker and first classman. Looking down at Brown's shoes, Dempsey remarked on "how important it is to maintain one pair of dress shoes to wear at any formation." First classmen traditionally helped plebes by offering such advice.[11]

Another first classman, John Van Velzer, counseled Brown about the hazing he would face. A Chicago native and midshipman ensign or "one-striper" and platoon leader in the Sixteenth Company in the fall set, Van Velzer lived down the hall from Brown. "I invited him to my room on the first day that he and the rest of the plebes joined the battalion," he recalled. "I told him that plebe year was extremely tough, and that he shouldn't think that he was being singled out when the normal 'bad stuff' occurred. I told him to inform me if the situation seemed [unclear]." If leaders among the first class had offered Johnson such support,[12]

Edward J. McCormack, Jr., a particularly popular and charismatic Sixteenth Company first classman, offered Brown his friendship. Son of a "saloon keeper" and "bookmaker" and nephew of Representative John W. McCormack (D-MA, later speaker of the House), Eddy McCormack was born and raised in South Boston. McCormack grew up amid prejudice toward every ethnic, racial, and religious group except Irish Catholics. Even so, he had never fully internalized those prejudices. As a young boy he had dreamed of becoming a priest and had read the Bible diligently, so his faith tended to mitigate the effects of prejudice on his outlook. His plebe year (1943–1944) roommate at the Academy was a Jewish kid from Brookline, Massachusetts, named Elliot Robert Rosenberg (later shortened to Rose). Since they had both grown up in the Boston area and both of their fathers were bookies, the two developed a close friendship. McCormack called him "Murph," which became Rosenberg's nickname throughout his time at the Academy. The first night that their plebe class joined the regiment, they received a visit from an anti-Semitic upperclassman who told Murph to "step outside" for a paddling.

"Can I ask a question, sir?" said Murph.
"Yeah," said the upperclassman.
"What have I done to warrant stepping outside and having you hit me
    with a broom?"
"Your name is Rosenberg, isn't it?"
"Yes."
"That's enough for me."

McCormack joined them. "He's my wife [Academy jargon for roommate]," he said to the upperclassman. "You beat his ass, you gotta beat my ass." The first classman obliged. "He beat our asses every night for,

I'd say, thirty days running," McCormack recalled. Despite the fact that
a prejudiced upperclassman was out to get Murph, McCormack stood by
his friend.[13]

Although Eddy McCormack had become a midshipman, he had never
envisioned a career in the Navy. His Uncle John had been grooming him
for a career in law. With that end in view, Eddy entered Colby College in
the fall of 1941. After the Japanese attack on Pearl Harbor, it seemed that
everybody McCormack knew in South Boston enlisted in the Navy, including his brother Jack. Eddy wanted to join the Navy too, but his
mother feared losing both of her sons at sea, so she and Eddy's sister prevailed upon him to enter the Naval Academy. He did so with an appointment from his uncle.

Eddy McCormack cut a memorable figure at the Academy. He was the
kind of guy who knew everybody and who everybody knew. Joe Flanagan remembered him as "one of the most incredibly foul-mouthed midshipmen who ever lived" and a "damned good" varsity lacrosse player.
Tom Hudner, also a classmate, remembered Eddy as "a little bit of a wise
guy" who was "picked on quite a bit" because of it. Eddy and Murph
"went around together all the time," he said. "Very often they would call
themselves by the other's name, just to pull the tails of the upperclassmen.
And because they both acted this way, they got their butts pounded a lot
more than if they had stayed more low key." McCormack's cockiness
stemmed from a feeling of invincibility because of his family's political
connections. He felt that nobody could touch him.[14]

As a result, McCormack always took hazing lightheartedly. "When I
became a youngster, and a first classman," he recalled,

if a plebe stepped out of line, and I was going to hit him with a broom, I
would do it by "swapping." I would let him hit me three times, which is
the normal thing, three whacks, and then I'd hit him three times. I did
that quite a bit. And more times than not, I did it with humor. I don't
ever remember hitting a plebe because I was bullshit at him or anything
like that. I generally liked the guy, and I would swap with him. And primarily because I thought I was really a good ass beater. I mean I got to
tell you, it was like almost doing the triple jump—hop, skip, and then
the whacking of the ass with the broom as you are coming into the
jump. And I don't care how big the guy was. I could lift him off the
ground. I was good. But I'd always make them hit me first because I did-

n't want them to see how I hit their ass. I had fun with hazing, you know, both as a hazer and a hazee.

It was during McCormack's Academy days that events combined with faith to banish racism from his psyche. During the summer cruise between his first and second academic years on the battleship *New York,* the chaplain gave a lesson about the good Samaritan. For the first time Mc-Cormack realized that Samaritans held a position in ancient society analogous to that of blacks in American society in terms of caste and segregation. Later that year, while he was driving home with a classmate for Christmas leave, McCormack's car got a flat tire. "We pulled into the median strip," he recalled.

It was tall grass. The jack would not raise the car up high enough to get the wheel off. A truck pulled off to the other side of the road. This fellow came over, a huge black truck driver. This guy had to be six foot four, six foot five. He had to weigh 280 pounds. I was, I will say, in awe or in fear of the size of this fellow. And he said, "What's the trouble?" And I said, "My jack won't raise the car high enough to change the tire." And he says, "Let me get my jack." So he got his jack. He raised the wheel and he changed the tire. And I took out ten dollars. Ten dollars was a lot of money in those days. And when he finished, I gave him the ten dollars and said, "I thank you very much. I don't know what we would have done without you. Take this as a sign of our appreciation." And this fellow said, "Oh, I couldn't take your money, because you're a fellow human being in need, and therefore it's my responsibility to help you." And I thought, "This is my good Samaritan."

Although McCormack never considered himself "born again," these incidents reshaped his attitude toward race in a seminal way. As a result, when Brown arrived at the Academy, McCormack was predisposed toward helping him. As a rule, upperclassmen did not speak to plebes outside the line of duty, but McCormack spooned on Brown and conversed with him regularly. "I think I got to know him fairly well," McCormack recalled.[15]

Two other first classmen also made Brown feel welcome in the Sixteenth Company. Roommates Frederick F. Jewett and Walter M. Meginnis "made an interesting North-South combination," as Jewett recalled.

Born in Schenectady, New York, and raised in four different states as a Navy junior, Jewett always wanted to be a naval officer like his father and never thought much about race relations before entering the Academy. Meginnis had dreamed of commanding a Navy ship since he was a boy. He was born and raised in Tallahassee, Florida, to parents who "stressed fairness and respect to all persons," as he put it. "There was never any emphasis that one race was superior to another. We were taught to be considerate of persons less fortunate than we and to be willing to help those in need." Neither Jewett nor Meginnis perceived Brown's coming to the Academy as a major event. "We agreed that if he were to keep his record clean and hold his own academically," recalled Jewett, "we were all for him. In fact, we 'spooned' on him and told him to keep us advised of any problems he encountered."[16]

Another Sixteenth Company first classman went a step further. Upon returning from his summer cruise, Howard Allen Weiss noticed that an African American plebe had joined his company. The legend about the black midshipman being found tied to a bell buoy in the Chesapeake back in the 1930s immediately leapt into his mind. "My God!" he thought. "This kid is going to have a terrible time."

Howie Weiss was born in Chicago and raised in the Jewish faith by parents who taught him that everybody was equal, regardless of race, creed, or color. Although his parents didn't keep kosher and only went to synagogue on high holidays, Howie at age nine began four years of Hebrew school to learn Hebrew and to prepare for the bar mitzvah. Despite the fact that he grew up in the thirties, the Depression had little impact on his youth because his father earned a comfortable living in the liquor business. After Hebrew school, Howie attended Pierce Grammar School on Chicago's north side, where he helped organize the school's first student government. After skipping ahead a year and graduating from Pierce in 1937, he entered Senn High School, also on the north side. It was a tough school, with a bad reputation for crime. After one year at Senn, Weiss entered Culver Military Academy in Culver, Indiana, thereby fulfilling a boyhood dream. Culver was a private prep school with a renowned equestrian program. Its students enrolled in the Army's Reserve Officer Training Corps (ROTC). "I really dearly wanted to go," Weiss recalled. "I loved everything about horses and Culver had a horse program that was incomparable." The program included polo, regular drill riding, rough riding, cross-country riding, and jumping. Culver's Black Horse Troop frequently went on tour and routinely rode in presidential inaugural parades. Weiss also loved the military discipline and regimentation at Culver, in contrast to many of his classmates, who hated it. Weiss excelled in both academics and horsemanship, becoming a lieutenant in the Black Horse Troop during his senior year.

Despite the fact that Culver groomed its students for the Army, Weiss had no ambition for a military career. During his senior year (1941) he applied for college, sending out only one application—to Harvard. His parents questioned the wisdom of applying to only one school, but Weiss was confident that he would be accepted. He was. He entered Harvard in the fall of 1941 and joined the Army ROTC program there. Toward the end of Weiss's second year at Harvard, his father Louis worried that the Army would perceive the need to call Howie and his classmates to active duty without first commissioning them (which is exactly what happened to Bill Sword). Louis reasoned that if his son got into the Naval Academy, he would get a decent education and would not be sent to war without a commission, so he arranged an appointment through his good friend, Representative Adolph Joachim Sabath (D-IL). Howie entered with the Class of 1947 in the summer of 1943.

Although Weiss loved the regimentation at the Naval Academy just as he had loved it at Culver, he regarded aspects of plebe indoctrination as nonsense, particularly paddling. He absolutely refused to let upperclassmen "beat his ass." Consequently, he spent much of his first year running the obstacle course before reveille and shoved out at mealtimes ("shoving out" involved pushing the chair away while maintaining a sitting position). "My memory is that I spent my whole plebe year shoved out," he said.

> I developed pretty good legs for kind of a skinny guy. I was known as an obstinate kid. People challenged that just automatically. I knew a dozen or more first classmen who were just on my tail all the time because of my obstinateness. So I made it far worse for myself than it was for most of my class. I really got very good at that obstacle course.

Nevertheless, Weiss survived plebe year, excelled in his studies, and began his senior year standing eleventh in a class of 852.[17]

Weiss had a gut feeling that some of his classmates would make trouble for Wesley Brown. Southerners, he recalled, could be "very charming fellows" and had many "good traits," but they could be "very wooden-headed about blacks." He figured Brown's presence would be "intolerable" to them. Although he had experienced anti-Semitism while growing up, it was not only a revulsion to prejudice that made him want to help Brown. The impulse also stemmed from Weiss's innate sense of fairness and love of challenges. "I just took one look at Brown and knew that there was trouble ahead," he said. "And I knew I could be helpful." Weiss spooned on Brown and decided to become his first classman.[18]

Custom dictated that every plebe was adopted by a first classman, who served as the newcomer's guide, mentor, and protector. "The relationship between them is unique," noted Kendall Banning in his primer on the Academy. It approximated

> that of a somewhat aloof older brother with his kid brother, without the fraternal tie and possibly without any special affection between them. The purpose of this odd relationship is to give the plebe a friend at court; an older counselor who is experienced in the ways of the Naval Academy and who may guard his younger charge in a semi-official capacity from running afoul of the rocks that beset his course.

A plebe usually visited his first classman a few minutes before each meal formation to have his appearance checked and to get advice.[19]

The relationship also usually had what Weiss described as a "mentor-slave" or "mentor–shoe shine" aspect, in which the plebe would shine his first classman's shoes, wash his gloves, or perform some other menial task in return for the first classman's guardianship. "Brown wasn't my plebe in that sense," recalled Weiss. "I didn't want him to shine my shoes. I wanted to help him, and see to it that things went all right. I don't think I was waving a flag for anything or anybody. I just knew there was going to be trouble."[20]

Captain Ingersoll also figured that there would be trouble. He determined to keep a close eye on the situation. Near the beginning of the semester he summoned Joe Flanagan to his office. Joe had recently been appointed midshipman captain or "six striper" in the fall set, making him the Academy's highest-ranking midshipman. Ingersoll asked him to look in on Brown from time to time, to see how he was doing.

Flanagan honored the commandant's request by deciding to become Brown's first classman, too. He paid Brown a visit, spooned on him, and asked him to be his plebe. Brown said that he already had a first classman, Howie Weiss. Flanagan explained that he had a direct wire to the commandant. Since they were in different companies, the only way for Brown to visit him legitimately, if Brown wanted to tell him something in confidence or to register a complaint, was as his plebe. So Brown had two first classmen.[21]

Joe Flanagan and Wesley Brown had an unusual first classman–plebe relationship. First, because of his responsibilities as brigade leader, a six-striper did not usually have a plebe. Second, a first classman and his plebe usually belonged to the same company, but Flanagan was in the Twenty-second Company and Brown, the Sixteenth. By taking Brown as his plebe—with the tacit support of the commandant—Flanagan reinforced the administration's message that it would not look the other way if anyone discriminated against Brown.[22]

Admiral Fitch involved another first classman in keeping watch on the situation. Born in Camden, Ohio, William Childs Patton was raised by parents who taught him to judge people on the basis of their accomplishments and the type of life they lived. He entered the Naval Academy for the education, but really wanted to become a Marine. He originally matriculated with the Class of 1946, but six weeks before he was to graduate, he failed a gunnery exam by three one-hundredths of a point and was turned back to '47. Now in his "second first class year," he was appointed midshipman lieutenant commander or "four striper" in the fall set. "Since I was the battalion commander of the 4th Battalion and because I lived diagonally across the corridor from Brown," he recalled,

> I was called to meet with the superintendent just prior to the new plebe class joining the brigade. The Admiral informed me that he anticipated there would be some harassment problems for Wesley. He emphasized several times that he wanted Wesley treated like any other plebe, "No easier, no harder!" He informed me that he was making me responsible for monitoring all instances where Wesley was put on report. To my knowledge my roommate [John Van Velzer] was the only other midshipman that was aware of this arrangement between me and the administration.[23]

Because he was a plebe, Wesley Brown began the semester unaware of who among the upperclassmen objected to his presence. He also remained unaware of the administration's actions to prevent anticipated discrimination against him. He expected to be hazed, like any other plebe. He figured that some upperclassmen might also haze him because of his race. As Van Velzer had advised, he decided that unless he could prove otherwise, he would assume that anyone who hazed him was doing so because he was a plebe. He figured that if anyone physically attacked him, he would fight back. Otherwise, as he had done during plebe summer, he would try to blend into the background and to conform to the regulations and plebe rates as closely as possible.[24]

Brown's effort to fit in impressed officers of the Executive Department. Commander Barham admired Brown's courage and the way he conducted himself. "Mr. Brown felt from the start and correctly so I think," Barham recalled, "that he would be under closer observation than his classmates, so he was meticulous in his efforts to comply with all Naval Academy regulations. He usually was first man at formations with an impeccable uniform and highly polished shoes. He felt like he had to do better than anybody else."[25]

Many of the upperclassmen in the Sixteenth Company also perceived Brown as a squared-away plebe. By and large, they found him to be quiet, unassuming, bright, decent, dedicated, and hard working.[26]

As the term began, Brown remained concerned primarily with following the rules and staying "sat," or satisfactory, in his classes. He joined the cross-country team and continued to play lots of tennis. One of his greatest fears was oversleeping. To ensure that he got up on time, he kept several alarm clocks and set them to go off at different times. Soon, he developed the habit of going swimming first thing in the morning. He lived in the wing next to the natatorium. He would get up as early as possible, throw on swimming trunks, a bathrobe, and a pair of slippers, walk to the pool, and hit the cold water. "That woke me up right away," he recalled. "I found that I was very, very alert for that first class."

Brown had no trouble academically. Although not a "star," Academy jargon for a top scholar, he steered clear of both the "tree" and the "bush," Academy lingo for, respectively, the posted lists of midshipmen who were failing a course and those who were barely passing. Brown enjoyed the humanities courses, especially history, more than the engineering and science courses. His best course was German. "Our language professor used to kid Wes about speaking German with a southern accent and me for using Yiddish words in place of German words," recalled classmate Harry Krantzman.[27]

Some of Brown's more difficult moments came at mealtimes, when upperclassmen subjected him to the usual round of plebe questioning. Occasionally Brown got the answers wrong and received orders to "come around." Sometimes he and his classmates had to "shove out." In one such instance Brown noticed one of the mess stewards watching him. Although Brown regarded this occasion as normal plebe hazing, the steward apparently thought otherwise, for he wore a serious expression on his face with tears in his eyes. Brown forgot his aching legs and worried that the steward might come over and punch out one of the upperclassmen. To his relief, the steward stayed put. The stewards did, however, tend to deliver extra desserts to Brown's table.[28]

When the fourth class had joined the brigade, the plebes had been distributed among different companies according to their foreign language preference. While Brown lost touch with classmates he had known during the summer, he made several new acquaintances among classmates in the Sixteenth Company. Brown's attitude and sense of humor helped his new acquaintances accept him. They were pleased to discover that he was not a vocal advocate of civil rights like Congressman Powell. "He never gave the impression he was fighting for a cause," recalled one plebe. Many of his Sixteenth Company classmates came to regard him as a stoic, diligent, likable, and cheerful fellow who always appeared positive and upbeat and who conducted himself in a gentlemanly and professional manner. A few considered themselves friends.[29]

Classmate Harry Meyer attributed the company's acceptance of Brown to its diversity. "Wes's being assigned to Sixteenth Company was for him a great step," he said. "That batch of 'kids' had so much mixed ethnic or breeding backgrounds that Wes could have been green or purple. My dad ran a gas station; another dad was a butcher; another a restauranteur; another a wealthy businessman."[30]

Having grown up in a segregated city, with limited exposure to Caucasians, Brown had thought of prejudice in terms of black and white. But at the Academy, he was surprised to learn that a white person, depending upon his own particular heritage, might also harbor prejudices towards those with Jewish, Catholic, Protestant, Mexican, Polish, Italian, or Irish backgrounds. He was particularly intrigued by the hatred that Irish Catholics and Protestants seemed to have for each other; he wondered how they could tell each other apart.[31]

Nevertheless, Brown did experience racial incidents at the Academy. Rumors about him ran rampant, the most common being that the NAACP was paying him to attend the Academy. One version had him drawing a monthly stipend, another had him receiving ten thousand dollars for each year he finished, and a third had him getting a lump sum upon graduation. Brown never received any such payment from the

NAACP; he was not a member at that time, nor did the organization ever contact him while he was at the Academy. Another rumor had it that Brown lacked genuine interest in becoming a naval officer and was trying to break the color barrier at the Naval Academy only for political reasons—that he was a "professional tradition breaker." Such rumors fueled animosity toward him.[32]

Upperclassmen who thought Brown was attending the Academy for political reasons occasionally confronted him. Some who believed he was on the NAACP payroll called him a mercenary and promised to make sure he *earned* the money. Others who believed that he was a "professional tradition breaker" or that a black Academy graduate would have no future in the Navy, bombarded him with questions. "Why are you here?" they would ask. "What are you trying to prove? What are you trying to accomplish? Do you really plan to serve in the Navy? If so, what will we do with you? Who's going to want you on board ship as part of the crew, or as part of the officers' mess? Don't you understand how people feel about this?"

"I expect to serve in the fleet," Brown would answer. "I'm not going to just graduate and disappear." Although Brown did, in fact, feel an obligation to his race to succeed, he truly wanted an engineering education and a career as a naval officer.

Sometimes Brown pointed out that the Navy had already commissioned blacks during the war, citing newspaper articles about the Golden Thirteen and other black naval officers. Many of his interrogators had been unaware of this fact. Some asked to see the articles. Fortunately, Brown had clipped and saved them and could produce them on demand. Even so, a few of the interrogators remained adamant that black officers had no place in the Navy. Brown never argued with them because he didn't want to make things harder for himself.[33]

Although Brown had prepared himself for such encounters, he found them disconcerting, for they underscored the awkwardness he sometimes felt living among whites. He often couldn't tell whether another midshipman was a bigot or not, so he reined in his outgoing nature and approached strangers cautiously. Rather than initiating friendships, he waited until others made the opening move. He later recalled that growing up under segregation had "burdened" him "with the problem of social readjustment" at the Academy. "It's like stepping into a new world. Unless you've had the experience, you have no idea what an impediment it is. It often makes you imagine nonexistent troubles and persecutions."[34]

Brown did, in fact, encounter hostility. A few prejudiced classmates shunned him. Some expressed their feelings openly by giving him dirty looks or by moving to another seat when he sat down beside them. Others ignored him when he spoke to them, acting as if he wasn't there.[35]

Worse, despite his best efforts to live by the book, Brown's name appeared early and often on the "frap sheet," the list of midshipmen with demerits, eerily echoing the experiences of Alonzo McClennan and James Lee Johnson. On the first day of the academic year, one first classman fried Brown three times, first for "Hat not squared," then for "Wearing dirty hat," finally for "Room in disorder." During the first few weeks, demerits rained down on him in bucketfuls. He noticed that "a small clique of upperclassmen" reported him frequently for minor infractions such as talking in ranks or marching out of step on the way to class.[36]

Nevertheless, Brown felt that the upperclassmen in his company were treating him fairly. To be sure, they would quiz him at mealtimes and have him do pushups at come arounds, but he never felt that they were discriminating against him because of race. Most of the demerits seemed to result from contact with upperclassmen from other companies. Brown tried to limit such "exposure" by remaining within his company area in Bancroft Hall whenever possible.[37]

A few plebes in the Sixteenth Company sensed that individual upperclassmen harbored negative attitudes about Brown. One perceived "hostility" toward him "from a lunatic southern fringe of upperclassmen." Harry Meyer occasionally overheard upperclassmen mutter derogatory remarks about Brown or express the hope that he wouldn't graduate.[38]

Still, many of the plebes in Brown's company saw nothing unusual in the way he was being treated. "I have no recollection of ever seeing him being hassled unduly by the upperclassmen," noted one classmate. "Of course I don't mean to imply that he didn't undergo the usual plebe training." Another classmate concurred. "The three upper classes treated Wesley just as they treated the rest of us—awful," he declared, "but there was never any discrimination, to my eyes."[39]

Several first classmen in the Sixteenth Company shared this view. "There was no effort made on the part of any midshipman or group of midshipmen to 'get him,' from within the Sixteenth Company or from outside the Sixteenth Company," asserted one Class of '47 alumnus. "In fact had there been such an effort, I am certain that the [first class] of the Sixteenth Company would not have permitted it." First classmen in other companies agreed. "I was not aware of any efforts to drum him out of the Academy," recalled Stansfield Turner, "and as Vice President of the Class and the Brigade Commander during the Spring Term, I believe I would have been aware of any such movements that represented more than an occasional disgruntled Southerner."[40]

Even William Patton saw nothing unusual about Brown's conduct record. Patton recalled that Admiral Fitch had ordered him to examine each delinquency report on Brown and to

> ascertain if it was within the regulation and fair. If it was suspect, I was to go to the upperclassman submitting the report and talk him out of it and, if I determined the report was not fair or legal, I was to destroy it if the submitting midshipman refused to withdraw it. That was what I did to the best of my ability. I probably made a mistake or two but I felt that if I erred I did so in Wesley's favor. I never saw any indication that he was hazed any more than most plebes.[41]

Several of Brown's classmates in the Sixteenth Company perceived the opposite, however. They felt that some of the upperclassmen were indeed discriminating against him. One classmate considered him a "marked man." "While Wesley had strong support from Academy officers and Midshipman officers," he recalled, "individual upperclassmen seemed to find ways to make things more difficult for Wesley than for the rest of us." Another plebe heard rumors that a number of upperclassmen were attempting to fry Brown "until he was 'chitted' out. That is, to place him on report for any number of minor violations until the amount of demerits accumulated to a point where he would be released for cause." Still another classmate characterized Brown as "a random target" for upperclassmen "who were down on him." "They would stop him when he was alone and just get on his case for no good reason," he recalled. Sometimes plebes in the Sixteenth Company were "also given a hard time by someone who just wanted to get on Wesley."[42]

The perception that Brown was a "marked man" caused many classmates to shy away from him. "People didn't want to be too closely associated with him," recalled a plebe in his company. Fellow fourth classmen generally sympathized with Brown, but tended to remain aloof because, as another plebe put it, "life was challenging enough." A classmate in the Thirteenth Company described the dynamics of the situation:

> The most desirable thing for a plebe to be was anonymous as possible, to remain in the shadows, not to be singled out or to be any more obvious than was absolutely necessary. Anything which drew attention to a plebe represented a special opportunity for hazing. We much preferred to make our trips down the halls when they were deserted, for example. Who knew what chance encounters with the "wrong" upper classmen might lead to? Wesley stood out like no one else. Ergo, he was a magnet for hazing, spontaneous, nefarious, what have you. Any direct contact with Wesley increased one's chances for more hazing, or so it was reasoned. No one told me to stay away; no one had to.[43]

Because so many plebes seem to have adopted this approach, some upperclassmen perceived Brown as a loner. "He appeared to have very few friends during his plebe year," recalled William Patton. "I got the impression that Wesley was a bit aloof and perhaps didn't make friends easily. This of course could have also been because other plebes were hesitant to associate with him." Joe Flanagan concurred. "He did not, as far as I can see, develop close relationships with any of his class," he said. "That must have made it terribly lonesome."[44]

Plebes in Brown's company made similar observations. "He made few close friends," recalled one. "I would characterize the general attitude toward Wes as friendly and supportive, but not necessarily overly so. He was largely a non-factor in Company activities, preferring his own counsel and company, perhaps to the relief of the rest of us." Another plebe described the relationship between Brown and his peers in the Sixteenth Company as "correct but not necessarily close." "This was partly us and partly him," he added. "Polite but distant."[45]

Nevertheless, some plebes did try to close the gap. "I went out of my way a little to be friendly with Wes," recalled company mate Harry Meyer. A plebe in the Thirteenth Company, William Thomas, did the same. "I felt very sorry for him during plebe year because he was so much alone," he recalled. "I knew how miserable I was and felt that his situation was that much worse because he lived alone and was probably a special target for some upper classmen. I did make a point of being pleasant to him whenever the opportunity presented itself for that reason."[46]

Other plebes befriended Brown simply because they liked him. These individuals were either undeterred by the extra attention Brown was receiving from upperclassmen or unaware of it. Kenneth Bott, from Jersey City, New Jersey, became friends with Brown early in plebe year and remained close to him throughout their time at the Academy. Despite his being in Annapolis, a naval career was the farthest thing from Bott's mind. He had gone to Rutgers during the 1942–1943 academic year, hoping to get into medical school, but his grades weren't good enough. To avoid being drafted, he joined the Marines. Although trained as an airborne radar technician, he opted on the spur of the moment for a fleet appointment to the Naval Academy. Since Bott's and Brown's last names began with "Bo" and "Br," respectively, they often sat near each other in class. "It didn't make any difference to me that he was black," recalled Bott. "We were pretty good friends." The son of a German immigrant butcher, Bott had grown up in Jersey City among people of diverse ethnic and racial backgrounds, so Brown wasn't a novelty to him. Being used to black people, having survived Marine basic training, and not necessarily thinking of the Navy as a career, Bott didn't care if some upperclassmen disapproved of his relationship with Brown.[47]

Harry Krantzman met Brown during plebe summer. A Jewish native of South Boston, Krantzman grew up among Irish Catholics, Syrians, Armenians, and African Americans. When prejudiced people called him "Jew," he shouted the rejoinder, "American Jew!" Such encounters with anti-Semitism imbued Krantzman with distaste for bigots. He had always wanted a military career and had enlisted in the Navy in 1943. While he was at Gunner's Mate School in Newport, Rhode Island, an announcement for a fleet appointment competition revived boyhood dreams of going to the Military Academy, so Krantzman applied to the Naval Academy. Of the three hundred sailors from the Schools Command who applied, only Krantzman and one other received the appointment. People like Bott and Krantzman had not only grown up in ethnically diverse neighborhoods; they had also seen much more of life before entering the Academy than most midshipmen who entered the Academy before the war had seen. Krantzman's two Academy roommates, Irving "Bob" Bobrick and Larry Washer, also happened to be Jewish. Brown frequently went to their room before formations and the four would make sure that each other's uniforms were in order.[48]

Brown perceived no social problems with the plebes in his company. He felt perfectly free during study hour to visit any of them if he had questions on assignments. He never knew that some of his company mates were deliberately maintaining their distance, since they all treated him with civility and several had befriended him. Besides, he was so busy studying, playing tennis, running, and keeping himself squared away that he didn't have time for a lot of friends anyway. Although many plebes and upperclassmen perceived him as a loner, Brown never considered himself one.[49]

As the semester wore on, Brown found himself spending more and more time marching extra duty tours. Despite his best effort at following the regulations and plebe rates, the demerits still piled up. Soon they numbered in dozens, then in scores, then over a hundred. "For weeks a small group of upperclassmen really worked me over," Brown recalled. "I thought this treatment would never stop, and it discouraged me." Brown suspected that some of the delinquency reports being filed on him were spurious—that in certain cases, the upperclassman who had reported him had lied. In virtually every such instance, Brown had no basis upon which to challenge the report. He was being fried for things that were nearly impossible to disprove, such as marching out of step on the way to class. In some cases, an upperclassman would file a report in the morning and Brown would sign it that afternoon, unsure of whether he had committed the alleged offense or not. In other cases, he was certain of his innocence, but if he challenged such reports, it would be his word against that of an upperclassman and, traditionally, the administration accepted the upperclassman's version. Often, Brown never knew whether a report was fair or not. An uneasy suspicion began to well up inside him: "I developed a feeling that maybe they were trying to run me out of the place."[50]

A number of upperclassmen reached the same conclusion. "I was aware that a small group of upperclass, primarily first class with the authority to place midshipmen on report, were out to get Brown," recalled a Class of '48A alumnus, "but I have no idea who they were, or any of their plans."[51]

Howie Weiss had a clearer picture of the situation. He knew that some of his classmates were filing false reports, and he also knew who they were. "A group of firstclassmen from the South," he recalled,

a very tight knot of them, you know, a dozen, dozen and a half, two dozen, were out to get him. They were just plain out to get him. And the way they were going to get him was through demerits. Which was very clever. You know, they weren't going to get him by tying him to the bell buoy, or by lynching him, or anything that could get them into terrible trouble. They were going to get him by demerits. And they were throwing demerits around. You just couldn't believe what he was getting demerits for. I mean, you know, where the ordinary person would be told to do this or that, and that would be the end of it, he'd get three demerits. This was a concerted effort. This was not haphazard. Now he didn't get 150 demerits in one day, which I suppose would be physically possible under the circumstances. But he got as many demerits in one day, or one week, as you'd expect somebody to get in one semester. Just for the pettiest, most ridiculous things that are overlooked in all other instances.

Weiss recalled that the "knot" of midshipmen out to get Brown were undistinguished in classwork, in sports, in leadership—indeed, in anything but prejudice.[52]

Occasionally an upperclassman would stop harassment of Brown in its tracks. In one such instance, Alfred G. Wellons, a second classman, confronted a group of third classmen. Born in Vicksburg, Mississippi, and raised in Memphis, Tennessee, Wellons was used to seeing blacks relegated to using separate bathrooms and water fountains and sitting in the back of the bus. Nevertheless, he objected to blatant mistreatment of any human being. "All plebes were required to square corners, walk in the center of the aisle, and so forth," he recalled. Brown

> came walking down a corridor as I was returning to my room, which was on a corner. And he squared the corner and made the turn and was walking straight toward me. There were some third class, who were former classmates of mine by then, they were the Class of '48B, started giving him a rough time about not squaring the corner, about not doing this, and not doing that, and his uniform looked so and so, and this and that, and I happened to walk up and said, "Look, he squared that corner just as perfect as any plebe I've ever seen. You guys are just taking it out on him because of who he is. Now let him alone."[53]

Robert Peniston, a classmate of Wellons who was born in Missouri and raised in Kansas, recalled a similar experience:

> I lived near the exit to the 2nd wing on the ground floor or "swabo" deck. One day I was near the exit when Mr. Brown was coming toward the exit in the middle of the passageway, finned out [hands open, fingers straight], eyes in the boat [looking straight ahead] and all that which

plebes are supposed to observe when outside their rooms. I heard some remarks coming from one of the rooms telling Mr. Brown to fin out, look more military, etc. Knowing this was coming from a room occupied by classmates of Mr. Brown, I entered and asked what in the hell these clowns had in mind in hazing a classmate and proceeded to give them a severe tongue lashing among other things.[54]

Once Brown returned from class and found all the linen pulled off his bed and his books scattered about the floor. Anger replaced shock as he realized that someone had set him up for demerits. On his desk lay a note to report to the battalion office. He did so. The officer of the day asked whether he had made his bed before going to class. Brown replied in the affirmative. "I thought so," said the officer. "Just forget it." In stark contrast to what would have happened to James Lee Johnson, no demerits resulted.[55]

When Eddy McCormack heard rumors that some of his classmates were trying to bilge Brown out on demerits, he remembered the parable of the good Samaritan and the black truck driver and offered Brown shelter. "I let it be known to him that if at any time he needed a place to hang out, a place to hide, if you will, that he was always welcome in my room," he recalled. "And on occasion, he would take advantage of that offer." Brown visited McCormack about twice a week, usually just to chat. He considered McCormack a friend, a "natural politician," and a "very warm guy." "If there was anybody in our company that I felt perfectly at ease with, it was Ed," Brown recalled. "He knew how to make people feel good."[56]

Sometimes those who encouraged Brown incurred the wrath of their peers. Brown ran on the cross-country team with a first classman from Plains, Georgia, Jimmy Carter. Class of '47 alumnus Walter Moyle recalled that Carter "came under a fair amount of heat" from fellow southerners because he was an "outspoken" proponent of equality. "He was treated as if he was a traitor," Moyle said, "because here he was from a small rural town in Georgia, and he was lined up with the others who were looking out for Brown."[57]

Brown remembered the future president as being friendly and supportive. One incident in particular came to mind. Brown had gone to a first classman's room outside his company area for a come around. The first classman made him do two or three sets of forty-nine pushups. Brown emerged from the room looking shaken and flustered. Carter

stopped him, put his arm around him, and offered a few words of encouragement. As they parted company, Brown heard someone call Carter
a "God damn nigger lover."[58]

Like Alfred Wellons, Jimmy Carter had grown up in a rigid racial-caste
society. All the white men in Carter's childhood were arch-segregation-
ists. His mother, Miss Lillian, was the exception. Unlike other white
women, she allowed black children to eat with Jimmy in her kitchen. She
was the only white person in town who went into black people's homes
to help out when they were sick. She happened to attend the first Brooklyn Dodgers game in which Jackie Robinson played and was the only person in her section of the bleachers to stand and applaud when he ran out
onto the field. Jimmy leaned toward his mother's views on race, even
though he knew they ran against the mainstream.[59] Nevertheless, when
Brown first came to the Academy, Carter struggled with the concept of
equality.[60] But when Carter sensed that certain classmates were out to get
Brown, images of how segregation had eroded boyhood friendships with
African Americans haunted his thoughts. A poem he wrote later in life
captures one of these images:

> This empty house three miles from town
> was where I lived. Here I was back,
> and found most homes around were gone.
> The folks who stayed here now were black,
> like Johnny and A.D., my friends.
>
> As boys we worked in Daddy's fields,
> hunted rabbits, squirrels, and quail,
> caught and cooked catfish and eels,
> searched the land for arrowheads,
> tried to fly the smallest kite,
> steered barrel hoops with strands of wire,
> and wrestled hard. At times we'd fight,
> without a thought who might be boss,
> who was smartest or the best,
> the leader for a few brief hours
> was who had won the last contest.
>
> But then—we were fourteen or so—
> as we approached the pasture gate,

they went to open it, and then
stood back. This made me hesitate,
sure it must have been a joke,
a tripwire, maybe, they had planned.
I reckon they had to obey
their parents' prompting. Or command.

We only saw it vaguely then,
but we were transformed at that place.
A silent line was drawn between
friend and friend, race and race.[61]

Such poignant memories led Carter not just to acknowledge Brown's right to equal treatment but to encourage him as well.[62]

After Fred Jewett and Walter Meginnis had spooned on Brown, they kept a weather eye on his progress. "At first everything seemed to go well," Jewett recalled, "but then the word started circulating around that a few of our classmates, including one or more members of the great football team, were out to 'get' Midshipman Brown." As with Howie Weiss, the image of the black plebe tied to the bell buoy popped into Jewett's mind. He had heard the story from his father, a Class of 1920 alumnus. "I put out the word—fully supported by my roommate," Jewett said, "that if Brown were to be given any kind of trouble, it would be over our dead bodies, or words to that effect." Classmate Tom Hartigan recalled that Jewett assembled the midshipman company officers "to discuss the manner in which Wesley Brown was to be treated." The upshot was, according to Hartigan, that the company officers "resolved to do everything in our power to see that Wesley Brown was treated fairly. We felt it would be unjust to treat him less than fairly because of race."[63]

Walter Moyle perceived the emergence of a "north-Midwestern contingent who made it a point to take Brown under their wing." "I picture the key element being from Minnesota, and Michigan, northern Midwest," he recalled. "They were very active." Another Class of '47 alumnus recalled that Howie Weiss gained a reputation among his classmates for being "diligent in seeing to it that Brown was NOT inappropriately treated or unreasonably physically hazed by over-zealous or bigoted upperclassmen."[64]

Weiss numbered Brown's supporters in the hundreds, compared to the dozen or two first classmen trying to fry him out. He perceived "a war going on" between those out to get him and those out to help him. Joe Flanagan considered Brown's presence a far less divisive issue. "It was only those with a sense of mission, one way or another, who were concerned about Brown, negatively or affirmatively," he recalled.[65]

From Flanagan's perspective, it was one individual in particular who was giving Brown the most grief. One day Flanagan discovered that a "wrestling companion from upstate Pennsylvania" had been filing false delinquency reports on Brown. The wiry six-striper confronted the perpetrator, nose to nose. "Now look," he said, "you keep doing this, you're going to get in a little problem. With me." Thereafter the wrestler treated Flanagan like a pariah, but stopped filing false reports. Those out to get Brown must have found it disconcerting that popular and respected first classmen like Flanagan, Weiss, McCormack, and Carter openly supported Brown.[66]

Joe Flanagan never heard a discouraging word from Brown. Because Flanagan was the brigade commander and in a different company, he had less contact with Brown than other first classmen had with their plebes. He certainly had less contact with Brown than Weiss did. Flanagan occasionally dropped in on Brown, and Brown, in turn, visited Flanagan's room about once a week. The two would discuss the weather, their families, or goings on at the Academy. Brown also got along well with Flanagan's roommates.[67]

Brown liked Flanagan, but sometimes seeing him proved troublesome. "When I left my battalion to go over to Joe's room," he recalled, "I had to go through several other company areas, and that was hostile territory." First classmen he didn't know stopped him for spot inspections or to ask questions. These encounters occasionally led to come arounds. Sometimes he was stopped en route to such a come around, resulting in yet another come around. "I was a moving target," he recalled. Nevertheless, he never complained to Flanagan.[68]

Brown never complained to Howie Weiss about unfair hazing, either. Since they both belonged to the same company, they had a more normal first classman–plebe relationship. Brown found Weiss to be extremely helpful in prepping him for the questions the first classmen were asking. Besides *Reef Points*, first classmen often quizzed plebes on subjects they were studying in their own classes. Weiss "was on top of everything that his class was studying," Brown recalled. In general he found Weiss to be an excellent mentor and "very protective." Weiss, in turn, found Brown to be a strong, upbeat individual. Brown regularly discussed his conduct record with Weiss, but never mentioned hazing and always remained circumspect with regard to his treatment. Weiss became upset when he suspected that a classmate had filed a false report. "That so and so," Brown remembers him saying. "He made that all up."[69]

Through these daily visits, Brown also got to know Weiss's roommates. Stan Schiller, an old friend of Weiss from Chicago, spooned on Brown and filled in as his first classman when Weiss was unavailable. Weiss's other two roommates, Barney Martin, another Chicago native, and Leroy Stafford, from Alexandria, Louisiana, were cordial but maintained their distance. Both were polite to Brown, but neither wanted to get involved.[70]

Weiss and to a lesser extent Schiller took heat from classmates for mentoring Brown. Brown recalled that "people were always saying to them, 'Why are you doing this?'" Weiss remained cool during such encounters, but Schiller became argumentative. Weiss knew that some of his classmates thought ill of him for helping Brown, but he didn't care what they thought.[71]

But Stafford did care. Suspicious of Brown at first, he warmed up as he got to know him. He realized that Brown genuinely wanted a naval career; he was not there just to make a political statement. Even so, he told Brown that he wouldn't go out of his way for him. "I still have my prejudices," Brown remembers him saying, and "I'm under enough pressure as it is from the other guys."[72]

Brown, too, felt pressure, especially on days when everything seemed to go wrong. Sometimes when he was section leader, he found himself on report for someone in his section talking. One day he received a package from home. He tore it open eagerly. When his gaze fell on a can of peaches, he froze. His mother had thought the peaches would be a nice treat. Little did she know that midshipmen were prohibited from keeping food in their room that required preparation, which, according to the regulations, included "opening of cans."[73] Brown stared at the can, wondering what to do. He decided to put it in the trash, uncovered. He then went off to class. When he returned, he found himself on report. Although he had never before challenged a delinquency report, he did so this time. The report did not stand.

Once Brown added up the number of days till graduation. It totaled more than a thousand. "Oh God," he thought. He never did that again. Instead, he took it one day at a time, viewed each day as a fresh start, and tried not to carry over the worries of a bad day into the next. He adhered to his policy of viewing hazing as normal plebe stuff instead of as being racially motivated. He assumed that other plebes were getting the same treatment, if not worse.

Mail from friends, visits from his parents, and social calls in town helped raise his spirits. One of his parents, usually his mother, visited him almost every week. On most Saturdays, Brown visited people in the black section of Annapolis, just off Church Circle between West and Northwest Streets. He had met several Annapolitans in Washington and at Highland Beach before coming to the Academy. He had become acquainted with Dr. Aris T. Allen, for example, at Howard, when both were going through the Army Specialized Training Reserve Program there. Dr. Allen introduced him to others in Annapolis's black community, where Brown's name was already well known from the publicity surrounding his matriculation. Several people stopped him in the street and invited him to drop by any time. Soon everyone in town, white or black, got to know him. Visiting people in Annapolis gave him a welcome respite from the usual pressures of being a plebe, as well as from the unique pressures of being the only black midshipman. No matter how bad things got, he always had Saturdays to look forward to.

He could also take comfort in the fact that a number of classmates and upperclassmen were rooting for him. It was obvious that people like Howie Weiss, Joe Flanagan, Eddy McCormack, Jimmy Carter, Fred Jewett, Walter Meginnis, Bill Patton, Harry Meyer, Harry Krantzman, and Ken Bott were on his side. There were others who, by a gleam in their eye or a nod of their head, signaled their support as well.

Sometimes it was fun to be a plebe. John Van Velzer devised a special order for indoor meal formations on rainy days. With the midshipmen at attention, he would give the command, "Groucho, MARCH," at which everyone began emulating the mannerisms of Groucho Marx. Such expressions of "authority" enlivened otherwise dull occasions. Brown and the other plebes liked the laid-back Van Velzer and his infectious brand of wry humor.[74]

All in all, Brown enjoyed the first year as much as any plebe could. He never seriously considered resigning. Because of chums and silent supporters at the Academy and friends in town, he never felt lonely. He seemed to be slowly winning acceptance throughout the brigade. His biggest concern remained the demerits.[75]

Weiss never believed that Brown was in danger of physical attack, as his Reconstruction-era predecessors had been. In fact, other than the demerit situation, Weiss thought Brown was having a normal plebe year. But awareness that demerits could get Brown expelled unsettled him. Occasionally, he discussed the situation with Joe Flanagan.

Weiss concluded that the flood of delinquency reports would have to be stopped if his plebe was to graduate. Because of the procedure by which demerits were issued, Executive Department officers were certainly aware that Brown was accumulating demerits at an unusually high rate. Since the total kept climbing, Weiss doubted that the officers were going to stanch the flow. He had no wish to bilge his shipmates, but he felt he had to do *something*. He telephoned Congressman Sabath's office. Although he never got through to Sabath, he described the situation in detail to the congressman's administrative assistant. According to Weiss, as a result of his call to Sabath's office, that October, or thereabouts, a congressional subcommittee launched a quiet investigation of Brown's treatment at the Academy.[76]

Commander Barham also took action. He did notice that first classmen were filing delinquency reports on Brown at a rate well above average for the fourth class. "They were coming through almost daily," he recalled. "He was getting reports on unmilitary conduct, talking in ranks, just anything they could find." Barham sensed that something was "amiss." "When a midshipman is put on report, you usually don't suspect the person putting him on the report," he explained. "You look at the circumstances." Since he considered Brown an "exemplary" plebe, he began to suspect that upperclassmen were singling him out because of who he was. "This was not an organized effort," he opined, "but it probably was discussed among the first classmen who were the participants."

Barham began examining reports on Brown more closely. Those he deemed legitimate, he let stand. If he thought a first classman had filed a spurious report, he tried to discourage him from doing it again. "For instance if Mr. Brown was reported for room in gross disorder," Barham recalled, "I would have the reporting midshipman accompany me and we would together inspect both Mr. Brown's room as well as that of the reporting midshipman." Barham always found Brown's room "in a superior condition." In such cases the commander discarded the report. "This flurry soon subsided when it became evident that this tactic would not be allowed," he said. Even though filing a false report was a Class "A" offense, Barham chose not to discipline midshipmen "for being unfair to Mr. Brown." Making "a big deal out of this thing only would exacerbate the situation," he reasoned.[77]

Adam Clayton Powell, however, decided that "making a big deal" out of it was exactly the thing to do. On 5 October 1945, Powell sent Secretary of the Navy Forrestal a letter alleging that he had received information from a "reliable source" that Brown was "not receiving fair and equal treatment." The letter said that a "concerted effort is being made to bring about his dismissal,—that his papers are being 'undergraded,'— and that he is not being informed in advance concerning offenses for which demerits are to be given." Forrestal ordered an investigation of Powell's charges.[78]

On 19 October the commandant summoned Brown to his office. Visibly angry, Captain Ingersoll showed him Powell's letter. "What's your problem?" he asked Brown. "Why didn't you come to us rather than go to your congressman?"

Brown was stunned. He had never even complained to Howie Weiss, Joe Flanagan, or anyone else about his treatment, let alone to Powell. Brown swore that he had nothing to do with the letter. Ingersoll asked him whether he felt his grades were fair. Brown said that he was satisfied with the results of his daily quizzes and that he had never seen his name on the "tree" or "bush." He said that Powell's letter seemed "silly." He offered to telephone the congressman right then and there, to tell him that the statements in his letter to Forrestal were false. Ingersoll advised him not to do so.[79]

The commandant took Brown at his word. He sent a memo to the superintendent outlining his meeting with the black plebe. "Midshipman Brown's conduct is handled in exactly the same manner as that of any other midshipman," Ingersoll wrote.

> For every one of his conduct cases the report has been referred to him in the customary manner, and he has in each and every case initialed the report signifying whether he did or did not wish to make a statement. His demerits at the present time are by no means excessive, and they were awarded for offenses which were clear-cut and absolutely fair.

He added that Brown was "very honest" and seemed more concerned about Powell's letter than about the demerits. The superintendent forwarded Ingersoll's memo to Forrestal. The secretary, in turn, used the memo as the basis of his reply to Powell, dated 23 October. "The work at the Naval Academy is far from easy," Forrestal wrote. "Midshipman Brown has apparently applied himself diligently, and to date his record has been satisfactory. It would seem unfortunate should the pursuance of his Naval career be further complicated by unusual and unnecessary publicity."[80]

The last sentence proved ironic indeed, for on the same date that Forrestal signed his reply to Powell, a story about the congressman's letter to the secretary appeared on the front page of the *Washington Post*. The story included most of the text of the 5 October letter. A similar story appeared in the *New York Times*.[81]

That day, 23 October 1945, marked the beginning of Brown's worst time at the Academy. Since the *Washington Post* was delivered to many rooms in Bancroft Hall in those days, virtually everyone knew about the Powell letter. When Brown stepped out of his room to pick up the paper, he noticed looks of "disapproval and hate" emanating from company mates down the hall. He wondered what was going on. Then he looked at the paper and saw the story. It absolutely mortified him. He realized that the other midshipmen would probably react as Captain Ingersoll had. They would assume that he had cried to his congressman, and they would despise him for "talking out of school."

Brown turned to his friends for help. "I was so shaken that I didn't want to be by myself," he recalled. First, he explained the situation to Howie Weiss. The thought that Brown had complained to Powell never crossed Weiss's mind. "I knew that he hadn't done anything like that," Weiss recalled. "It would be totally out of character for him." But Weiss realized that the Powell letter put Brown "in an extremely bad light." Still, Weiss told him not to worry about the article, since he had nothing to do with it.

Brown then called on Eddy McCormack. On the verge of tears, he told McCormack and Harry Krantzman, who happened to be in the room visiting his own first classman, that the article was baseless. He expressed concern that it would reverse the acceptance he was slowly gaining. He asked for help. McCormack promised to spread the word among the first class that Brown had nothing to do with the story. He advised Brown to tell the truth if anyone asked.

After leaving McCormack's room, Brown, Krantzman, Larry Washer, and Bob Bobrick lined up and "chopped" or trotted down the fourth wing's spiral staircase to formation and fell into ranks. A first classman approached, but before he could say anything to Brown, the platoon commander faced them into a column and marched them off to breakfast. They entered the mess hall, chopped to their table, and braced up.

"Well," said another first classman, "I see you made the papers this morning, Mr. Brown." Before Brown could reply, Howie Weiss politely nudged him away. Thereafter the meal proceeded as usual, except for Brown's heightened tension.[82]

Later that day, Brown talked to Joe Flanagan about the Powell letter. Flanagan found it inconceivable that Brown would have had anything to do with it. He told him not to worry.[83]

After reading the article in the *Washington Post,* Fred Jewett had a talk with Brown. Brown expressed misgivings that other plebes believed that he had indeed cried to Powell; some even thought he had planted the article in the *Post.* Jewett counseled Brown to ignore the pettiness of his classmates, carry on, and do his best.[84]

Other midshipmen reacted to the Powell letter in various ways. Some hardly noticed it. Others launched into intense discussions about Brown's presence at the Academy. Many read the allegations about Brown's mistreatment and thought, "Poor baby." A few upperclassmen made the plebes at their table in the mess hall shout "Mr. Congressman! I'm being picked on!" and similar taunts. Brown never heard such razzing, but classmates from other companies told him about it.[85]

The Powell letter prompted Midshipman 3/c Donald R. Morris and several other upperclassmen from New York to ask their congressmen to get Powell to stop meddling in Brown's affairs, for it was embarrassing Brown. It also prompted Morris to spoon on Brown and offer him support.[86]

A number of midshipmen took a dim view of Brown, undoubtedly believing that he had indeed complained to his congressman. For some, the Powell letter confirmed the rumor that Brown was attending the Academy only for political reasons. New rumors sprang up that Brown was merely a political "tool" of Powell and that certain midshipmen were ratting out abusers of Brown to Powell. One rumor even had it that the FBI was on the lookout for abusers. Such rumors angered a group of southern plebes outside the Sixteenth Company, who began referring to Brown among themselves as "that damned nigger."[87]

From Brown's perspective, the Powell letter did more harm than good. Brown wanted others to accept him not as an African American midshipman but as just another midshipman. He feared that Powell's letter was interfering with that goal. "Everybody was really angry and disgusted at me," he recalled. If anything mitigated such feelings, it was the fact that the *Washington Post* article included a statement from Brown's mother: "Wesley hasn't said a thing to me except that he was getting along fine." Rosetta's words supported Brown's contention that he had never complained to anyone, especially Powell. Still, months passed before the distrust aroused by the incident evaporated.[88]

It turns out that Adam Clayton Powell had lied to Forrestal. "I deliberately fabricated that letter in order to make sure that nothing would happen to Wesley Brown," Powell wrote in his autobiography. Neither Brown nor anyone in his family had complained to him. Powell probably got the idea to make accusations concerning grades and demerits from the James Lee Johnson case. It was by sheer coincidence that he had mentioned demerits. But he had stumbled onto a genuine problem.[89]

Despite the unease it caused Brown, however, Powell's letter might well have had its intended effect, perhaps in conjunction with the investigation precipitated by Weiss's call to Sabath's office. In any case, several upperclassmen recall that sometime after the story appeared in the *Washington Post,* a special meeting of the first class was convened. Accounts vary as to the date of the meeting, whether it involved the first class in the Sixteenth Company, Fourth Battalion, or the entire brigade, and whether the commandant, Fourth Battalion officers, or midshipman officers presided. By all accounts, however, the bottom line was clear. The Executive Department put out the word that it would tolerate no spurious delinquency reports on Brown. Nobody was to put Brown on report, unless it was for a legitimate, clear-cut infraction. Anyone who did otherwise would be jeopardizing his future in the Navy. The meeting supposedly brought the run of spurious demerits against Brown to a screeching halt.[90]

Whether a big, dramatic meeting stopped them suddenly, or subtler action like that taken by Commander Barham ended them gradually, efforts to fry Brown out on demerits ceased because of decisive action by the Executive Department. Brown received 103 demerits during the first semester and only five during the second, totaling 108 for plebe year.[91]

After the Executive Department squelched the campaign against Brown, rumors of reverse discrimination sprouted throughout the brigade. Some midshipmen believed that first classmen had become afraid to fry Brown for real offenses, enabling him to "get away with murder." Others believed that Executive Department officers were tearing up legitimate delinquency reports on Brown. One rumor even alleged that the administration had empowered Brown himself to approve or disapprove delinquency reports against him! Another rumor had it that he was going to graduate regardless of his performance. "Brown was so closely watched by faculty, administration, and Washington politicians," recalled a second classman, "that he could not bilge out if he tried." Some midshipmen heard that Eleanor Roosevelt was applying political pressure on the administration to ensure Brown's graduation. Others heard that midshipmen were being put on report for harassing Brown.[92]

Peer pressure not to harry Brown flourished alongside the rumors and probably exacerbated them. Midshipman 2/c Randolph F. Patterson, a Norfolk native with a "first family of Virginia" background, once found himself on the receiving end of such pressure. "I felt so sorry for [Brown], alone, seldom spoken to," he recalled, "that I stopped him in front of Bancroft Hall one day to ask how he was doing and lend encouragement. That night, I was called to a first classman's room and told to back off if I planned to graduate. I did. That's the extent of my association with Wesley Brown." Although Patterson had meant well, this particular first classman had misconstrued his intention. In fact, it seems that the first classman had discriminated against Patterson because he was a southerner.[93]

Some who believed that Brown was receiving preferential or special treatment from the administration resented him for it. Others figured it was necessary for Brown to get a fair chance.[94]

Brown, in fact, did receive special treatment. Executive Department intervention had been necessary to end the demerit campaign. Dozens of first classmen, both for and against him, had involved themselves in his life. After the rain of demerits stopped, upperclassmen in other companies treated him like any other plebe or, fearing the wrath of the Executive Department, kept their distance. While most first classmen in the Sixteenth Company treated him no better or worse than they did his classmates, Brown had gotten more spoons and made more friends among upperclassmen than did most of his classmates.[95] And Brown had fewer friends among classmates than other plebes, owing to the perceptions that being his friend would make life more difficult for them, or that he had indeed complained to Powell. But Brown did have friends; he was no hermit. Given the situation, special treatment was inevitable.

Brown was not privy to the Executive Department's warning to the upperclassmen about the consequences of filing false delinquency reports. Although the demerits stopped coming before Christmas, Brown's conduct record remained a matter of concern throughout the rest of the first semester, which ended on 1 February 1946. "I don't know what happened," he said. "I do know that at some point, things leveled off. But, now, my conduct was no different." He knew that he had done some "dumb" things for which he had been rightfully fried. He also knew that many of his demerits had resulted from false delinquency reports.[96]

Despite the fact that many of them were undeserved, the demerits adversely affected Brown's class standing. At the end of the first term, he stood 1,030th out of 1,049 fourth classmen in conduct. Academically, he stood in the bottom half of his class in all subjects, except German. He had not lived up to his academic potential because the extra duty resulting from unfair delinquency reports had robbed him of time he could have spent studying. Moreover, his demerit situation increased his general anxiety, often causing him to "clutch" or tense up and miss questions he would have otherwise gotten right during quizzes and exams in the latter half of the first semester. The problem was emotional, not intellectual. "I became known as a 'super-clutcher' because I worried so over the prospects of failing," he recalled. "Often I missed easy questions because of anxiety."[97]

During the second semester, however, Brown relaxed a little more each week as his name stayed off the "frap sheet." His grades improved as his anxiety abated. On academic work alone for the second semester, he stood in the top half of his class. He finished plebe year 617th of 953 midshipmen remaining in the Class of 1949 in "order of merit," a ranking derived from a formula combining classwork and conduct.[98]

June Week relieved whatever remained of Brown's anxiety about surviving plebe year. Mothers, fathers, brothers, sisters, aunts, uncles, friends, well-wishers, and future brides from all across America poured into Annapolis for six days of athletic events, parades, ceremonies, concerts, boat demonstrations, air shows, and garden parties under the glow of colored Chinese lanterns, capped by the graduation of the first class.

As they prepared for the big day, Howie Weiss, Joe Flanagan, and Eddy McCormack reflected on Wesley Brown. "I figured if he got by the plebe year, he had it made," recalled Eddy McCormack. "Once he had finished his plebe year, their opportunity to knock him out of the ball game was gone." Joe Flanagan concurred. "After he got through the first year, which is more than any black plebe had ever done up to that time," he said, "I knew that a whole new world opened up, and it would just become easier and easier." Howie Weiss agreed. "It seemed to me absolutely assured that he was going to get through," he recalled. "There was no longer any doubt. I felt absolutely confident that he was going to make it through the next three years."[99]

On 5 June 1946, the Class of 1947 filed into Dahlgren Hall amid a welcoming roar from the assembled crowd of family, friends, and underclassmen. For the first time four fleet admirals—Nimitz, Leahy, King, and Halsey—attended the graduation ceremony, along with five admirals, ten vice admirals, and nine rear admirals. After the invocation by the chaplain and a brief introduction by Vice Admiral Fitch, Fleet Admiral Nimitz delivered an address and distributed the diplomas. Then, Fleet Admiral Halsey administered the oath of office, after which the newly minted ensigns and second lieutenants flung their hats skyward with a resounding cheer.

Immediately following the ceremony, Wesley Brown and his classmates in '49 turned their hats backwards and their coats inside out and snaked danced through the previously forbidden walkways "Lover's Lane" and "Youngster Cut-Off" to the Herndon Monument. There they formed a human pyramid, up which one of their number scrambled to replace a plebe's "Dixie cup" cap on top of the greased obelisk with an upperclassman's cover, symbolically ending plebe year.[100]

The newly minted third classmen felt a tremendous sense of relief. First classmen still outranked them, but could no longer run them. There would be no more memorizing menus, looking up answers to silly questions, coming around, and walking braced up and down the center of corridors. They now rated dragging and going to hops, appearing outside their rooms in bathrobes, and eating meals in peace. They had survived one of the most rigorous weeding-out processes in America.

Although Wesley Brown experienced the same joyous feelings as his classmates, his transformation into a third classman carried a deeper significance. He had become the first African American midshipman to survive plebe year. James Conyers had served a full year in time, but had not met the academic requirements, bilging out upon failing the reexamination in the fall of what would have been youngster year. Brown, on the other hand, had successfully passed all of the academic, military, and athletic tests of the first year and had become a full-fledged third classman. Decisive action by the Executive Department and individuals in the Class of 1947 had crushed the campaign to fry him out on demerits. Brown now had a much more level playing field. Whether he would succeed in graduating or not now depended entirely on his own abilities.

Why did Wesley Brown become the first black midshipman to survive plebe year? His character played a decisive role. Throughout the year, Brown kept his nose to the grindstone and his upper lip stiff. His intellect enabled him to handle the academic work without undue difficulty. The habits he had learned in junior high and high school—working hard, working smart, budgeting his time—enabled him to maintain good grades, meet the military requirements, play sports, and engage in extracurricular activities. The self-reliance, self-discipline, self-esteem, and self-confidence instilled in him by his family and community enabled him to withstand the buffeting of racism, whether manifested in the relative social isolation from peers or the extra attention from prejudiced upperclassmen.

Brown's positive attitude and low-key approach contributed almost as much to his survival as his intelligence and mental toughness. It was patently obvious to any objective observer that Brown was squared away, trying his best to conform, and genuinely interested in a naval career. Throughout his plebe year, Brown never complained and sought to remain inconspicuous, an excellent survival strategy for any midshipman. Had Brown been a flamboyant, outspoken proponent of civil rights like Adam Powell or Dennis Nelson, fewer classmates and upperclassmen would have tried to help him.

At the same time, the Naval Academy was finally ready to accept a black midshipman. Unlike James Conyers, Alonzo McClennan, Henry Baker, James Lee Johnson, and George Trivers, Wesley Brown enjoyed support at all levels in the Academy hierarchy. Just before he was sworn in, the Navy Department, then in the midst of articulating its equal opportunity policy, ordered the Executive Department to ensure that he receive fair treatment. In 1945 it would have been politically infeasible for the Navy to condone unfair treatment of a black midshipman as it had done in the thirties.

But even without pressure from above, Aubrey Fitch, the superintendent, Stuart Ingersoll, the commandant, and Eugene Barham, the Fourth Battalion officer, would not have tolerated unfair treatment of any squared-away midshipman for any reason. Fitch, Ingersoll, and Barham had commanded men in combat, where anything that interfered with a subordinate's ability to get the job done threatened the whole command. None of these men intended to permit racism from preventing Brown from accomplishing his mission. On the broad canvas of their life experience, racist objections to a black midshipman and racist concerns over the implications of a black Academy graduate for the Navy paled into trivial insignificance.

From the start, the superintendent, commandant, and Fourth Battalion officer each took action designed to give Brown an even chance. Fitch had William Patton covertly monitor Brown's progress. Ingersoll's request that Joe Flanagan look in on Brown signaled the administration's support when the six-striper became the black plebe's first classman. Even Barham, who had been born into a social class whose very foundation was the racial caste system, remained adamant that Brown get a fair shake. When the demerits began piling up, Barham paid extra attention to Brown's delinquency reports, carefully reviewing the validity of each one. This action also signaled the administration's intention that Brown receive fair treatment.

Many midshipmen supported Brown as well. Popular or well-respected first classmen like Howie Weiss, Joe Flanagan, Eddy McCormack, and Jimmy Carter anticipated trouble and offered Brown help before it started. These men possessed unusually high levels of moral courage and had no fear of acting upon their principles, regardless of what others might say or do. Their open support of Brown helped prevent those out to get him from succeeding and doubtless discouraged other bigots from acting against him.

For plebes like Harry Krantzman, Harry Meyer, and Ken Bott, Brown's race simply didn't matter. Having grown up with black people and possessing more maturity than the average prewar plebe, they befriended Brown because they enjoyed his company and, like Weiss, McCormack, Flanagan, and Carter, they too possessed unusually high levels of moral courage and didn't care what others might think or do about it. Such midshipmen personified the general decline of racial prejudice in America during the forties.

Whatever pressure was placed on the fourth class to silence Brown was doomed to fail. Graham Leonard responded to such pressure by rebelling against it and befriending Brown. Likewise Bill Sword refused to cave in, because his Army experience and friendship with Joe Flanagan negated any fear of upper classmen he might otherwise have had. Those who offered to room with Brown either ignored the pressure to silence him or remained unaware of it.

Brown's most trying period at the Academy occurred during first semester, plebe year, after the upperclassmen returned from summer activities and the demerits began piling up. Acting alone or perhaps in small groups, some one to two dozen first classmen, largely southerners but also a sprinkling of northerners, tried to prevent Brown from graduating by frying him as often as possible, so that he would bilge out on demerits. Throughout the Academy's history, midshipmen had used this tactic to rid the Academy of plebes who, in their eyes, didn't fit in, for whatever reason. Midshipmen who survived plebe year were far less vulnerable to this tactic, because upperclassmen had far less power over one another than they had over plebes. This tactic proved decisive in the departures of McClennan and Johnson and landed scores of demerits on Brown's conduct record, undermining his morale and preventing his academic performance from reaching its full potential. The bigots' actions illustrate the fact that although racism was declining among some Americans, it remained as strong as ever among others.

The message that the administration would not tolerate unfair treatment of Brown drove efforts to "get" him underground. These efforts were so subtle, well camouflaged, and uncoordinated that many plebes and upperclassmen believed that Brown was being treated no differently than anyone else. Nevertheless, most plebes seemed to realize that Brown was indeed a "marked man." Consequently the majority of plebes minimized their interaction with him to prevent the ill treatment he was receiving from rubbing off on them. Most fourth classmen remained civil to Brown, however, and a few maintained their friendships with him despite the risk.

Several upperclassmen who perceived that Brown was being discriminated against took action to stop it. A few, like Alfred Wellons, witnessed and immediately stopped single instances of discrimination, but did not necessarily perceive any concerted efforts against Brown. Jimmy Carter knew that Brown was having a hard time and offered him moral support, despite taking heat from classmates for doing so. Fred Jewett and Walter Meginnis publicly declared their support for Brown and made it known that anyone who treated him unfairly would have to deal with them. Joe Flanagan, in a nose-to-nose confrontation, stopped a classmate from filing false delinquency reports on Brown. Howie Weiss went to his congressman to try to put an end to the demerit campaign against Brown. Support by well-respected first classmen severely undermined efforts to get Brown.

All in all, Wesley Brown enjoyed far more support from midshipmen—both classmates and upperclassmen—than had James Lee Johnson. The administration's message that it would not tolerate mistreatment of

Brown certainly facilitated this support. But it was largely a shift in the motivations and racial attitudes of midshipmen that accounted for the difference in the experiences of James Lee Johnson and Wesley Brown.

Midshipmen who entered the Academy during World War II differed from prewar midshipmen in several respects. A higher proportion had grown up with black people and had come to the Academy from the enlisted service. They were better educated; many had entered the Academy from the V-12 program with several semesters of college already under their belts. And like Howie Weiss, Joe Flanagan, and Eddy McCormack, many would never have entered the Academy if not for the war. Because of their maturity, because they were not committed to a naval career, or because prior enlisted service exposed them to experiences beside which plebe indoctrination paled, these World War II midshipmen were less vulnerable to pressure from upperclassmen or peers who wanted to rid the Academy of a black plebe than prewar midshipmen had been.

The decisive blow to the movement to get Brown resulted from Adam Clayton Powell's letter to Secretary Forrestal. By sheer coincidence, Powell exposed the demerit campaign against his appointee to full public scrutiny, thereby making it potential political dynamite. His letter to Forrestal spurred the Academy administration into action to head off trouble. The Executive Department spread the word, by whatever means, that it would not tolerate spurious delinquency reports on Brown. Because those who wanted to rid the Academy of Brown were unwilling to risk the wrath of the administration to achieve their goal, the demerit campaign ended. After plebe year Brown had much greater control over his own destiny.

9

Success and Celebrity

On 5 June 1946, the newly minted third classmen departed Annapolis for four weeks of leave. No longer being a plebe made Wesley Brown feel "like a human being," as he put it. He spent a week in New York City visiting a jazz musician he had met through a friend in Annapolis and getting to know Harlem. He spent the rest of the time at home.[1]

Youngster Leave, Academy jargon for the brief vacation following plebe year, expired at 4:00 P.M. on the Fourth of July. Two days later, the third classmen embarked on the battleships *North Carolina* (BB-55) and *Washington* (BB-56) for their first summer practice cruise. These cruises introduced the midshipmen to life at sea and to the various branches of the service while providing practical experience in gunnery, navigation, seamanship, engineering, and communications. Wesley Brown's group sailed on board the *North Carolina*. For three months the battleship steamed in the Chesapeake Bay, along the East Coast, and in the Caribbean, with stops at Newport, Rhode Island; New York City; Norfolk; Cristobal, Panama; and Guantanamo, Cuba. At sea, the duties of youngsters, as third classmen or sophomores were called, paralleled those of recently recruited enlisted men. When not attending lectures or drilling, Brown and his classmates spent their time standing watches or "turning to," becoming intimately familiar with holystones, chipping hammers, scrapers, wire brushes, and bright work polish. Friday—"field day"—they dreaded most, for they spent the whole day scrubbing and polishing the ship in preparation for a rigorous inspection by the skipper on Saturday morning.[2]

At first, Brown was a little apprehensive about how he would be received on board the *North Carolina*. From his point of view, racial integration of the fleet had not yet proceeded very far. To be sure, some of the African American sailors on the battleship had general service ratings, but most were messmen or stewards. How would the old salts among the crew react to a black midshipman?

Brown need not have worried. He and his classmates had little contact with the sailors on the *North Carolina*. One or two of the first classmen who supervised the youngsters treated Brown harshly, but Brown didn't feel singled out, for they were nasty to everybody. It seemed to Brown that he spent the entire cruise holystoning the wooden deck outside the skipper's cabin.[3]

The youngsters disembarked from the battleships on 27 September and classes began promptly the next day. Not being a plebe enabled Brown to focus more attention on his studies. As a result his grades improved, averaging 3.28 during the first semester and 3.25 the second. In the absence of efforts to "get" him, he received only eighty-three demerits that year, including the summer. His conduct grades were 3.37 for the first term and 3.55 for the second.[4]

Brown did not score as highly in "aptitude for the service." Midshipmen received an aptitude rating each term and on practice cruises. Along with academic and conduct grades, aptitude ratings determined a midshipman's class standing or "order of merit." According to the regulations, the aptitude rating was supposed to reflect a midshipman's "officerlike qualities; that is, those qualities which reflect his ability as a leader, his sense of duty, his military attitude and bearing, and his desirability in time of war." A midshipman's aptitude rating for each term was derived from "grease chits" received from his instructors, Executive Department officers, and every first classman in his company. There was no specified set of objective criteria for determining grease marks. Indeed, the whole process was rather arbitrary. Some midshipmen considered it little more than a popularity contest.[5]

Brown received a 2.90 in aptitude for the first semester and a 3.0 for the second and finished the year standing 770th out of 860. "Now I don't believe as an individual I was that bad, or off the ball, or showed lack of leadership," he recalled. Most of the low grease marks, he believed, came from midshipmen who probably had nothing against him personally but who still objected to blacks being midshipmen or naval officers. "I might have been a few numbers higher in class standing if I'd received even an average evaluation," he said.[6]

Prejudice still stalked him in other quarters as well. Some midshipmen continued to glare at him or get up and leave when he sat next to them. He tried to join the choir, but the director very apologetically informed him that the Academy just wasn't ready for a black tenor. Thus the administration denied him equal access to Academy opportunities.

Nevertheless, the year passed quickly and uneventfully, compared to plebe year. Youngsters enjoyed more leisure time and more privileges than plebes. Although barred from the choir, Brown found extracurricular activities that did not involve public appearances open to him and joined the Chess Club, Photo Club, and German Club. He continued to run cross country, which he did for the remainder of his time at the Academy. And he got to know his classmates better. Several of those who had been apprehensive about associating with a "marked man" during plebe year now spoke to him without reservation.

Following the graduation of the Class of 1948A in June 1947, the midshipmen of '49 became second classmen. Since the Academy had returned to the usual schedule of leave at the end of the summer, the second class boarded the carrier *Randolph* (CV-15) for the first overseas summer practice cruise since before the war. The *Randolph* departed Annapolis on 7 June, bound for northern Europe, making ports of call at Rosyth, Scotland; Goteborg, Sweden; and Portsmouth, England. She left Portsmouth on 18 July, stopping at Guantanamo Bay before arriving on 12 August at Hampton Roads.[7]

Brown and several classmates took a side trip to Copenhagen, Denmark. Few Americans had visited Denmark during or after the war, so the Danes gave the midshipmen heroes' welcomes in gratitude for America's role in defeating Nazi Germany. The Danes invited uniformed Americans into their homes for meals. Owners of many pubs, restaurants, and other businesses refused to accept money from them. The Brits and Swedes also welcomed the midshipmen warmly. "It was a good feeling to be an American," Brown recalled. "People respected us. They appreciated the war effort." The cleanliness, modernity, and prosperity of Sweden, which had escaped the ravages of World War II, contrasted markedly with the austerity and bomb-damaged buildings of postwar Britain, whose people had sacrificed so much in the fight against fascism. No racial incidents marred the cruise for Brown, and if he had any thoughts on the differences between the way Europeans and Americans treated black people, he kept them to himself.[8]

The carrier cruise aimed at interesting midshipmen in aviation, but for Brown the experience on board the *Randolph* had the opposite effect. The idea of a moveable floating airport had fascinated him as a child and he had looked forward to the carrier cruise thinking he might go into

naval aviation. While he did enjoy catapult launches and tail-hook re-
coveries, he disliked the "non-reg" approach and devil-may-care attitude
he observed among many of the World War II veterans of Carrier Air
Group 17. Nevertheless, he was gratified to see that one of the enlisted
plane captains and some of the mechanics were African Americans, billets that black sailors could never have held just five years earlier. But
what really turned him away from a career in naval aviation was the dive-
bombing exercise. Going into the dive excited him, but when the plane
pulled up, it felt like his stomach kept going down. He realized then and
there that he couldn't fly for a living.[9]

On 12 August, the second class disembarked at Hampton Roads. For
the next dozen days they participated in joint amphibious training near
Norfolk with their counterparts from West Point, and then they took four
weeks' leave.[10]

As was routine in those days, the second classmen were reassigned to
new companies at the beginning of the academic year. Brown and most of
his classmates from the Fourth Battalion, Sixteenth Company moved
over to the First Battalion, Fourth Company.[11]

During his second class year Brown improved his overall standing to
317 in a class of 802, while his standing in aptitude rose to 613. He received twenty demerits for the year.[12]

The social highlight of second class year was the Ring Dance, held on
29 May 1948, the Saturday preceding Graduation Day Friday. Brown attended the dance with Sylvia Hicks Johnson, a friend from Annapolis.[13]

For Sylvia, seeing the Naval Academy on a midshipman's arm was a
dream come true. Born in Baltimore on 25 November 1926, she came to
Annapolis with her family when she was about four or five, when her father, Charles E. Hicks, Jr., opened the Hicks Funeral Home, which eventually became the largest black-owned business in Annapolis. Sylvia's
mother, Ethel Hicks, worked periodically as a domestic. When Charles
died in 1939, Ethel took over the funeral home and Sylvia assumed the
responsibility of running the house.[14]

Charles and Ethel never talked about race or discrimination with
Sylvia and her brother. When she was a little girl, before she became
aware of race or the existence of prejudice, she often imagined going to a
hop at the Academy. "We used to sit on the step when the midshipmen
had their dances," she said. "We would watch the midshipmen and their
dates go by. Childlike, we would select one of the women to be us. We
would say, 'That one's me. That one's me.' You know, just childlike. We

didn't even have sense enough to know what discrimination was." Sylvia soon learned. The route she took to Wiley Bates High School, the black school, came within two blocks of Annapolis High School, the white school. "The white kids would come by on their school bus and spit out the window on the black kids as they passed," she recalled. After graduating high school in 1942, Sylvia continued to take care of the family home.

During World War II black Annapolitans still perceived the Academy only as a workplace and a source of entertainment—football games, basketball games, watching the midshipmen exercise in the gym on weekends—rather than as an opportunity for an education or a step toward a naval career. News that an African American had entered the Academy in the summer of 1945 electrified black Annapolis and thrilled Sylvia. "There's one of us in the Naval Academy!" she thought.

Dr. Aris Allen introduced Sylvia Hicks Johnson to Wesley Brown during Brown's plebe year. Sylvia and Wesley developed a friendship rather than a romance. Wesley visited her about twice a month throughout his time at the Academy. Since dating was forbidden during plebe year, Wesley visited her at home, but the two did not go out together. Even when he rated dragging, Wesley and Sylvia didn't go out in Annapolis much because the segregated town didn't have much for a black couple to do, so they spent most of their time together at her home. Wesley got to know Sylvia's mother and brother quite well. The young couple occasionally went to Washington, so Sylvia became acquainted with Wesley's mother, too.

Wesley never told Sylvia about the prejudice he encountered at the Academy, even during plebe year. Instead, he said things that bespoke his determination to succeed. "When I get to be an officer, . . ." he would say. He told her about things that all plebes had to do, such as eating square meals. "But he didn't talk about anything that wasn't fun," she recalled.

Sylvia was thrilled when Wesley asked her to the Ring Dance. Ever since she had been a little girl, she had longed to see the Academy from the inside. She never gave a thought to how she might be received as the first black woman to go to the Ring Dance—or to any Academy social function, for that matter. Her mother had taught her all the social graces, so she had no doubt that she could handle herself properly.

The Ring Dance, with all its attendant pageantry and spectacle, was the Academy's most colorful and important hop. Although well prepared in terms of politesse, Sylvia was still a little awestruck by the ambiance and the pretty dresses. A dinner in the mess hall preceded the dance. It was the only time midshipmen were permitted to entertain dates inside Bancroft Hall. Every other place at the tables included an orchid corsage, a souvenir bracelet, and two lengths of narrow ribbon, one blue and one gold. The date took her host's class ring, strung it on the blue and gold ribbons, and hung it around her neck.

The class ring was and is one of a graduate's most treasured possessions. It symbolized the midshipman's success, fidelity to classmates, and service to the nation. Only midshipmen who had completed three full years at the Academy rated wearing rings, and only those who graduated were permitted to keep them.

The dance itself took place in the gymnasium in Macdonough Hall. Streamers and Chinese lanterns brightened up the normally spartan room. Tables, chairs, and a small picket fence, arranged to look like an outdoor café, complete with vines and flowers, adorned the fencing loft. Bandleader Claude Thornhill and his orchestra supplied the music.

The crowning event of the evening arrived when each couple mounted the carpeted dais and passed through a large, gilded replica of the class ring, surmounted by a glowing globe of crystals that simulated the jewel. As each couple approached the archway, the woman took her host's ring from around her neck and christened it by dipping it into a binnacle containing water from the Seven Seas, symbolizing the journey that lay ahead. She then placed the ring on her host's finger, kissed him, then together they passed through the archway.[15]

Despite being the only black woman at the Ring Dance, Sylvia never felt uncomfortable. The other couples that she and Wesley sat with at the dinner table and the dance floor treated them warmly and naturally. Sylvia never got the sense that anyone was being nice to her because they felt they had to. No doubt Brown's general acceptance by his classmates made it easier for their dates to accept Sylvia. Also, the people they socialized with were Brown's friends.

Afterward, Sylvia's attendance at the Ring Dance became a big topic of conversation among her friends. They bombarded her with questions about what it was like. She filled them in on the details. Several who didn't think that they could have gone themselves admired her courage.[16]

For Wesley Brown, receiving his class ring made him feel that he had hit the "home stretch." The Ring Dance and Graduation Day marked his transformation into a first classman. On 5 June 1948 he and his classmates left Annapolis for Hampton Roads. Brown embarked on the destroyer *Ernest G. Small* (DD-838), which departed for the Mediterranean on the seventh, calling at Lisbon, Genoa, and Casablanca and returning to Norfolk on 21 July.

During the latter part of the cruise, the first classmen embarked in submarines and destroyers for six days of training in submarine and anti-submarine warfare. Brown sailed on the submarine *Finback* (SS-230). The closeness and degree of affection between the officers and men on the *Finback* impressed him.[17]

After returning from sea, Brown did well academically during his first class year, averaging 3.19 in his classwork. Although he tallied only twenty-five demerits, he continued to receive low grades in aptitude, standing 761 out of 791 in grease for the last semester. Still, he achieved the rank of midshipman lieutenant commander and led a platoon during Harry S. Truman's inaugural parade in January 1949. Possibly as a result of photos of Brown marching with his classmates that appeared in the newspapers, the First Battalion acquired the nickname "Black Dot Battalion."[18]

While Brown didn't haze plebes, he did participate in their indoctrination, quizzing them on *Reef Points,* naval history, and shipboard customs. He found that plebes and underclassmen respected him as much as any of his classmates.[19]

In the spring of 1949, the first classmen made their selections for their preferred branch of service. In keeping with his long-standing "edifice complex," Brown selected the Navy's Civil Engineer Corps (CEC). "My main interest was building buildings, roads, and bridges," he recalled. Also, the CEC seemed to offer the best training for a civilian engineering career should his naval career not work out. He drew lots with more than one hundred classmates for a commission in the CEC. He picked one of 18 lucky numbers, so the Navy granted his wish and slated him to continue his education at the Rensselaer Polytechnic Institute in Troy, New York.[20]

As graduation day drew near, the media spotlight began to focus on Brown. The press had been hounding the Academy for a story on him for years. During Brown's third class year, *Ebony Magazine* approached the Academy's public relations office, seeking to do a picture story on the black midshipman, while Lester Granger tried to obtain an interview with Brown for *Our World* magazine through Secretary Forrestal. During Brown's second class year, both Keystone Pictures, Inc. and *Today's World* magazine tried to obtain interviews with him. The Executive Department usually frowned upon singling out individuals for interviews but was willing to make an exception in Brown's case. Brown, however, declined. "I didn't want celebrity status that others would resent," he recalled. Such status would "probably make it a lot tougher to try to be an average Joe. So I didn't grant any interviews at all." But he did consent to be photographed for an article on the Cadet Corps in the Washington *Afro-American* with fellow Dunbar alumnus Edward Howard, then a second classman at West Point, and Brigadier General Benjamin O. Davis, Sr.[21]

Despite Brown's refusal to sit for an interview, Morris A. Bealle, writer and author of several books on sports teams, did a story on Brown for *Today's World,* a rabidly anticommunist magazine. The story had nothing to do with communism, however. It opened with discussions of African American sports "firsts": Jackie Robinson, the first black major league baseball player; Marion Motley, the first black professional football player; and others. "They have opened wide the door to negroes in professional sports," wrote Bealle. "They are outstanding colored men who have held their own with the best the white race has to offer."

Bealle then came to Wesley Brown. "But for our money," he wrote, "the colored boy who came up the hardest way . . . is a studious little chap who doesn't weigh 140 pounds soaking wet." The article provided few details about Brown's performance and nothing beyond speculation about his experience at the Academy. Bealle concluded nevertheless that Brown was "the colored race's champion of champions."[22]

In the spring of 1948, Garnet C. Wilkinson, first assistant superintendent of the D.C. public schools, sought to have Brown detailed as the reviewing officer for the regimental parade following the annual competitive drill among Washington's black high schools. Rear Admiral James L. Holloway, Jr., who had relieved Admiral Fitch as superintendent on 15 January 1947, turned him down because final exams were scheduled at that time. The Academy did, however, grant Florence Murray's request for information about the black midshipman for the next issue of *The Negro Handbook.*[23]

During Brown's first class year, the clamoring by reporters intensified. The *Minneapolis Tribune* ran a brief story on Brown, including a picture from the Academy's public relations office, as did the *New York Star. Ebony* and *Our World* magazines again requested interviews with Brown. *Life* magazine asked the secretary of the Navy's office for permission to do a photo story on Brown. Brown turned down all but one of the interview requests, as he wanted no publicity until graduation. Although he did speak to a reporter from the *New York Star,* he said nothing about the difficulties he had encountered during plebe year. The resulting article mentioned only that Brown had to walk a "social tightrope" but included no details. Otherwise Brown clung tenaciously to his no-interview policy.[24]

John P. Davis, publisher of *Our World* magazine, refused to take no for an answer. On 13 January 1949 he wrote directly to Brown, asking him to reconsider, explaining that national magazines needed some three months' lead time to prepare an edition for publication. "From another point of view," Davis added,

> the fact that it is likely that you will be the first Negro graduate of the United States Naval Academy, is a fact of extreme importance to all American people for it raises the hopes of first-class citizenship for several million Negro American youth. It is a demonstration to the whole world—at a time when America needs increasingly to give such a demonstration—that America is fulfilling its destiny as a democratic nation. Neither you nor the Naval Academy have the right to overlook the legitimate desire of a national publication, such as ours, to give wholesome and constructive publicity to such an event.[25]

The volume of inquiries from reporters about Brown reaching the Navy Department grew so high that in January 1949, the Bureau of Naval Personnel's Office of Public Relations assigned Lieutenant Dennis D. Nelson to coordinate publicity. Nelson was one of the original "Golden Thirteen" who had been commissioned in 1944 and became the second black naval officer to receive a regular commission after the war. He used his berth in the Bureau of Naval Personnel to see that the Navy implemented its new racial policy as quickly as possible. Although too junior to make things happen on his own, he functioned effectively as a thorn in the side of authority. When he saw various doors of opportunity closed to black sailors and officers, he did his best to kick them in, perhaps sacrificing his own chances for promotion in the process. Nicknamed "Dennis the Menace" by fellow members of the Golden Thirteen, he was proud, egotistical, flamboyant, debonair, and gregarious. Meticulous about his appearance, he only carried new money and always wore a clean and pressed uniform. His strangest idiosyncrasy involved his car. He was a fanatic about washing it. He washed it every day, regardless of the weather. But most significantly, he was an outspoken proponent of fairness and equal opportunity. "He felt that he was equal to anybody," recalled fellow Golden Thirteen alumnus Graham Martin. "And he carried himself in that peacock fashion. But make no mistake about it, he was a brilliant man." And he loved the Navy.[26]

Lieutenant Nelson warned Brown that reporters had a way of twisting a person's words to convey an unintended meaning. "You never know what they're going to say," he told Brown. Still, Nelson and other public relations officers in the Navy Department and the Academy agreed that Brown would have to talk to the press. After all, John Davis had a point.

Nelson and Brown worked out a solution. The public relations people wrote press releases and arranged for a Navy photographer to take pictures of Brown, depicting a typical day at the Academy, for distribution to "interested parties" during graduation week. To prevent reporters from misconstruing statements made in an interview, Nelson suggested that Brown himself write an article about his experience at the Academy. Brown liked the idea, so Nelson introduced him to Commander William J. Lederer, Jr., a fellow public relations officer, freelance writer, and future coauthor of *The Ugly American*. Brown had already received offers from several magazines to write his story. He discussed the offers with Lederer, who reiterated Nelson's warning about the press. "I would trust the *Saturday Evening Post* the most," Lederer advised. "They will give you a chance to look the article over and make sure it's what you want. And they won't change a word in it without your permission." Brown took the advice. On 10 May, he signed a contract with the *Saturday Evening Post*. The magazine agreed to pay him one thousand dollars for the article, a sizable sum for the time. To prevent complaints from the black newspapermen whose requests for interviews he had been declining for years, the public relations people suggested that Brown hold a press conference. That way he could deal with all of the reporters at once. The pictures of Brown taken by the Navy photographer would be distributed at the conference. Then, when his article appeared in the *Saturday Evening Post,* the black press could not criticize him for giving an exclusive story to a white publication. Brown agreed.[27]

The press conference took place on 26 May 1949. Reporters from the Associated Negro Press, the Associated Press, the *Chicago Defender,* the *Pittsburgh Courier,* the *Afro-American,* the *Washington Post,* the *Times-Herald,* the *Evening Star,* and *Time* magazine attended. The commandant and Lieutenant Nelson sat with Brown throughout the conference.

Brown answered the questions without prompting or restraint, sometimes making slight gestures with his left hand, sometimes pausing in thought before answering.

"Were you given the 'silent treatment' at the Academy?" asked one reporter.

"I've had a lot of people ask me that," replied Brown. "I can't say about the others before me. If you mean did the fellows speak to me— well, most of them did."

The reporter pressed. "But when you first came to the Academy—were the other midshipmen unfriendly to you?"

"It's very hard to say this or that is happening to me because I am who I am," Brown replied. "It was more like being the new kid in the class in high school. . . . Other than the fact of being new or different I'd say no to that question."

Another reporter asked Brown if the staff had been hostile to him. "The officers, professors and civilians here have been completely impartial," Brown declared.

Someone else asked Brown if he liked the publicity. Brown said no. He said that the press conference was not his idea. He didn't think he rated a press conference. He said that his record demonstrated that he was "just an average Joe around here." National media attention, he said, was a "cross" that he had had to bear for four years. "I hope the . . . fellows who come in later years will be spared," he said. "I feel it is unfortunate the American people have not matured enough to accept an individual on the basis of his ability and not regard a person as an oddity because of his color." The questioning lasted about an hour. Reporters found Brown "shy, modest, and retiring" yet able to answer "frankly and with a sincerity that would have done credit to vice admirals."[28]

June Week began three days later with the traditional baccalaureate service for the graduating class in the chapel. Brown took a different date to each June Week event.

Graduation day for Brown and his classmates came on Friday, 3 June 1949. Graduation exercises commenced at 11:00 A.M. in Dahlgren Hall. Brown's mother and father, aunt Harriet, uncle Granville, and Sylvia Hicks Johnson sat in the audience. Following an invocation by Chaplain Commander R. E. Bishop, and an address by Secretary of the Navy Francis P. Matthews, Admiral Louis E. Denfeld, the Chief of Naval Operations, administered the oath of office to the newly minted ensigns and second lieutenants, who then flung their hats into the air. Brown felt like he was throwing his hat over the moon. He graduated 372nd in a class of 790. Doubtless, he would have stood higher if certain upperclassmen had not tried to run him out during plebe year and if his peers had graded him fairly on aptitude for the service. He and his classmates had thirty days leave to celebrate and relax before reporting to their first duty station.

After the ceremony, reporters and photographers hounded the Academy's first black graduate. Brown eluded them for about half an hour, until one of them spotted him in Bancroft Hall and persuaded him to pose on the lawn with his mother. A reporter asked Brown how he felt. "I'm glad that it's all over!" he replied. Once outside, he was fair game for autograph seekers and photographers. Dennis Nelson and James C. Evans, a civilian assistant to the secretary of defense, had attended the ceremony and were photographed with Brown and his mother. Sylvia Hicks Johnson was photographed performing the traditional duty of placing Wesley's shoulder boards on his uniform and sealing the task with a kiss.

Finally, Brown managed to break away. He raced back to Washington in his recently purchased brand-new black 1949 Chevrolet business coupe to attend Howard University's graduation ceremony at Griffith Stadium. Frederic Stanton, secretary of Howard University, had invited him. While there, he had the opportunity to speak with Ralph Bunche, the African American diplomat, and Vijaya Lakshmi Pandit, India's ambassador to the United States and one of the most accomplished women of the twentieth century, both of whom received honorary doctorates that day. Brown sat through the entire ceremony in a state of emotional shock, while 917 individuals received diplomas in the largest commencement in Howard's history.

Afterward some two dozen of Brown's high school classmates came over to his parents' house to celebrate. The strain of a week's worth of high points, starting with the press conference, soon caught up to Brown. He went to bed well before midnight, exhausted. Many of his friends stayed. When he got up the next morning, a couple of the guys were just leaving.

The next day, Sunday, Wesley Brown went to church. Wearing his Navy uniform, he strode proudly through the doors. Just inside he saw his godfather, Sergeant Hewlett Smith, wearing his Army uniform. With tears in his eyes, Sergeant Smith saluted the young ensign. Wesley Brown was not only the first African American to graduate from the Academy, but the first in his family to attend and to graduate from college. He symbolized hope for a better future. With tears in his own eyes, Brown returned the salute.[29]

News about Brown's graduation quickly hit the street. Articles appeared in the *New York Times, Pittsburgh Courier, Afro-American, Time* magazine, and a host of other publications. Most of the articles included a brief account of Brown's predecessors, background information on Brown himself, statements from the press conference, and photographs supplied by the Navy. Some contained an account of the graduation ceremony along with pictures taken that day. They all put a positive spin on the event.

The black press put a political spin on Brown's graduation. "Ensign Brown represents more than an ordinary 'first,'" declared the *Pittsburgh Courier.*

> The granting of his commission should graphically illustrate that the United States has already lost the services of uncounted millions of talented youths whose potentialities have been stultified by bias and discrimination. Ensign Brown is ample proof that Negroes can deliver the goods if given an opportunity to do so. His name should rightfully be placed alongside those Negroes who have blazed notable trails in various fields of national endeavor.

An editorial in the *Afro-American* lamented that so many news organizations deemed it necessary to cover Brown's graduation. Were he white, argued the writer, the event would not have been newsworthy. "The fact that Ensign Brown is the first to break down this traditional barrier," it said, "made his graduation significant and made of him, as he put it, 'an oddity.' It has been ever thus with pioneers, regardless of race." The writer looked forward to the day when graduation of black midshipmen would become "commonplace," too ordinary an event to attract media attention.

The editorial then commented on how Brown got to the Academy in the first place. "Newspapers, national organizations and local groups have been fighting for over 50 years to get a colored youth through Annapolis," it said.

> Ensign Brown would never have entered Annapolis had it not been for this sustained campaign for representation. He could not have remained

there but for their prayers, counsel and personal intercession. He should be forever mindful of the obligation that he has and accept the fact that in his graduation, he becomes a symbol of victory of which all of us are proud and like to talk about.

A cartoon accompanied the editorial. It depicted Brown standing alone atop a wall labeled "U.S. Naval Academy," looking seaward at the fleet. Labels attached to each rung of a ladder propped against the wall suggested how Brown made the climb: "will power," a testament to Brown's abilities; "U.S. Congressmen," a reference to Adam Clayton Powell and evidently to others, perhaps Congressman Sabath; "press," a reference to how coverage of racism in the military drew political attention to the issue; and "other groups," presumably civil rights organizations.[30]

Brown's article in the *Saturday Evening Post* appeared in the 25 June 1949 issue. "I am the first Negro to be graduated from the United States Naval Academy," it began,

> but I don't see why this should excite a lot of attention. Thousands of other Negroes have accomplished far more. I wouldn't be writing this at all if there hadn't been so many queries and rumors. It seemed to me that if I wrote one article and personally gave all the facts—not hearsay and misinterpretations—it might make it easier for me to live a normal life in the Navy and enjoy being an anonymous cog in a machine.

Brown had written the article with Bill Lederer's help. Lederer suggested that Brown grease the flow of the prose with a bit of artistic license. For example, the article states that Brown had been "thinking about the Navy" since he was eight or ten, when he pinned a picture of the aircraft carrier *Lexington* (CV-2) to his wall. He did, in fact, have the picture, but only because the idea of a floating airport fascinated him, not because he wanted to be in the Navy. The article portrays his entry into the Academy as the result of a long-term plan, when actually it was much more a spur-of-the-moment decision. Stenciling his clothes was not the ordeal he portrayed it as in print. And he wrote about his graduation before it actually happened, using Lederer's own graduation with the Class of 1936 as a model.

Otherwise the article rang true. Brown had worried that the article might hurt his career, but Lederer had assured him that everything would be all right as long as he cast the Academy in a positive light. Brown generally did so, but did not dodge the issue of his treatment during plebe year. "For weeks a small group of upperclassmen really worked me over," he said. "I developed a feeling that maybe they were trying to run me out of the place. During my first month the demerits rained on me in bucketfuls. . . . A small clique of upperclassmen tried to work me over by reporting me for minor offenses."

But instead of attributing this treatment to racism, Brown blamed himself. "I guess the fact that I could be so easily identified in a crowd made my breaking of regulations stand out," he said. "Most of the demerits I received as a midshipman I got because I deserved them. I was no angel and broke my share of the regulations. When I got into hot water, I kept reminding myself, *Brown, you're in trouble because you're a dumb cluck and have made a mistake. You're getting the same treatment as your classmates.*"

This statement did not gibe with the reality of Brown's first semester, plebe year. Although he knew that some of the upperclassmen in the "clique" that "worked him over" had filed false delinquency reports, he ignored the subject of racism in the article. More than three years had passed since that awful first semester. To be sure, he had since received nasty looks from time to time, but for the most part, he had experienced the same things and received the same treatment as other midshipmen. The instances of discrimination—the false delinquency reports, not being permitted to sing in the choir, the open displays of disdain by a minority of racists, the low grease marks—were overshadowed by the positive experiences—making friends, lettering in cross country, playing lots of tennis, spending Saturday afternoons in town, getting ensign's stripes. To be sure, Brown avoided the subject of racism, at least in part, because he didn't want the trouble that could arise from an article denouncing the Academy stalking him during his career. But to dwell on the subject would simply have been out of character for Brown. He had never wanted to be seen as a black midshipman, but simply as a midshipman, a sentiment reflected in the advice he offered future black midshipmen. "The most important thing is fervently to desire a naval career," he declared at the end of the article. "Remember that while you are in the Navy you are an American naval officer first and a Negro second."[31]

In the weeks following graduation and the article's appearance in the *Saturday Evening Post,* Brown received hundreds of letters, cards, and telegrams from people around the world, congratulating him on his achievements. Many came from people he knew: Colonel Atwood; Lieutenant Benjamin Hunton, a military instructor at Dunbar; Lieutenant (j.g.) Edith DeVoe, the first black regular Navy nurse; and numerous friends and acquaintances. Many came from people he didn't know. W. Sylvester White, Jr., one of the Golden Thirteen, wrote, "We, as reservists strove for a standard of conduct and performance which, at least, would not prejudice the chances of the Negro we hoped the Academy would some day graduate. Your graduation has fulfilled those hopes." Francis J. Myers, a U.S. Senator from Pennsylvania, sent Rosetta Brown a telegram declaring that the example set by her son "will stand as a bright beacon to light the way toward a better future for all Americans."[32]

Brown received more than five hundred letters from people who read his article in the *Saturday Evening Post*. Most offered kind words. "Congratulations and God-speed to you in your career," wrote one white person whom Brown had never met. "No matter what my color were, I'd take my hat off to you." Ralph M. Jaeger, a graduate of the Class of 1908, echoed these sentiments. "Somehow I cannot help but feel that maybe your four years in the Academy were tougher than your story would indicate," he said. Ensign Ta-Tsai Liu of the Republic of China (Taiwan) Navy found Brown's article so moving that he had it translated into Chinese and published in his navy's official magazine. Only a handful of letters contained negative sentiments: "there's no place in the Navy for a black officer," "you should know your place," "now you'll want to marry a white woman," and the like.[33]

In addition to publicity and fan mail, Brown was feted at luncheons and dinners. On the evening of 20 June, the John Wesley Church held a banquet in Brown's honor. A few days later, he took a trip to Chicago for a two-day visit under the auspices of the Chicago Urban League. Dennis Nelson had arranged the event as part of a Bureau of Naval Personnel effort to recruit blacks into the NROTC program, so he drove Brown to the Windy City in his gray Studebaker convertible, stopping every hundred miles or so to wash it. They arrived on the twenty-ninth and checked in at the DuSable Hotel. That evening Brown attended a ball in his honor at the Parkway Ballroom, cosponsored by the American Legion and the Illinois National Guard. The next morning, Thursday, Brown and Nelson took part in a conference at Dunbar Trade School for young people interested in a naval career.

The climax of the trip was a luncheon sponsored by the Chicago Urban League that afternoon at the Blackstone Hotel, with Brown as guest of honor. Brown and Nelson were running late, so Nelson parked his car right in front of the entrance to the Blackstone. They hurried inside to the Crystal Room and took their seats. "I've been anxious to meet you," said a voice behind Brown. Brown looked up. Standing there was Jesse Owens, the African American hero of the 1936 Olympics in Berlin whose four gold medals and record-setting performances on a global stage symbolized the utter fallacy of Hitler's master-racism. Struck momentarily speechless, Brown stood up to shake Owens's hand. Owens then handed Brown his program. "Would you autograph this for me?" he asked. Brown was dumbfounded. Why on earth would a man of Jesse Owens's stature want his autograph? Brown recovered quickly and signed the program. Owens handed him several more and Brown autographed them, too. Brown then grabbed his own program and asked Owens to autograph it. Owens did so. "To Ensign Brown," he wrote. "My Best Wishes to a first. Good Luck Always." He then signed his name. Brown sat there in amazement while the president and the executive secretary of the Chicago Urban League and Dennis Nelson each made a few remarks. Brown spoke too, then he and Nelson went outside.

To his horror, Nelson saw a police officer writing him a parking ticket. It was not the ticket that mortified him. The officer had a foot propped on the Studebaker's running board. Nelson walked over. "Well," he said jovially, "I see Chicago's finest is right on the ball." Nelson admitted that he had parked illegally, adding that he had been late for an engagement in the hotel with the mayor. The officer continued writing without looking up. "Would you mind," Nelson said, gesturing. The policeman removed his foot. Nelson pulled out a handkerchief and wiped the footprint off the running board. With timing that couldn't have been scripted better, a limousine pulled up at the moment Mayor Martin D. Kennelly emerged from the Blackstone. Nelson sauntered over and struck up a conversation with Mayor Kennelly like he was an old friend. The police officer finished writing the ticket and finally looked up. The sight of Nelson chatting with Mayor Kennelly and his entourage took him aback momentarily. Then, without a word, he tore up the ticket.[34]

Six months later, the *Chicago Defender* named Wesley Brown and fourteen others, including politicians, Hollywood celebrities, and Jackie Robinson, to its "honor roll" for "outstanding contributions in advancing the frontier of American democracy in 1949." John Sengstacke sent Brown a letter of congratulations. "America can only grow through *Complete Citizenship* for all its citizens," he said. "Your efforts have played a major role in helping all Americans attain this goal." By break-

ing the color barrier at the U.S. Naval Academy, Wesley Brown symbolized black people's hope that one day they would attain full civil rights.[35]

Wesley Brown spent almost forty years acting out his "edifice complex." After graduating from the Naval Academy, he served briefly at the
Boston Naval Shipyard before attending Rensselaer Polytechnic Institute
in Troy, New York, where he received his bachelor's degree in civil engineering in 1951. He spent the next eighteen years in the Civil Engineer
Corps, building houses in Hawaii, a nuclear power plant in Antarctica,
and a desalinization plant at Guantanamo Bay, Cuba. The largest-scale
projects that he worked on were in the Philippines: construction of the air
station at Cubi Point, which, at the time, was the largest earth-moving
undertaking in the world after the Panama and Suez Canals, and construction of the aircraft carrier wharf at Subic Bay, where he served as
project officer and operations officer. His career included special assignments to Liberia, Chad, the Central African Republic, and Costa Rica, for
which he received a commendation for achievement from Secretary of the
Navy Paul H. Nitze in 1964. He retired a lieutenant commander on 30
June 1969 after twenty years of service. He believed that an unfair fitness
report from a racist commanding officer had kept him from making commander. Otherwise, he never had racial problems with any other Seabees.

After retirement Brown continued working as an engineer, first for the
State University of New York at Stony Brook, Long Island, until 1976,
then in the facilities planning department at Howard University, until his
second retirement in 1988. Since then he has lectured at college campuses,
played tennis, traveled with his wife, Crystal, and spent time with his four
children and six grandchildren. Public service remained an important
part of his life throughout his career and retirement. He was a member of
the Association for the Study of African American Life and History; the
NAACP; the American Civil Liberties Union; the John Wesley AME Zion
Church; and the National Naval Officers Association. He served as a
Naval Academy Alumni Trustee and a member and chairman of the D.C.
delegate's Congressional Nominations Review Board for U.S. Service
Academies. To recognize his pioneering role and to thank him for his con-
tinuing involvement with the Academy, in the spring of 2002, Vice Ad-
miral John R. Ryan, the superintendent, named a new field house after
him. Lately it seems to Brown that every February, during Black History
Month, some reporter or group asks him to recount his experiences as the
Naval Academy's first African American graduate.[36]

After he cleared the hurdle of plebe year, the rest of Brown's time at the Academy was relatively uneventful, racially speaking. Decisive action by the Executive Department had leveled the playing field, enabling him to succeed or fail on his own merit. After first semester, plebe year, he never encountered any further attempts to prevent him from graduating. At the same time, his social circle widened as more of his classmates proved willing to associate with him. Brown never had to endure complete social segregation, as did his Reconstruction predecessors at Annapolis or Benjamin O. Davis, Jr., at West Point.

Nevertheless, racial prejudice and discrimination continued to dog Brown during his upper-class years. He received lower grease marks than he probably deserved, a number of bigoted classmates still shunned him, and the administration barred him from the choir. Complete professional and social equality eluded Brown and would continue to elude black midshipmen for decades. Until the Naval Academy developed a formal equal-opportunity policy and institutionalized an associated organizational infrastructure in the 1970s, black midshipmen remained a token presence, were denied full access to Academy opportunities, endured partial social segregation, and maintained a black subculture to facilitate their adaptation to Academy life and to acquire what the larger culture denied them.[37]

Brown became a celebrity because in graduating, he had struck a blow against segregation. His success marked the culmination of a four-score-year effort to break the color barrier at the Naval Academy that had begun with the matriculation of James Conyers in 1872 and constituted a milestone on the road to freedom for African Americans.

Conclusion

Whether or not black midshipmen could succeed at the Naval Academy in any given period depended on national politics, the Navy's racial policy, other midshipmen's racial attitudes, and black midshipmen's own abilities.

Throughout its history, the state of race relations at the Naval Academy reflected American society. With Jim Crow fully ensconced in American culture throughout most of the period between the end of the Civil War and the end of World War II, only a handful of congressmen proved willing to appoint African Americans to the Naval Academy and only about two dozen black young men received appointments in that period.

During Reconstruction, national politics demanded that the secretary of the Navy and the Academy's top officers at least attempt to level the playing field for the three black midshipmen appointed during the 1870s. Nevertheless, these three suffered racially motivated mistreatment at the hands of racist white classmates. While the Academy's leaders tried to stop physical assaults, they condoned social silencing. Both forms of mistreatment exacerbated the black midshipmen's academic difficulties. Academic work was hard enough for the majority of midshipmen but was particularly difficult for black midshipmen, born in a time and place where it was against the law to educate black people. Because the Academy's leaders condoned social segregation, white midshipmen succeeded in using intimidation and harassment to prevent black midshipmen from graduating.

During the Jim Crow era, segregation in all of its manifestations returned African Americans to a state that closely resembled slavery, and opportunities for black sailors plummeted to their nadir. Between 1919 and 1933, the Navy barred black civilians from entering the service altogether. The only ratings available to black sailors who enlisted during the remaining years between the world wars were as cooks and stewards. Throughout this era, the Naval Academy maintained an insurmountable color barrier against blacks seeking to become naval officers.

By the 1930s, the Great Migration had given African Americans in Chicago enough political clout to seat black congressmen in the House of Representatives. These congressmen and other black activists targeted the Naval Academy as a symbol of American apartheid and sought to break the color barrier as a step toward securing full equal rights for African Americans. Washington, D.C.'s black community figured prominently in these efforts because of Dunbar High School's national reputation. Furthermore, Colonel Henry O. Atwood wanted to break the color barrier at Annapolis and to create symbols of black pride in the tradition of Colonel Charles Young, who had graduated from the U.S. Military Academy in 1889.

More African American appointees would have become midshipmen between 1929 and 1941 had they passed the Naval Academy's entrance exams. Evidence suggests, however, that Navy officials falsified examination results to exclude African Americans during this period.

While the two African Americans who did matriculate during the 1930s received support from some midshipmen, met resistance from others, and were studiously avoided by most, they received less than no support from the officers in the Academy's Executive Department. In fact, the Executive Department's policy of malign neglect ensured that the two black midshipmen would never graduate. Since there was no place in the Navy for black officers, the Academy's leadership reasoned, there was no place at the Academy for black midshipmen. The commandant of midshipmen even said as much to one black plebe. No African American, however well qualified, could have graduated under these circumstances. From the standpoint of the Navy's racial policy, blacks remained persona non grata in every level of the officer corps.

World War II wrought profound changes in the economic, political, social, and cultural lives of African Americans, accelerating their transformation from a predominantly rural, agrarian population into an urban, industrial one. Mobilization for total war forced American industry and the U.S. armed forces to tap previously underutilized sources of labor, particularly African Americans and women. The exigencies of the war effort, coupled with increasing militancy among African American leaders, organizations, and the population in general, accelerated the emigration of black people from the South, increased their political power, afforded them unprecedented economic opportunities, and broadened their participation in the armed services.

Because of the need to mobilize all of America's labor power, and because of political pressure on the Roosevelt and Truman administrations from civil rights advocates, the Navy revolutionized its written racial policy during World War II. The political pressures and manpower imperatives of global war, along with an innate sense of fairness, inspired Secretary Forrestal to spearhead the transformation. Under his leadership, segregation by occupation gave way to limited integration. By the end of the war black sailors were no longer restricted to the messman's branch but found most enlisted billets open to them, at least in writing. Most significantly, the Navy commissioned its first African American officers. It would take decades and another upheaval in American society, however, before the Navy's actual racial practices caught up with its racial policy.

The movement within the black community to break the color barrier at the Academy stalled during World War II. With thousands of African Americans pouring into the enlisted service and only a few dozen trickling into the officer corps, activists shifted their attention from the Naval Academy to the much larger goal of eliminating discrimination against black sailors.

Nevertheless, what remained of the movement to break the Academy's color barrier resulted in the matriculation of a lone black midshipman. Like the African Americans appointed in the 1930s, Wesley Brown received support from some midshipmen, met resistance from others, and was avoided by most. Unlike his predecessors, however, he had more friends than enemies. The small minority of upperclassmen who didn't want to see a black midshipman graduate and were willing to do something about it mounted a campaign to run Brown out on demerits, just as their racist predecessors had done to ensure that Brown's African American predecessors didn't graduate.

This time, however, the administration was bent on giving the black midshipman the chance to succeed or fail on his own merit. Pressure along the entire chain of command—from fellow plebes, upperclassmen, midshipmen officers, Executive Department officers, the secretary of the Navy, and congressmen—crushed the effort to run Brown out and leveled the playing field. As a result, Brown became the first black midshipman to succeed.

Although some might argue that the graduation of an African American from the Naval Academy was inevitable, Brown's ability, attitude, and timing decisively affected the outcome. James Conyers had enjoyed some support from the administration but did not have the scholastic training necessary to survive. James Lee Johnson had possessed all the requisite academic, athletic, and social qualities, but lacked support from the Academy's hierarchy. Wesley Brown had both the requisite talent and administrative support, the latter stemming in part from political pressure. Yet, by making the adjustments necessary to make Brown's graduation possible, the Academy took the first step in transforming itself from a racist institution to one that today ranks equal opportunity among its fundamental tenets.

Notes

Abbreviations

BD MacGregor, Morris J., and Bernard C. Nalty, eds. *Blacks in the United States Armed Forces: Basic Documents.* 13 vols. Wilmington, DE: Scholarly Resources, 1977

BMPJ Midshipman Personnel Jacket, s.v. Wesley A. Brown, Class of 1949, box 4, Special Collections and Archives Division, Nimitz Library, United States Naval Academy, Annapolis, MD

BMS Wesley A. Brown Papers, Moorland-Spingard Research Center, Howard University, Washington, DC

BOSMR Official Service and Medical Record, s.v. Wesley Anthony Brown, service number 521291, National Personnel Records Center, St. Louis, MO

FDRL Franklin Delano Roosevelt Library, Hyde Park, NY

JMPJ Midshipman Personnel Jacket, s.v. James L. Johnson, Jr., Class of 1940, box 8, Special Collections and Archives Division, Nimitz Library, United States Naval Academy Archives, Annapolis, MD

LC Library of Congress, Washington, DC

MCHS Arthur Wergs Mitchell Papers, Chicago Historical Society, Chicago, IL

MPJ Midshipmen Personnel Jackets, Special Collections and Archives Division, Nimitz Library, United States Naval Academy, Annapolis, MD

NA National Archives and Records Administration, Washington, DC

NAACPLC National Association for the Advancement of Colored People Papers, Library of Congress, Washington, DC

NHC Naval Historical Center, Washington, DC

OA Operational Archives, Naval Historical Center, Washington, DC

OF Roosevelt, Franklin D., Papers as President, Official File, Franklin Delano Roosevelt Library, Hyde Park, NY

PPF Roosevelt, Franklin D., Papers as President, President's Personal File, Franklin Delano Roosevelt Library, Hyde Park, NY

PSF Roosevelt, Franklin D., Papers as President, President's Secretary's File, Franklin Delano Roosevelt Library, Hyde Park, NY

RG 24 Record Group 24, Records of the Bureau of Navigation and the Bureau of Naval Personnel, National Archives, Washington, DC

RG 45 Record Group 45, Naval Records Collection of the Office of Naval Records and Library, National Archives, Washington, DC

RG 80 Record Group 80, General Records of the Department of the Navy, National Archives, Washington, DC

RG 405 Records of the United States Naval Academy, Special Collections and Archives Division, Nimitz Library, United States Naval Academy, Annapolis, MD

USNA United States Naval Academy, Annapolis, MD

NOTES TO THE PREFACE

1. The term "midshipman" was used originally by the Royal Navy to designate an experienced seaman stationed amidships to relay orders fore and aft. In the seventeenth century it became a rank for officer apprentices. Midshipmen went to sea at ages twelve to sixteen and literally grew into officers. The U.S. Navy adopted the Royal Navy's usage of the term and, with the founding of the Naval Academy in 1845, applied it to students of that institution. Jack Sweetman, *The U.S. Naval Academy: An Illustrated History* (Annapolis: Naval Institute Press, 1979), 4–6.

NOTES TO CHAPTER 1

1. Eric Foner, *Reconstruction: America's Unfinished Revolution, 1863–1877* (New York: Harper and Row, 1988); Eric Foner and Olivia Mahoney, *America's Reconstruction: People and Politics after the Civil War* (New York: Harper-Collins, 1995).

2. Peggy Lamson, *The Glorious Failure: Robert Brown Elliott and the Reconstruction in South Carolina* (New York: Norton, 1973), 12–13.

3. Herbert Aptheker, "The Negro in the Union Navy," *Journal of Negro History* 32 (April 1947): 169–200; W. Jeffrey Bolster, *Black Jacks: African American Seamen in the Age of Sail* (Cambridge, MA: Harvard University Press, 1997); Frederick S. Harrod, *Manning the New Navy: The Development of a Modern Naval Enlisted Force, 1899–1940* (Westport, CT: Greenwood Press, 1978), 3–4; Bernard C. Nalty, *Strength for the Fight: A History of Black Americans in the Military* (New York: Free Press, 1986), 14–28, 43, 79–80; Joseph P. Reidy, "Black Jack: African American Sailors in the Civil War Navy," in *New Interpretations in Naval History: Selected Papers from the Twelfth Naval History Symposium,* ed. William B. Cogar (Annapolis, MD: Naval Institute Press, 1997);

and David L. Valuska, *The Afro-American in the Union Navy: 1861–1865* (New York: Garland, 1993). Approximately 18 percent of the 115,000 men who served in the Union navy were black, for a total of 20,700 African American sailors.

4. Park Benjamin, *The United States Naval Academy* (New York: Putnam's, 1900), 284–85.

5. U.S. Department of the Navy, *Regulations of the United States Naval Academy as Approved by the Secretary of the Navy, March 4, 1869* (Washington: Government Printing Office, 1869), 9; Peter Karsten, *The Naval Aristocracy: The Golden Age of Annapolis and the Emergence of Modern American Navalism* (New York: Free Press, 1972), 5–7, quote from 7.

6. Foner, *Reconstruction,* 352, 443; Lamson, *The Glorious Failure;* Bruce Ragsdale and Joel D. Treese, *Black Americans in Congress, 1870–1989* (Washington: Government Printing Office, 1990), 45–47.

7. Benjamin, *United States Naval Academy,* 291–92; file 2202, "James H. Conyers," box 40, Entry 403, RG 24, NA; Edmund L. Drago, *Initiative, Paternalism, and Race Relations: Charleston's Avery Normal Institute* (Athens: University of Georgia Press, 1990), 43.

8. Quoted in Karsten, *The Naval Aristocracy,* 37.

9. U.S. Department of the Navy, *Regulations,* 5; Paolo E. Coletta, ed., *American Secretaries of the Navy,* 2 vols. (Annapolis, MD: Naval Institute Press, 1980), 1:369–77; William S. McFeely, *Grant: A Biography* (New York: Norton, 1981), 301.

10. Later "commandant of midshipmen."

11. U.S. Department of the Navy, *Regulations,* 5–7.

12. Benjamin, *United States Naval Academy,* 284; William N. Still, Jr., *Ironclad Captains: The Commanding Officers of the USS Monitor* (Washington: National Oceanic and Atmospheric Administration, 1988), 3–12; Jack Sweetman, *The U.S. Naval Academy: An Illustrated History* (Annapolis, MD: Naval Institute Press, 1979), 102.

13. Karsten, *The Naval Aristocracy,* 8–16, 385.

14. U.S. Department of the Navy, *Regulations,* 7–11, 15–26; United States Naval Academy Alumni Association, Inc., *Register of Alumni: Graduates and Former Midshipmen and Naval Cadets* (Annapolis, MD: U.S. Naval Academy Alumni Assoc., 1997).

15. Benjamin, *United States Naval Academy,* 275; U.S. Department of the Navy, *Regulations,* esp. 33–41. The next edition of the regulations was published in 1876.

16. U.S. Department of the Navy, *Regulations,* 105–7, 114–21; Sweetman, *U.S. Naval Academy,* 94.

17. Worden, Orders 105 (28 September 1871), 117 (6 October 1871), 109 (28 September 1872), and 132 (22 October 1872), "orders" file, Worden Papers,

LC; Worden to Robeson, 5 and 8 June 1874, vol. 36, Entry 33A, RG 45, NA; Benjamin, *United States Naval Academy,* 288; Karsten, *The Naval Aristocracy,* 38–40; Sweetman, *U.S. Naval Academy,* 50, 67, 104.

18. Charles Todorich, *The Spirited Years: A History of the Antebellum Naval Academy* (Annapolis, MD: Naval Institute Press, 1984), 33–34, 126.

19. Parker to Toucey, 20 March 1857, target 3, roll 3, Microcopy 949, RG 405, NA; William H. Parker, *Recollections of a Naval Officer, 1841–1865* (Annapolis, MD: Naval Institute Press, 1985), 187.

20. Philip L. Brown, *The Other Annapolis, 1900–1950* (Annapolis, MD: Annapolis Publishing Company, 1994), 33; Todorich, *Spirited Years,* 153.

21. Craig L. Symonds, *Confederate Admiral: The Life and Wars of Franklin Buchanan* (Annapolis, MD: Naval Institute Press, 1999), 129–30, 170.

22. Jean Alice Ponton, "Rear Admiral Louis M. Goldsborough: The Formation of a Nineteenth-Century Naval Officer" (Ph.D. dissertation, Catholic University, 1996), 126–27, 141, 386.

23. Quoted in Todorich, *Spirited Years,* 155.

24. Todorich, *Spirited Years,* 156.

25. Todorich, *Spirited Years,* 190.

26. Karsten, *Naval Aristocracy.*

27. U.S. Department of the Navy, *Official Records of the Union and Confederate Navies in the War of the Rebellion,* ed. Richard Rush, et al., 31 vols. (Washington: Government Printing Office, 1894–1922), Series I, vol. 24, 678, vol. 23, 449–50, vol. 25, 327–38, and vol. 11, 90–91.

28. Still, *Ironclad Captains,* 12; Sweetman, *The U.S. Naval Academy,* 104.

29. *Baltimore American and Commercial Advertiser,* September 1872, 24–26.

30. Robley D. Evans, *A Sailor's Log: Recollections of Forty Years of Naval Life* (Annapolis, MD: Naval Institute Press, 1993), xiii–xix, 169.

31. *Army and Navy Journal,* 7 June 1873, 683; Evans, *A Sailor's Log,* 170; Willard B. Gatewood, Jr., "Alonzo Clifton McClennan: Black Midshipman from South Carolina, 1873–1874," *South Carolina Historical Magazine* 89 (January 1988): 32; Karsten, *The Naval Aristocracy,* 38; Sweetman, *U.S. Naval Academy,* 42, 84–87.

32. Robeson to Worden, 12 December 1872, 242–43, vol. 3, Entry 17, RG 45, NA; Benjamin, *United States Naval Academy,* 291; Evans, *A Sailor's Log,* 169.

33. Evans, *A Sailor's Log,* 170; Benjamin, *United States Naval Academy,* 290–91.

34. "Moke" was slang for "ass" and one of the almost endless synonyms for "nigger."

35. "Proceedings of a Board," 17 October 1872, doc. 78, vol. 33, Entry 33A, RG 45, NA. One of the racist stereotypes about blacks was that they had terrible

body odor. Thus, those who held their noses in Conyers's presence were making a racial slur.

36. Order No. 45, 18 April 1872, "Orders" file, John L. Worden papers, LC; file 1915, box 32, file 2116, box 37, and file 2140, box 38, Entry 403, RG 24, NA.

37. "Proceedings of a Board," 17 October 1872, doc. 78, vol. 33, Entry 33A, RG 45, NA; "Summary of Testimony," doc. 79, vol. 33, Entry 33A, RG 45, NA.

38. Sawyer to Robeson, 18 October 1872, with extract from James Conyers to Catherine Conyers, 11 October 1872, in file 2202, "James H. Conyers," box 40, Entry 403, RG 24, NA; Bruce Ragsdale, ed., *Biographical Directory of the United States Congress, 1774–1989* (Washington: Government Printing Office, 1989), 1770.

39. "Proceedings of a Board," 17 October 1872, doc. 78, vol. 33, Entry 33A, RG 45, NA.

40. Unprovenanced newspaper clippings, folder 9a, box 5, Entry 39B, Records of the Superintendent, General Records, Midshipmen, Brigade of Midshipmen, RG 405, USNA; *Baltimore American and Commercial Advertiser,* 15 and 29 October 1872.

41. *Army and Navy Journal,* 19 October 1872, 153.

42. Case to Worden, 18 October 1872, 148, vol. 3, Entry 17, RG 45, NA.

43. Worden to McNair, Yates, and Schley, 16 October 1872, doc. 77, "Proceedings of a Board," 17 October 1872, doc. 78, and "Summary of Testimony," doc. 79, vol. 33, Entry 33A, RG 45, NA; Robeson to Digges, 21 October 1872, folder 8, box 2, Entry 75, RG 405, USNA; Winfield Scott Schley, *Forty-Five Years under the Flag* (New York: Appleton, 1904), 106–7.

44. Worden to Case, 29 October 1872, doc. no. 76, vol. 33, Entry 33A, RG 45, NA.

45. Robeson to Worden, 12 December 1872, 242–43, vol. 3, Entry 17, RG 45, NA.

46. Poland to Robeson, 8 January 1873, Goodfellow to Robeson, 10 January 1873, Collamore to Robeson, 10 January 1873, "Copy of Endorsements on foregoing," n.d., Parker to Robeson, 10 January 1873, and Robeson to Worden, 15 January 1873, folder 3, box 17, Entry 25, RG 405, USNA; Goodfellow to Grant, February 1873, file 2140, box 38, Entry 403, RG 24, NA; Ragsdale, ed., *Biographical Directory,* 838, 1503, 1610, 1657.

47. Testimony of Percival J. Werlich, "Proceedings of a Board to investigate a report against Cad. Mids. Thos. H. Taylor & Conyers for fighting," 13 October 1873, folder 4, box 2, Entry 75, RG 405, USNA; *Army and Navy Journal,* 19 October 1872, 153; R. L. Field, "The Black Midshipman at the U.S. Naval Academy," *Proceedings* 99 (April 1973): 28.

48. Gatewood, "Alonzo Clifton McClennan," 30–31.

49. *Baltimore American and Commercial Advertiser,* 13 June 1873; U.S. De-

partment of the Navy, *Regulations*, 7, 26–31; Sawyer to Robeson, 18 October 1872, in file 2202, box 40, Entry 403, RG 24, NA; "Minutes of the Academic Board, No. 4, U.S. Naval Academy, 1867–74," 420–25, Entry 204, RG 405, USNA; *Army and Navy Journal*, 7 June 1873, 683; Robeson to Worden, 9 June 1873, folder 3, box 17, Entry 25, RG 405, USNA.

50. *Baltimore American and Commercial Advertiser*, 5 June 1873; Evans, *A Sailor's Log*, 169–70.

51. File 1917, box 32, file 2055, box 36, file 2152, box 38, file 2180, box 39, files 2212, 2215, 2222, and 2230, box 40, and file 2243, box 41, Entry 403, RG 24, NA; *Baltimore American and Commercial Advertiser*, 28 September 1872.

52. "Proceedings of a Board investigating the conduct of Cadet O'Keefe & others against Cadet Conyers," June 1873, folder 4, box 2, Entry 75, RG 405, USNA.

53. Worden to Robeson, 10 June 1873, doc. no. 115, vol. 35, Entry 33A, RG 45, NA; Robeson to Butterfield, Cheek, Duer, Ewing, Fletcher, Lockett, O'Keefe, Rowan, and Young, and Robeson to Crittenden, et al., 13 June 1873, folder 3, box 17, Entry 25, RG 405, USNA.

54. *Baltimore American and Commercial Advertiser*, 13 and 20 June 1872; *New York Daily Tribune*, 6 June 1873; *New York Times*, 6 June 1873; Butterfield to Robeson, 14 June 1873, doc. no. 169, vol. 35, Entry 33A, RG 45, NA.

55. Butterfield to Robeson, 14 June 1873, Stewart to Robeson, 19 June 1873, and Worden to Robeson, 28 July 1873 (doc. no. 169), Worden to Robeson, 16 June 1873 (doc. no. 117), Worden to Robeson, 27 June 1872 (doc. no. 142), Worden to Reynolds, 27 September 1873 (doc. no. 193), vol. 35, Entry 33A, RG 45, NA; Reynolds to Worden, 19 September 1873, 417, vol. 3, Entry 17, RG 45, NA; file 2152, box 38, and file 2243, box 41, Entry 403, RG 24, NA; Andrew Summers Rowan, *How I Carried the Message to Garcia* (San Francisco: Walter D. Harney, c. 1922); Elbert Hubbard, *A Message to Garcia and Other Essays* (Westwood, NJ: Fleming H. Revell, 1959); Ragsdale, ed., *Biographical Directory*, 1177, 1689–90, 1877; U.S. Naval Academy Alumni Association, *Register of Alumni*; Robert Timberg, *The Nightingale's Song* (New York: Simon and Schuster, 1995), 25.

56. McFeely, *Grant*, 71–72, 375–79, 422–25.

57. File 2222, box 40, Entry 403, RG 24, NA; U.S. Naval Academy Alumni Association, *Register of Alumni*, 1:50–51.

58. Worden to Robeson, 14 June 1873, doc. no. 122, vol. 35, Entry 33A, RG 45, NA; Robeson to Worden, 14 June 1873, 407, vol. 3, Entry 17, RG 45, NA.

NOTES TO CHAPTER 2

1. Maude Thomas Jenkins to author, June 1999; "Alonzo C. McClennan," file no. 2421, box 45, Entry 403, RG 24, NA; William B. Gatewood, "Alonzo

Clifton McClennan"; "Black Midshipman from South Carolina, 1873–1874," *South Carolina Historical Magazine* 89 (January 1988): 24–39; Willard B. Gatewood, *Aristocrats of Color: The Black Elite, 1880–1920* (Bloomington: Indiana University Press, 1990), 81; Maude Thomas Jenkins, "Alonzo McClennan, M.D." (unpublished family paper, 1983). Gatewood's "Alonzo Clifton McClennan" contains the full text of an account by McClennan of his experience at the Naval Academy published in the *Charleston News and Courier,* 25 April 1897. McClennan penned the article to correct an erroneous story about him that appeared in the *New York Times* on 18 April 1897 on the occasion of the appointment of a black youth to the Naval Academy that year.

2. *Dictionary of American Biography,* s.v., "Richard Harvey Cain"; Eric Foner, *Reconstruction: America's Unfinished Revolution, 1863–1877* (New York: Harper and Row, 1988), 426; Gatewood, "Alonzo Clifton McClennan"; Thomas Cleveland Holt, *Black over White: Negro Political Leadership in South Carolina during Reconstruction* (Urbana: University of Illinois Press, 1977), 18, 112; Bruce Ragsdale, ed., *Biographical Directory of the United States Congress, 1774–1989* (Washington: Government Printing Office, 1989), 726.

3. *Baltimore American and Commercial Advertiser,* 25 September 1873, 4; Gatewood, "Alonzo Clifton McClennan," McClennan quoted on 32.

4. Gatewood, "Alonzo Clifton McClennan," quotes on 33.

5. Testimony of Conyers, "Proceedings of a Board to investigate a report against Cad. Mids. Thos. H. Taylor & Conyers for fighting," 13 October 1873, folder 4, box 2, Entry 75, RG 405, USNA.

6. *Army and Navy Journal,* 14 June 1873, 701; Worden to Robeson, 9 October 1873, doc. no. 204, vol. 35, Entry 33A, RG 45, NA; Robeson to Worden, 8 November 1873, 440, "Minutes of the Academic Board, No. 4, U.S. Naval Academy, 1867–74," Entry 204, RG 405, USNA; Conyers to Robeson, 10 November 1873, file 2202, box 40, Entry 403, RG 24, NA; Robeson to Conyers, 11 November 1873, folder 4, box 17, Entry 25, RG 405, USNA.

7. Gatewood, "Alonzo Clifton McClennan," 35.

8. Gatewood, "Alonzo Clifton McClennan," 34–35.

9. Breese to Worden, 3 January 1874, unnumbered doc. following doc. no. 4, and Breese to Robeson, 7 January 1874, doc. no. 5, vol. 36, Entry 33A, RG 45, NA.

10. "Minutes of the Academic Board, No. 4, U.S. Naval Academy, 1867–74," 454–59, Entry 204, RG 405, USNA. The limit of demerits allowed a plebe was three hundred.

11. McClennan to Breese, 2 January 1874, and Breese to Worden, 3 January 1874, unnumbered docs. following doc. no. 4, vol. 36, Entry 33A, RG 45, NA.

12. "Proceedings of a Board," 6 January 1874, unnumbered doc. preceding doc. no. 4, vol. 36, Entry 33A, RG 45, NA.

13. Breese to Robeson, 7 January 1874, doc. no. 5, vol. 36, Entry 33A, RG 45, NA.

14. Cain to Robeson, 5 February 1874, file 2421, box 45, Entry 403, RG 24, NA; Gatewood, "Alonzo Clifton McClennan," 35–36.

15. Mooney, James L., et al., eds., *Dictionary of American Naval Fighting Ships* (Washington: Government Printing Office, 1959–), s.v. *"Santee"*; Gatewood, "Alonzo Clifton McClennan," 36–37.

16. Gatewood, "Alonzo Clifton McClennan," 38. Quote from Cain to Robeson, 5 February 1874, file 2421, box 45, Entry 403, RG 24, NA.

17. Thompson to McClennan, 6 March 1864, file 2421, box 45, Entry 403, RG 24, NA; Gatewood, "Alonzo Clifton McClennan," 38–39.

18. File 2421, box 45, Entry 403, RG 24, NA; Gatewood, "Alonzo Clifton McClennan," 39.

19. James B. Edwards and Thomas C. Rowland, Jr., "Resolution for McClennan-Banks Ambulatory Care Center," n.d., author's files; Gatewood, "Alonzo Clifton McClennan," 25–27, 39; *Post and Courier* (Savannah), 15 August 1992.

20. William C. Harris, *The Day of the Carpetbagger: Republican Reconstruction in Mississippi* (Baton Rouge: Louisiana State University Press, 1979), 117–18; Ragsdale, ed., *Biographical Directory,* 582–83.

21. File 2492, box 47, Entry 403, RG 24, NA; *Army and Navy Journal,* 3 October 1874, 118.

22. Moore to Mitchell, 16 July 1937, folder 1, box 2, MCHS.

23. Rodgers to Sampson, McCormick, and Walker, 28 October 1874, and "Proceedings of a Board," 28 October 1874, folder 3, box 1, Entry 75, RG 405, USNA; Stephen D. Brown, "Christopher Raymond Perry Rodgers: Mentor of the New Navy," in *Naval History: The Sixth Naval History Symposium,* ed. Daniel Masterson (Wilmington, DE: Scholarly Resources, 1986); Jack Sweetman, *The U.S. Naval Academy: An Illustrated History* (Annapolis, MD: Naval Institute Press, 1979), 57, 108–11; United States Naval Academy Alumni Association, *Register of Alumni: Graduates and Former Midshipmen and Naval Cadets* (Annapolis, MD: U.S. Naval Academy Alumni Association, 1997).

24. Rodgers to Sampson et al., 14 November 1874, and "Proceedings of a Board . . . ," 16 November 1874, folder 3, box 1, Entry 75, RG 405, USNA.

25. "Minutes of the Academic Board, No. 5, U.S. Naval Academy, 1874–77," 34–39, Entry 204, RG 405, USNA.

26. File 2473, box 47, and file 2562, box 49, Entry 403, RG 24, NA; "Minutes of the Academic Board, No. 5, U.S. Naval Academy, 1874–77," 34–35, Entry 204, RG 405, USNA; Ragsdale, ed., *Biographical Directory,* 1823.

27. White to Terry, 7 February 1875, Rodgers to Howell et al., 8 February 1875, and Hood to Terry, 8 February 1875, folder 3, box 1, Entry 75, RG 405, USNA; Baker to Terry, 8 February 1875, doc. no. 19, vol. 38, Entry 33A, RG 45, NA.

28. Melton to Terry, 8 February 1875, folder 3, box 1, Entry 75, RG 405, USNA.

29. Rodgers to Robeson, 8 February 1875, doc. no. 20, vol. 38, Entry 33A, RG 45, NA; Robeson to Rodgers, 9 February 1875, vol. 5, Entry 17, RG 45, NA.

30. "Various Naval Matters," *Army and Navy Journal,* 6 March 1875, 470.

31. File 2473, box 47, Entry 403, RG 24, NA; William B. Cogar, ed., *Dictionary of Admirals of the U.S. Navy.* Vol. 1, *1862–1900* (Annapolis, MD: Naval Institute Press, 1989), 132–33; Ragsdale, ed., *Biographical Directory,* 1181; United States Naval Academy Alumni Association, *Register of Alumni.*

32. Order No. 37, 9 February 1875, unnumbered doc. following doc. no. 20. vol. 38, Entry 33A, RG 45, NA.

33. *New York Times,* 27 February 1875. No jacket appears in Entry 403, RG 24, NA, for the cadet named in the article, Gordon Claude. The name "Gordon Handy Claude" is listed as a nongraduate of the Class of 1878 in the Naval Academy Alumni Association's *Register of Alumni.*

34. Rodgers to Robeson, 26 October 1875, doc. no. 111, vol. 39, Entry 33A, RG 45, NA.

35. "Minutes of the Academic Board, No. 5, U.S. Naval Academy, 1874–77," 60–61, 80–85, Entry 204, RG 405, USNA.

36. Breck to Rodgers, 24 June 1875, in doc. 92, vol. 38, Entry 33 A, RG 45, NA.

37. Robeson to Rodgers, 22 June 1875, folder 4, box 17, Entry 25, RG 405, USNA; Rodgers to Robeson, doc. no. 92, vol. 38, Entry 33A, RG 45, NA.

38. Rodgers to Robeson, 23 October 1875, doc. no. 109, vol. 39, Entry 33A, RG 45, NA.

39. File 2540, box 46, Entry 403, RG 24, NA; "Proceedings of a Board," 22 October 1875, doc. no. 109, vol. 39, Entry 33A, RG 45, NA.

40. Rodgers to Robeson, 26 October 1875, doc. no. 111, vol. 39, Entry 33A, RG 45, NA; "Various Naval Items," *Army and Navy Journal,* 13 November 1875, 214; R. L. Field, "The Black Midshipman at the U.S. Naval Academy," *Proceedings* 99 (April 1973): 30.

41. Robert Ewell Greene, *Black Defenders of America, 1775–1973: A Reference and Pictorial History* (Chicago: Johnson Publishing Co., 1974), 110–12; Thomas Truxtun Moebs, *Black Soldiers, Black Sailors, Black Ink: Research Guide on African Americans in U.S. Military History, 1526–1900* (Chesapeake Bay: Moebs Publishing Co., 1994), 14–15.

42. Quoted in Holt, *Black over White,* 209.

43. George L. Andrews, "West Point and the Colored Cadets," *International Review* (November 1880): 480.

44. Goodfellow to Grant, February 1873, file 2140, box 38, Entry 403, RG 24, NA.

Notes to Chapter 3

1. According to historian William Katz,
the phrase "Jim Crow" dates to 1830. Thomas Rice, a famous white en-
tertainer, walked out of his Baltimore theater to observe a Black singer-
dancer performing in the alley. Rice "borrowed" the man's dance routine
and costume and enlarged on the song he was singing. He made the words
famous all over the world—"wheel about, turn about, dance jest so—
every time I wheel about I shout Jim Crow!" Like another white invention,
"Uncle Tom," which Blacks used to describe a man afraid to stand up for
his rights, "Jim Crow" came to mean the many kinds of racial discrimination Blacks faced in America.
William Loren Katz, *Eyewitness: A Living Documentary of the African American Contribution to American History* (New York: Simon and Schuster, 1995),
318.

2. "History of Negro Midshipmen or Negro Candidates for Midshipmen,"
21 September 1944, "Black Midshipmen" reference file, Special Collections,
Nimitz Library, USNA. The exact number of blacks appointed to the Academy
during this period will probably never be known. The compilers of the source
cited above did not know whether every person they named in the document was
black. Other sources disagree as to the race of particular individuals. Finally, one
or more Academy alumni who were taken for white might actually have been
black, as was the case with Oscar Holmes, now believed to be the first African
American naval aviator. See Robert J. Schneller, Jr., "Oscar Holmes: A Place in
Naval Aviation," *Naval Aviation News* 80 (January–February 1988): 26–27.

3. Quoted in Morris J. MacGregor, *Integration of the Armed Forces,
1940–1965* (Washington: Government Printing Office, 1981), 478.

4. Joel Williamson, "Wounds Not Scars: Lynching, the National Conscience,
and the American Historian," *Journal of American History* 83 (March 1997):
1236.

5. Harry A. Ploski and Ernest Kaiser, *Afro USA: A Reference Work on the
Black Experience* (New York: Bellwether, 1971), 267–68.

6. William H. Chafe, "The Gods Bring Threads to Webs Begun," *Journal of
American History* 86 (March 2000): 1534; Pete Daniel, *The Shadow of Slavery:
Peonage in the South, 1901–1969* (Urbana: University of Illinois Press, 1990);
John Hope Franklin and Alfred A. Moss Jr., *From Slavery to Freedom*, 6th ed.
(New York: McGraw-Hill, 1988), 361, 376; Gunnar Myrdal, *An American
Dilemma: The Negro Problem and Modern Democracy*, 2 vols. (New York:
Harper, 1944), 38, 60–61, 100–108, 191, 205–7, 304–19, 335, 365, 476–78,
559, 592–97, 608–24, 677, 1142–43, quote on 100–101; Williamson, "Wounds
Not Scars," 1228, 1235; C. Vann Woodward, *The Strange Career of Jim Crow*
(New York: Oxford University Press, 1955), 1–113.

7. Quoted in Bernard C. Nalty, *Strength for the Fight: A History of Black Americans in the Military* (New York: Free Press, 1986), 107.

8. Wesley A. Brown, "Eleven Men of West Point," *Negro History Bulletin* 19 (April 1956): 152; Florette Henri, *Bitter Victory: A History of Black Soldiers in World War I* (Garden City, NY: Doubleday, 1970), 30, 40–51; Franklin and Moss, *From Slavery to Freedom*, 291–318, Klansman quoted on 312; Nalty, *Strength for the Fight*, 64, 77, 107–24.

9. David M. Kennedy, *Freedom from Fear: The American People in Depression and War, 1929–1945* (New York: Oxford University Press, 1999), 163–64; John B. Kirby, *Black Americans in the Roosevelt Era: Liberalism and Race* (Knoxville: University of Tennessee Press, 1980), 3–5, 97; Woodward, *Strange Career of Jim Crow*, 114–15, 118.

10. Frederick S. Harrod, *Manning the New Navy: The Development of a Modern Naval Enlisted Force, 1899–1940* (Westport, CT: Greenwood Press, 1978), 3–7.

11. Harrod, *Manning the New Navy*, 10–11.

12. T. P. Magruder, "The Enlisted Personnel," *Proceedings* 36 (June 1910): 385; *Army and Navy Journal* 44 (19 January 1907): 563, and 50 (21 June 1913): 1296.

13. Harrod, *Manning the New Navy*, 57–58; Nalty, *Strength for the Fight*, 81.

14. Quoted in Harrod, *Manning the New Navy*, 59.

15. *Pittsburgh Courier*, 8 August 1936; Harrod, *Manning the New Navy*, 58–60; MacGregor, *Integration of the Armed Forces*, 58; Nalty, *Strength for the Fight*, 84–86; Leedell W. Neyland, "The Messman's/Steward's Branch: A Haunting Chapter in the History of the U.S. Navy, 1919–1942," lecture given at the Naval Historical Center, 17 May 1994; L. D. Reddick, "The Negro in the United States Navy during World War II," *Journal of Negro History* 32 (1947): 203.

16. Krewasky Antonio Salter, "'Sable Officers': African-American Military Officers, 1861–1948" (Ph.D. dissertation, Florida State University, 1996), 53–54; *Afro-American*, 27 February 1937.

17. Henry Ossian Flipper, *The Colored Cadet at West Point: Autobiography of Lieut. Henry Ossian Flipper, U.S.A., First Graduate of Color from the U.S. Military Academy* (New York: Johnson Reprint Corp., 1968); Salter, "'Sable Officers,'" 64; William P. Vaughn, "West Point and the First Negro Cadet," *Journal of Military History* 35 (October 1971): 101; Ezra J. Warner, "A Black Man in the Long Gray Line," *American History Illustrated* 4 (January 1970): 30–35.

18. Willard B. Gatewood, Jr., "John Hanks Alexander of Arkansas: Second Black Graduate of West Point," *Arkansas Historical Quarterly* 41 (Summer 1982): 103–123.

19. Brown, "Eleven Men of West Point," 150; Salter, "'Sable Officers,'" 82–84.

20. George L. Andrews, "West Point and the Colored Cadets," *International Review* 9 (November 1880); John F. Marszalek, Jr., "A Black Cadet at West Point," *American Heritage* 22 (August 1971): 30–37, 104–6; Salter, "'Sable Officers,'" 53–87.

21. Brown, "Eleven Men of West Point," 149–50; Gatewood, "John Hanks Alexander," 123–28; Greene, *Black Defenders of America, 1775–1973: A Reference and Pictorial History* (Chicago: Johnson Publishing, 1974), 113–14; Nalty, *Strength for the Fight,* 51, 60; Warner, "A Black Man in the Long Gray Line," 34; "Lieutenant Henry Ossian Flipper, U.S. Army, 1856–1940," http://www.army.mil/cmh-pg/topics/afam/flipper.htm, 18 June 2003.

22. Quoted in Brown, "Eleven Men of West Point," 150.

23. Quoted in Nalty, *Strength for the Fight,* 66.

24. Draft press release dated 4 May 1949, "Atwood, A–Z" file, Washingtoniana Division, Martin Luther King Jr., Branch, D.C. Public Library; "Minutes of the Board of Education of the District of Columbia," vol. 75, 6 June 1951, 87, Charles Sumner School Museum and Archives; Frank Johnson, interview by author, 23 July 1998; Brown, "Eleven Men of West Point," 150–52, Atwood quoted on 151; Henri, *Bitter Victory,* 26–29; Nalty, *Strength for the Fight,* 98–99, 110–11.

25. *Afro-American,* 27 February 1937; Brown, "Eleven Men of West Point," 152.

26. File 5817, box 114, Entry 403, RG 24, NA; Bruce Ragsdale, ed., *Biographical Directory of the United States Congress, 1774–1989* (Washington: Government Printing Office, 1989), 2038.

27. File 6064, box 118, Entry 403, RG 24, NA; *New York Times,* 20 May 1897, 14 June 1897, 31 August 1897, and 4 September 1897.

28. *New York Times,* 15 April 1897 and 25 April 1897; Ragsdale, ed., *Biographical Directory,* 1797.

29. *New York Times,* 23 April 1897.

30. Cooper to Long, 11 May 1897, in *BD,* 3:154.

31. Cotten to Henderson, 18 April 1897, Cotten Family Papers, Southern Historical Society Collection, University of North Carolina library; *New York Times,* 25 April 1897.

32. *New York Times,* 31 August 1897, 2 September 1897, 5 September 1897.

33. Marvin E. Fletcher, *America's First Black General: Benjamin O. Davis, Sr., 1880–1970* (Lawrence: University Press of Kansas, 1989), 18–19.

34. Smalls to the President, 8 March 1911, courtesy of Wesley A. Brown.

35. Lee Finkle, *Forum for Protest: The Black Press during World War II* (Cranbury, NJ: Fairleigh Dickinson University Press, 1975), 89–90; Franklin and Moss, *From Slavery to Freedom,* 286–89, 340; Thomas C. Holt, "African-American History," in Eric Foner, ed., *The New American History* (Philadelphia: Temple University Press, 1990), 224; James R. Grossman, *Land of Hope: Chicago,*

Black Southerners, and the Great Migration (Chicago: University of Chicago Press, 1989), 3–17; Kirby, *Black Americans in the Roosevelt Era,* 98–102; Manning Marable, *Race, Reform and Rebellion: The Second Reconstruction in Black America* (Jackson: University Press of Mississippi, 1984), 8–9; Myrdal, *American Dilemma,* 744, 750–52; Woodward, *The Strange Career of Jim Crow,* 124–29.

36. *Pittsburgh Courier,* 16 March 1929 and 1 June 1929; *Dictionary of American Biography,* s.v. "Oscar Stanton DePriest"; Franklin and Moss, *From Slavery to Freedom,* 342–48; Grossman, *Land of Hope,* 130; Dennis S. Nordin, *The New Deal's Black Congressman: A Life of Arthur Wergs Mitchell* (Columbia: University of Missouri Press, 1997), 57, 70–71, 87; Ragsdale, ed., *Biographical Directory,* 899–900.

37. U.S. Navy Department, Bureau of Navigation, *Regulations Governing the Admission of Candidates into the U.S. Naval Academy as Midshipmen* (Washington: Government Printing Office, 1921), 4–5; Nimitz to Mitchell, 30 March 1936, folder 1, box 18, MCHS; *Pittsburgh Courier,* 11 May 1929, 18 May 1929, and 29 June 1929; "History of Negro Midshipmen or Negro Candidates for Midshipmen," 21 September 1944, "Black Midshipmen" reference file, Special Collections, Nimitz Library, USNA; unprovenanced newspaper clipping, "DePriest, Rep. Oscar (ILL.)" file, Washingtoniana Division, Martin Luther King Branch, D.C. Public Library. In 1929 DePriest also appointed two other candidates to the Naval Academy whose race is not known.

38. Jervis Anderson, "A Very Special Monument," *New Yorker,* 20 March 1978, 97–107; Francine Curro Cary, ed., *Urban Odyssey: A Multicultural History of Washington, D.C.* (Washington: Smithsonian, 1995), 211; Lillian G. Dabney, *The History of Schools for Negroes in the District of Columbia, 1807–1947* (Washington: Catholic University of America Press, 1949), 243–53; Willard B. Gatewood, Jr., *Aristocrats of Color: The Black Elite, 1880–1920* (Bloomington: Indiana University Press, 1990), 258–62; Constance McLaughlin Green, *The Secret City: A History of Race Relations in the Nation's Capital* (Princeton, NJ: Princeton University Press, 1967), 210–12; Thomas Sowell, "Black Excellence: A History of Dunbar High," *Washington Post,* 28 April 1974, C3.

39. Nimitz to Mitchell, 30 March 1936, folder 1, box 18, MCHS; *Pittsburgh Courier,* 11 May 1929, 18 May 1929, and 29 June 1929; "History of Negro Midshipmen or Negro Candidates for Midshipmen," 21 September 1944, "Black Midshipmen" reference file, Special Collections, Nimitz Library, USNA.

40. Wiltsie to the Secretary of the Navy, 17 February 1930 and Jahncke to Wiltsie, 20 February 1930, file OL11 330–429, box 754, Entry 90, RG 24, NA.

41. See for example Eugene A. Barham, Class of 1935, interview by author, 29 April 1997; Philip E. Baylor, Class of 1947, to author, 20 September 1996; Joseph P. Flanagan, Jr., Class of 1947, interview by author, 23 September 1996;

Walter G. Moyle, Jr., Class of 1937, interview by author, 12 August 1997; Robert K. Ripley, Class of 1949, to author, 23 October 1996; and Howard A. Weiss, Class of 1947, interview by author, 11 May 1996.

42. Unprovenanced newspaper clipping, 2 July 1929, "DePriest, Rep. Oscar (ILL.)" file, Washingtoniana Division, Martin Luther King, Jr., Branch, D.C. Public Library; Salter, "'Sable Officers,'" 212.

43. Kirby, *Black Americans in the Roosevelt Era,* 132; Myrdal, *American Dilemma,* 908.

44. *Pittsburgh Courier,* 5 August 1926 and 14 September 1940.

45. *Pittsburgh Courier,* 17 March 1930.

46. "Candidates Nominated for the U.S. Military Academy from the 1st Congressional District of Illinois by ex-Congressman DePriest," n.d., folder 4, box 72, MCHS; "History of Negro Midshipmen or Negro Candidates for Midshipmen," 21 September 1944, "Black Midshipmen" reference file, Special Collections, Nimitz Library, USNA; Nimitz to Mitchell, 30 March 1936, folder 1, box 18, MCHS; *Pittsburgh Courier,* 17 May 1930 and 8 November 1930; United States Navy Department, Bureau of Personnel, *Regulations Governing the Admission of Candidates into the United States Naval Academy as Midshipmen and Sample Examination Papers, June 1945* (Washington: Government Printing Office, 1945), 18–30.

47. *New York Times,* 19 October 1968; U.S. Congress, *Official Congressional Directory for the Use of the United States Congress, 71st Congress, 3d Session, Beginning December 1, 1930* (Washington: Government Printing Office, 1930), 75; Charles V. Hamilton, *Adam Clayton Powell, Jr.: The Political Biography of an American Dilemma* (New York: Atheneum, 1991), 139; Ragsdale, ed., *Biographical Directory,* 1049.

48. *Pittsburgh Courier,* 8 March 1930, 15 March 1930, and 17 May 1930; "History of Negro Midshipmen or Negro Candidates for Midshipmen," 21 September 1944, "Black Midshipmen" reference file, Special Collections, Nimitz Library, USNA.

49. Benjamin O. Davis, Jr., *American: An Autobiography* (Washington: Smithsonian Institution Press, 1991), 18–50; Fletcher, *America's First Black General.*

50. Davis, *American,* 44; "History of Negro Midshipmen or Negro Candidates for Midshipmen," 21 September 1944, "Black Midshipmen" reference file, Special Collections, Nimitz Library, USNA; Nimitz to Mitchell, 30 March 1936, folder 1, box 18, MCHS.

51. Quoted in Franklin and Moss, *From Slavery to Freedom,* 344.

52. Walter White, *A Man Called White: The Autobiography of Walter White* (New York: Viking, 1948), 104.

53. Quoted in Kirby, *Black Americans in the Roosevelt Era,* 131, 136.

54. Franklin and Moss, *From Slavery to Freedom,* 342–51; Kirby, *Black*

Americans in the Roosevelt Era, 21–22, 83–84; Woodward, *The Strange Career of Jim Crow,* 129.

55. William J. Grimshaw, *Bitter Fruit: Black Politics and the Chicago Machine, 1931–1991* (Chicago: University of Chicago Press, 1992), 26; "Historical Notes," *Journal of Negro History* 53 (July 1968): 281–82.

56. Nordin, *The New Deal's Black Congressman,* 61, 294–99, ANP writer quoted on 292.

57. *Afro-American,* 17 November 1934; "Historical Notes," 281–82; Nordin, *The New Deal's Black Congressman,* vii, x, 28, 71, 292, 297.

58. Nordin, *The New Deal's Black Congressman,* xiii–ix, 1–39, 140–41, 194, 196, 209–10, 294–98.

59. *Washington Tribune,* 14 August 1935; Nordin, *The New Deal's Black Congressman,* 138, 176–81, 190, 195, 201–24, 294; Mitchell quoted in *Afro-American,* 26 January 1935.

60. *Afro-American,* 24 November 1934.

61. Mitchell to Schaefer, 28 January 1937, folder 10, box 26; Mitchell to Svorb, 1 March 1938, folder 1, box 37; Mitchell to Hedger, 1 March 1938, folder 1, box 37; Mitchell to Gilbert, 2 March 1938, folder 1, box 37, MCHS; Nordin, *The New Deal's Black Congressman,* 224. George Tittinger failed the entrance exam.

62. Mitchell to Vickery, 15 July 1935, folder 7, box 12, MCHS.

63. "Congressman Mitchell Announces Appointments to Military Academy," undated press release, folder 4, box 72, MCHS; Mitchell to Vickery, 15 July 1935, folder 7, box 12, MCHS; Nimitz to Mitchell, 19 July 1937, folder 2, box 32, MCHS; *Washington Tribune,* 20 March 1935; Nordin, *The New Deal's Black Congressman,* 226.

64. Mitchell's papers in the Chicago Historical Society are peppered with applications from young black men for Military Academy appointments, but letters from those seeking Naval Academy nominations are few and far between.

65. Mitchell to Houston, 14 March 1938, folder 6, box 37, MCHS.

66. Holman to Mitchell, 4 January 1935 [sic, 1936], folder 3, box 15, MCHS; *Afro-American,* 9 March 1935; Andrews to Mitchell, 29 October 1935, folder 1, box 14, MCHS; Mitchell to Austin, Mitchell to Evans, Mitchell to Williams, Mitchell to Griffin, and Mitchell to Brown, 21 and 26 December 1935, folder 6, box 14, MCHS; Nordin, *The New Deal's Black Congressman,* 226.

67. Gerald R. Brown, "Military Training in the Public Schools of the District of Columbia" (M.A. thesis, Howard University, 1963), 2; Barnett Broughton, "Excerpts from the History of the Cadet Corps," *The Adjutant* (1940), Washingtoniana Division, Martin Luther King, Jr., Branch, D.C. Public Library; Edith W. Edwards, "Drilling for the Future," *Washington Log* (April 1943), clipping in "Public Schools, High Schools, Cadets—1971, Pamphlets & Pictures" file,

Washingtoniana Division, Martin Luther King, Jr., Branch, D.C. Public Library; Andrea P. Sckoppeglia, "The Washington High School Cadet Corps," *Nation's Capital Magazine,* April 1931, clipping in "Public Schools, High Schools, Cadets before 1940" file, Washingtoniana Division, Martin Luther King, Jr., Branch, D.C. Public Library; clipping from *Washington Daily News,* 20 May 1946, "Public Schools, High School Cadets, 1940–49" file, Washingtoniana Division, Martin Luther King, Jr., Branch, D.C. Public Library; Catherine Theresa Wold, "A History of the Washington High School Cadet Corps, 1882–1934" (M.A. thesis, University of Maryland, 1935), 83; *Washington Post,* 29 November 1932, clipping in "Public Schools, High Schools, Cadets before 1940" file, Washingtoniana Division, Martin Luther King, Jr., Branch, D.C. Public Library.

68. Baker to Fleetwood, 14 February 1889, "testimonial concert, 1889" file, and "Biography of Christian A. Fleetwood," "Miscellany" file, box 1, Christian Alexander Fleetwood Papers, Library of Congress; Greene, *Black Defenders,* 67; Mary Gibson Hundley, *The Dunbar Story, 1870–1955* (New York: Vantage Press, 1965), 19, 56; Jesse J. Johnson, ed., *Black Armed Forces Officers, 1736–1971: A Documented Pictorial History* (Hampton, VA: Hampton Institute, 1971), 61.

69. "Biography of Christian A. Fleetwood," "Miscellany" file, box 1, Christian Alexander Fleetwood Papers, Library of Congress; Brown, "Military Training," 5; Brown, "Eleven Men of West Point," 153; Cary, ed., *Urban Odyssey,* 217; *Washington Tribune,* 10 June 1939, clipping in "Public Schools, High Schools, Cadets before 1940" file, Washingtoniana Division, Martin Luther King, Jr., Branch, D.C. Public Library; program, *Fifty-Sixth Annual Competitive Drill, Twenty-Fourth Regiment, Washington High School Cadets,* 20 May 1948, Charles Sumner Museum School and Archives; Hundley, *The Dunbar Story,* 19, 56.

70. Brown, "Eleven Men of West Point," 153; Lawrence C. Chambers, Class of 1952, interview by author, 7 November 1996; Paul P. Cooke, interview by author, 2 April 1997; Elmer Jones, telephone conversation with author, 13 May 1997; "Minutes of the Board of Education of the District of Columbia," vol. 75, 6 June 1951, 86–88, Charles Sumner School Museum and Archives; "Col. Henry O. Atwood, Eighty-eight, District Military Instructor," *Evening Star,* 11 July 1969; "Twenty-one Military Tutors Have Trained Cadets since 1888," *Afro-American* (Washington), 17 April 1947; Wesley Anthony Brown, telephone conversation with author, 29 October 1997; Mu-So-Lit Club Collection, Moorland-Spingarn Research Center, Howard University; Sandra Fitzpatrick and Maria R. Goodwin, *The Guide to Black Washington: Places and Events of Historical and Cultural Significance in the Nation's Capital,* rev. ed. (New York: Hippocrene Books, 1999), 146.

71. Wesley Anthony Brown, Class of 1949, interview by author, 23 January

1997 (2d interview); Atwood quoted in Brown, "Eleven Men of West Point," 152.

72. Brown, "Eleven Men of West Point," 153; Brown, 2d interview; Chambers interview.

73. Brown, 2d interview; Chambers interview; U.S. Department of Defense, *The Negro Officer in the Armed Forces of the United States of America* (Washington: Department of Defense, 1960), 18–19.

NOTES TO CHAPTER 4

1. Atwood to Mitchell, 14 February 1936, folder 9, box 16, MCHS; "James Daniel Fowler," *Assembly* 47 (July 1988): 181–82; *Liber Anni 1933* (Washington: Dunbar High School, 1933), 20, 24, 45, 59, 62, 73, 74, 84; Paul P. Cooke, telephone conversation with author, 8 June 1998.

2. Paul P. Cooke, interview by author, 2 April 1997; *Liber Anni 1933,* 22, 59, 77, 84.

3. "Annapolis: Negro Midshipman Finds Race Trouble at Academy," *Newsweek,* 27 February 1937, 12; William M. Carpenter, Class of 1940, to author, c. June 1997; Case School of Applied Science, transcript of James Lee Johnson, Jr., 20 March 1936, JMPJ; Cooke interview; Frank Johnson, interview by author, 23 July 1998; James Lee Johnson, Jr., Class of 1940, interview by Dennis Nordin, 29 September 1974; *Liber Anni 1933,* 28, 73, 79, 84; "Middy's Mother Breaks Silence," unprovenanced newspaper clipping, folder 9A, box 5, Entry 39B, Records of the Superintendent, General Records, Midshipmen, Brigade of Midshipmen, RG 405, USNA; Dennis S. Nordin, *The New Deal's Black Congressman: A Life of Arthur Wergs Mitchell* (Columbia: University of Missouri Press, 1997), 228.

4. "Congressman Arthur W. Mitchell, Who Has Made an Enviable Record During His Term In Congress, Scores Another Signal Victory," undated press release, folder 4, box 72, MCHS; *Afro-American,* 28 March 1936; *Pittsburgh Courier,* 28 March 1936; Johnson, interview by Nordin.

5. No psychological examinations were administered to candidates.

6. "Certificate Methods of Admission," JMPJ. Between 1938 and 1948, 43 percent of midshipmen entered by the college certificate method, 22 percent by the certificate with substantiating exam method, and 35 percent by regular exam. Earl Wentworth Thomson, "The Naval Academy as an Undergraduate College," *Proceedings* 74 (March 1948): 274.

7. Cooke to Mitchell, 15 February 1936, folder 9, box 16, MCHS; Nimitz to Mitchell, 19 July 1937, folder 2, box 32, MCHS; "History of Negro Midshipmen or Negro Candidates for Midshipmen," 21 September 1944, "Black Midshipmen" reference file, Special Collections, Nimitz Library, USNA; Paul P.

Cooke, telephone conversation with author, 8 June 1998; Cooke interview, 2 April 1997.

8. Midshipman nomination form, 25 February 1936, folder 1, box 17, MCHS; "Certificate Action Slip," 26 March 1936, ltr., president, Medical Examining Board, to superintendent, 15 June 1936, and "Oath of Office," 15 June 1936, JMPJ.

9. *Pittsburgh Courier,* 27 June 1936.

10. Todd to Mitchell, 21 July 1936, JMPJ.

11. U.S. Navy Department, *Annual Report of the Secretary of the Navy for the Fiscal Year 1936* (Washington: Government Printing Office, 1936), 25; U.S. Naval Academy, *Regulations of the United States Naval Academy, 1933* (Annapolis: U.S. Naval Academy, 1933), 1–2; Richard S. West, Jr., "The Superintendents of the Naval Academy," *Proceedings* 71 (July 1945): 801.

12. U.S. Naval Academy, *Regulations of the United States Naval Academy, 1933,* 5–6.

13. Officer Biographical Files, s.v. "David Foote Sellers," OA.

14. David F. Sellers, "The United States Naval Academy: It Belongs to the Fleet," *Proceedings* 62 (October 1936): 1427–34; West, "Superintendents," 808.

15. W. D. Puleston, *Annapolis: Gangway to the Quarterdeck* (New York: Appleton-Century, 1942), 202.

16. Park Benjamin, *The United States Naval Academy* (New York: Putnam's, 1990), 362.

17. Officer Biographical Files, s.v. "Forde Anderson Todd," OA.

18. U.S. Naval Academy, *Regulations of the U.S. Naval Academy, 1933,* 28–31, 48–49; Sellers, "The United States Naval Academy," 1433.

19. U.S. Naval Academy, *Regulations of the U.S. Naval Academy, 1933,* 46–55, 96–98; Kendall Banning, *Annapolis Today,* 5th ed. (Annapolis, MD: U.S. Naval Institute, 1957), 21.

20. See for example Reeves R. Taylor, Class of 1953, interview by author, 2 December 1996.

21. Ross Mackenzie, *Brief Points: An Almanac for Parents and Friends of U.S. Naval Academy Midshipmen* (Annapolis, MD: Naval Institute Press, 1993), 39–55.

22. Sellers, "The United States Naval Academy," 1429; Morris Janowitz, *The Professional Soldier: A Social and Political Portrait* (New York: Free Press, 1971), 81–101. Between 1938 and 1948, 70 percent of midshipmen entered the Academy with prior college or prep school work or tutoring. During the Depression, since most families could not afford to pay for education beyond what the public school system provided, it stands to reason that most midshipmen probably came from middle- or upper-class families. Thomson, "The Naval Academy as an Undergraduate College," 274–75.

23. Janowitz, *The Professional Soldier,* 104–16.

24. William M. Carpenter, Class of 1940, interview by author, 17 June 1997.

25. U.S. Naval Academy, *Reef Points 1936–1937* (Annapolis, MD: U.S. Naval Academy, 1936), 155–59.

26. The Trident Society, ed., *The Book of Navy Songs* (New York: Doubleday, 1937), 22, 118–19.

27. U.S. Naval Academy, *Reef Points 1936–1937*, 157; Trident Society, *Book of Navy Songs*, 32, 126; U.S. Congress, Senate, *Centennial of the United States Naval Academy, 1845–1945*, S. Doc. 91, 79th Cong., 1st sess., 1945, 11; Puleston, *Annapolis: Gangway to the Quarterdeck*, 237.

28. *Washington Tribune*, 27 February 1937; Seymour Einstein, Class of 1941, to author, 28 May 1997; Harvey B. Seim, Class of 1940, telephone conversation with author, 27 June 1997.

29. Todd to Sellers, 19 July 1937, "general correspondence, Jan. 1937–Oct. 1937" file, box 4, David F. Sellers Papers, Library of Congress.

30. U.S. Naval Academy, *Annual Register of the United States Naval Academy, 1936* (Washington: Government Printing Office, 1936), 2, 76; Mackenzie, *Brief Points, 39–55*; Puleston, *Annapolis*, 201. In 1929, the Academy established a "second-class summer," in which second classmen remained at the Yard for additional classwork. In 1936 the schedule included three four-week destroyer cruises, with one-third of the class sent on each cruise.

31. Johnson, interview by Nordin.

32. Reed to Mitchell, 28 July 1936, folder 5, box 20, MCHS.

33. Johnson to Mitchell, 6 August 1936, folder 7, box 20, and memo titled "Agenda," 15 June 1937, folder 5, box 31, MCHS.

34. "Abstract of Conduct . . . Plebe Summer," JMPJ; Johnson to Mitchell, 6 August 1936, folder 7, box 20, MCHS; Johnson, interview by Nordin.

35. Undated memo titled "first year midshipmen," folder 2, box 27, MCHS; Johnson, interview by Nordin; Nordin, *The New Deal's Black Congressman*, 229.

36. Johnson to Mitchell, 6 August 1936, folder 7, box 20, MCHS; Banning, *Annapolis Today*, 22.

37. Mitchell to Johnson, 4 August 1936, folder 7, box 20, and Reed to Mitchell, 28 July 1936, folder 5, box 20, MCHS.

38. Reed to Mitchell, 28 July 1936, folder 5, Mitchell to Reed, 4 August 1936, folder 7, and Johnson to Mitchell, 6 August 1936, folder 7, box 20, MCHS.

39. Johnson to Mitchell, 6 August 1936, folder 7, box 20, MCHS.

40. U.S. Congress, Senate, *The United States Naval Academy: A Sketch Containing the History, Entrance Requirements, Curriculum, Athletics, After Graduation Service, and Other Factual Information*, S. doc. 181, 75th Cong., 3d sess., 1938, 32–34.

41. Puleston, *Annapolis*, 206.

42. Banning, *Annapolis Today,* 37–46; Norlin J. Jankovsky, ed., *Reef Points, 1945–1946* (Annapolis, MD: United States Naval Academy, 1945), 88.

43. Norlin J. Jankovsky, ed., *Reef Points, 1945–1946* (Annapolis, MD: United States Naval Academy, 1945), 39.

44. For specific anecdotes, see Warren Johnson, transcriber, "Excerpts from President Carter's Speech in the Naval Academy Chapel, Tuesday, 4 June 1996" *Shipmate* (September 1996), 12; Jimmy Carter, *Why Not the Best?* (Nashville, TN: Broadman Press, 1975), quoted on 43; Joseph P. Flanagan, Class of 1947, interview by author, 23 September 1996; Edward J. McCormack, Jr., Class of 1947, interview by author, 23 October 1996; Howard A. Weiss, Class of 1947, interview by author, 11 May 1996; Richard E. Whiteside, Class of 1949, interview by author, 9 October 1996; Seymour Einstein, Class of 1941, to author, 28 May 1997.

45. Francis B. Carlon, Class of 1948A, to author, 12 October 1996; Lawrence C. Chambers, Class of 1952, interview by author, November 1996; Carter, *Why Not the Best?* 43.

46. Undated memo titled "first year midshipmen," folder 2, box 27, MCHS; "Annapolis: Negro Midshipman Finds Race Trouble at Academy," 12; *Washington Tribune,* 27 February 1937; press release entitled "Midshipman Johnson's Dismissal Upheld," 1 March 1937, folder 3, box 315, Claude Barnett Papers, Chicago Historical Society; Johnson, interview by Nordin.

47. *Afro-American,* 27 February 1937, clipping in folder 9A, box 5, Entry 39B, Records of the Superintendent, General Records, Midshipmen, Brigade of Midshipmen, RG 405, USNA; Wilson to the President, 11 April 1938, folder 8, box 5, Entry 39B, Records of the Superintendent, General Records, Midshipmen, Brigade of Midshipmen, RG 405, USNA; Carpenter interview.

48. *Washington Tribune,* 27 February 1937; Johnson, undated memo titled "significant facts," folder 2, box 35, MCHS; Bruce P. Hayden, Class of 1938, interview by author, 29 October 1997.

49. "Abstract of Conduct . . . Fourth Class Year," JMPJ; Johnson, undated memo dated "significant facts," folder 2, box 35, MCHS; memo titled "Agenda," 15 June 1937, folder 5, box 31, MCHS; "Annapolis: Negro Midshipman Finds Race Trouble at Academy," 12; ltr., Bruce P. Hayden to the editor, *Proceedings* 99 (August 1973): 98.

50. Mark H. Jordan, Class of 1937, telephone conversation with author, 25 August 1998.

51. Robert B. Erly, Class of 1937, to author, 28 October 1998.

52. Memo titled "Agenda," 15 June 1937, folder 5, box 31, MCHS; "Annapolis: Negro Midshipman Finds Race Trouble at Academy," 12; Johnson, interview by Nordin; Nordin, *The New Deal's Black Congressman,* 229. Many documents in the Mitchell papers indicate that Johnson was aware of the efforts against him. See for example the memo titled "agenda," 15 June 1937, folder 5,

box 31, and two different memos written by Johnson titled "significant facts," folder 2, box 35, MCHS.

53. "An Annapolis Dad" to Mitchell, 27 February 1937, folder 6, box 28, MCHS; Joseph P. Morray, Class of 1940, to author, 20 May 1997.

54. Ltr., Bruce P. Hayden to the editor, *Proceedings* 99 (August 1973): 98; Bruce P. Hayden, Class of 1938, to author, 22 October 1997. See also Bruce P. Hayden, Class of 1938, interview by author, 29 October 1997.

55. "Annapolis: Negro Midshipman Finds Race Trouble at Academy," 12; Robert J. Celustka, Class of 1941, telephone conversation with author, 18 June 1997; Hayden to author, 22 October 1997; Carpenter interview.

56. "An Annapolis Dad" to Mitchell, 27 February 1937, folder 6, box 28, MCHS; ltr., Bruce P. Hayden to the editor; Robert J. Celustka, Class of 1941, to author, c. 1997.

57. Sellers to Mitchell, 30 January 1937, folder 1, box 27, MCHS.

58. "Abstract of Conduct . . . Fourth Class Year," JMPJ; Johnson, "Statement of Facts," n.d., folder 2, box 35, MCHS.

59. Note appended to "Statements of Lt. Com. Padgett," 4 February 1937, folder 2, box 27, MCHS; memo concerning Johnson's English grade and Christmas leave, 17 February 1937, JMPJ; Johnson, "Significant Facts," 1937, folder 2, box 35, MCHS; *Washington Tribune*, 27 February 1937; Johnson, interview by Nordin.

60. Sellers to Johnson, 27 January 1937, JMPJ, folder 10, box 26, MCHS, and OF 2567, FDRL.

61. James Lee Johnson, Sr., to Sellers, 2 February 1937, JMPJ.

62. Mitchell to Roosevelt, 29 January 1937, folder 10, box 26, MCHS and OF 2567, FDRL.

63. Mitchell to Sellers, 29 January 1937, folder 10, box 26, MCHS and OF 2567, FDRL.

64. Sellers to Mitchell, 30 January 1937, folder 1, box 27, MCHS.

65. Sellers, memorandum, 8 February 1937, JMPJ.

66. Mitchell to Sellers, 3 February 1937, folder 2, box 27, MCHS; "Statements of Lt. Com. Padgett," 4 February 1937, MCHS; Padgett, memorandum for the Commandant of Midshipmen, 8 February 1937, JMPJ. Emphasis added.

67. Todd, memorandum for the superintendent, 11 February 1937, JMPJ.

68. Hart to Chief of the Bureau of Navigation, 25 July 1934, file 550–639, box 755, Entry 90, RG 24, NA; undated documents titled "Physical Record" and "1st Term 1936–37," JMPJ; Byrd to Swanson, 5 January 1937, file OL11 730–809, box 756, Entry 90, RG 24, NA; Carpenter interview.

69. Minutes of the meeting of the Naval Academy Academic Board, 9–10 February 1937, 189–90, part 2, vol. 31, Entry 204, RG 405, USNA; Todd to Johnson, Sr., 15 February 1937, folder 6, box 27, MCHS; Sellers, memo dated 23 February 1937, JMPJ.

70. "Significant Facts," 1937, folder 2, box 35, and Johnson, "The Circumstances of My Resignation," 11 February 1937, folder 4, box 27, MCHS; Johnson to the superintendent, 11 February 1937, and Secretary of the Navy to Johnson, 12 February 1937, JMPJ; Johnson, interview by Nordin.

71. Johnson, Sr., to Mitchell, 13 February 1937, folder 5, box 27, MCHS; Johnson, Sr., to Todd, 14 February 1937, JMPJ; Todd to Johnson, Sr., 15 February 1937, JMPJ.

72. Mitchell to Sellers and Mitchell to Roosevelt, 13 February 1937, folder 5, and Mitchell to the *Pittsburgh Courier,* 15 February 1937, folder 6, box 27, MCHS; Mitchell to Roosevelt, 13 February 1937, OF 2567, FDRL.

73. Mitchell to the *Pittsburgh Courier,* 15 February 1937, folder 6, box 27, MCHS.

74. *Baltimore Sun,* 14 February 1937; *Washington Times,* 16 February 1937.

75. Nordin, *The New Deal's Black Congressman,* 232–33.

76. Swanson, memorandum for the President, 13 February 1937, JMPJ and OF 2567, FDRL; Sellers, memorandum for the files, 15 February 1937, JMPJ; Henry C. Ferrell, author of *Claude A. Swanson of Virginia: A Political Biography* (Lexington: University of Kentucky Press, 1985), to author, 10 June 1998.

77. Sellers, memo dated 18 February 1937, JMPJ.

78. "Journal of the Academic Board, 1936–1938," 193, part 2, vol. 31, Entry 204, RG 405, USNA; Sellers, "memorandum for the files," and Sellers to the Secretary of the Navy, 18 February 1937, JMPJ; memo, 24 February 1937, OF 2567, FDRL; King to Johnson, Sr., 19 February 1937, JMPJ; *Afro-American,* 27 February 1937.

79. *Pittsburgh Courier,* 6 March 1937.

80. Mitchell to Young, 25 February 1937, folder 4, box 28, MCHS.

81. *Pittsburgh Courier,* 20 February 1937; *Afro-American* (Washington edition), 27 February 1937; "Annapolis: Negro Midshipman Finds Race Trouble at Academy," 11–12.

82. *Afro-American* (Washington edition), 27 February 1937; *Washington Tribune,* 27 February 1937.

83. *Afro-American* (Washington edition) and *Washington Tribune,* 27 February 1937.

84. Unprovenanced clipping, folder 9a, box 5, Entry 39B, Records of the Superintendent, General Records, Midshipmen, Brigade of Midshipmen, RG 405, USNA.

85. Mitchell to Vickery, 16 February 1937, folder 7, box 27, Mitchell, draft of a House resolution, 23 February 1937, folder 3, box 28, Mitchell to Garvin, 5 March 1937, folder 9, box 28, Mitchell to Houston, 8 March 1937, folder 1, box 29, Mitchell to Bluford, n.d., folder 4, box 29, Mitchell to the Secretary of the Navy, 7 July 1937, folder 8, box 31, Leahy to Mitchell, 13 July 1937, folder 9, box 31, Mitchell to the Secretary of the Navy, 19 July 1937 (two letters this

date), folder 2, box 32, and Andrews to Mitchell, 24 July 1937 (two letters this date), folder 3, box 32, MCHS.

86. Drake to superintendent, n.d., "Black Midshipmen" reference file, Special Collections, Nimitz Library, USNA.

87. Gillem to Mitchell, 16 February 1937, folder 7, box 27, Wiseman to Mitchell, 16 February 1937, folder 7, box 8, Hamilton to Mitchell, 17 February 1937, folder 8, box 27, Lochard to Mitchell, 17 February 1937, folder 8, box 27, Davis to Mitchell, 17 February 1937, folder 7, box 27, American Society for Race Tolerance to Mitchell, 18 February 1937, folder 8, box 27, Douglass to Mitchell, 28 February 1937, folder 7, box 28, and James and Gertrude Johnson to Mitchell, 28 February 1937, folder 7, box 28, MCHS.

88. Young to Mitchell, 22 February 1937, folder 3, and "An Annapolis Dad" to Mitchell, 27 February 1937, folder 6, box 28, MCHS.

89. Anon. to Mitchell, 17 February 1937, folder 8, box 27, MCHS; anon. to Mitchell, 11 March 1937, folder 3, box 29, MCHS; unprovenanced clipping, folder 9a, box 5, Entry 39B, Records of the Superintendent, General Records, Midshipmen, Brigade of Midshipmen, RG 405, USNA.

90. Mitchell to O'Connell, 17 February 1937, folder 7, box 27, MCHS; Mitchell to Wiseman, 25 February 1937, folder 4, box 28, MCHS.

91. William M. Carpenter, ed., *The Class of Forty—After Fifty Years* (Annapolis, MD: U.S. Naval Academy, c. 1990), s.v., James Lee Johnson, Jr.; William M. Carpenter, Class of 1940, to author, c. June 1997.

92. Cooke interview; Johnson, interview by Nordin; Frank Johnson interview; Elmer Jones, Tuskegee airman who served with James Lee Johnson, Jr., telephone conversation with author, 25 April 1997; Kurt Johnson, son of James Lee Johnson, Jr., telephone conversation with author, 14 July 1998.

93. William M. Carpenter, Class of 1940, to author, c. June 1997; Carpenter interview.

NOTES TO CHAPTER 5

1. Andrews to Mitchell, 18 February 1937, folder 8, box 27, MCHS; *Pittsburgh Courier,* 20 March 1937.

2. Doc. titled "Col. Atwood's Delegation," 13 February 1937, folder 5, box 27, MCHS; Mitchell to the Bureau of Navigation, 10 March 1937, folder 2, box 29, MCHS; *Washington Tribune,* 13 March 1937; George Joseph Trivers, Class of 1941, interview by author, 1997.

3. *Liber Anni 1933* (Washington: Dunbar High School, 1933), 31, 84; *Washington Tribune,* 13 and 20 March 1937.

4. *Washington Tribune,* 13 March 1937; transcript of George Trivers, Miner Teachers College, 23 March 1937, MPJ, s.v. George Joseph Trivers, Class of 1941; *Time,* 19 July 1937, 15; Trivers interview; Cooke interview, 2 April 1997;

Thomas J. Cantwell, "Anacostia: Strength in Diversity," in *Records of the Columbia Historical Society of Washington, D.C., 1973–1974,* ed. Francis Coleman Rosenberger (Washington: Columbia Historical Society, 1976), 330–57; Francine Curro Cary, ed., *Urban Odyssey: A Multicultural History of Washington, D.C.* (Washington: Smithsonian, 1995), 221–22.

5. Minutes of the meeting of the Academic Board, 30 March 1937, part 2, vol. 31, Entry 204, RG 405, USNA; Trivers interview.

6. *Pittsburgh Courier,* 20 March and 26 June 1937.

7. *Washington Tribune,* 17 July 1937; Trivers interview.

8. Nimitz to Mitchell, 22 June 1937, folder 6, box 31, MCHS; Trivers interview.

9. Jackson to Mitchell, 18 June 1937, folder 5, box 31, MCHS; anon. to Mitchell, 18 June 1937, folder 5, box 31, MCHS; *Pittsburgh Courier,* 26 June 1937.

10. Trivers interview.

11. *Washington Tribune,* 17 July 1937; Trivers interview.

12. *Washington Tribune,* 17 July 1937; Trivers interview.

13. *Washington Tribune,* 10 July 1937; *Time,* 19 July 1937, 15; Trivers interview; Ronald Trivers, telephone conversation with author, 4 September 1997; CDR Paul H. Backus, USN (Ret.), Class of 1941, Oral History, USNA.

14. Todd to Sellers, 19 July 1937, "general correspondence Jan.–Oct. 1937" file, box 4, David F. Sellers Papers, LC; Trivers interview.

15. Claudine to George Trivers, n.d., MPJ, s.v., George Joseph Trivers, Class of 1941; Trivers interview.

16. Trivers to the Secretary of the Navy, 3 July 1937, MPJ, s.v., George Joseph Trivers, Class of 1941; Trivers interview.

17. Mitchell, undated memo, folder 8, box 31, MCHS; Todd to Sellers, 19 July 1937, "general correspondence Jan.–Oct. 1937" file, box 4, David F. Sellers Papers, LC.

18. Leahy to Trivers, 7 July 1937, and Todd to Trivers, 8 July 1937, MPJ, s.v., George Joseph Trivers, Class of 1941.

19. Mitchell, undated memo, folder 8, box 31, MCHS.

20. Mitchell to Young, 9 July 1937, folder 9, box 31, MCHS.

21. *Washington Post,* 24 July 1937.

22. *Washington Tribune,* 10 July 1937.

23. Clipping attached to Gay to Mitchell, 16 July 1937, folder 1, box 32, MCHS; *Time,* 19 July 1937, 15; *Pittsburgh Courier* and *Washington Tribune,* 24 July 1937; undated *Boston Herald* clipping attached to Douglass to Mitchell, 27 July 1937, folder 3, box 32, MCHS.

24. Strong to Swanson, 12 July 1937, file OL11 730–809, box 756, Entry 90, RG 24, NA; Stauffer to the Commanding Officer, U.S. Naval Academy, 24 July 1937, MPJ, s.v., George Joseph Trivers, Class of 1941.

25. Todd to the Chief of the Bureau of Navigation, 17 July 1937, file OL11 730–809, box 756, Entry 90, RG 24, NA; MPJ, s.v., George Joseph Trivers, Class of 1941.

26. Unprovenanced clipping, folder 8, box 66, MCHS.

27. Todd to Sellers, 19 July 1937, "general correspondence Jan.–Oct. 1937" file, box 4, David F. Sellers Papers, LC.

28. Draemel, memorandum for the superintendent, 28 April 1938, folder 8, box 5, Entry 39B, Records of the Superintendent, General Records, Midshipmen, Brigade of Midshipmen, RG 405, USNA.

29. Trivers interview; Ming to White, 10 March 1941, file "District of Columbia, Washington, 1941," box II C27, NAACPLC; *Washington Post,* 6 August 2000.

30. Gavagan to White, 13 January 1938, file "Navy 1935–38," box I C377, NAACPLC.

31. *Pittsburgh Courier,* 3 September 1938.

32. "History of Negro Midshipmen or Negro Candidates for Midshipmen," originally dated 21 September 1944, "Black Midshipmen" reference file, Special Collections, Nimitz Library, USNA.

33. Mitchell to Douglass, 29 July 1937, folder 4, box 32, MCHS; Mitchell to Bordley, 17 August 1937, folder 7, box 32, MCHS.

34. Mitchell to Houston, 14 March 1938, folder 6, box 37, Houston to Mitchell, 18 March 1938, folder 7, box 37, and Mitchell to Diggs and Lochard, 27 March 1939, folder 8, box 43, MCHS.

35. War Department press release, 14 July 1945, folder 3, box 315, Claude Barnett papers, Chicago Historical Society; "James Daniel Fowler," *Assembly* 47 (July 1988): 181–82.

36. "James Daniel Fowler," *Assembly* 47 (July 1988): 182.

37. Mitchell to Benedict, 18 June 1938, Mitchell to Roosevelt, 23 June 1938, and Roosevelt to Watson, 9 July 1938, file "War Dept., U.S. Military Academy 1937–39," box 18, OF 25C, FDRL.

38. Wilby to Mitchell, 4 June 1942, folder 4, box 66, MCHS; War Department press release, 14 July 1945, folder 3, box 315, Claude Barnett papers, Chicago Historical Society; "James Daniel Fowler," 181–82; Dennis S. Nordin, *The New Deal's Black Congressman: A Life of Arthur Wergs Mitchell* (Columbia: University of Missouri Press, 1997), 237–38. Classmates who encountered Fowler after graduation found him gracious and outgoing, not bitter. Fowler remained in the Army until 1967, retiring as a colonel. He died in 1985. Fowler's two sons also graduated from the Military Academy.

39. Robert B. Tresville, Jr., admitted 1 July 1939, graduated 19 January 1943; Henry Minton Francis, admitted 1 July 1941, graduated 6 June 1944; Ernest J. Davis, Jr., admitted 20 July 1942, graduated 5 June 1945. Press release entitled "28 Negroes Have Been admitted to United States Military Acad-

emy," 14 July 1945, folder 3, box 315, Claude Barnett Papers, Chicago Historical Society.

40. Mitchell to Gilmer, 13 June 1939, folder 9, box 45, MCHS.

41. Gadsden to Mitchell, 15 January 1941, and Kingsley to Mitchell, 16 January 1941, folder 8, Mitchell to Kingsley, 20 January 1941, and Mitchell to Gadsden, 20 January 1941, folder 9, box 57, Mitchell to Braddan, 3 February 1941, undated memo titled "Toussaint Gadsden, Jr.," folder 3, undated flier titled "Berean Says 'Thanks A Million!'", folder 4, box 58, MCHS.

42. Undated memo titled "Alvin Jerome Thompson," folder 4, box 58, MCHS; *Pittsburgh Courier,* 15 February 1941.

43. "History of Negro Midshipmen or Negro Candidates for Midshipmen," originally dated 21 September 1944, "Black Midshipmen" reference file, Special Collections, Nimitz Library, USNA; undated clipping titled "Qualified, But Barred From Naval School," folder 3, box 315, Claude Barnett papers, Chicago Historical Society.

44. Mitchell to White, 20 April 1941, "Annapolis and West Point Appointment 1941" file, box II A18, NAACPLC.

45. *Pittsburgh Courier,* 8 July 1939; Mitchell to White, 20 April 1941, "Annapolis and West Point Appointment 1941" file, box II A18, NAACPLC; press release entitled "28 Negroes Have Been Admitted to United States Military Academy," 14 July 1945, folder 3, box 315, Claude Barnett papers, Chicago Historical Society. The Military Academy graduated Davenport's class early on account of the war; hence the unusual date.

46. Mitchell to White, Mitchell to Rabout, Tenerowicz, Dingell, Lesinski, Dondero, and Brown, 18 April 1941, Mitchell to O'Brien, 18 April 1941, file "Annapolis and West Point Appointments 1941," box II A18, NAACPLC.

47. O'Brien to Mitchell, 21 April, Dondero to Mitchell, 23 April, Rabaut to Mitchell, 28 April, Lesinski to Mitchell, 29 April, Brown to Mitchell, 19 May 1941, "Annapolis and West Point Appointments 1941" file, box II A18, NAACPLC.

48. Dingell to Mitchell, 23 April 1941, "Annapolis and West Point Appointments 1941" file, box II A18, NAACPLC; press release entitled "28 Negroes Have Been Admitted to United States Military Academy," 14 July 1945, folder 3, box 315, Claude Barnett papers, Chicago Historical Society.

49. "Dingell, Hon. John D.," 12 June 1941, "X-refs. 1941" file, box 4, OF 93, FDRL.

50. Tenerowicz to Diggs, 17 April, and to Mitchell, 21 April 1941, "Annapolis and West Point Appointments 1941" file, box II A18, NAACPLC.

51. Mitchell to White, 23, 24, and 26 April and 1, 3, and 24 May 1941, and White to Mitchell, 30 April and 7 and 28 May 1941, "Annapolis and West Point Appointments 1941" file, box II A18, NAACPLC.

52. White, memorandum for Wilkins and Crump, 19 July 1941, file "Annapolis and West Point Appointments 1941," box II A18, NAACPLC.

53. Johnson, interview by Nordin.

NOTES TO CHAPTER 6

1. *All Hands,* October 1945, 33, 47; Julius Augustus Furer, *Administration of the Navy Department in World War II* (Washington: Government Printing Office, 1959), 34; U.S. Navy Department, "United States Naval Administration in World War II, Bureau of Naval Personnel, History of the Enlisted Personnel Activity" (Washington: Navy Department, 1946), enlisted distribution section, 43–48.

2. Roosevelt established the committee to investigate charges of discrimination in the employment of workers in defense industries and government. Although the committee had no power to punish violators, employers often changed their policies to avoid the embarrassment of a public appearance.

3. Quoted in Neil A. Wynn, *The Afro-American and the Second World War* (New York: Holmes and Meier, 1976), 71.

4. Robert A. Hill, et al., eds., *The FBI's RACON: Racial Conditions in the United States during World War II* (Boston: Northeastern University Press, 1995), 3.

5. "Increasing Militancy and Unity of Negroes," *Washington Post,* 6 January 1942; Walter White, *A Rising Wind* (Garden City, NY: Doubleday, 1945; reprint ed., Westport, CT: Negro Universities Press, 1971), 123; Walter White, *A Man Called White: The Autobiography of Walter White* (New York: Viking, 1948), 220–22; Russell A. Buchanan, *Black Americans in World War II* (Santa Barbara, CA: Clio Books, 1983), 118–31; Lewis A. Erenberg and Susan E. Hirsch, eds., *The War in American Culture: Society and Consciousness during World War II* (Chicago: University of Chicago Press, 1996), 315; Eric Foner, ed., *The New American History* (Philadelphia: Temple University Press, 1990), 133–35; John Hope Franklin and Alfred A. Moss, Jr., *From Slavery to Freedom,* 6th ed. (New York: McGraw-Hill, 1988), 399–406; Hill, et al., eds., *The FBI's RACON,* 35, 407–12; Brenda L. Moore, *To Serve My Country, to Serve My Race: The Story of the Only African American WACs Stationed Overseas during World War II* (New York: New York University Press, 1996), 24–25; Gunnar Myrdal, *An American Dilemma: The Negro Problem and Modern Democracy,* 2 vols. (New York: Harper and Bros., 1944), 2:1003–4, quote on 1003; Wynn, *The Afro-American and the Second World War,* 6–21, 39–78, 99–123; http://www.southerncouncil.org/about/timeline.html, 19 May 2004.

6. White to Roosevelt, 14 July 1937, enclosing "Resolutions Adopted by the Twenty-Eighth Annual Conference," file 1936–39, box 2, OF 2538, FDRL;

Houston to Swanson, 8 October 1937, file "Navy 1935–38," box I C377, NAACPLC; "Houston, Charles H., Special Counsel," 8 October 1937, file 1936–39, box 2, OF 2538, FDRL; *Pittsburgh Courier,* 23 October 1937; White to Roosevelt, 14 July 1938, enclosing "a set of the Resolutions Adopted by the 29th Annual Conference," file 1936–39, box 2, OF 2538, FDRL; White to Roosevelt, 15 September 1939, file 1936–39, box 2, OF 2538, FDRL.

7. Watson to White, 17 October 1939, file 1936–39, box 2, OF 2538, FDRL; White to Wilkins, October 1939, and Wilkins to White, 23 October 1939, 504–5, vol. 4, *BD;* Frank Freidel, *Franklin D. Roosevelt: A Rendezvous with Destiny* (Boston: Little, Brown, 1990), 244–48; David M. Kennedy, *Freedom from Fear: The American People in Depression and War, 1929–1945* (New York: Oxford University Press, 1999), 774–75; Morris J. MacGregor, *Integration of the Armed Forces, 1940–1965* (Washington: Government Printing Office, 1981), 14–15; George McJimsey, *The Presidency of Franklin Delano Roosevelt* (Lawrence: University Press of Kansas, 2000), 162–63; Wynn, *The Afro-American and the Second World War,* 112.

8. Watson to White, 17 October 1939, file 1936–39, box 2, OF 2538, FDRL; MacGregor, *Integration of the Armed Forces,* 14–15.

9. Wilkins, memo to White, 17 May 1940, file "United States Army, Integration in the Armed Services, 1940–55," box II A647, NAACPLC; Marshall to Knox, 26 July 1940, file "United States National Defense Program," box II A654, NAACPLC.

10. Knox to Capper, 1 August 1940, 3, vol. 6, *BD.*

11. Paolo Enrico Coletta, ed., *American Secretaries of the Navy,* 2 vols. (Annapolis, MD: Naval Institute Press, 1980), 2:677–722; MacGregor, *Integration of the Armed Forces,* 59. Knox quoted in *Time,* 7 September 1942, 25.

12. Whiting to Marshall, 2 August 1940, file "United States National Defense Program," box II A654, Marshall, memo to the Secretary, 9 August 1940, file "United States Army, Integration in the Armed Services, 1940–55," box II A647, NAACPLC.

13. Walter White, telegram to Knox, 9 December, and Bureau of Navigation, telegram to White, 16 December 1941, file "United States Navy, Changes in Navy Policy, 1941–44," box II A654, NAACPLC; "Presidential Memorandum for the Secretary of the Navy," 9 January 1942, file 1942–45, box 2, OF 2538, FDRL; NAACP press release, 17 December 1941, "Colonel Watson Committee" file, and clipping from Washington *Afro-American,* "Discrimination—Newspaper Clippings" file, box 2, Entry 131D, RG 80, NA; U.S. Navy Department, "United States Naval Administration in World War II, Bureau of Naval Personnel, The Negro in the Navy in World War II" (Washington: Navy Department, 1947), 4–5.

14. "Negro Editorial Opinion concerning the Navy," 13 December 1941–28

February 1942, "Addison Walker—Miscellaneous Discrimination" file, box 2, Entry 131D, RG 80, NA.

15. Houston to Knox, 12 December 1941, file "U.S. Navy Discrimination Policy, 1943–46," box II B195, NAACPLC.

16. *Pittsburgh Courier,* 14 February 1942; Lee Finkle, "The Conservative Aims of Militant Rhetoric: Black Protest during World War II," *Journal of American History* 60 (December 1973): 692, 705, 713.

17. *Pittsburgh Courier,* 26 March 1938; Lee Finkle, *Forum For Protest: The Black Press during World War II* (Cranbury, NJ: Fairleigh Dickinson University Press, 1975), 9, 10, 156–62. The 23 October 1943 issue of the *Pittsburgh Courier* contains an article summarizing its fight to change Navy policy.

18. *Pittsburgh Courier,* 14 December 1940.

19. Finkle, "The Conservative Aims of Militant Rhetoric," 704–5, 713.

20. Roosevelt, memo for the Secretary of the Navy, 9 January 1942, file "Navy 1942," box 7, PSF confidential, FDRL; Roosevelt, memo for the Secretary of the Navy, 22 February 1943, 43–44, vol. 6, *BD;* U.S. Navy Department, "The Negro in the Navy," 4–5.

21. Knox to Pinchot, 19 January 1942, 13–14, vol. 6, *BD.*

22. Press release, 7 April 1942, 103, vol. 6, *BD;* MacGregor, *Integration of the Armed Forces,* 66.

23. *Pittsburgh Courier,* 18 April 1942; various postcards, "Negro R" file, box 1, Entry 131-O, RG 80, NA.

24. Douglass to Walker, 1 February 1942, "Discrimination D" file, box 1, Entry 131-N, RG 80, NA; extract from the Cleveland *Call and Post,* 18 April 1942, "Addison Walker—Miscellaneous Discrimination" file, box 1, Entry 131D, RG 80, NA.

25. Keating to Knox, 19 March 1942, "Discrimination K" file, box 1, Entry 131-N, RG 80, NA; extract from the Norfolk *Journal and Guide,* 18 April 1942, "Addison Walker—Miscellaneous Discrimination" file, box 1, Entry 131D, RG 80, NA; *Washington Tribune,* 11 April 1942.

26. Knox to Smathers, 6 February 1942, 17, vol. 6, *BD;* "Report of the Board of Visitors to the United States Naval Academy—1942," 23 April 1942, folder 1, box 2, Entry 209A, RG 405, USNA.

27. Smathers to Beardall, 16 March 1942, folder 8, box 5, Entry 39B, Records of the Superintendent, General Records, Midshipmen, Brigade of Midshipmen, RG 405, USNA; extract from the *Newark Herald News,* 21 March 1942, "Addison Walker—Miscellaneous Discrimination" file, box 1, Entry 131D, RG 80, NA; *New York Times,* 25 September 1955.

28. Beardall to Smathers, 19 March 1942, folder 8, box 5, Entry 39B, Records of the Superintendent, General Records, Midshipmen, Brigade of Midshipmen, RG 405, USNA.

29. Knox to Walsh, 21 May 1942, 118, vol. 6, *BD.*

30. Unless otherwise stated, this section on Doris Miller comes from the "Doris Miller" file, Blacks in the Navy, World War II, Ready Reference Files, OA, especially USS *West Virginia,* Action Report, 11 December 1941; *New York Times,* 22 December 1941; undated United States Pacific Fleet press release; *Washington Post,* 14 July 1990; and Jesse Pond, "The Doris Miller Story," *The Pearl Harbor History Associates, Incorporated Newsletter* 23 (Summer 1994): 1–2. See also Vickie Gail Miller, *Doris Miller: A Silent Medal of Honor* (Austin, TX: Eakin Press, 1997). Doris Miller was proud of his first name, given to him by his mother, and refused to give it up. The Navy, concerned about image, masculinized the name to "Dorie" in correspondence and press releases.

31. White to Roosevelt, 24 December 1941, "Citation of Negro Mess Attendants" file, box 1, Entry 131D, RG 80, NA, and file "United States Navy, Dorie Miller, 1942," box II A655, NAACPLC; Knox to White, 31 December 1941, "Citation of Negro Mess Attendants" file, box 1, Entry 131D, RG 80, NA, and file "United States Navy, Dorie Miller, 1942," box II A655, NAACPLC.

32. Allen to White, 5 March 1942, "Citation of Negro Mess Attendants" file, box 1, Entry 131D, RG 80, NA, and file "United States Navy, Dorie Miller, 1942," box II A655, NAACPLC; Walker, memo for Bard, 13 May 1942, "Addison Walker—Miscellaneous Discrimination" file, box 2, Entry 131D, RG 80, NA; *Pittsburgh Courier,* 14 March 1942; Wilkins to Knox, 13 March 1942, "Citation of Negro Mess Attendants" file, box 1, Entry 131 D, RG 80, NA, and file "United States Navy, Dorie Miller, 1942," box II A655, NAACPLC; extracts from the *Chicago Sunday Bee,* 22 March 1942, and from the *Hartford Courant,* 23 March 1942, "Addison Walker—Miscellaneous Discrimination" file, box 1, Entry 131D, RG 80, NA; *Congressional Record,* 77th Cong., 2d sess., vol. 88, part 2, 2411; excerpts from various black newspapers, "Addison Walker—Miscellaneous Discrimination" file, box 1, Entry 131D, RG 80, NA.

33. *Amsterdam Star News,* 21 March 1942; "Dorie Miller" file, box 1, Entry 131D, RG 80, NA.

34. Walker to "Dear Sir," 6 April 1942, "Dorie Miller" file, box 1, Entry 131D, RG 80, NA.

35. Biddle, Memorandum for the President, 1 May 1942, "Addison Walker—Miscellaneous Discrimination" file, box 2, Entry 131D, RG 80, NA, and OF 4936, FDRL.

36. See OF 4936, FDRL, and file "United States Navy, Dorie Miller, 1942," box II A655, NAACPLC.

37. *Pittsburgh Courier,* 11 April and 30 May 1942.

38. Lewis to Mitchell, 1 June 1942, Apter to Mitchell, 3 June 1942, and Service to Mitchell, 8 June 1942, folder 4, box 66, MCHS.

39. Anon. to White, 21 July, White to Willson, 30 July, and Beardall to

White, 31 July 1942, folder 8, box 5, Entry 39B, Records of the Superintendent, General Records, Midshipmen, Brigade of Midshipmen, RG 405, USNA.

40. Draper to Mitchell, 15 July, folder 9, and Draper to Mitchell, 16 July 1942, folder 10, box 66, MCHS; Ford to Murray, 22 July 1943, folder 8, box 5, Entry 39B, Records of the Superintendent, General Records, Midshipmen, Brigade of Midshipmen, RG 405, USNA.

41. Clipping from *Detroit Tribune,* 6 June 1942, folder 3, box 315, Claude Barnett papers, Chicago Historical Society; Draper to Mitchell, 19 November 1942, folder 7, box 66, Mitchell to Kelly, 16 December 1942, Draper to Mitchell, 17 December 1942, folder 9, box 67, Draper to Mitchell, 6 January 1943, folder 2, box 68, MCHS.

42. MacGregor, *Integration of the Armed Forces,* 67–68.

43. Conference of Presidents of Negro Land Grant Colleges to Knox, 23 June, and memorandum to the editor, 3 July 1942, file "United States Army and Navy Reserve (V-1) Program, 1942–43," box II A653, NAACPLC; *Pittsburgh Courier,* 21 November 1942; Finkle, *Forum for Protest,* 161.

44. White, *A Rising Wind,* 128.

45. U.S. Navy Department, "The Negro in the Navy," 9–14; MacGregor, *Integration of the Armed Forces,* 68–71; Dennis D. Nelson, *The Integration of the Negro into the U.S. Navy* (New York: Farrar, Straus, and Young, 1951), 18. As a result of these measures, the percentage of blacks in the enlisted service skyrocketed to about 5 percent, but then it hovered there for the rest of the war despite the efforts of the War Manpower Commission and President Roosevelt to raise it to 10 percent. The number of black sailors reached 101,573 at the end of 1943. The figure peaked on 30 June 1945 at 165,500, approximately 45 percent of whom were steward's mates.

46. Roosevelt, memo for Knox, 22 February 1943, file "Navy 1943," box 7, PSF confidential, FDRL; "Knox, Hon. Frank," 25 February 1943, file "Abstracts Jan.–April 1943," box 10, OF 18, FDRL; Bureau of Personnel circular, 1 March 1943, 134, vol. 6, *BD;* U.S. Navy Department, "The Negro in the Navy," 13.

47. *Pittsburgh Courier,* 27 February, 18 September, and 23 October 1943; MacGregor, *Integration of the Armed Forces,* 72.

48. Sengstacke to Roosevelt, 29 December 1943, Lovette, memorandum for the Secretary of the Navy, 6 January 1944, and Jacobs, "Comments on the Letter," n.d., file "Jan.–March 1944," box 6, OF 93, FDRL. Italics added.

49. "Notes taken during conference with Petty Officer Carroll, M1/c on 19 March 1945," file 54-1, box 93, Entry 131P, RG 80, NA; U.S. Navy Department, "The Negro in the Navy," 36; Nelson, *The Integration of the Negro into the U.S. Navy,* 27–34. DuFau quoted in Mary Pat Kelly, *Proudly We Served: The Men of the USS Mason* (Annapolis, MD: Naval Institute Press, 1995), 117.

50. Quoted in Mary Penick Motley, ed., *The Invisible Soldier: The Experi-*

ence of the Black Soldier, World War II (Detroit: Wayne State University Press, 1975), 106.

51. U.S. Navy Department, "The Negro in the Navy," 67, 75–80; MacGregor, *Integration of the Armed Forces,* 75.

52. Bernard C. Nalty, *Strength for the Fight: A History of Black Americans in the Military* (New York: Free Press, 1986), 190–93; MacGregor, *Integration of the Armed Forces,* 75–78.

53. Nimitz to McClendon, 4 March 1941, file "U.S. Navy General 1940–47," box II B195, NAACPLC.

54. *Pittsburgh Courier,* 4 July 1942; MacGregor, *Integration of the Armed Forces,* 79, n. 69; Robert J. Schneller, Jr., "Oscar Holmes: A Place in Naval Aviation," *Naval Aviation News* 80 (January–February 1998): 26–27.

55. The Navy merged all of its previous college training programs into the V-12 program, including the NROTC, V-1, and V-7 programs.

56. U.S. Navy Department, "The Negro in the Navy," 34, 43; U.S. Navy Department, "United States Naval Administration in World War II, Bureau of Naval Personnel, Officer Personnel" (Washington: Navy Department, 1945), I, procurement section, 24, 33–46, 94–97, 108; U.S. Navy Department, "United States Naval Administration in World War II, Bureau of Naval Personnel, Training Activity, Part 4, Vol. 1, Standards and Curriculum Division" (Washington: Navy Department, 1946), 111–29, 152; U.S. Navy Department, "United States Naval Administration in World War II, Bureau of Naval Personnel, Part 4, Vol. 4, Training Activity, College Training Program" (Washington: Navy Department, 1946), 2–7, 46–67, 83, 94, 123–25; James G. Schneider, "'Negroes Will Be Tested!'—FDR," *Naval History* 7 (Spring 1993): 15; James G. Schneider, *The Navy V-12 Program: Leadership for a Lifetime* (Boston: Houghton Mifflin, 1967), xi, 68–74, 87, 102, 123, 150–59. The test was administered twice more, in November 1943 and April 1944.

57. Stevenson to Knox, 29 September 1943, 141, vol. 6, *BD.*

58. U.S. Navy Department, "The Negro in the Navy," 32–33.

59. *Pittsburgh Courier,* 5 February 1944; U.S. Navy Department, "The Negro in the Navy," 33–34; Finkle, *Forum for Protest,* 161; MacGregor, *Integration of the Armed Forces,* 81–82; Nelson, *The Integration of the Negro into the United States Navy,* 159; Paul Stillwell, ed., *The Golden Thirteen: Recollections of the First Black Naval Officers* (Annapolis, MD: Naval Institute Press, 1993), xxii–xxiv.

60. Townsend Hoopes and Douglas Brinkley, *Driven Patriot: The Life and Times of James Forrestal* (New York: Knopf, 1992), 3–9, 36, 61, 73, 83, 109–29, 140, 179–86, 452–65, 478. Forrestal's workaholic nature, combined with the tremendous stresses arising from his wartime responsibilities and role in the post-war defense reorganization, fatally wounded his mental health. On 22 May 1949, he climbed out a window and plummeted thirteen stories to his death.

61. Forrestal, "Remarks . . . at a Dinner Meeting of the National Urban League," 12 February 1948, box 32, James V. Forrestal Papers, Seeley G. Mudd Library, Princeton University; L. D. Reddick, "The Negro in the United States Navy during World War II," *Journal of Negro History* 32 (1947): 214; Hoopes and Brinkley, *Driven Patriot*, 181.

62. Quoted in MacGregor, *Integration of the Armed Forces*, 88–89.

63. Knox to Mowrer, 1 May 1942, file "General Correspondence 1942," Franklin Knox papers, LC; Forrestal, Memorandum for the President, 20 May 1944, 245, vol. 6, *BD;* MacGregor, *Integration of the Armed Forces*, 85–86.

64. Jacobs to All Ships and Stations, 7 August 1944, 172, vol. 6, *BD;* MacGregor, *Integration of the Armed Forces*, 86–91.

65. U.S. Navy Department, Bureau of Personnel, *Guide to Command of Negro Naval Personnel*, 12 February 1945, 275–93, vol. 6, *BD*.

66. Buchanan, *Black Americans in World War II*, 86–87; MacGregor, *Integration of the Armed Forces*, 92–93; Nalty, *Strength for the Fight*, 190–96.

67. Quoted in White, *A Man Called White*, 272–73.

68. MacGregor, *Integration of the Armed Forces*, 94–97.

69. MacGregor, *Integration of the Armed Forces*, 95–97.

70. "Statement by Mr. Lester Granger," 13 July 1945, "Minorities in the Military/Blacks in the Navy, World War II" file, Ready Reference Files, OA.

71. Granger to Forrestal, 26 August 1948, 695, vol. 8, *BD*.

72. U.S. Navy Department, *Annual Report, Fiscal Year 1945* (Washington: Navy Department, 1946), A-19; T. L. Sprague, memo to the Under Secretary of the Navy, 1 May 1947, file P16-1/MM Jan. 1945–Dec. 1948, box 259, Entry 1001, RG 24, NA; MacGregor, *Integration of the Armed Forces*, 98.

73. U.S. Navy Department, *Annual Report, Fiscal Year 1945*, A-19; Paul to Granger, 27 July 1945, file "U.S. Navy, General, 1940–47," box II B145, NAACPLC; T. L. Sprague, memo to the Under Secretary of the Navy, 1 May 1947, file P16-1/MM Jan. 1945–Dec. 1948, box 259, Entry 1001, RG 24, NA; Nelson, *The Integration of the Negro into the United States Navy*, 166–67; Regina Akers, "The Integration of Afro-Americans into the WAVES, 1942–1945" (M.A. thesis, Howard University, 1993).

74. Ulysses Lee, *The Employment of Negro Troops* (Washington: Government Printing Office, 1994), 211, 415–16.

75. War Department press release, 14 July 1945, folder 3, box 315, Claude Barnett papers, Chicago Historical Society; U.S. Department of Defense, *Black Americans in Defense of Our Nation: A Pictorial Documentary of the Black American Male and Female Participation and Involvement in the Military Affairs of the United States of America* (Washington: Government Printing Office, 1991), 241.

76. During the war the curriculum at the Military Academy was shortened to three years.

292 | *Notes to Chapter 6*

77. Undated data sheet titled "H. Minton Francis," folder 4, box 58, Wilby to Mitchell, 4 June 1942, folder 4, box 66, MCHS; Salter, Krewasky Antonio Salter, "'Sable Officers': African-American Military Officers, 1861–1948" (Ph.D. dissertation, Florida State University, 1996), 223–36.

78. LCDR Wesley Anthony Brown, CEC, USN (Ret.), USNA Class of 1949, Oral History, United States Naval Institute, Annapolis, MD; Wesley Anthony Brown, Class of 1949, interview by author, 19 December 1995; Wesley Anthony Brown, Class of 1949, interview by author, 23 January 1997, 21–34; Wesley A. Brown, conversation with author, 19 November 1998; Wesley A. Brown, "The First Negro Graduate of Annapolis Tells His Story," *Saturday Evening Post,* 25 June 1949, 111; Draper to Brown, 20 June 1945, BMPJ; memo, 22 October 1945, folder 8, box 5, Entry 39B, Records of the Superintendent, General Records, Midshipmen, Brigade of Midshipmen, RG 405, USNA; Adam Clayton Powell, *Adam by Adam: The Autobiography of Adam Clayton Powell, Jr.* (New York: Dial Press, 1971), 78; Hill, ed., *The FBI's RACON,* 190–91; Hamilton, *Adam Clayton Powell,* 1–6, 59, 81–185; Wil Haygood, "Keeping the Faith," *American Legacy* 3 (Winter 1998): 23–28; Wil Haygood, *King of the Cats: The Life and Times of Adam Clayton Powell, Jr.* (Boston: Houghton Mifflin, 1993), 118.

NOTES TO CHAPTER 7

1. Unless otherwise cited, this chapter is based upon the following sources: LCDR Wesley Anthony Brown, CEC, USN (Ret.), USNA Class of 1949, Oral History (unpublished), U.S. Naval Institute, Annapolis, MD; Wesley Anthony Brown, Class of 1949, interview by author, 19 December 1995 (1st interview), 23 January 1997 (2d interview), 17 October 1997 (3d interview), 17 December 1998 (4th interview), 16 September 1999 (5th interview); Wesley A. Brown, interview by Jean-Paul Reveyoso and Martha Dey, 8 May 1991, General Accounting Office, Washington, D.C.; Wesley Brown's high school transcript, "Dunbar High School" folder, box 1, BMS; "Statement of Personal History," n.d., BOSMR.

2. John Kalivretenos (grandson of the founder), telephone conversation with author, 7 January 1999.

3. Sandra Fitzpatrick and Maria R. Goodwin, *The Guide to Black Washington: Places and Events of Historical and Cultural Significance in the Nation's Capital,* rev. ed. (New York: Hippocrene Books, 1999), 149–50.

4. Constance McLaughlin Green, *The Secret City: A History of Race Relations in the Nation's Capital* (Princeton, NJ: Princeton University Press, 1967), vii, 4, 199–231; Harry S. Wender, "An Analysis of Recreation and Segregation in the District of Columbia," May 1949, unpublished ms., Historical Society of Washington, D.C.

5. *Minutes of the Board of Education of the District of Columbia*, vol. 32, 11 January 1939, 30, and vol. 44, 19 May 1943, 64–67, Charles Sumner School Museum and Archives, Washington, DC; *Liber Anni 1944* (Washington: Dunbar High School, 1944), 25, 53; *Afro-American* (Washington edition), 17 April 1948; Atwood to Brown, 1949, "U.S. Naval Academy Graduation—Congratulatory Cards" folder, box 1, BMS.

6. U.S. Congress, House, *Memorial Services Held in the House of Representatives and Senate of the United States, Together with Tributes Presented in Eulogy of William L. Dawson, Late a Representative from Illinois* (Washington: Government Printing Office, 1971); clipping from *Cleveland Call and Post*, 29 January 1949, "Correspondence 1948–49" file, and typescript biographical sketch, "Army Segregation Speech" file, and clipping from the *Philadelphia Tribune*, 17 March 1945, "News Articles about Dawson" file, William L. Dawson Papers, Moorland-Spingarn Research Center, Howard University; William J. Grimshaw, *Bitter Fruit: Black Politics and the Chicago Machine, 1931–1991* (Chicago: University of Chicago Press, 1992), 31, 72, 75, quote on 66; Dennis S. Nordin, *The New Deal's Black Congressman: A Life of Arthur Wergs Mitchell* (Columbia: University of Missouri Press, 1997), 247.

7. William H. Chafe, "America since 1945," in Eric Foner, ed., *The New American History* (Philadelphia: Temple University Press, 1990), 152.

8. Transcript, "Howard University" folder, BMS; Brown to Chief of Naval Personnel, 8 March 1954, BOSMR.

9. Brown oral history; Brown, 1st interview; Brown, 2d interview; Adam Clayton Powell, Jr., *Adam by Adam: The Autobiography of Adam Clayton Powell, Jr.* (New York: Dial, 1971), 78. Powell's account of how he selected Brown for the Naval Academy differs from Brown's. This account relies on Brown's.

10. *Pittsburgh Courier*, 31 March 1945; "Certificate Action Slip," 25 May 1945, BMPJ; "Memorandum for Mr. Duvall," 22 October 1945, folder 8, box 5, Entry 39B, Records of the Superintendent, General Records, Midshipmen, Brigade of Midshipmen, RG 405, USNA; U.S. Navy Department, Bureau of Naval Personnel, *Regulations Governing the Admission of Candidates into the United States Naval Academy as Midshipmen and Sample Examination Questions, June 1945* (Washington: Government Printing Office, 1945), 8–10. The *Courier* reports that Powell nominated eleven African Americans that year; the memorandum cited above lists ten.

11. *Pittsburgh Courier*, 29 January 1944; "Memorandum for Mr. Duvall," 22 October 1945, folder 8, box 5, Entry 39B, Records of the Superintendent, General Records, Midshipmen, Brigade of Midshipmen, RG 405, USNA; U.S. Office of War Information, Division of Public Inquiries, *United States Government Manual* (Washington: Government Printing Office, 1945); *Dictionary of American Biography*, s.v. Clarence James Brown.

12. Brown to Superintendent, 22 March 1945, BMPJ; Wesley A. Brown,

"The First Negro Graduate of Annapolis Tells His Story," *Saturday Evening Post,* 25 June 1949, 111; Kendall Banning, *Annapolis Today,* 5th ed. (Annapolis, MD: U.S. Naval Institute, 1957), Leland Pearson Lovette, *School of the Sea: The Annapolis Tradition in American Life* (New York: Frederick A. Stokes, 1941), quote on 99; Writers' Program of the Works Projects Administration in the State of Maryland, *A Guide to the United States Naval Academy* (New York: Devin-Adair, 1941).

13. Brown oral history.

14. Press release, 18 February 1941, file "District of Columbia, Washington, 1941," box II C27, Lomack to Wilkins, 4 April 1945, file "District of Columbia, Washington, Jan.–July 1945," and Reed to White, 20 October 1945, file "District of Columbia, Washington, Aug.–Dec. 1945," box II C28, NAACPLC.

15. Powell to Brown, 2 May 1945, "Report of Physical Examination," 8 May 1945, McIntire to Powell, 19 May 1945, "Dental Record," 25 June 1945, BOSMR; President, Permanent Medical Examining Board to Superintendent, 26 June 1945, BMPJ; Brown oral history; Brown, 2d interview.

16. Brown, "The First Negro Graduate," 112; *New York Times,* 8 July 1945; "Oath of Office," 30 June 1945, BMPJ; Brown oral history.

17. Writers' Program, *Guide to the United States Naval Academy,* 31–32; United States Naval Academy Alumni Association, Inc., *Register of Alumni: Graduates and Former Midshipmen and Naval Cadets* (Annapolis, MD: U.S. Naval Academy Alumni Association, 1997), 176–252; Jack Sweetman, *The U.S. Naval Academy: An Illustrated History* (Annapolis, MD: Naval Institute Press, 1979), 197. The 1946 and 1947 *Lucky Bags* reflect the change in the organization of midshipmen from a regiment to a brigade.

18. Sweetman, *U.S. Naval Academy,* 196–97.

19. Officer Biographical Files, s.v. "Stuart H. Ingersoll," OA (quote from incompletely provenanced newspaper clipping); U.S.S. *Monterey,* "History of the U.S.S. Monterey, 17 June 1943 to 2 September 1945" (unpublished manuscript, U.S.S. *Monterey,* c. 1945); Eugene P. Barham, Class of 1935, interview with author, 29 April 1997.

20. Barham interview; Eugene A. Barham, "The 228 Days of the United States Destroyer *Laffey* DD 459" (unpublished ms., Naval Historical Center, 1988), Evins quoted on 1; Richard B. Frank, *Guadalcanal* (New York: Random House, 1990), 428–61, skipper quoted on 441.

21. See *1947 Lucky Bag* (Annapolis, MD: United States Naval Academy, 1946) for interesting details about their time in Annapolis.

22. *Echo of '49,* 2, box 1, BMS; "Midshipmen Having Prior Military Service," 17 April 1946, folder 18, box 4, Entry 39B, Records of the Superintendent, General Correspondence, Midshipmen, Policy and Administration, RG 405, USNA.

23. Thomas T. Seelye, Jr., Class of 1949, to author, 25 November 1996.

24. "Midshipmen Having Prior Military Service," 17 April 1946, folder 18, box 4, Entry 39B, Records of the Superintendent, General Correspondence, Midshipmen, Policy and Administration, RG 405, USNA.

25. Randall Jacobs, "A Post-War Plan for Training Naval Officers," n.d., box 20, James V. Forrestal papers, Seeley G. Mudd Manuscript Library, Princeton University; William Albert Vogele, Class of 1949, to author, 25 October 1996; Matthew A. Chiara, Class of 1948B, to author, May 1997; James H. Doyle, Jr., Class of 1947, to author, 19 May 1997; Kenneth O. Ekelund, Jr., Class of 1947, to author, 17 May 1997; Robert W. Crouter, Class of 1948A, to author, 5 June 1997; John T. Metcalf, Jr., Class of 1949, to author, 24 June 1997; Walter Grechanik, Class of 1948A, to author, 30 July 1997. "We considered the upper classes as staunch draft dodgers," recalled one Class of 1949 alumnus. Robert K. Ripley, Class of 1949, to author, 23 October 1996. While an obvious exaggeration, Ripley's view echoes that put forth by many other alumni from that time.

26. "Chart: United States Naval Academy Attendance—Subdivisions by Religions," folder 8, box 5, Entry 39B, Records of the Superintendent, General Records, Midshipmen, Brigade of Midshipmen, RG 405, USNA.

27. J. C. G. Wilson, Class of 1935, to author, 12 May and 10 June 1997. A "pass-down-the-line" order (PDL) was an orally transmitted instruction.

28. See, for example, the *New York Times,* 8 July 1945. ·

29. See, for example, Graham W. Leonard, Class of 1949, interview by author, 16 April 1997.

30. Brown oral history; Brown, 1st interview; Leonard interview.

31. Brown, 2d interview; Edward S. Briggs, Class of 1949, to author, 2 October 1996; James V. Ferrero, Class of 1949, interview by author, 16 May 1997; William A. Armstrong, Class of 1949, to author, 17 May 1997; Ivan L. Roenigk, Class of 1949, to author, 21 May 1997.

32. Anonymous former midshipman, interview by author, 28 October 1996.

33. Leonard interview.

34. Leonard interview; MPJ, s.v. Graham Weaver Leonard, Class of 1949.

35. U.S. Naval Academy, *Annual Register of the United States Naval Academy, 1945–1946* (Washington: Government Printing Office, 1945), 142.

36. Fitch to Flanagan, 1 June 1946, MPJ, s.v. Joseph Patrick Flanagan, Jr.

37. Joseph P. Flanagan, Jr., Class of 1947, interview by author, 23 September 1996; MPJ, s.v. Joseph Patrick Flanagan, Jr., Class of 1947; Joseph P. Flanagan, Class of 1947, to author, 19 March 1997.

38. Flanagan interview; William H. Sword, Class of 1949, interview by author, 24 October 1996.

39. MPJ, s.v. Donald Boone Whitmire, Class of 1947; Baltimore *Evening Sun,* 4 December 1986; Jack Clary, *Navy Football: Gridiron Legends and Fighting Heroes* (Annapolis, MD: Naval Institute Press, 1997), 90–100.

40. Flanagan interview; quote from Flanagan to author, 19 March 1997.

41. Flanagan interview.

42. MPJ, s.v. Donald Boone Whitmire, Class of 1947.

43. Sword interview.

44. Brown, 2d interview; Sword interview; Flanagan to author, 19 March 1997.

45. Brown, 1st interview; Brown, 2d interview; Brown oral history; Brown, "The First Negro Graduate," 112.

46. John Long, "Here's How the Middies Celebrated Jap Armistice," *Shipmate* 8 (October 1945): 30–31, 77–78; *Lucky Bag 1947* (Annapolis, MD: Naval Academy, 1946); Sweetman, *The U.S. Naval Academy,* 200.

47. Philip L. Brown, *The Other Annapolis, 1900–1950* (Annapolis, MD: Annapolis Publishing Co., 1994).

48. Brown, 1st interview.

49. Harry M. Krantzman, Class of 1949, to author, 27 September 1996; Leonard interview; Brown, 1st interview.

50. Richard S. West, Jr., "The Superintendents of the Naval Academy," *Proceedings* 71 (July 1945): 809, emphasis added; Barham interview.

51. Louis J. Gulliver, "Air Admiral at Academy Controls," *Shipmate* 8 (September 1945): 19, 59–62; various documents, Officers' Biographies File, s.v. Aubrey Wray Fitch, OA.

52. U.S. Navy Department, Bureau of Personnel, *Catalog of Course of Instruction at the United States Naval Academy, Annapolis, Md., the One Hundred and First Academic Year, 1945–1946* (Washington: Government Printing Office, 1946), 5; Brown oral history; Brown, 1st interview.

NOTES TO CHAPTER 8

1. U.S. Naval Academy, *Annual Register of the United States Naval Academy, 1945–1946* (Washington: Government Printing Office, 1945), 142; U.S. Navy Department, Bureau of Naval Personnel, *Catalog of Course of Instruction at the United States Naval Academy, Annapolis, Md., the One Hundred and First Academic Year, 1945–1946* (Washington: Government Printing Office, 1946), 5.

2. Earle K. McLaren, Class of 1934, to author, 20 May 1997.

3. Eugene A. Barham, Class of 1935, interview by author, 29 April 1997.

4. Beaumont M. Buck, Class of 1948B, to author, 30 May and 14 June 1997; James H. Doyle, Jr., Class of 1947, to author, 19 May 1997; Walter M. Meginniss, Class of 1947, to author, 4 June 1997; Ralph E. Moon, Jr., Class of 1947, telephone conversation with author, 21 May 1997; William A. Spencer, Class of 1947, to author, 17 October 1996.

5. Joseph P. Flanagan, Jr., Class of 1947, interview by author, 23 September 1996; William H. Barnes III, Class of 1948B, to author, 20 October 1996; Robert C. Peniston, Class of 1947, to author, 26 May 1997; James H. Forbes,

Class of 1947, to author, 18 June 1997; Stansfield Turner, Class of 1947, to author, 26 August 1996.

6. Philip E. Baylor, Class of 1947, to author, 20 September 1996; Donald R. Morris, Class of 1948B, to author, 19 October 1996; Wade Hampton Harris, Class of 1948B, to author, 7 April 1999; Edward J. McCormack, Jr., interview by author, 23 October 1996.

7. Thomas J. Hudner, Jr., Class of 1947, to author, 29 August 1996; Thomas J. Hudner, Jr., Class of 1947, interview by author, 21 October 1996.

8. Wesley A. Brown, "The First Negro Graduate of Annapolis Tells His Story," *Saturday Evening Post,* 25 June 1949, 111.

9. William H. Barnes III, Class of 1948B, to author, 20 October 1996; Alfred G. Wellons, Jr., Class of 1948A, audiotape sent to author, postmarked 28 May 1997.

10. Thomas L. Hartigan, Class of 1947, to author, 27 September 1996; Edwin Heminger, Class of 1949, to author, 7 October 1996; Joseph P. Flanagan, Jr., Class of 1947, to author, 19 March 1997; Flanagan interview.

11. John J. Dempsey, Class of 1947, to author, 11 June 1997.

12. John B. Van Velzer, Class of 1947, to author, June 1997.

13. McCormack interview.

14. Flanagan interview; Hudner interview; Howard A. Weiss, Class of 1947, interview by author, 22 October 1997 (2d interview).

15. McCormack interview.

16. Frederick F. Jewett, Class of 1947, to author, 1 September 1997; Walter M. Meginnis, Class of 1947, to author, 4 June 1997.

17. Howard A. Weiss, Class of 1947, interview by author, 11 May 1996 (1st interview); U.S. Naval Academy, *Annual Register . . . 1945–1946,* 94.

18. Weiss, 1st interview.

19. Kendall Banning, *Annapolis Today,* 5th ed. (Annapolis, MD: U.S. Naval Institute, 1957), 24–25. See also Norlin J. Jankovsky, ed., *Reef Points, 1945–1946* (Annapolis, MD: United States Naval Academy, 1945), 39.

20. Weiss, 1st interview.

21. Wesley A. Brown, Class of 1949, interview by author, 23 January 1997 (2d interview); Flanagan interview.

22. Flanagan interview.

23. William C. Patton, Class of 1947, to author, 5 June 1997.

24. Brown, "The First Negro Graduate," 112; LCDR Wesley Anthony Brown, CEC, USN (Ret.), USNA Class of 1949, Oral History (unpublished), U.S. Naval Institute, Annapolis, MD.

25. Eugene A. Barham, Class of 1935, to author, 21 September 1996; Earle K. McLaren, Class of 1934, to author, 6 October 1996; Barham interview.

26. Francis Brandon Carlon, Class of 1948B, to author, 12 October 1996; John J. Dempsey, Class of 1947, to author, 11 June 1997; William C. Patton,

Class of 1947, to author, 5 June 1997; Kenneth M. Robinson, Class of 1947, to author, c. May 1997.

27. Brown oral history; Harry M. Krantzman, Class of 1949, to author, 27 September 1996.

28. Brown oral history.

29. Brown oral history; Weiss, 1st interview; Thomas F. Lechner, Class of 1949, to author, 25 September 1996; Harry M. Krantzman, Class of 1949, to author, 27 September 1996; Claude E. Swecker, Class of 1949, to author, 29 September 1996; Kenneth A. Bott, Class of 1949, interview by author, 3 October 1996; Robert M. Douglass, Class of 1949 to author, 3 October 1996; Edwin Heminger, Class of 1949, to author, 7 October 1996; Willard S. Peterson, Class of 1949, to author, 7 October 1996; James R. Juncker, Class of 1949, to author, 9 October 1996; Francis B. Carlon, Class of 1948B, to author, 12 October 1996; William Albert Vogele, Class of 1949, to author, 25 October 1996; Thomas T. Seelye, Jr., Class of 1949, to author, 25 November 1996.

30. Harry B. Meyer, Class of 1949, to author, 28 September 1996.

31. Wesley A. Brown, Class of 1949, interview by author, 19 December 1995 (1st interview); Brown, 2d interview.

32. Brown oral history; Brown, 1st interview; James H. Forbes, Class of 1947, to author, 22 May 1997. For different versions of the rumor, see Lawrence H. Derby, Jr., Class of 1949, to author, 23 July 1997; Otto E. Krueger, Class of 1949, to author, 27 July 1997; John Sheehan, Class of 1952, telephone conversation with author, 1 October 1996; Wilburn A. Speer, Class of 1948B, to author, 12 June 1997; J. C. G. Wilson, Class of 1935, to author, 12 May 1997.

33. Brown oral history; Wesley A. Brown, Class of 1949, interview by author, 17 October 1997 (3d interview).

34. Brown, "The First Negro Graduate," 111.

35. Brown oral history.

36. Brown, "The First Negro Graduate," 112; Brown, 1st interview; Brown oral history.

37. Brown, 2d interview.

38. James R. Juncker, Class of 1949, to author, 9 October 1996; Harry B. Meyer, Class of 1949, to author, 28 September 1996.

39. Thomas F. Lechner, Class of 1949, to author, 25 September 1996; William A. Vogele, Class of 1949, to author, 25 October 1996. See also Harry M. Krantzman, Class of 1949, to author, 27 Sept. 1996.

40. Stansfield Turner, Class of 1947, to author, 26 August 1996; Nye G. Rodes, Class of 1947, to author, 4 June 1997. See also Philip E. Baylor, Class of 1947, to author, 8 October 1996; William D. Chandler III, Class of 1948B, telephone conversation with author, 17 June 1997; John J. Dempsey, Class of 1947, to author, 11 June 1997.

41. William C. Patton, Class of 1947, to author, 5 June 1997.

42. Irving Bobrick, Class of 1949, to author, c. October 1996; Edwin L. Heminger, Class of 1949, to author, 7 October 1996; Otto E. Krueger, Class of 1949, to author, 27 July 1997.

43. Claude E. Swecker, Class of 1949, to author, 29 September 1996; Edwin Heminger, Class of 1949, to author, 7 October 1996; John R. Kint, Class of 1949, to author, 10 June 1997.

44. Flanagan interview; William C. Patton, Class of 1947, to author, 5 June 1997.

45. Donald A. Gairing, Class of 1949, to author, 13 October 1996; Robert K. Ripley, Class of 1949, to author, 23 October 1996.

46. Harry B. Meyer, Class of 1949, to author, 28 September 1996; Wallace J. Thomas, Class of 1949, to author, 19 May 1997.

47. Bott interview.

48. Brown oral history; Harry M. Krantzman, Class of 1949, to author, 27 September 1996.

49. Brown, 3d interview.

50. Brown, "The First Negro Graduate," 112; Brown oral history.

51. Oliver L. Norman, Jr., Class of 1948A, to author, 28 July 1997.

52. Weiss, 1st and 2d interviews.

53. Alfred G. Wellons, Jr., Class of 1948A, audiotape sent to author, postmarked 28 May 1997.

54. Robert C. Peniston, Class of 1947, to author, 26 May 1997.

55. Brown oral history.

56. McCormack interview; Brown, 2d interview.

57. Walter G. Moyle, Jr., Class of 1947, interview by author, 12 August 1997.

58. Brown, 2d interview.

59. Peter G. Bourne, *Jimmy Carter: A Comprehensive Biography from Plains to Postpresidency* (New York: Scribner's, 1997), 25, 29–30, 284.

60. Warren Johnson, transcriber, "Excerpts from President Carter's Speech in the Naval Academy Chapel, Tuesday, 4 June 1996," *Shipmate* (September 1996): 13.

61. Jimmy Carter, "The Pasture Gate," in *Always a Reckoning and Other Poems* by Jimmy Carter (New York: Random House, 1995), 33–34. Copyright (c) 1995 by Jimmy Carter. Illustrations Copyright (c) 1995 by Sarah Elizabeth Chuldenko. Used by permission of Times Books, a division of Random House, Inc.

62. Jimmy Carter, Class of 1947, to author, 24 September 1997.

63. Thomas L. Hartigan, Class of 1947, to author, 27 September 1996; Frederick F. Jewett, Class of 1947, to author, 18 June 1997.

64. Chester H. Shaddeau, Jr., Class of 1947, to author, c. July 1997; Moyle interview. Moyle didn't remember any names of those in this group.

65. Weiss, 1st interview; Flanagan interview.

66. Flanagan interview.

67. Flanagan interview.

68. Brown, 2d interview; Flanagan interview.

69. Brown oral history; Brown, 2d interview; Brown, 3d interview; Weiss, 1st interview; Weiss, 2d interview.

70. Brown, 1st interview; Brown, 2d interview; Weiss, 1st interview.

71. Brown oral history; Weiss, 1st interview.

72. Brown oral history.

73. U.S. Naval Academy, *Regulations of the United States Naval Academy, 1945* (Annapolis, MD: U.S. Naval Academy, 1945), 119.

74. Wesley A. Brown, telephone conversation with author, 25 May 1999; John J. Dempsey, Class of 1947, to author, 11 June 1997; John B. Van Velzer, Class of 1947, to author, June 1997.

75. Brown oral history; Brown, 3d interview.

76. Weiss, 1st interview; Weiss, 2d interview.

77. Barham interview; Eugene A. Barham, Class of 1935, to author, 21 September 1996.

78. Powell to Forrestal, 5 October 1945, Forrestal to Powell, 13 October 1945, and Fechteler to Superintendent, U.S. Naval Academy, 15 October 1945, BMPJ.

79. Eugene A. Barham, Class of 1935, to author, 21 September 1996; Brown, 1st interview; Brown, 2d interview; Brown oral history; Ingersoll, memo for the superintendent, 19 October 1945, BMPJ.

80. Brown, 2d interview; Ingersoll, memo for the superintendent, 19 October 1945, and Fitch to Fechteler, 22 October 1945, BMPJ; Forrestal to Powell, 23 October 1945, file P8-5 (7-1-45 to 6-30-46), box 338, RG 80, NA.

81. *Washington Post* and *New York Times,* 23 October 1945.

82. Brown oral history; Brown, 2d interview; McCormack interview; Harry M. Krantzman, Class of 1949, to author, 27 September 1996; Krantzman, telephone conversation with author, 24 September 1996; Weiss, 2d interview.

83. Flanagan interview.

84. Walter M. Meginniss, Class of 1947, to author, 4 June and 13 July 1997.

85. Arthur H. F. Barlow, Class of 1947, to author, 4 July 1997; Brown, 2d interview; David W. Fischer, Class of 1947, telephone conversation with author, 22 May 1997; Flanagan interview; Donald R. Morris, Class of 1948B, to author, 19 October 1996.

86. Donald R. Morris, Class of 1948B, to author, 19 October 1996.

87. Arthur H. F. Barlow, Class of 1947, to author, 4 July 1997; Matthew A. Chiara, Class of 1948B, to author, 9 June 1997; James V. Ferrero, Class of 1949, interview by author, 16 May 1997; James H. Forbes, Class of 1947, to author, 22 May and 18 June 1997.

88. Brown oral history; Brown, 3d interview; McCormack interview; *Washington Post,* 23 October 1945.

89. Adam Clayton Powell, Jr., *Adam by Adam: The Autobiography of Adam Clayton Powell, Jr.* (New York: Dial, 1971), 78–79.

90. Philip E. Baylor, Class of 1947, to author, 20 September and 8 October 1996; Beaumont M. Buck, Class of 1948B, to author, 14 June 1997; James B. Davidson, Class of 1947, to author, 17 May 1997; Robert M. Douglass, Class of 1949, to author, 3 October 1996; Kenneth O. Ekelund, Jr., Class of 1947, to author, 17 May and June 3 1997; David W. Fischer, Class of 1947, telephone conversation with author, 22 May 1997; Thomas L. Hartigan, Class of 1947, to author, 27 September 1996; Walter M. Meginniss, Class of 1947, to author, 4 June and 13 July 1997; Ralph E. Moon, Jr., Class of 1947, telephone conversation with author, 21 May 1997; Moyle interview.

91. "Academic Record," BMPJ.

92. Hudner interview; William H. Barnes III, Class of 1948B, to author, 20 October 1996; Eugene S. Bowers, Class of 1948B, to author, c. July 1997; William D. Chandler III, Class of 1948B, telephone conversation with author, 17 June 1997; James H. Forbes, Class of 1947, to author, 22 May 1997; Otto E. Krueger, Class of 1949, to author, 27 July 1997; William McKinley, Class of 1948A, to author, 25 June 1997; Charles Mertz III, Class of 1948B, telephone conversation with author, 29 May 1997; Moyle interview; Oliver L. Norman, Class of 1948A, to author, 22 May 1997; Richard U. Scott, Class of 1948B, to author, 1997.

93. Randolph F. Patterson, Class of 1948A, to author, 11 June 1997.

94. Forbes to author, 22 May and 18 June 1997; Walter Grechanik to author, 30 July 1997; William McKinley to author, 25 June 1997.

95. Brown, 2d interview.

96. U.S. Naval Academy, *Catalog . . . 1945–1946*, 5; Brown, 3d interview.

97. "Academic Record," BMPJ; Brown, "The First Negro Graduate," 111.

98. "Academic Record," BMPJ; Brown, 1st interview.

99. Flanagan interview; McCormack interview; Weiss, 1st interview.

100. Wesley A. Brown, telephone conversation with author, 25 May 1999; John E. Long, "The Complete Story of June Week 1946 at the Naval Academy," *Shipmate* 9 (July 1946): 31–50; Banning, *Annapolis Today*, 231–46.

NOTES TO CHAPTER 9

1. U.S. Navy Department, Bureau of Naval Personnel, *Catalog of Course of Instruction at the United States Naval Academy, Annapolis, Md., The One Hundred and Second Academic Year, 1946–1947* (Washington: Government Printing Office, 1946), 5; Wesley A. Brown, Class of 1949, interview by author, 16 September 1999 (5th interview).

2. Kendall Banning, *Annapolis Today*, 5th ed. (Annapolis, MD: U.S. Naval Institute, 1957), 149–59; U.S. Naval Academy, *Annual Register of the United*

States Naval Academy, 1946 (Washington: Government Printing Office, 1946), 130–31; U.S. Naval Academy, *Lucky Bag 1949,* 390–93; U.S. Navy Department, Bureau of Naval Personnel, *Catalog, 1946–1947,* 5.

3. LCDR Wesley Anthony Brown, CEC, USN (Ret.), USNA Class of 1949, Oral History (unpublished), U.S. Naval Institute, Annapolis, MD; Wesley A. Brown, Class of 1949, interview by author, 23 January 1997 (2d interview); Brown, 5th interview.

4. "Academic Record," BMPJ; U.S. Naval Academy, *Catalog . . . 1946–1947,* 5–6.

5. U.S. Naval Academy, *Regulations of the United States Naval Academy, 1945,* 46–48; Reeves R. Taylor, Class of 1953, interview by author, 2 December 1996.

6. U.S. Naval Academy, *Annual Register of the United States Naval Academy, 1947* (Washington: Government Printing Office, 1947), 64; "Academic Record," BMPJ; Wesley A. Brown, Class of 1947, interview by author, 19 December 1995 (1st interview).

7. U.S. Naval Academy, *Annual Register,* 1947, 122.

8. Brown oral history; quote in Brown, 1st interview.

9. Brown oral history; Brown, 5th interview; Wesley A. Brown, "The First Negro Graduate of Annapolis Tells His Story," *Saturday Evening Post,* 25 June 1949, 111.

10. U.S. Naval Academy, *Annual Register,* 1947, 122.

11. See U.S. Naval Academy, *Lucky Bag 1948A* and *Lucky Bag 1948B.*

12. U.S. Naval Academy, *Annual Register of the United States Naval Academy, 1948* (Washington: Government Printing Office, 1948), 47; "Academic Record," BMPJ.

13. U.S. Naval Academy, *Lucky Bag* 1949, 414–15.

14. Sylvia Hicks Johnson, interview by author, 6 August 1997; Philip L. Brown, *The Other Annapolis* (Annapolis, MD: Annapolis Publishing Company, 1994), 144–45.

15. Banning, *Annapolis Today,* 136–38.

16. Wesley A. Brown, Class of 1949, interview by author, 17 October 1997 (3d interview); Sylvia Hicks Johnson interview.

17. Brown oral history; Brown, "The First Negro Graduate," 111; U.S. Naval Academy, *Annual Register,* 1948, 119.

18. BMPJ; Brown oral history; unprovenanced clipping, "Articles About Brown" folder, box 1, BMS; William Sandkuhler, Class of 1949, to author, c. June 1997.

19. Brown oral history.

20. Brown, "The First Negro Graduate," 111; Brown oral history; Brown, 1st interview; *Evening Star,* 27 May 1949; clipping, "Naval Academy to Give

Ensign Boards to Negro," folder 3, box 315, Claude Barnett papers, Chicago Historical Society.

21. Brown, 1st interview; Chapnick to Public Relations Department, 3 October 1946, Fitch to Chapnick, 11 October 1946, Granger to Forrestal, 10 June 1947, Gurnette to Chief of Naval Personnel, 11 July 1947, Weintraub to Public Relations Officer, 3 November 1947, Bealle to Holloway, 22 November 1947, Burke to Weintraub and Burke to Bealle, 24 December 1947, BMPJ; clipping, Washington *Afro-American,* file "Public Schools, High School Cadets, 1940–1949," Washingtoniana Division, Martin Luther King, Jr., Branch, D.C. Public Library.

22. Morris A. Bealle, "The Color Line Slackens," *Today's World* 2 (February 1948): 20–21, copy in BMPJ.

23. Wilkinson to Superintendent, 5 March 1948, and Holloway to Wilkinson, 12 March 1948, BMPJ; Murray to Registrar, 19 May 1948, and Hiese to Murray, 25 May 1948, folder 8, box 5, Entry 39B, Records of the Superintendent, General Records, Midshipmen, Brigade of Midshipmen, RG 405, USNA.

24. Guthrie to Public Relations Dept., 15 September 1948, Chapnick to Superintendent, 17 September 1948, Kelleher to Guthrie, 27 September 1948, clipping, *Minneapolis Tribune,* 3 October 1948, Sears to Superintendent, 27 October 1948, Ward to Superintendent, 4 November 1948, Hepburn to Public Relations Dept., 28 December 1948, and Cooper to Hepburn, 10 January 1949, BMPJ; *New York Star,* 9 September 1948.

25. Davis to Brown, 13 January 1949, BMPJ.

26. Hope to Chief of Bureau of Personnel, 17 January 1947, 252–59, vol. 8, *BD;* Nelson to Cooper, 25 January 1949, BMPJ; Brown oral history; Paul Stillwell, ed., *The Golden Thirteen: Recollections of the First Black Naval Officers* (Annapolis, MD: Naval Institute Press, 1993), 21–22, 42, 58, 186–89, 267–69, Martin quoted on 22; Morris J. MacGregor, *Integration of the Armed Forces, 1940–1965* (Washington: Government Printing Office, 1981), 246.

27. Brown oral history; Brown, 1st interview; Nelson to Cooper, 25 January 1949, BMPJ; folder "The First Negro Graduate of Annapolis . . . Contract," BMS; press release, "Midshipman Wesley A. Brown," 28 May 1949, file "United States Navy, General, 1945–49," box II A 654, NAACPLC; U.S. Navy Department, *Register of Commissioned and Warrant Officers of the United States Navy and Marine Corps, January 1, 1950* (Washington: Government Printing Office, 1950), 36. *The Ugly American* (New York: Norton, 1958) is a collection of fictionalized short stories whose collective message was that the United States was losing ground to the Communists in Southeast Asia because of its tactless, ignorant, and ethnocentric diplomats.

28. Brown oral history; *Evening Star,* 27 May 1949; clipping, "Naval Academy to Give Ensign Boards to Negro," folder 3, box 315, Claude Barnett papers,

Chicago Historical Society; unprovenanced clipping, personal papers of Wesley A. Brown; *Pittsburgh Courier,* 4 June 1949; Holloway to the Chief of Naval Personnel, 7 June 1949, BMPJ.

29. *Afro-American* (Baltimore), 11 June 1949; *Pittsburgh Courier,* 11 June 1949; "Annapolis' First," *Time,* 13 June 1949, 19–20; *Echo of '49,* folder "U.S. Naval Academy Graduation Memorabilia June 1949" and folder "News Articles About Brown re. Graduation," box 1, BMS; Brown oral history; Brown, 1st interview; Wesley A. Brown, Class of 1949, interview by author, 17 December 1998 (4th interview).

30. *New York Times,* 27 May 1949; *Pittsburgh Courier,* 28 May and 4 and 11 June 1949; *Afro-American* (Baltimore), 4 and 11 June 1949; "Annapolis' First," 19–20.

31. Brown, "The First Negro Graduate"; Brown oral history.

32. Myers to Rosetta Brown, 27 May 1949, White to Brown, 3 June 1949, and various other correspondence, folder "U.S. Naval Academy Graduation—Congratulatory Cards," box 1, BMS.

33. Brown, note attached to an unprovenanced article, folder "News Articles About Brown," and Gartensleben to Brown, 24 June 1949, Jaeger to Brown, 22 August 1949, Ta-Tsai Liu to Brown, 10 December 1950, folder "Naval Academy Graduation, Letters of Congratulation," box 1, BMS; Brown, 1st interview.

34. Brown oral history; Spottswood to Holloway, 27 May 1949, and unprovenanced article titled "Plan Fetes Here for 1st Negro Annapolis Grad," BMPJ; program signed by Jesse Owens, Chicago Urban League luncheon program, 30 June 1949, folder "U.S. Naval Academy Graduation Memorabilia, June, 1949," box 1, BMS.

35. *New York Times,* 31 December 1949; Sengstacke to Brown, 16 January 1950, folder "Naval Academy Graduation, Letters of Congratulation," box 1, BMS.

36. Brown oral history; Brown, 1st interview; various documents, BOSMR; *Baltimore Sun,* 17 March 1998; resume and ltr., Ryan to Brown, 5 June 2002, courtesy of Wesley A. Brown.

37. Robert J. Schneller, Jr., *Racial Integration of the U.S. Naval Academy* (forthcoming).

Bibliography

PRIMARY SOURCES

Archives, Manuscripts, and Special Collections:

Charles Sumner School Museum and Archives, Washington, DC
   General Research Files
   Minutes of the Board of Education of the District of Columbia
Chicago Historical Society, Chicago, IL
   Claude Barnett Papers
   Arthur Wergs Mitchell Papers
D.C. Public Library, Martin Luther King, Jr., Branch, Washingtoniana Division
Dunbar Senior High School, Washington, DC
   Liber Anni, 1930–1944 (yearbooks)
Library of Congress, Washington, DC
   Christian Alexander Fleetwood Papers
   Franklin Knox Papers
   National Association for the Advancement of Colored People Papers
   David Foote Sellers Papers
   John Lorimer Worden Papers
Moorland-Spingarn Research Center, Howard University, Washington, DC
   Wesley Anthony Brown Papers
   Mu-So-Lit Club Collection
Seeley G. Mudd Library, Princeton University, Princeton, NJ
   James Vincent Forrestal Papers
National Archives and Records Administration, Washington, DC
   RG 24: Records of the Bureau of Navigation and the Bureau of Naval Personnel
      Entry 90. "General Correspondence, 1935–1940."
      Entry 403. "Jackets of Naval Cadets, November 1862–July 1910."
   RG 45: Naval Records Collection of the Office of Naval Records and Library
      Entry 33-A. "Naval Academy Letters, 1847–1884."
      Entry 17. "Letters to Naval Academy, Commanding, and Other Officers, Nov. 1869–Aug. 1884."

Microcopy 124. "Miscellaneous Letters Received by the Secretary of the Navy, 1801–1884."

RG 80: General Records of the Department of the Navy

Entry 131-D. "Assistant Secretary of the Navy Ralph Bard, Correspondence Relating to Discrimination in the Navy, 1941–1944."

Entry 131-N. "Special Assistant Addison Walker, Correspondence Concerning Discrimination in the Navy."

Entry 131-O. "Correspondence on Negroes (Negro Spindle File), Feb.–Sept. 1942, Special Assistant Addison Walker."

Entry 131-P. "Records of the Secretary of the Navy, James Forrestal, 1940–47."

Entry 131-R. "Records of the Secretary of the Navy, James Forrestal, Correspondence Relating to Meetings of the Top Policy Group, 1944–47."

RG 319: Records of the Army Staff

Entry "Integration of Armed Forces 1940–1965."

RG 405: Records of the United States Naval Academy Microcopy 949. "U.S. Naval Academy, Superintendent, Letters Received 1845–1887."

National Personnel Records Center, St. Louis, MO

Official Service and Medical Record, s.v. Wesley Anthony Brown, service number 521291.

Nimitz Library, United States Naval Academy, Annapolis, MD

RG 405: Records of the United States Naval Academy

Entry 25. "Letters Received by the Superintendent, 1845–1887."

Entry 39-B. "Records of the Superintendent."

Entry 75. "Letters and Reports Received by the Superintendent Relating to Individual Midshipmen, 1846–1888; Office of the Superintendent, Administrative Records, Relating to Midshipmen and Cadets, 1846–1925."

Entry 204. "Journals of the Academic Board, 1845–1979."

Entry 209A. "Records of Boards and Committees, Board of Visitors, Reports of the Board of Visitors, 1936–77."

Special Collections and Archives Division

"Black Midshipmen" reference file.

Midshipmen Personnel Jackets.

Franklin Delano Roosevelt Library, Hyde Park, NY

Roosevelt, Franklin D., Papers as President

Official File

President's Personal File

President's Secretary's File

United States Naval Institute, Annapolis, MD

CDR Paul H. Backus, USN (Ret.), Class of 1941, Oral History.

LCDR Wesley Anthony Brown, CEC, USN (Ret.), Class of 1949, Oral History.
University of North Carolina Library, Chapel Hill, NC
Southern Historical Collection, Cotten Family Papers.

*Author Correspondence Files (all correspondence is addressed to the author
and includes letters, faxes, e-mails, and audiotapes sent by individuals):*

William A. Armstrong, Class of 1949, 17 May 1997.
Eugene A. Barham, Class of 1935, 21 September 1996.
Arthur H. F. Barlow, Class of 1947, 4 July 1997.
William H. Barnes III, Class of 1948B, 20 October 1996.
Philip E. Baylor, Class of 1947, 20 September 1996.
Irving Bobrick, Class of 1949, October 1996.
Eugene S. Bowers, Class of 1948B, c. July 1997.
Edward S. Briggs, Class of 1949, 2 October 1996.
Ernest B. Brown, Class of 1949, 26 July 1999.
Beaumont M. Buck, Class of 1948B, 30 May and 14 June 1997.
Francis B. Carlon, Class of 1948A, 12 October 1996.
William M. Carpenter, Class of 1940, c. June 1997.
Jimmy Carter, Class of 1947, 10 April 1996 and 24 September 1997.
Robert J. Celustka, Class of 1941, c. 1997.
Matthew A. Chiara, Class of 1948B, c. May 1997.
Donald E. Craig, Class of 1949, 20 September 1996.
Robert W. Crouter, Class of 1948A, 5 June 1997.
James B. Davidson, Class of 1947, 17 May 1997.
John J. Dempsey, Class of 1947, 11 June 1997.
Lawrence H. Derby, Jr., Class of 1949, 23 July 1997.
Robert M. Douglass, Class of 1949, 3 October 1996.
James H. Doyle, Jr., Class of 1947, 19 May 1997.
Seymour Einstein, Class of 1941, 28 May 1997.
Kenneth O. Ekelund, Jr., Class of 1947, 17 May 1997.
Robert B. Erly, Class of 1937, 28 October 1998.
Joseph P. Flanagan, Class of 1947, 19 March 1997.
James H. Forbes, Class of 1947, 18 June 1997.
Donald A. Gairing, Class of 1949, 13 October 1996.
Walter Grechanik, Class of 1948A, 30 July 1997.
Milton Gussow, Class of 1949, 18 September 1997.
Wade Hampton Harris, Class of 1948B, 7 April 1999.
Thomas L. Hartigan, Class of 1947, 27 September 1996.
Bruce P. Hayden, Class of 1938, 22 October 1997.
Edwin Heminger, Class of 1949, 7 October 1996.

Thomas J. Hudner, Jr., Class of 1947, 29 August 1996.
Frederick F. Jewett, Class of 1947, 1 September 1997.
James R. Juncker, Class of 1949, 9 October 1996.
John R. Kint, Class of 1949, 10 June 1997.
Harry M. Krantzman, Class of 1949, 27 September 1996.
Otto E. Krueger, Class of 1949, 27 July 1997.
Thomas F. Lechner, Class of 1949, 25 September 1996.
Shannon L. Matheny, Jr., Class of 1949, 28 October 1996.
William McKinley, Class of 1948A, 25 June 1997.
Earle K. McLaren, Class of 1934, 20 May 1997.
Walter M. Meginniss, Class of 1947, 4 June 1997.
John T. Metcalf, Jr., Class of 1949, 24 June 1994.
Harry B. Meyer, Class of 1949, 28 September 1996.
Joseph P. Morray, Class of 1940, 20 May 1997.
Donald R. Morris, Class of 1948B, 19 October 1996.
Oliver L. Norman, Jr., Class of 1948A, 28 July 1997.
Randolph F. Patterson, Class of 1948A, 11 June 1997.
William C. Patton, Class of 1947, 5 June 1997.
Robert C. Peniston, Class of 1947, 26 May 1997.
Willard S. Peterson, Class of 1949, 7 October 1996.
Robert K. Ripley, Class of 1949, 23 October 1996.
Kenneth M. Robinson, Class of 1947, c. May 1997.
Nye G. Rodes, Class of 1947, 4 June 1997.
Ivan L. Roenigk, Class of 1949, 21 May 1997.
William Sandkuhler, Class of 1949, c. June 1997.
Richard U. Scott, Class of 1948B, c. 1997.
Thomas T. Seelye, Jr., Class of 1949, 25 November 1996.
Chester H. Shaddeau, Jr., Class of 1947, c. July 1997.
Wilburn A. Speer, Class of 1948B, 12 June 1997.
William A. Spencer, Class of 1947, 17 October 1996.
Claude E. Swecker, Class of 1949, 29 September 1996.
Wallace J. Thomas, Class of 1949, 19 May 1997.
Stansfield Turner, Class of 1947, 26 August 1996.
John B. Van Velzer, Class of 1947, June 1997.
William A. Vogele, Class of 1949, 25 October 1996.
Alfred G. Wellons, Jr., Class of 1948A, c. May 1997.
J. C. G. Wilson, Class of 1935, 12 May and 10 June 1997.

Oral Histories (all interviews by author unless otherwise stated):

Eugene A. Barham, Class of 1935, 29 April 1997.
Kenneth A. Bott, Class of 1949, 3 October 1996.

Wesley Anthony Brown, Class of 1949, 19 December 1995 (1st interview), 23 January 1997 (2d interview), 17 October 1997 (3d interview), 17 December 1998 (4th interview), 16 September 1999 (5th interview).

Wesley Anthony Brown, Class of 1949, interview by Jean-Paul Reveyoso and Martha Dey, 8 May 1991, General Accounting Office, Washington, DC

William M. Carpenter, Class of 1940, 17 June 1997.

Lawrence C. Chambers, Class of 1952, 7 November 1996.

Paul P. Cooke, 2 April 1997.

Robert E. Fellowes, 21 May 1997.

James V. Ferrero, Class of 1949, 16 May 1997.

Joseph P. Flanagan, Jr., Class of 1947, 23 September 1996.

Milton Gussow, Class of 1949, 27 October 1997.

Bruce P. Hayden, Class of 1938, 29 October 1997.

Thomas J. Hudner, Jr., Class of 1947, 21 October 1996.

Frank Johnson, 23 July 1998.

James Lee Johnson, Jr., Class of 1940, interview by Dennis Nordin, 29 September 1974.

Sylvia Hicks Johnson, 6 August 1997.

Graham W. Leonard, Class of 1949, 16 April 1997.

Edward J. McCormack Jr., Class of 1947, 23 October 1996.

Walter G. Moyle, Jr., Class of 1947, 12 August 1997.

William H. Sword, Class of 1949, 24 October 1996.

Reeves R. Taylor, Class of 1953, 2 December 1996.

George Joseph Trivers, Class of 1941, 1997.

Howard A. Weiss, Class of 1947, 11 May 1996 (1st interview), 22 October 1997 (2d interview).

Richard E. Whiteside, Class of 1949, 9 October 1996.

Published Documents and Reports:

Johnson, Warren, transcriber. "Excerpts from President Carter's Speech in the Naval Academy Chapel, Tuesday, 4 June 1996." *Shipmate* (September 1996): 12–13, 45.

MacGregor, Morris J., and Bernard C. Nalty, eds. *Blacks in the United States Armed Forces: Basic Documents.* 13 vols. Wilmington, DE: Scholarly Resources, 1977.

U.S. Congress. *Official Congressional Directory for the Use of the United States Congress, 71st Congress, 3d Session, Beginning December 1, 1930.* Washington: Government Printing Office, 1930.

———. House. *Memorial Services Held in the House of Representatives and Senate of the United States, Together with Tributes Presented in Eulogy of*

William L. Dawson, Late a Representative from Illinois. Washington: Government Printing Office, 1971.

———. House. Office of the Historian. *Women in Congress, 1917–1990.* Washington: Government Printing Office, 1991.

———. Senate. *Centennial of the United States Naval Academy, 1845–1945.* S. Doc. 91, 79th Cong., 1st sess., 1945.

———. Senate. *The United States Naval Academy: A Sketch Containing the History, Entrance Requirements, Curriculum, Athletics, after Graduation Service, and Other Factual Information.* S. Doc. 181, 75th Cong., 3d sess., 1938.

U.S. Department of Defense. *Black Americans in Defense of Our Nation: A Pictorial Documentary of the Black American Male and Female Participation and Involvement in the Military Affairs of the United States of America.* Washington: Government Printing Office, 1991.

———. *The Negro Officer in the Armed Forces of the United States of America.* Washington: Government Printing Office, 1960.

U.S. Department of the Navy. *Official Records of the Union and Confederate Navies in the War of the Rebellion.* Edited by Richard Rush, et al. 31 vols. and index. Washington: Government Printing Office, 1894–1922.

U.S. Naval Academy. *Annual Register of the United States Naval Academy, 1936–1949.* Washington: Government Printing Office, 1936–1949.

———. *Lucky Bag* (yearbook), various years.

———. *Reef Points, 1936–1937.* Annapolis, MD: U.S. Naval Academy, 1936.

———. *Regulations of the United States Naval Academy, 1933.* Annapolis, MD: U.S. Naval Academy, 1933.

———. *Regulations of the United States Naval Academy, 1945.* Annapolis, MD: U.S. Naval Academy, 1945.

United States Naval Academy Alumni Association, Inc. *Register of Alumni: Graduates and Former Midshipmen and Naval Cadets.* Annapolis, MD: U.S. Naval Academy Alumni Assoc., 1997.

U.S. Navy Department. *Annual Report of the Secretary of the Navy for the Fiscal Year 1936.* Washington: Government Printing Office, 1936.

———. *Annual Report, Fiscal Year 1945.* Washington: Government Printing Office, 1946.

———. *Regulations of the United States Naval Academy as Approved by the Secretary of the Navy,* March 4, 1869. Washington: Government Printing Office, 1869.

———. Bureau of Naval Personnel. *Catalog of Course of Instruction at the United States Naval Academy, Annapolis, Md., the One Hundred and First Academic Year, 1945–1946.* Washington: Government Printing Office, 1946.

———. Bureau of Naval Personnel. *Catalog of Course of Instruction at the United States Naval Academy, Annapolis, Md., the One Hundred and Sec-*

ond Academic Year, 1946–1947. Washington: Government Printing Office, 1946.

———. Bureau of Naval Personnel. *Regulations Governing the Admission of Candidates into the United States Naval Academy as Midshipmen and Sample Examination Questions, June 1945.* Washington: Government Printing Office, 1945.

———. Bureau of Navigation. *Regulations Governing the Admission of Candidates into the U.S. Naval Academy as Midshipmen.* Washington: Government Printing Office, 1921.

U.S. Office of War Information. Division of Public Inquiries. *United States Government Manual.* Washington: Government Printing Office, 1945.

United States Statutes at Large. Washington: Government Printing Office, 1874–.

Memoirs and Contemporary Publications:

Andrews, George L. "West Point and the Colored Cadets." *International Review* 9 (November 1880): 477–98.

"Annapolis' First." *Time* (13 June 1949): 19–20.

"Annapolis: Negro Midshipman Finds Race Trouble at Academy." *Newsweek* (27 February 1937): 11–12.

Banning, Kendall. *Annapolis Today,* 5th ed. Annapolis, MD: U.S. Naval Institute, 1957.

Bealle, Morris A. "The Color Line Slackens." *Today's World* (February 1948): 20–21.

Benjamin, Park. *The United States Naval Academy.* New York: Putnam's, 1900.

Bowers, Ingrid. *A Greater Challenge: U.S. Naval Academy Black History.* Bethesda, MD: Phase II Productions, 1979 (video documentary).

Brown, Wesley A. "The First Negro Graduate of Annapolis Tells His Story." *Saturday Evening Post* (25 June 1949): 26–27, 110–12.

Carpenter, William M., ed. *The Class of Forty—After Fifty Years.* Annapolis, MD: U.S. Naval Academy, c. 1990.

Carter, Jimmy. *Always a Reckoning and Other Poems.* New York: Random House, 1995.

———. *Why Not the Best?* Nashville, TN: Broadman Press, 1975.

Davis, Benjamin O., Jr. *American: An Autobiography.* Washington: Smithsonian Institution Press, 1991.

Evans, Robley D. *A Sailor's Log: Recollections of Forty Years of Naval Life.* Introduction and notes by Benjamin Franklin Cooling. Annapolis, MD: Naval Institute Press, 1993.

Flipper, Henry Ossian. *The Colored Cadet at West Point: Autobiography of Lieut. Henry Ossian Flipper, U.S.A., First Graduate of Color from the U.S.*

Military Academy. New York: Homer Lee & Co., 1878. Reprint ed. New York: Johnson Reprint Corp., 1968.

Gulliver, Louis J. "Air Admiral at Academy Controls." *Shipmate* (September 1945): 19, 59–62.

Hubbard, Elbert. *A Message to Garcia and Other Essays.* Westwood, NJ: Fleming H. Revell, 1959.

"James Daniel Fowler." *Assembly* (July 1988): 181–82.

Jankovsky, Norlin J., ed. *Reef Points, 1945–1946.* Annapolis, MD: United States Naval Academy, 1945.

Johnson, Warren, transcriber. "Excerpts from President Carter's Speech in the Naval Academy Chapel, Tuesday, 4 June 1996." *Shipmate* (September 1996): 12–13, 45.

Long, John E. "The Complete Story of June Week 1946 at the Naval Academy." *Shipmate* (July 1946): 31–50.

———. "Here's How the Middies Celebrated Jap Armistice." *Shipmate* (October 1945): 30–31, 77–78.

Lovette, Leland Pearson. *School of the Sea: The Annapolis Tradition in American Life.* New York: Frederick A. Stokes, 1941.

Magruder, T. P. "The Enlisted Personnel." *Proceedings* 36 (June 1910): 375–89.

Powell, Adam Clayton, Jr. *Adam by Adam: The Autobiography of Adam Clayton Powell, Jr.* New York: Dial, 1971.

Rowan, Andrew Summers. *How I Carried the Message to Garcia.* San Francisco: Walter D. Harney, c. 1922.

Schley, Winfield Scott. *Forty-Five Years under the Flag.* New York: Appleton, 1904.

Sellers, David F. "The United States Naval Academy: It Belongs to the Fleet." *Proceedings* 62 (October 1936): 1427–34.

Thomson, Earl Wentworth. "The Naval Academy as an Undergraduate College." *Proceedings* 74 (March 1948): 271–85.

The Trident Society, ed. *The Book of Navy Songs.* New York: Doubleday, 1937.

White, Walter. *A Man Called White: The Autobiography of Walter White.* New York: Viking, 1948.

———. *A Rising Wind.* Garden City, NY: Doubleday, 1945. Reprint ed. Westport, CT: Negro Universities Press, 1971.

Writers' Program of the Works Projects Administration in the State of Maryland. *A Guide to the United States Naval Academy.* New York: Devin-Adair, 1941.

Newspapers and Periodicals:

Afro-American
All Hands

Army and Navy Journal
Baltimore American and Commercial Advertiser
Chicago Defender
Cleveland Call and Post
Evening Star (Washington)
Evening Sun (Baltimore)
New York Daily Tribune
New York Star
New York Times
Newsweek
Pittsburgh Courier
Post and Courier (Savannah, GA)
Time
Washington Post
Washington Times
Washington Tribune

SECONDARY SOURCES

Books:

Allen, Robert L. *The Port Chicago Mutiny.* New York: Warner Books, 1989.

Astor, Gerald. *The Right to Fight: A History of African Americans in the Military.* Novato, CA: Presidio, 1998.

Bolster, W. Jeffrey. *Black Jacks: African American Seamen in the Age of Sail.* Cambridge, MA: Harvard University Press, 1997.

Bourne, Peter G. *Jimmy Carter: A Comprehensive Biography from Plains to Postpresidency.* New York: Scribner's, 1997.

Brown, Philip L. *The Other Annapolis.* Annapolis, MD: Annapolis Publishing Company, 1994.

Buchanan, A. Russell. *Black Americans in World War II.* Santa Barbara, CA: Clio Books, 1983.

Cary, Francine Curro, ed. *Urban Odyssey: A Multicultural History of Washington, D.C.* Washington: Smithsonian, 1995.

Chambers, John Whiteclay II, et al., ed. *The Oxford Companion to American Military History.* New York: Oxford University Press, 1999.

Clary, Jack. *Navy Football: Gridiron Legends and Fighting Heroes.* Annapolis, MD: Naval Institute Press, 1997.

Clayton, Obie, Jr., ed. *An American Dilemma Revisited: Race Relations in a Changing World.* New York: Russell Sage Foundation, 1996.

Cogar, William B. *Dictionary of Admirals of the U.S. Navy.* Vol. 1, *1862–1900.* Annapolis, MD: Naval Institute Press, 1989.

Coletta, Paolo Enrico, ed. *American Secretaries of the Navy.* 2 vols. Annapolis, MD: Naval Institute Press, 1980.

Dabney, Lillian G. *The History of Schools for Negroes in the District of Columbia, 1807–1947.* Washington: Catholic University of America Press, 1949. Published Ph.D. dissertation.

Daniel, Pete. *The Shadow of Slavery: Peonage in the South, 1901–1969.* Urbana: University of Illinois Press, 1990.

Dictionary of American Biography. 10 vols. plus supplements. New York: Scribner's, c. 1964.

Drago, Edmund L. *Initiative, Paternalism, and Race Relations: Charleston's Avery Normal Institute.* Athens: University of Georgia Press, 1990.

Erenberg, Lewis A., and Susan E. Hirsch, eds. *The War in American Culture: Society and Consciousness during World War II.* Chicago: University of Chicago Press, 1996.

Ferrell, Henry C. *Claude A. Swanson of Virginia: A Political Biography.* Lexington: University of Kentucky Press, 1985.

Finkle, Lee. *Forum for Protest: The Black Press during World War II.* Cranbury, NJ: Fairleigh Dickinson University Press, 1975.

Fitzpatrick, Sandra, and Maria R. Goodwin. *The Guide to Black Washington: Places and Events of Historical and Cultural Significance in the Nation's Capital,* rev. ed. New York: Hippocrene Books, 1999.

Fletcher, Marvin E. *America's First Black General: Benjamin O. Davis, Sr., 1880–1970.* Lawrence: University Press of Kansas, 1989.

Foner, Eric. *Reconstruction: America's Unfinished Revolution, 1863–1877.* New York: Harper and Row, 1988.

Foner, Eric, ed. *The New American History.* Philadelphia: Temple University Press, 1990.

Foner, Eric, and Olivia Mahoney. *America's Reconstruction: People and Politics after the Civil War.* New York: HarperCollins, 1995.

Frank, Richard B. *Guadalcanal.* New York: Random House, 1990.

Franklin, John Hope, and Alfred A. Moss, Jr. *From Slavery to Freedom,* 6th ed. New York: McGraw-Hill, 1988.

Freidel, Frank. *Franklin D. Roosevelt: A Rendezvous with Destiny.* Boston: Little, Brown, 1990.

Furer, Julius Augustus. *Administration of the Navy Department in World War II.* Washington: Government Printing Office, 1959.

Gatewood, Willard B., Jr. *Aristocrats of Color: The Black Elite, 1880–1920.* Bloomington: Indiana University Press, 1990.

Green, Constance McLaughlin. *The Secret City: A History of Race Relations in the Nation's Capital.* Princeton, NJ: Princeton University Press, 1967.

Greene, Robert Ewell. *Black Defenders of America, 1775–1973: A Reference and Pictorial History.* Chicago: Johnson Publishing, 1974.

Grimshaw, William J. *Bitter Fruit: Black Politics and the Chicago Machine, 1931–1991.* Chicago: University of Chicago Press, 1992.

Gropman, Alan L. *The Air Force Integrates, 1945–1964.* Washington: Office of Air Force History, 1985.

Grossman, James R. *Land of Hope: Chicago, Black Southerners, and the Great Migration.* Chicago: University of Chicago Press, 1989.

Hamilton, Charles V. *Adam Clayton Powell, Jr.: The Political Biography of an American Dilemma.* New York: Atheneum, 1991.

Harris, William C. *The Day of the Carpetbagger: Republican Reconstruction in Mississippi.* Baton Rouge: Louisiana State University Press, 1979.

Harrod, Frederick S. *Manning the New Navy: The Development of a Modern Naval Enlisted Force, 1899–1940.* Westport, CT: Greenwood Press, 1978.

Haygood, Wil. *King of the Cats: The Life and Times of Adam Clayton Powell, Jr.* Boston: Houghton Mifflin, 1993.

Henri, Florette. *Bitter Victory: A History of Black Soldiers in World War I.* Garden City, NY: Doubleday, 1970.

Hill, Robert A., et al., eds. *The FBI's RACON: Racial Conditions in the United States during World War II.* Boston: Northeastern University Press, 1995.

Holt, Thomas Cleveland. *Black over White: Negro Political Leadership in South Carolina during Reconstruction.* Urbana: University of Illinois Press, 1977.

Hoopes, Townsend, and Douglas Brinkley. *Driven Patriot: The Life and Times of James Forrestal.* New York: Knopf, 1992.

Hundley, Mary Gibson. *The Dunbar Story, 1870–1955.* Introduction by Robert C. Weaver. New York: Vantage Press, 1965.

Janowitz, Morris. *The Professional Soldier: A Social and Political Portrait.* New York: Free Press, 1971.

Johnson, Jesse J., ed. *Black Armed Forces Officers, 1736–1971: A Documented Pictorial History.* Hampton, VA: Hampton Institute, 1971.

Karsten, Peter. *The Naval Aristocracy: The Golden Age of Annapolis and the Emergence of Modern American Navalism.* New York: Free Press, 1972.

Katz, William Loren. *Eyewitness: A Living Documentary of the African American Contribution to American History.* New York: Simon and Schuster, 1995.

Kelly, Mary Pat. *Proudly We Served: The Men of the USS Mason.* Annapolis, MD: Naval Institute Press, 1995.

Kennedy, David M. *Freedom from Fear: The American People in Depression and War, 1929–1945.* New York: Oxford University Press, 1999.

Kirby, John B. *Black Americans in the Roosevelt Era: Liberalism and Race.* Knoxville: University of Tennessee Press, 1980.

Lamson, Peggy. *The Glorious Failure: Robert Brown Elliott and the Reconstruction in South Carolina.* New York: Norton, 1973.

Lee, Ulysses. *The Employment of Negro Troops.* Washington: Government Printing Office, 1994.

MacGregor, Morris J. *Integration of the Armed Forces, 1940–1965*. Washington: Government Printing Office, 1981.

Mackenzie, Ross. *Brief Points: An Almanac for Parents and Friends of U.S. Naval Academy Midshipmen*. Annapolis, MD: Naval Institute Press, 1993.

Marable, Manning. *Race, Reform, and Rebellion: The Second Reconstruction in Black America, 1945–1982*. Jackson: University Press of Mississippi, 1984.

McFeely, William S. *Grant: A Biography*. New York: Norton, 1981.

McJimsey, George. *The Presidency of Franklin Delano Roosevelt*. Lawrence: University Press of Kansas, 2000.

Miller, Vickie Gail. *Doris Miller: A Silent Medal of Honor*. Austin, TX: Eakin Press, 1997.

Moebs, Thomas Truxtun. *Black Soldiers, Black Sailors, Black Ink: Research Guide on African Americans in U.S. Military History, 1526–1900*. Chesapeake Bay, VA: Moebs Publishing, 1994.

Mooney, James L., et al., eds. *Dictionary of American Naval Fighting Ships*. Washington: Government Printing Office, 1959–.

Moore, Brenda L. *To Serve My Country, to Serve My Race: The Story of the Only African American WACs Stationed Overseas during World War II*. New York: New York University Press, 1996.

Motley, Mary Penick, ed. *The Invisible Soldier: The Experience of the Black Soldier, World War II*. Detroit: Wayne State University Press, 1975.

Myrdal, Gunnar. *An American Dilemma: The Negro Problem and Modern Democracy*. 2 vols. New York: Harper & Brothers, 1944.

Nalty, Bernard C. *Strength for the Fight: A History of Black Americans in the Military*. New York: Free Press, 1986.

Nelson, Dennis D. *The Integration of the Negro into the U.S. Navy*. New York: Farrar, Straus, and Young, 1951.

Nordin, Dennis S. *The New Deal's Black Congressman: A Life of Arthur Wergs Mitchell*. Columbia: University of Missouri Press, 1997.

Osur, Alan M. *Blacks in the Army Air Forces during World War II*. Washington: Government Printing Office, 1977.

Pfeffer, Paula F. *A. Philip Randolph, Pioneer of the Civil Rights Movement*. Baton Rouge: Louisiana State University Press, 1990.

Ploski, Harry A., and Ernest Kaiser. *Afro USA: A Reference Work on the Black Experience*. New York: Bellwether Publishing, 1971.

Puleston, W. D. *Annapolis: Gangway to the Quarterdeck*. New York: D. Appleton-Century, 1942.

Ragsdale, Bruce, ed. *Biographical Directory of the United States Congress, 1774–1989*. Washington: Government Printing Office, 1989.

Ragsdale, Bruce, and Joel D. Treese. *Black Americans in Congress, 1870–1989*. Washington: Government Printing Office, 1990.

Schneider, James G. *The Navy V-12 Program: Leadership for a Lifetime*. Boston: Houghton Mifflin, 1967.

Still, William N., Jr. *Ironclad Captains: The Commanding Officers of the USS Monitor*. Washington: National Oceanic and Atmospheric Administration, 1988.

Stillwell, Paul, ed. *The Golden Thirteen: Recollections of the First Black Naval Officers*. Annapolis, MD: Naval Institute Press, 1993.

Sweetman, Jack. *The U.S. Naval Academy: An Illustrated History*. Annapolis, MD: Naval Institute Press, 1979.

Symonds, Craig L. *Confederate Admiral: The Life and Wars of Franklin Buchanan*. Annapolis, MD: Naval Institute Press, 1999.

Timberg, Robert. *The Nightingale's Song*. New York: Simon and Schuster, 1995.

Todorich, Charles. *The Spirited Years: A History of the Antebellum Naval Academy*. Annapolis, MD: Naval Institute Press, 1984.

Valuska, David L. *The Afro-American in the Union Navy: 1861–1865*. New York: Garland, 1993.

Williams, Michael S., ed. *The African American Encyclopedia*. 6 vols. New York: Marshall Cavendish, 1993.

Woodward, C. Vann. *The Strange Career of Jim Crow*. New York: Oxford University Press, 1955.

Wynn, Neil A. *The Afro-American and the Second World War*. New York: Holmes and Meier, 1976.

Articles:

Anderson, Jervis. "A Very Special Monument." *New Yorker* (20 March 1978): 97–121.

Aptheker, Herbert. "The Negro in the Union Navy." *Journal of Negro History* 32 (April 1947): 169–200.

Bodnar, John W. "How Long Does It Take to Change a Culture? Integration at the U.S. Naval Academy." *Armed Forces and Society* 25 (Winter 1999): 289–306.

Brown, Stephen D. "Christopher Raymond Perry Rodgers: Mentor of the New Navy," in *Naval History: The Sixth Naval History Symposium*, ed. Daniel Masterson. Wilmington, DE: Scholarly Resources, 1986.

Brown, Wesley A. "Eleven Men of West Point." *Negro History Bulletin* 19 (April 1956): 147–57.

Cantwell, Thomas J. "Anacostia: Strength in Diversity," in *Records of the Columbia Historical Society of Washington, D.C., 1973–1974*, ed. Francis Coleman Rosenberger. Washington: Columbia Historical Society, 1976.

Chafe, William H. "America since 1945," in *The New American History*, ed. Eric Foner. Philadelphia: Temple University Press, 1990.

———. "The Gods Bring Threads to Webs Begun." *Journal of American History* 86 (March 2000): 1531–51.

Field, R. L. "The Black Midshipman at the U.S. Naval Academy." *Proceedings* 99 (April 1973): 28–36.

Finkle, Lee. "The Conservative Aims of Militant Rhetoric: Black Protest during World War II." *Journal of American History* 60 (December 1973): 692–713.

Fitzgerald, John A. "Changing Patterns of Officer Recruitment at the U.S. Naval Academy." *Armed Forces and Society* 8 (Fall 1981): 111–28.

Gatewood, Willard B., Jr. "Alonzo Clifton McClennan: Black Midshipman from South Carolina, 1874–1874." *South Carolina Historical Magazine* 89 (January 1988): 24–39.

———. "John Hanks Alexander of Arkansas: Second Black Graduate of West Point." *Arkansas Historical Quarterly* 41 (Summer 1982): 103–28.

Haygood, Wil. "Keeping the Faith." *American Legacy* 3 (Winter 1998): 23–28.

Holt, Thomas C. "African-American History," in *The New American History,* ed. Eric Foner. Philadelphia: Temple University Press, 1990.

Marszalek, John F., Jr. "A Black Cadet at West Point." *American Heritage* 22 (August 1971): 30–37, 104–6.

Pond, Jesse. "The Doris Miller Story." *Pearl Harbor History Associates, Incorporated Newsletter* 23 (Summer 1994): 1–2.

Reddick, L. D. "The Negro in the United States Navy during World War II." *Journal of Negro History* 32 (1947): 201–19.

Reidy, Joseph P. "Black Jack: African American Sailors in the Civil War Navy," in *New Interpretations in Naval History: Selected Papers from the Twelfth Naval History Symposium,* ed. William B. Cogar. Annapolis, MD: Naval Institute Press, 1997.

Robinson, Henry S. "The M Street High School, 1891–1916." *Records of the Columbia Historical Society of Washington, D.C.* 51 (1984): 119–43.

Schneider, James G. "'Negroes Will Be Tested!'—FDR." *Naval History* (Spring 1993): 11–15.

Schneller, Robert J., Jr. "Oscar Holmes: A Place in Naval Aviation." *Naval Aviation News* (January–February 1998): 26–27.

Sowell, Thomas. "Black Excellence: A History of Dunbar High." *Washington Post* (28 April 1974): C3.

Vahsen, Penny. "Blacks in White Hats." *Proceedings* 113 (April 1987): 65–71.

Vaughn, William P. "West Point and the First Negro Cadet." *Journal of Military History* 35 (October 1971): 100–102.

Warner, Ezra J. "A Black Man in the Long Gray Line." *American History Illustrated* 4 (January 1970): 30–38.

West, Richard S., Jr. "The Superintendents of the Naval Academy." *Proceedings* 71 (July 1945): 800–809.

Williamson, Joel. "Wounds Not Scars: Lynching, the National Conscience, and the American Historian." *Journal of American History* 83 (March 1997): 1221–53.

Unpublished Works:

Akers, Regina. "The Integration of Afro-Americans into the WAVES, 1942–1945." M.A. thesis, Howard University, 1993.

Barham, Eugene A. "The 228 Days of the United States Destroyer *Laffey* DD 459." Naval Historical Center, Washington, DC, 1988.

Brown, Gerald R. "Military Training in the Public Schools of the District of Columbia." M.A. thesis, Howard University, 1963.

Forney, Todd Alan. "Four Years Together by the Bay: A Study of the Midshipman Culture at the United States Naval Academy, 1946–1976." Ph.D. dissertation, Ohio State University, 2000.

Jenkins, Maude Thomas. "Alonzo McClennan, M.D." Unpublished paper, Naval Historical Center, Washington, DC, 1983.

"Lieutenant Henry Ossian Flipper, U.S. Army 1856–1940." http://www.army.mil/cmh-pg/topics/afam/flipper.htm. 18 June 2003.

Neyland, Leedell W. "The Messman's/Steward's Branch: A Haunting Chapter in the History of the U.S. Navy, 1919–1942." Lecture given at the Naval Historical Center, 17 May 1994.

Ponton, Jean Alice. "Rear Admiral Louis M. Goldsborough: The Formation of a Nineteenth-Century Naval Officer." Ph.D. dissertation, Catholic University, 1996.

Salter, Krewasky Antonio. "'Sable Officers': African-American Military Officers, 1861–1948." Ph.D. dissertation, Florida State University, 1996.

U.S. Navy Department. "United States Naval Administration in World War II, Bureau of Naval Personnel, History of the Demobilization Activity." Washington: Navy Department, 1946.

———. "United States Naval Administration in World War II, Bureau of Naval Personnel, History of the Enlisted Personnel Activity." 2 vols. Washington: Navy Department, 1946.

———. "United States Naval Administration in World War II, Bureau of Naval Personnel, Officer Personnel." Washington: Navy Department, 1945.

———. "United States Naval Administration in World War II, Bureau of Naval Personnel, The Negro in the Navy in World War II." Washington: Navy Department, 1947.

———. "United States Naval Administration in World War II, Bureau of Naval Personnel, Training Activity, Part 4, Vol. 1, Standards and Curriculum Division." Washington: Navy Department, 1946.

————. "United States Naval Administration in World War II, Bureau of Naval Personnel, Training Activity, Part 4, Vol. 4, College Training Program." Washington: Navy Department, 1946.

USS *Monterey*. "History of the USS *Monterey*, 17 June 1943 to 2 September 1945." Unpublished manuscript, USS *Monterey*, c. 1945.

Wender, Harry S. "An Analysis of Recreation and Segregation in the District of Columbia." Unpublished manuscript, Historical Society of Washington, DC, May 1949.

Wold, Catherine Theresa. "A History of the Washington High School Cadet Corps, 1882–1934." M.A. thesis, University of Maryland, 1935.

Index

About the Author

Robert J. Schneller, Jr., is an official historian in the Contemporary History Branch of the U.S. Navy's Naval Historical Center and holds a Ph.D. in military history from Duke University. An award-winning biographer and historian, he has published five books on American naval history, including *Shield and Sword: The United States Navy and the Persian Gulf War; A Quest for Glory: A Biography of Rear Admiral John A. Dahlgren; Farragut: America's First Admiral;* and *Cushing: Civil War Seal.* He also edited the memoir of John W. Grattan, titled *Under the Blue Pennant; or, Notes of a Naval Officer, 1863–1865.*